The Laws of Hammurabi

The Laws of Hammurabi

At the Confluence of Royal and Scribal Traditions

PAMELA BARMASH

OXFORD
UNIVERSITY PRESS

OXFORD
UNIVERSITY PRESS

Oxford University Press is a department of the University of Oxford. It furthers the University's objective of excellence in research, scholarship, and education by publishing worldwide. Oxford is a registered trade mark of Oxford University Press in the UK and certain other countries.

Published in the United States of America by Oxford University Press
198 Madison Avenue, New York, NY 10016, United States of America.

Library of Congress Cataloging-in-Publication Data
Names: Barmash, Pamela, 1966– author.
Title: The laws of Hammurabi : at the confluence of royal and
scribal traditions / Pamela Barmash.
Description: New York : Oxford University Press, 2020. |
Includes bibliographical references and index.
Identifiers: LCCN 2020010796 (print) | LCCN 2020010797 (ebook) |
ISBN 9780197525401 (hardback) | ISBN 9780197525425 (epub)
Subjects: LCSH: Code of Hammurabi—Influence. |
Law, Assyro-Babylonian—Sources. | Scribes—Iraq—Babylonia—History—To 1500. |
Babylonia—Politics and government.
Classification: LCC KL2212.1 .B37 2020 (print) |
LCC KL2212.1 (ebook) | DDC 349.35—dc23
LC record available at https://lccn.loc.gov/2020010796
LC ebook record available at https://lccn.loc.gov/2020010797

1 3 5 7 9 8 6 4 2

Printed by Integrated Books International, United States of America

Contents

List of Illustrations vii
List of Abbreviations ix

Introduction 1

1. The Stela of the Laws of Hammurabi and the Representation of Political Power 19

2. Royal Legitimization through the Establishment of Justice 49

3. The Laws of Hammurabi as a Royal Inscription 87

4. Scribes and Statutes 137

Excursus: Scribes and Scribal Education 203

5. Adoption in the Laws of Hammurabi 219

6. The Legal Authority of the Laws of Hammurabi 231

7. The Afterlife of the Laws of Hammurabi: The Continuation of Scribal Improvisation outside Mesopotamia and the Creation of Commentaries in Mesopotamia 251

Conclusion 279

Bibliography 285
Index of Subjects and Authors 307
Index of Texts 315

Illustrations

Image I.1	Photograph of the excavation of the Stela of the Laws of Hammurabi at Susa, 1901–1902. Credit Gustave Jéquier (1868–1946). © Archive Musée du Louvre / département des antiquités orientales.	2
Image 1.1	The Stela of the Laws of Hammurabi. Diorite, 2.250 m × 0.650 m. Sb 8. Photo: Franck Raux. Musée du Louvre. © RMN-Grand Palais / Art Resource, NY.	21
Image 1.2	Presentation scene from the Stela of the Laws of Hammurabi. Musée du Louvre. Photo Credit: Erich Lessing / Art Resource, NY.	23
Image 1.3	Stela depicting a king pouring a libation before a god, 20th–19th c. BCE. Found in Susa, Iran. Sb 7. Limestone, 67 × 62 cm. Musée du Louvre. © RMN-Grand Palais / Art Resource, NY.	24
Image 1.4	Detail of a stela depicting the king Ur-Namma pouring a libation before the god Nanna (the Ur-Namma stela fragment). Courtesy of the Penn Museum, image no. 141417, object no. B16676.	25
Image 1.5	The Victory Stela of Naram-Sin, c. 2270 BCE. Pink limestone, h. 198 cm. Found in Susa, Iran. Sb 4. Photo: Franck Raux. © RMN-Grand Palais / Art Resource, NY.	28
Map 1	Central cities of Babylonia	107
Map 2	Peripheral cities to the East	109
Map 3	Cities to the North	112

Abbreviations

AASOR	Annual of the American Schools of Oriental Research
AbB	Altbabylonische Briefe
AHw	Wolfram von Soden, *Assyrisches Handwörterbuch* (Wiesbaden: Otto Harrassowitz, 1959–1981)
ANET	William B. Pritchard, *Ancient Near Eastern Texts Relating to the Old Testament*, 3rd edition (Princeton, N.J.: Princeton University Press, 1955)
AOAT	Alter Orient und Altes Testament
AOS	American Oriental Series
ARM	*Archives royales de Mari* (Paris: Paul Guethner, 1942–)
AS	Assyriological Studies
BAL	Rykle Borger, *Babylonisch-Assyrisch Lesestücke* (Rome: Pontifical Biblical Institute, 1979)
BIN	Babylonian Inscriptions in the Collections of James B. Nies
BM	tablets in the collections of the British Museum
BWL	W. G. Lambert, *Babylonian Wisdom Literature* (Oxford: Oxford University Press, 1960)
CAD	*The Assyrian Dictionary of the University of Chicago* (Chicago: Oriental Institute, 1956–2010)
CANE	Jack M. Sasson, ed., *Civilizations of the Ancient Near East* (New York: Scribners, 1995)
CT	Cuneiform Texts from Babylonian Tablets
ETCSL	Electronic Text Corpus of Sumerian Literature
GMTR	Guides to the Mesopotamian Textual Record
HL	Hittite Laws
JAOS	*Journal of the American Oriental Society*
JCS	*Journal of Cuneiform Studies*
JEOL	*Jaarbericht Ex oriente lux*
JESHO	*Journal of the Economic and Social History of the Orient*
JNES	*Journal of Near Eastern Studies*
LE	Laws of Eshnunna
LH	Laws of Hammurabi

LL	Laws of Lipit-Ishtar
LOx	Laws about Rented Oxen
LU	Laws of Ur-Namma
MAL	Middle Assyrian Laws
mng.	meaning
NABU	*Nouvelles Assyriologiques Brèves et Utilitaires*
NS	New Series
OEBL	Brent Strawn, editor-in-chief, *The Oxford Encyclopedia of the Bible and Law* (Oxford: Oxford University Press, 2015)
OIP	Oriental Institute Publications
Or	*Orientalia*, NS
PBS	Publications of the Babylonian Section
RA	*Revue d'Assyriologie*
RIDA	*Revue internationale des droits de l'antiquité*
RIME	The Royal Inscriptions of Mesopotamia, Early Periods
RLA	*Reallexikon der Assyriologie und vorderasiatische Archäologie* (Berlin: de Gruyter, 1932–)
SANER	Studies in Ancient Near Eastern Records
SDIOAP	Studia et documenta ad iura orientis antiqua pertinentia
SLEx	Sumerian Laws Exercise Tablet
SLHF	Sumerian Laws Handbook of Forms
TJA	E. Szlechter, *Tablettes juridiques et administratives de la IIIe Dynastie d'Ur et de la 1re Dynastie de Babylone* (Paris: Librairie Orientaliste Paul Geuthner, 1963)
UAZP	M. Schorr, *Urkunden des altbabylonische Zivil- und Prozessrechts* (Leipzig: Hinrichs, 1913)
UET	Ur Excavations, Texts
WO	*Welt des Orients*
YOS	Yale Oriental Series
ZA	*Zeitschrift für Assyriologie*
ZAR	*Zeitschrift für altorientalische und biblische Rechtsgeschichte*

Introduction

Of the people known to us from preclassical antiquity, the ancient Babylonian king Hammurabi is among the best recognized and most esteemed. His fame and reputation are due to the collection of laws written under his patronage, recovered by the fortuitousness of archaeological excavation. Other figures from antiquity are mostly known for their military conquests and political success, and Hammurabi excelled in those as well. But without his collection of laws, he would be just one more royal figure whose achievements have faded into oblivion.

The Laws of Hammurabi was recopied for more than a thousand years after it was promulgated, and when the text of the Laws of Hammurabi was lost to history, the style and content exemplified in it left traces on the laws of other cultures. Statutes in the Bible were articulated in the literary technique of the Laws of Hammurabi, and legal cases and concepts of biblical law were shaped in reaction to the legal culture epitomized by the Laws of Hammurabi. The formal law collection of the Hittite Empire manifests the influence of Mesopotamian law. Early Greek law and Roman law bear a definite resemblance to the Laws of Hammurabi, and they may serve as evidence demonstrating the far-reaching influence of Mesopotamian law. Certain legal concepts that are evident in Western law, such as the significance of written evidence and the use of protocols through which property could be transferred, appear to be already attested in the Laws of Hammurabi. So while the Laws of Hammurabi vanished in antiquity until it was rediscovered in modern times, the legal culture epitomized in the Laws of Hammurabi continued to exercise influence, however muted and oblique.

The image of Hammurabi the lawgiver and his law collection are familiar to us nowadays, but until 1902 almost nothing was known of his law collection. A few fragments containing law articulated as statutes from Mesopotamia had been found and studied in the 1890s, and one scholar surmised that the fragments might be part of a law code from the time of Hammurabi.[1] In

[1] Otto Peiser was the first to publish fragments of the Laws of Hammurabi before the discovery of the Stela of the Laws of Hammurabi (*Jurisprudentiae Babylonicae quae supersunt*, Ph.D. dissertation,

The Laws of Hammurabi. Pamela Barmash, Oxford University Press (2020). © Oxford University Press.
DOI: 10.1093/oso/9780197525401.001.0001.

Image I.1 Photograph of the excavation of the Stela of the Laws of Hammurabi at Susa, 1901–1902. Credit Gustave Jéquier (1868–1946). © Archive Musée du Louvre / département des antiquités orientales.

December 1901–January 1902, during an excavation of Susa in present-day Iran, French archaeologist Jacques de Morgan discovered the pieces of the Stela (stone monument) on which an official copy of the Laws of Hammurabi was inscribed, as shown in image I.1. The find attracted wide publicity and interest. A scholarly edition of the Stela of the Laws of Hammurabi was published within the year,[2] and the Stela is now on display at the Louvre, its lasting fame assured.

University of Berlin, 1890). Bruno Meissner published more fragments and surmised that they might be part of a civil code from Hammurabi's reign ("Altbabylonische Gesetze," *Beiträge zur Assyriologie* 3 [1898], 493–523). The tablets containing the Laws of Lipit-Ishtar, a text dating from a century before Hammurabi, were excavated in 1889–1900, but their poor state of preservation and their presence among a large mass of other material recovered from Nippur prevented their identification as a law collection until more than thirty years later. See Francis R. Steele, *The Code of Lipit-Ishtar* (Museum Monographs; Philadelphia: The University Museum, 1948), 3–4.

[2] Victor Scheil, *Textes élamites-sémitiques* (Mémoires de la Délégation en Perse IV; Paris: Ernest LeRoux, 1902), 11–162, plates 3–15.

The Laws of Hammurabi derives from the nature of monarchy in Mesopotamia. Establishing and maintaining justice was a major aspect of royal activity in Mesopotamia, and presenting the king as overseeing the legal system was central to royal ideology. Kings were portrayed as deeply involved in legal affairs, and the tradition that a king commission a collection of law had started centuries before Hammurabi. But Hammurabi's law collection surpasses the earlier collections in scope and sophistication.

In order to comprehend the place of the Laws of Hammurabi in its own time and its legacy for later cultures, I offer in this volume a "histoire totale"[3] of the Laws of Hammurabi. I combine the analysis of the origins of the Laws of Hammurabi with investigating its influence on later generations of scribes. I examine the Laws of Hammurabi from its birth in a scribal workshop, amid examples of royal inscriptions and the study of scribal exercises and model legal texts, to its official promulgation and circulation through recopying. I illuminate its reception in its own time as a monument of royal authority, its commandeering by a foreign conqueror, and then its afterlife as reflected in biblical, Hittite, and classical law.

I argue that the Laws of Hammurabi is both the culmination of one stream of tradition and a witness to the start of another. The tradition of a law collection associated with a royal patron appeared for the first time in the late third millennium BCE in Sumer (southern Mesopotamia). This tradition employs the form of a royal inscription, a composition extolling its royal patron and threatening those who might deface the inscription with a litany of curses, and infuses it with a set of statutes describing a case and prescribing a remedy. The inclusion of certain legal topics became the norm, and scribes would demonstrate their legal flair by composing statutes on a repertoire of traditional cases. The Laws of Hammurabi is the most developed of this stream of tradition, containing the most lengthy exaltation of the king, the most cases treated in the form of statutes, and the most extended series of threats. It was also the most well known in Mesopotamian culture: the Laws of Hammurabi has been excavated in more than fifty copies, attesting to its place in the scribal curriculum, unlike its predecessors, of which only a scant few copies remain. It is an extraordinary law collection, and it is also one of the longest texts extant in general from Mesopotamia.

[3] Ann Blair developed this approach for a natural philosopher of the late Renaissance (*The Theater of Nature* [Princeton, NJ: Princeton University Press, 1997], 9).

We also glimpse the beginning of another stream of tradition: the Laws of Hammurabi became a fixed text, and as a fixed text, scribes related to it in ways that were different from earlier attitudes. No longer was a law collection an improvisation frozen momentarily in written form. The text was transformed into a classic, and it became the subject of a formal commentary. If the text underwent any changes, it was either inadvertent or a one-time fix by a puzzled scribe.[4]

This change in attitude to the Laws of Hammurabi is radical. It is a Copernican revolution in intellectual life, and this study probes the causes of this revolution that enabled, if not necessitated, the rise of formal interpretation. The Laws of Hammurabi did not launch this intellectual revolution, but it was absorbed into its flow. While understanding any text requires an implicit act of interpretation, the development of interpretation that names itself as dependent on another text is more than the rise of a new genre. It is the sharp disjunction between seeing texts as equal and elevating one text above another. It is a profound conceptual and ideological change.

Situating the Laws of Hammurabi in both those traditions contextualizes it as part of cuneiform culture. This culture is known to us through the writing of social and professional groups that utilized the particular writing technology of Mesopotamia that is not only fundamental to a modern academic understanding of the region but that also linked its ancient inhabitants into a shared set of ways of understanding and managing their world.[5] Placing the Laws of Hammurabi in its context in cuneiform culture emphasizes the elements of long-term continuity while shedding light on its individual manifestation of literate culture. It allows for an understanding of what law collections meant to those who composed, memorized, and copied them. It illuminates the relationship between political power, law, and education: it identifies where and under what social and political conditions knowledge was generated, how that knowledge radiated, and where and under what circumstances.

Beyond the Laws of Hammurabi's place in cuneiform culture, it is crucial evidence for the history of law and for understanding the human experience in general. Hans Julius Wolff, one of modern times' most distinguished

[4] See Pamela Barmash, "Scribal Initiative in the Clarification and Interpretation of Mesopotamian Law Collections," in *Birkat Shalom: Studies in Honor of Shalom M. Paul* (ed. Chaim Cohen et al.; Winona Lake, Ind.: Eisenbrauns, 2008), 553–565.

[5] Karen Radner and Eleanor Robson, "Introduction," in *The Oxford Handbook of Cuneiform Culture* (ed. Karen Radner and Eleanor Robson; New York: Oxford University Press, 2011), xxvii.

scholars of Roman law, argued that the reason of greatest importance for the continuing study of Roman law is the light it may shed on the human experience:

> Roman law is not only the best-known, the most highly developed, and the most influential of all the legal systems of the past; apart from English law, it is the only one whose entire and unbroken history can be traced from early and primitive beginnings to a stage of elaborate perfection in the hands of skilled specialists. If studied in the light of modern historical-comparative method, it is particularly suited to give insight into the interrelations of law and other social processes that contribute to the growth and process of law.[6]

While the Laws of Hammurabi and Mesopotamian law do not rival the place of Roman law in the history of Western law, they are the first documentation we have of law in human society, thousands of years earlier than Roman law. Mesopotamian law never attained the systematization and sophistication of Roman law, yet it continued for millennia, achieving a modicum of advancement, and may have exerted a strong influence on the earliest strata of Roman law. Mesopotamian law, too, can "give insight into the interrelations of law and other social processes that contribute to the growth and process of law," as Wolff wrote about Roman law, and the Laws of Hammurabi is a nodal point at which law changed.

The Laws of Hammurabi is greater than the sum of its parts. It is worthy of serious study, and through synchronic and diachronic vectors, this book guides the reader through its multiple dimensions. Mesopotamian royal ideology presented the king as establishing and maintaining justice, and the tradition that a king commission a collection of law had started centuries before Hammurabi. The statutes incorporated in it are shaped by the learning and experience of scribes and express what they deemed fair and just. But the Laws of Hammurabi surpasses earlier law collections in sophistication, length, and scope. The legal culture manifested in the Laws of Hammurabi exercised influence outside of Mesopotamia, although modest and at times indirect.

[6] Hans Julius Wolff, *Roman Law: An Historical Introduction* (Norman: University of Oklahoma, 1951), 5.

I.1. What Is the Laws of Hammurabi?

When the Laws of Hammurabi was first discovered, it was surmised that it was royal legislation, whether a codification of existing law or a reform modifying and overturning it. But because none of the statutes in the law collections was ever cited in legal texts, whether in private legal agreements or in documents that stemmed from court proceedings, a new theory developed that removed the link between the Laws of Hammurabi and law as practiced. This new theory was devised primarily by F. R. Kraus and Jean Bottéro. They argued that the Laws of Hammurabi was never intended for use in legal proceedings but was entirely a product of scribes meant solely for academic purposes. A major area of scribal activity was the creation and transmission of lists, and the Laws of Hammurabi is a manifestation of this phenomenon. The statutes were almost purely academic. However, the pendulum has swung again, and a number of scholars have argued for a mixed characterization, one in which the imprint of law as practiced is evident amid the influence of scholastic concerns.

I.1.1. The Laws of Hammurabi as Royal Legislation

G. R. Driver, a professor of biblical studies, and John Miles, a lawyer and expert on the common law, in their commentary on the Laws of Hammurabi are representative of the view that the Laws of Hammurabi was royal legislation. They considered it to be a series of royal amendments and restatements of existing Old Babylonian law as it was enforced:[7]

> [Hammurabi] was a reformer of law and a legislator, and he did not claim to codify or republish the whole existing law in an improved form. His work, then, is not a collection of existing laws with the amendments and adjustments necessitated by their codification; it is a series of amendments and restatements of parts of the law in force when he wrote. There is therefore no attempt to deal with the law exhaustively and the subjects with which he deals are chosen simply because in his opinion they call for amendment or require to be emphasized by republication.[8]

[7] G. R. Driver and John C. Miles, *The Babylonian Laws* (Oxford: Clarendon, 1952), 1.41–53.
[8] Driver and Miles, *The Babylonian Laws*, 1.45.

Driver and Miles contended that the omission of matters of major importance and lack of systematic presentation demonstrate that the Laws of Hammurabi was not a code in the modern sense. They argued that it is to be compared to the English "Statutes of the Realm," which amends the common law and in so doing serves to codify it. Driver and Miles saw another parallel in English law:

> [The Laws of Hammurabi consisted of statutes that] were something like English case-law, which lays down a rule or a norm of which the purpose is to be followed and regarded is to be had in the spirit and not to the letter of the law. In fact, they set forth what Hammurabi recommended and desired as the law to be followed in his realm.[9]

Driver and Miles argued that the statutes of the Laws of Hammurabi were akin to (English) case law, which presents a rule whose spirit is to be followed, not its letter. The Laws of Hammurabi was to guide the manner and judgments made by courts, but it was not legislation to be followed exactly.

Driver and Miles were aware that the Laws of Hammurabi was never cited,[10] and they adduced other evidence as to the legal applicability of the Laws of Hammurabi. The term *ṣimdatum*, usually translated as "ordinance," appears twice in the Laws of Hammurabi in the phrase "according to the king's ordinance." LH 51 prescribes that if a farmer has borrowed money but cannot repay in silver, he may repay it in grain or sesame at their market value in relation to silver "according to the king's ordinance." LH U also prescribes that if a debtor cannot repay in silver, he may repay a debt in grain, "according to the king's ordinance," and the interest charge for the grain will be the same interest charge for silver, 20 percent, not the interest charge for grain, 33 percent. Both statutes deal with the rate of exchange for grain and silver. Driver and Miles argued that *ṣimdatum*, "ordinance," appeared only once before Rim-Sin and Hammurabi, but that after Hammurabi, it appeared often because the Laws of Hammurabi repealed or affirmed his predecessors' ordinances.[11] Its frequent use after Hammurabi's era demonstrates that the Laws of Hammurabi served to confirm or repeal existing law. It served as a way of signaling a modification.

[9] Driver and Miles, *The Babylonian Laws*, 1.52.
[10] Driver and Miles, *The Babylonian Laws*, 1.53.
[11] It is not so clear why Driver and Miles thought that the phenomenon of restating or modifying law occurred only in Hammurabi's reign and not before (*The Babylonian Laws*, 1.18–22).

I.1.2. The Laws of Hammurabi as Scientific Literature

Other scholars have a distinctly different viewpoint. The most influential of the revisionists, F. R. Kraus and Jean Bottéro, both Assyriologists, argued that the statutes of the Laws of Hammurabi are similar in literary form and origin to omens, a genre of Mesopotamian literature that modern scholars call "scientific" or "scholastic" literature.[12] The statutes were articulated in casuistic form as detailed cases expressed in conditional sentences containing a protasis starting with "if" and an apodosis. This literary pattern is used in omen literature, especially the extispicy omens, omens that deal with oddities in the internal organs of sacrificed animals. A key aspect of omen literature is that the overwhelming majority of omens do not originate from empirical observation. A single omen derived from actual events would be supplemented by variants, whose corollaries were extrapolated by analogy. Actual observations were recorded in a number of these omens, but the omen lists themselves were expanded to make the observations symmetrical, stylistically complete, and artistically elegant.[13] Specific predictions and outcomes were generalized, and a tendency toward paronomasia dictated that a word in the protasis was echoed in the apodosis. Similarly, Kraus and Bottéro argued, a few statutes were based on actual cases on which variants were created to demonstrate the justice of the king. The success of the literary expansion is reflected in the fact that the Laws of Hammurabi was copied in schools for over a thousand years. But the Laws of Hammurabi had nothing to do with the adjudication of law. The Laws of Hammurabi was a scholastic endeavor, divorced from law as practiced.

[12] F. R. Kraus, "Ein zentrales Problem des altmesopotamischen Rechtes: Was ist der Kodex Hammurabi?" *Genava* N.S. 8 (1960): 283–296; Jean Bottéro, "The 'Code' of Hammurabi," in *Mesopotamia: Writing, Reasoning, and the Gods* (trans. Zainab Bahrani and Marc Van De Mieroop; Chicago: University of Chicago Press, 1992 <1982>), 156–184.

[13] A. Leo Oppenheim, *Ancient Mesopotamia: Portrait of a Dead Civilization* (revised edition completed by Erica Reiner; Chicago: University of Chicago Press, 1977), 210–211; Jerrold Cooper, "Apodotic Death and the Historicity of 'Historical' Omens," in *Death in Mesopotamia: Papers Read at the XXVIe Roncontre Assyriologique Internationale* (ed. Bendt Alster; Copenhagen: Akademisk Forlag, 1980), 101–102. Recent analyses of the generative principles of omen texts may be found in Abraham Winitzer, *The Generative Paradigm in Old Babylonian Divination* (Ph.D. dissertation, Harvard University, 2006) and *Early Mesopotamian Divination Literature: Its Organizational Framework and Generative and Paradigmatic Characteristics* (Ancient Magic and Divination 12; Leiden: Brill, 2017).

I.1.3. The Laws of Hammurabi as Royal Propaganda

A significant variant on the royal connection to the Laws of Hammurabi is to deny that it was royal legislation but rather that it was employed for the sake of royal propaganda. Perhaps the most cited of the proponents of this viewpoint is J. J. Finkelstein, who argued that the motivation for the composition of the Laws of Hammurabi was to demonstrate before the public, future kings and posterity, and above all the gods that the king had fulfilled his duty, ordained by the gods, to carry out justice and be reckoned a just king.[14] The law collections were royal apologia, not legislation. They did not need to contain an adjuration to officials to pay heed to their statutes because the Laws of Hammurabi was not legislation. The promulgation of the Laws of Hammurabi was not an event of consequence to Hammurabi's contemporaries, according to Finkelstein: it was directed only at posterity and the gods. Many of the statutes of the Laws of Hammurabi are little more than moral pronouncements that were not intended to be implemented. A litigant could appeal to the provisions of the Laws of Hammurabi if they were appropriate to his case, but citing them served as moral suasion rather than as legal authority. Therefore, the Laws of Hammurabi was not quoted or referenced in records of legal disputes. In contrast, the *mīsharum* acts, edicts of equity, proclaimed at the beginning of a king's reign, were the means by which the king attempted to influence the legal system through socio-economic reforms.

Finkelstein argued that the *mīsharum* acts, the edicts of equity, may have been the "primary inspirational source" for the genre of law collections. He proposed the theory that in the first full year of his reign, a monarch proclaimed a *mīsharum*, an edict remitting specific types of debts for a narrow span of time. The edict might also include a number of procedural regulations meant to be in force during a longer duration. Perhaps at the same time or later there were rules enacted dealing with other legal matters that included remedies, whether financial or physical punishments: these did not include rules that modified the socio-economic system substantially in the way that the *mīsharum* edicts did, but they were intended to promote the king's image as a just king. At a later time, an official text was drafted to include all the pronouncements, and eventually that official text could have served as a source for a law collection.

[14] J. J. Finkelstein, "Ammiṣaduqa's Edict and the Babylonian 'Law Codes,'" *JCS* 15 (1961): 102–104.

Finkelstein argued that any reflection of actual law in the Laws of Hammurabi is purely accidental: when a norm in the Laws of Hammurabi concurs with a document from an actual court case, it must be inferred that the statute in the Laws of Hammurabi reflected legal practice but that it did not prescribe legal practice.[15] Many statutes in the Laws of Hammurabi reflected prevailing legal rules. But Finkelstein observed that at the same time there are many examples among the thousands of legal documents from the Old Babylonian period of situations covered in the Laws of Hammurabi where the legal provisions contradict what is in the Laws of Hammurabi.

I.1.4. More Recent Theories

Raymond Westbrook integrated the two viewpoints and argued that, on the one hand, there is a close connection between the king's legal activities and the Laws of Hammurabi. He contended that the Laws of Hammurabi is an account of past activities of the king in the administration of justice, following Finkelstein.[16] Hammurabi himself is quoted in the epilogue as stating that the preceding rules are "the just judgments" that the king established. However, the judgments were not limited to decisions in litigation: the Old Babylonian kings established rates and prices for services, which were incorporated in LH 241–243 and LE 1–4.

The extensive role of the king in the administration of justice yielded a number of rules on procedure included in the Laws of Hammurabi. Hammurabi's correspondence with his senior officials provides ample evidence for his role as an arbiter and administrator of law. However, Hammurabi's role in the legal arena does not sufficiently explain the statutes in the Laws of Hammurabi. The majority of the statutes belong not to royal judgments but to the genre of scientific literature, where a single example is amplified into many variants. Westbrook followed Kraus's view that the statutes are articulated in the casuistic form characteristic of "scientific literature" and argued for the position that through theoretical speculation, systematic collections of scholastically related cases were devised.

[15] J. J. Finkelstein, "Mishpaṭ, ha-mishpat ba-mizrah ha-qadmon," in *Encyclopaedia Miqra'it* (Jerusalem: Mossad Bialik, 1968), 5.610–611.

[16] Raymond Westbrook, *Old Babylonian Marriage Law* (Archiv für Orientforschung 23; Horn, Austria: Berger & Söhne, 1988), 2–3.

In contrast, I argue that what is crucial to note about the statutes of the Laws of Hammurabi is that *the statutes reflected how a scribe assessed what was just and legally fair because scribes were trained in legal cases, terminology, and concepts and served as legal functionaries.* The statutes were not purely academic. There was a repertoire of standard cases on which a scribe would demonstrate his legal flair, and the standard cases are evident in the statutes of the Laws of Hammurabi. This realization sheds a new light on the legal authority of the Laws of Hammurabi. Searching for legal texts that cite the Laws of Hammurabi is fruitless and misguided. The authority of the Laws of Hammurabi was based on the nature of scribal activities in the legal realm, not on the king's domination over his territory or over the court system. During their education, scribal students copied law collections and model court cases and contracts, and they wrote legal exercises. This educational process instilled a sense of what was just and equitable, and scribes developed an ability to detect and weigh the crucial variables in disputes. Scribes were also involved in legal matters, and their experience affected their thinking about justice and fairness as well. The Laws of Hammurabi manifests how a scribe articulated justice in a repertoire of traditional cases, and its authority lies in how it highlights the factors that need to be taken into account in remedying a wrong and how a wrong or dispute should be adjudicated.

I also argue that the overall structure of the Laws of Hammurabi is that of a royal inscription, in which a set of statutes has been incorporated, and that the imagery of the Stela and content of the royal inscription were configured innovatively to enhance the king's legitimacy. The physical appearance of the Stela served to manifest the political authority of the king, and the artist skillfully manipulated elements standard to a royal presentation scene in order to exalt the king. Concomitantly, the scribe exploited the content of the royal inscription in order to affirm and augment royal authority and jurisdiction.

I.2. The Plan of the Book

In chapter 1, I analyze how the Stela of the Laws of Hammurabi was employed as a manifestation of political power. An investiture scene is at the top of the Stela, and the artist manipulated the imagery cleverly to enhance the legitimacy and authority of Hammurabi. Standard imagery is skillfully reconfigured to exalt him. The king stands alone before Shamash, the god of justice, and the direct gaze between them symbolizes their close bond and the near equality of their status. Other elements in the imagery vividly promoted the message that the gods had exalted Hammurabi and authorized him as king. It is not surprising, then, that a number of stelas inscribed with the Laws of Hammurabi were set up. (Ironically, the Stela itself was seized centuries later by another king wanting to manifest his authority, and then by a modern state displaying its cultural power.)

I examine in chapter 2 how establishing justice was a crucial aspect of a king's legitimacy in Mesopotamian culture. The gods were seen as attentively governing the cosmos and establishing justice, and guaranteeing justice was seen as a duty enjoined upon a king by the gods. This is reflected in three textual genres: acts of equity commemorated in royal inscriptions and hymns, social reform edicts, and law collections. The relationship between these three genres is complex and nuanced, and I sketch out how they intersect and interact.

In chapter 3, I explore how the Laws of Hammurabi employs a rich treasury of rhetorical devices to present its message. It is structured in the form of a royal inscription, but it is not an ordinary agglomeration of hackneyed bromides repeating standard wording. It is inventive and subtle in the way it fuses together a number of models from Hammurabi's royal inscriptions, amplifying the authority of the king and demonstrating his devotion to justice. It incorporates a collection of statutes and presents them as being promulgated by the king immediately after his accession to the throne, rather than decades later: his pious actions are portrayed as timeless and unassailable achievements, rather than in chronological format. Verbal maps depict Hammurabi's domination over different regions.

I analyze in chapter 4 how the statutes in the Laws of Hammurabi are informed by the legal thinking of scribes. Scribes would demonstrate their legal talent and skills by revising and reworking a repertoire of standard cases. Scribes had the freedom and prerogative to compose statutes as they thought they should be: statutes reflected the scribes' personal determination as to which elements in a dispute were decisive and what solutions should be deemed just and equitable. In this way, the statutes refracted law as it was practiced, or at least how individual scribes thought it should be. The scribe composing the Laws of Hammurabi improvised on a repertoire of typical cases in the same way that the scribes who composed earlier law collections had done, but he went beyond the scope and sophistication of the previous compositions.

Mesopotamian scribes were unwilling or perhaps unable to articulate principles, but the scribe composing the statutes in the Laws of Hammurabi projected an intrinsic sense of implicit concepts. The scribe organized them in sets of incremental variants and aimed toward greater conceptualization and systematization, producing a more comprehensive treatment of a legal situation. Cases that share an implicit connection in the mind of the scribe are classed together, and in a few instances I offer explanatory comments that articulate the reasoning behind a ruling.

In the excursus to chapter 4, I use groundbreaking studies of scribal education produced by scholars in order to shed light on the way Mesopotamian scribes composed the statutes of the Laws of Hammurabi: the way they improvised on a shared repertoire of cases develops out of Mesopotamian scribal education. Scribes used what they had learned as building blocks of various kinds—whether of phraseology, textual structures, or concepts—in composing a new work. It is important to move away from the image of a scribe mindlessly copying text: that was not the reality of Mesopotamian scribes. Scribes who mastered Mesopotamian tradition used phraseology, topics, or textual structures in composing a new work. They learned and absorbed legal terminology, model contracts, court records, and administrative documents. This allowed scribes to find employment in many realms, whether in institutions or as freelance scribes working for private individuals, because they could compose whatever legal or administrative document was needed.

In chapter 5, I use the example of the statutes on adoption, a prominent institution in Mesopotamian society, to illustrate how the scribe employed a number of compositional techniques to demonstrate his flair for legal reasoning and conceptualization. The scribe utilized incremental variants, the incorporation of explanation, and the application of specific types of punishment as methods of composition. Legal records demonstrate the artificiality of the statutes because the extant records are about the adoption of adults. By contrast, the statutes are about the adoption of minor children, a sampling that does not accord with reality.

I address the legal authority of the Laws of Hammurabi in chapter 6 by examining whether Hammurabi issued the law collection that bears his name as legislation modifying existing law, as a summation of royal decrees, or as a collection of judicial decisions, whether of the king or of judges. At most, searching for evidence that the Laws of Hammurabi was applied in actual cases or derives from verdicts has yielded mesmerizing hints but no definitive evidence. A legal record provides for the same punishment as a provision in the Laws of Hammurabi, but it is not clear that they are informed by the same principle. Another legal document records the same circumstances as a provision in the Laws of Hammurabi, but while the statute has a striking and singular remedy, the legal record registers a case in progress without the remedy stated. Other legal records also seem to have a tantalizing link to the Laws of Hammurabi, but a mismatch between the cases makes it impossible to make a firm claim.

However, the question that must be examined is whether an approach that seeks to assign a relationship between the Laws of Hammurabi and legal records accurately and effectively illuminates the nature of the legal authority of the Laws of Hammurabi. There is no reason for law to be limited to the logical application of a discrete set of standardized rules, and debating whether the Laws of Hammurabi was legislation or a recapitulation of royal decrees or judicial verdicts is a misplaced effort. The nature of the authority of the Laws of Hammurabi was not based on the king's authority and dominion but on scribal activities in the legal realm. During scribal training, students copied law collections and model court cases and contracts, and they wrote legal exercises. Many scribes worked as legal professionals. This instilled a sense of justice in them. The conflicting rulings they may have learned during training and their experience in legal affairs helped them to think through competing examples of what constitutes justice and to weigh the variables in a particular dispute or offense. The interpretive flair that a scribe exhibited in composing the statutes of the Laws of Hammurabi allowed the scribe to demonstrate expertise in legal reasoning and decision-making and to articulate what he deemed fair and just.

In chapter 7, on the legacy of the Laws of Hammurabi, I examine how the tradition of law collections continued outside of Mesopotamia for more than a millennium after Hammurabi. The Laws of Hammurabi was the culmination of this tradition in Mesopotamia, but this tradition of statutes composed on a repertoire of traditional cases continued in the Hittite Laws and biblical law, even though the royal inscription format was no longer used. I probe the possible influence that the Laws of Hammurabi and Mesopotamian law had on ancient Greek and Roman law. In the second part of chapter 7, I analyze how the Laws of Hammurabi is also a witness to the start of another stream of tradition. The Laws of Hammurabi became a classic text, and no other law collection was copied so often and for so long. The Laws of Hammurabi served as the subject of formal commentaries. The rise of classic texts and formal commentaries signaled a profound cultural shift. Scribes related to the Laws of Hammurabi in ways that diverged from prior attitudes: the Laws of Hammurabi was no longer an improvisation on traditional cases frozen momentarily in written form but itself became an object of study. It became the object of commentary, a genre that names itself as dependent on another text: one text is elevated above another, and that text's obscurities and contradictions are affirmed and explained.

I.3. A Few Technical Notes

One issue debated in scholarship is whether the Laws of Hammurabi and the other law collections should be called "law codes." The objection is that calling these texts by the term "law codes" would denote that they were binding and comprehensive; therefore, it has been argued that they should be called "law collections," not "law codes."[17] This objection has been subject to a counter-argument: it has been claimed that the word "code" is rarely used to refer to a country's comprehensive body of law and that restatements of laws already in force are generally considered to be codifications of law even if the restatements themselves have no binding force.[18] Legal organizations have also drafted model codes, such as the English Draft Criminal Code.

The formal definition of "law code" in the authoritative English-language law dictionary, *Black's Law Dictionary*, is

> A complete system of positive law, carefully arranged and officially promulgated, a systematic collection or revision of laws, rules, or regulations <the Uniform Commercial Code>. Strictly a code is a compilation not just of existing statutes, but also of much of the unwritten law on a subject, which is newly enacted as a complete system of law.[19]

[17] See J. J. Finkelstein, *The Ox That Gored* (prepared for publication by Maria deJ. Ellis; Transactions of the American Philosophical Society 71/2; Philadelphia: American Philosophical Society, 1981), 15–16; Bottéro, "The 'Code' of Hammurabi," 156–184; Kraus, "Ein zentrales Problem des altmesopotamischen Rechts," 292. What is ironic about this stricture is that often enough when a pre-modern law code is studied, it is compared unfavorably to other law codes, which appear to be binding and comprehensive in comparison. See the lament about *Grágás*, the Icelandic laws, by Andrew Dennis, Peter Foote, and Richard Perkins, *Laws of Early Iceland: Grágás* (University of Manitoba Icelandic Studies III; Winnipeg: University of Manitoba Press, 1980), 9.

[18] James Lindgren, "Measuring the Value of Slaves and Free Persons in Ancient Law," *Chicago-Kent Law Review* 71/1 (1995), 150–151, n. 3.

[19] *Black's Law Dictionary* (ninth edition; Bryan A. Garner, editor in chief; St. Paul, Minn.: West/Thomson Reuters, 2009), 292.

These two sentences articulate a definition that marks the term "law code" as aiming at comprehensiveness.[20] The question is whether it is fair to judge the earliest collections of law by a modern standard of comprehensiveness, and I argue in this book that the Laws of Hammurabi is a serious and ambitious attempt at composing a comprehensive collection of law, especially in comparison to its predecessors. The following page in *Black's Law Dictionary* in fact does call the Laws of Hammurabi a "code."[21] A strict definition of "law code" does not capture the nature of the Laws of Hammurabi and the other Mesopotamian law collections, and the debate over whether to term them "law codes" or "law collections" is a red herring. In this study, I call them "law collections" for convenience.

I have termed the legal paragraphs of the Laws of Hammurabi as "statutes." This is no way implies that they were used as rules applied in legal disputes. The term "statutes" is appropriate for sentences or paragraphs that present a legal case or dispute and prescribe a remedy. A genre of Mesopotamian literature analogous to the law collections is omen texts, and the term "omen" is regularly used for the individual paragraphs, even though the overwhelming majority of omens were derived deductively, not through empirical observation, without objection that the term "omen" means that omens originated in observation. It must be noted as well that the text of the Laws of Hammurabi refers to the statutes as *dinâtum*, "verdicts; lawsuits; articles of law," and this term should not be taken as probative that they were used in legal cases.[22]

The references to scribes in this volume should not be mistaken for scribal copyists, especially those of the Middle Ages in Europe. Rather, Mesopotamian scribes evinced a wide range of levels of expertise and were employed in positions with varying levels of autonomy and authority.

In this volume, Sumerian is transliterated in lower case with periods separating each sign. Whole words in Akkadian are normalized in italics. Akkadian syllables are transliterated in lower-case, logograms in capitals, and semantic determinants and phonetic complements in superscript.

[20] This definition also states that a "code" must involve official promulgation, an effort that may include researching and gathering legal resources, selecting and editing them, and officially publishing them in a single text, with the presumption that the text will have an impact on the society in which it is promulgated. The Laws of Hammurabi was officially promulgated, and it may have had an impact in its own time, even though it was not decisive in legal matters, as seen in the number of copies from the Old Babylonian period during which it was composed. See Martha T. Roth, "The Law Collection of King Hammurabi: Toward an Understanding of Codification and Text," in *La Codification des Lois dans l'Antiquité* (ed. Ed Lévy; Paris: De Boccard, 2000), 12–14, 17–19.

[21] *Black's Law Dictionary*, 293.

[22] See CAD D 151–153, s.v. dīnum mngs. 1, 2, 3.

This book follows Martha T. Roth's numbering of statutes in the law collections[23]. Joachim Oelsner also discussed the problems with numbering in "Zur Einteilung des Kodex Ḫammu-rāpi im Altertum," *ZAR* 18 (2012), 79–81.

A number of sigla are used in the translation. Parentheses are used for additional information that clarifies the translation. Square brackets are for reconstructions of an unreadable original text. Angle brackets indicate the correction of a scribal error.

I.4. A Note on the Date of Hammurabi the King

The date of Hammurabi's reign is conventionally given as 1792–1750 BCE according to a chronology termed "the middle chronology." A Belgian-American team of scholars has suggested lowering the chronology by a century, eliminating a hundred years for which we have little documentation, a so-called dark age.[24] But is the lack of evidence sufficient to signify that a period of time did not exist? Perhaps. However, reliable evidence for the elimination of a century should come from new excavations with fresh data, not a possibility during the last three decades; with the renewed use of radiocarbon dating; and from better correlation with chronologies outside of Mesopotamia.[25]

I.5. A Note on the Name of Hammurabi

Whether Hammurabi's name should be normalized as Hammurabi or Hammurapi has been debated. Scholars are evenly divided on this issue.[26] Since the Library of Congress list of subject headings uses "Hammurabi", this volume does so as well for the sake of convenience, even though this author is inclined to argue that "Hammurapi" is the more likely normalization of the king's name.

[23] Martha T. Roth, *Law Collections from Mesopotamia and Asia Minor* (second edition; Society of Biblical Literature Writings from the Ancient World; Atlanta: Scholars Press, 1997), with an explanation of the issues with numbering the statutes, 74–75.

[24] H. Gasche, J. A. Armstrong, S. W. Cole, and V. G. Gurzadyan, *Dating the Fall of Babylon: A Reappraisal of Second Millennium Chronology* (Mesopotamian History and Environment 4; Ghent and Chicago: University of Ghent and the Oriental Institute of the University of Chicago, 1998).

[25] Mario Liverani, "Review of H. Gasche et al., *Dating the Fall of Babylon*," *JNES* 64 (2003): 214–215.

[26] Jack M. Sasson, "King Hammurabi of Babylon," in *CANE* 902; Michael P. Streck, "Hammurabi oder Hammurapi?" *Archiv Orientalni* 67 (1999): 665–669. See also Heather D. Baker, *The Prosopography of the Neo-Assyrian Empire* 2/I (University of Helsinki: Neo-Assyrian Text Corpus Project, 2000), 448.

1

The Stela of the Laws of Hammurabi and the Representation of Political Power

When visitors walk through the Louvre Museum in Paris, a number of objects exert a magnetic attraction on them. They throng to glimpse the *Mona Lisa*. They imagine the *Winged Victory* poised for flight at the top of a grand staircase, and in the halls devoted to art from pre-classical antiquity, the Stela of the Laws of Hammurabi commands their attention. The Stela is a stone monument more than two meters tall, and the platform on which it stands makes it seem even more elevated. The ceiling lights converge on it from across the room, and the curators and museum designers have made it the centerpiece of the room and the adjoining cluster of halls.

Nonetheless, the attention paid to the Stela of the Laws of Hammurabi in the Louvre today is a pale shadow of its significance in its own time. It was a representation of political power, manifesting the political order that the ruler sought to normalize. The Stela conveyed its message through its physical appearance and inscribed text. Its monumentality and decoration sought to substantiate the authority of the king, and its written inscription aimed at legitimizing the king through his establishment of justice. Ironically, the Stela itself was commandeered as booty six centuries later by an invader as a way to exhibit his dominion and authority, and then again three thousand years later by a modern European country wanting to display its political and cultural power.

1.1. The Physical Appearance of the Stela

The Stela of the Laws of Hammurabi is well preserved and basically undamaged.[1] It was originally found in three separate blocks, but it was clear to the

[1] Prudence O. Harper, "Mesopotamian Monuments Found at Susa," in *The Royal City of Susa: Ancient Near Eastern Treasures in the Louvre* (ed. Prudence O. Harper, Joan Aruz, and Françoise

The Laws of Hammurabi. Pamela Barmash, Oxford University Press (2020). © Oxford University Press.
DOI: 10.1093/oso/9780197525401.001.0001.

excavators that the blocks fit together to make a single monument. The Stela is made of diorite, a stone difficult to carve but desirable for public monuments because it can be polished to a radiant gloss.[2] The physical dimensions of the Stela also serve to make it eye-catching: it is 2.25 meters high, 65 centimeters wide, and 1.9 meters in circumference at the base, curving in to 1.65 meters at the top. The base that serves as a support was left blank, but otherwise the Stela was entirely carved with words and images in its original form, as shown in Image 1.1. (When the Stela was taken by the Elamites, a section at its lower front was smoothened for a rededication inscription that was never inscribed.)

The text and imagery are dual reflexes of the message of the Stela.[3] Its design is not clichéd and humdrum: it is innovative and vivid. At the top of the Stela is a scene of an encounter between the god Shamash,[4] the sun god and the god of justice, and Hammurabi, the king.[5] In this depiction, the king is receiving the symbols of royal authority from Shamash.[6] The god stretches out

Tallon; New York: Metropolitan Museum of Art, 1992), 162. Other objects found at Susa, the site at which the Stela was excavated, were defaced and smashed.

[2] Stone was rare in Mesopotamia, but its durability and beauty made it worth the effort of importing it and the arduous task of inscribing it. Most scholars have identified the stone as diorite. See Tallay Ornan, "Unfinished Business: The Relief on the Hammurabi Louvre Stele Revisited," *Journal of Cuneiform Studies* 71 (2019): 85–109.

[3] For insight into the dialectic between text and image, see W. J. T. Mitchell, *Iconology: Image, Text, Ideology* (Chicago: University of Chicago Press, 1986).

[4] This is clearly Shamash because of the rays projecting out of the god's shoulders. Contra Bottéro, "The 'Code' of Hammurabi," 157.

[5] The artistic excellence of the image, done in high relief, is debated. Henri Frankfort argued that the rendering possesses "a fresh awareness of its extraordinary nature" (*The Art and Architecture of the Ancient Orient* [fourth edition; New Haven, Conn.: Yale University Press, 1970], 119), while Denise Schmandt-Besserat highlighted the clumsiness of the portrayal (*When Writing Met Art* [Austin: University of Texas Press, 1997], 95–96). The evaluation depends on whether contortions in the imagery are attributable to the skill, or lack thereof, of the sculptor. The distorted portraiture may be due to the artist attempting to make the features of the characters more visible to those observing it from below (due to the monument's height). The king's shoulders are shown both in front view and in profile, and his fingers that should otherwise be perpendicular to the viewer are depicted frontally. It is debatable whether these distortions are a sign of genius or dullness on part of the sculptor.

[6] Shalom M. Paul correctly noted that the king is depicted as receiving the symbols of authority from the god, not displaying his laws for inspection by the god, as was sometimes commented (*Studies in the Book of the Covenant in Light of Cuneiform and Biblical Law* [Supplements to Vetus Testamentum 18; Leiden: Brill, 1970], 7). The measuring rod and coil of rope were used as a convention in royal investiture scenes (on stelas: Harper, "Mesopotamian Monuments Found at Susa," pp. 169–171, number 110 and fig. 47, and p. 181, number 117; and on seals: Joan Aruz, "Seals of the Old Elamite Period," in *The Royal City of Susa: Ancient Near Eastern Treasures in the Louvre*, pp. 117–118, numbers 76–77; Dominique Collon, *First Impressions: Cylinder Seals in the Ancient Near East* [Chicago: University of Chicago Press, 1987], p. 133, figures 560 and 561). The deities were portrayed in these scenes as the ones holding the rod and coil of rope in their own hands (Collon, *First Impressions*, title page; p. 53, figure 209; p. 127, figure 547). Thorkild Jacobsen argued persuasively that the measuring rod and coil of rope were signs that a god was entrusting the king with works of peace because the building of temples and other monumental structures could only be done during

Image 1.1 The Stela of the Laws of Hammurabi. Diorite, 2.250 m × 0.650 m. Sb 8. Photo: Franck Raux. Musée du Louvre. © RMN-Grand Palais / Art Resource, NY.

his arms and extends a measuring rod and coil of rope toward Hammurabi, symbolizing the transfer of the god's authority and responsibility to the king.

As shown in Image 1.2, the god and the king are highlighted at the climax of the investiture, at the moment the god makes the consequential action. The characters, their clothing, and the pictorial setting are employed to communicate the essential information about the investiture to the onlooker. This genre of imagery, an investiture scene in which a king stands before a deity and receives the deity's favor, is typical of Mesopotamian art. However, the sculptor of the Stela of the Laws of Hammurabi adjusted the images and layout in order to emphasize Hammurabi's status.

Space represents importance: how space was allotted in the image testifies to the significance of each figure.[7] On the Stela of the Laws of Hammurabi, there are only two figures, the god Shamash and Hammurabi, a departure from the typical scene in which a number of figures stand before a divine figure. The god occupies about three-fifths of the image: while that proportion testifies to his superiority over Hammurabi, the fact that the mortal king

peacetime, with the army otherwise occupied with military activities during wartime. The rod and coil of rope were used for the correct orientation and measure of architecture. See Thorkild Jacobsen, "Pictures and Pictorial Language (The Burney Relief)," in *Figurative Language in the Ancient Near East* (London: School of Oriental and African Studies, University of London, 1987), 4. It may also be that these signs of authority were taken both as actual measuring instruments and as a metaphorical measuring device of justice. See Mary Abram, "A New Look at the Mesopotamian Rod and Ring: Emblems of Time and Eternity," *Studia Antiqua* 10 (2011): 15–36; E. Ascalone and L. Peyronel, "Two Weights from Temple N at Tel Mardikh-Ebla: A Link between Metrology and Cultic Activities in the Second Millennium BC?" *JCS* 53 (2001), 7 n.20; Kathryn P. Slanski, "The Mesopotamian 'Rod and Ring': Icon of Righteous Kingship and Balance of Power Between Palace and Temple," in *Regime Change in the Ancient Near East and Egypt: From Sargon of Agade to Saddam Hussein*, (ed. Harriet Crawford, Proceedings of the British Academy; Oxford: University Press, 2007), 37–59; and F. A. M. Wiggerman, "Ring und Stab," RLA 11 (2007): 414–421. Other scholars have argued that the god is dictating the laws to the king or that the king is showing the laws to the god—this seems far-fetched because neither is holding a tablet, either to read to, or bestow upon, the other.

[7] While the relief at the top of the Stela has attracted scholarly attention since the Stela was discovered, I would argue that Schmandt-Besserat's analysis is the most significant advance in its study, and I utilize a number of criteria she has devised to analyze the imagery. See *When Writing Met Art*, 24–25, 36–39. Important contributions have also been made by Dominique Charpin, Le statut des "codes de lois" des souverains babyloniens. in *Le législateur et la loi dans l'Antiquité.Hommage à Françoise Ruzé. Actes du colloque de Caen, 15–17 mai 2003* (ed. P. Sineux. Caen: Presses Universitaires de Caen, 2005), 93–107; Gabriele Elsen-Novák and Mirko Novák, "Der König der Gerechtigkeit.'Zur Ikonologie und Teleologie des '*Codex*' *Hammurapi*," *Baghdader Mitteilungen* 37 (2006): 131–55; Marian Feldman, "Object Agency? Spatial Perspective, Social Relations, and the Stele of Hammurabi," in *Agency and Identity in the Ancient Near East: New Paths Forward*, (ed. Sharon R Steadman and Jennifer C. Ross; London: Equinox, 2010), 148–65; Ornan, "Unfinished Business: The Relief on the Hammurabi Louvre Stele Revisited," 85–109; Katherine E. Slanski, "The Law of Hammurabi and Its Audience," *Yale Journal of Law and the Humanities* 24 (2012): 97–110; Marc Van De Mieroop, "Hammurabi's Self-Presentation," *Orientalia* 80 (2011): 305–338; and I. J. Winter, "Touched by the Gods: Visual Evidence for the Divine Status of Rulers in the Ancient Near East," in *Religion and Power: Divine Kingship in the Ancient World and Beyond* (ed. N. Brisch; Chicago: Oriental Institute, 2008), 75–101.

Image 1.2 Presentation scene from the Stela of the Laws of Hammurabi. Musée du Louvre. Photo Credit: Erich Lessing / Art Resource, NY.

is allocated so much space by himself signals his significance. Typically, such a scene includes other human beings subservient to the god or depicts a god leading the king before a seated deity. But on the Stela, Hammurabi stands alone worshipping Shamash without a retinue of fellow mortals or a divine intermediary. His solo appearance makes him stand out as a hero, near equal in importance to the god.

The Stela diverges from other investiture scenes in another striking way.[8] Other scenes have an element intervening between the king and the deity, as shown in Images 1.3 and 1.4. A king may be pouring a libation onto an altar with a palm frond extending upward from its top, or a star may occupy the space between the two.[9] In the image on the Stela of the Laws of Hammurabi, the background is empty. Nothing intervenes between the god and the king,

[8] Schmandt-Besserat, *When Writing Met Art*, 94.

[9] In Image 1.4, a detail from the "Ur-Namma" Stela, see Jeanny Vorys Canby, *The "Ur-Nammu" Stela* (University Museum Monographs 110; Philadelphia: University of Pennsylvania Museum of Archaeology and Anthropology, 2001).

Image 1.3 Stela depicting a king pouring a libation before a god, 20th–19th c. BCE. Found in Susa, Iran. Sb 7. Limestone, 67 × 62 cm. Musée du Louvre. © RMN-Grand Palais / Art Resource, NY.

and they gaze at one another directly and intensely, without interruption. The artist has streamlined the composition, and by reducing the number of elements, the artistry of the image expresses the relationship between the king and the deity more emphatically.

The scene on the Stela has been simplified in two ways: there are no other figures, and the other objects in the scene are reduced. There is a divine throne without a podium. No altar or other objects intrude on the scene or intervene between the king and the deity. Shamash and Hammurabi are the only ones to appear on a blank background, with the focus on the direct and intense eye contact between the two, highlighting the warm bond and near equality between them.[10]

The direct gaze between king and god is all the more striking in contrast to other exempla of Mesopotamian imagery. Visual compositions often exhibit

[10] Schmandt-Besserat, *When Writing Met Art*, 95.

Image 1.4 Detail of a stela depicting the king Ur-Namma pouring a libation before the god Nanna (the Ur-Namma stela fragment). Courtesy of the Penn Museum, image no. 141417, object no. B16676.

a central image with mirror side images, and the location of a figure signifies its place in social and religious hierarchy. Here in the center is the relationship between Shamash and Hammurabi, exemplified in the direct gaze between near equals.[11] The king's eyes are even on a higher plane than those of the god.[12]

The image mirrors the wording of one of Hammurabi's royal inscriptions, attested in more than a dozen copies: "When Shamash with his shining face looked joyfully upon me, his obedient shepherd, Hammurabi."[13] And it also

[11] Frankfort, *The Art and Architecture of the Ancient Orient*, 119.

[12] Ornan, "Unfinished Business," 90.

[13] There are nine copies of the Sumerian version of this inscription and four copies of the Akkadian versions. For more details, see Douglas Frayne, *Old Babylonian Period (2002–1595 B.C.)* (RIME 4; Toronto: University of Toronto Press, 1990), E4.3.6.2; Arthur Ungnad, *Babylonian Letters of the Hammurapi Period* (Publications of the Babylonian Section 7; Philadelphia: University Museum, 1915), 30–33; Edmond Sollberger and Jean-Robert Kupper, *Inscriptions Royales Sumériennes et Akkadiennes* (Littératures anciennes du Proche-Orient; Paris: Cerf, 1971), 214–215; H. Winckler,

illustrates the declaration of Hammurabi in the text inscribed on the Stela (in the prologue to the Laws of Hammurabi): "I am a prudent king, who listens obediently to Shamash." The image puts Hammurabi's assertion of a warm bond with the deity into visual form: Shamash gazes at him, and Hammurabi makes obeisance to the god.

The size of the two figures of Shamash and Hammurabi demonstrates rank. The god Shamash is depicted only as slightly larger than his human worshipper, and the figure of Hammurabi is not much reduced in size from that of the god. Hammurabi's proportions show that he is lesser in rank than the god, but not by much. There is near equality between the two figures.

Many components of the image signal the close relationship of the king and the god. At the same time, elements depicting the god's dominance, traditional features of a presentation scene, remain. The god is seated, while Hammurabi is standing. This positioning indicates the superiority and dominance of the god over Hammurabi. The physical appearance of the two figures attests to the god's higher status. The god's fuller beard—a square beard with fifteen rows of curls—and thick hair indicates his superior rank over Hammurabi, whose beard has only four rows of curls and hangs below his chin with parallel lines suggesting curly whiskers.[14] Shamash has voluminous hair, while Hammurabi's hair dangles limply below the back of his cap. The god's clothes, a flounced garment with diagonal and horizontal lines suggesting a design, are more elaborate than the mortal king's, whose pleated garment flairs slightly at his ankles without a suggestion of a design. The god's jewelry, twin bracelets and torque, reflect his superior status over a king who has only a single bracelet and a single torque. The god is depicted as sitting on a throne with a footstool, with a three-horned crown on his head and sun rays emanating from his shoulders, as befitting the sun god. Hammurabi stands before him, with his hand covering his mouth, attesting to his submission to the god.

The image contains elements that exemplify Hammurabi's subordination to the god as well as other elements that exalt him to a level near that of the god. But the image is more than a congeries of isolated elements. The image is

"Einige neuveröffentliche texte Hammurabis, Nabopolassars und Nebukadnezars," *ZA* 2 (1887): 122–123; S. Langdon, *Sumerian and Semitic Religious and Historical Texts* (Oxford Editions of Cuneiform Texts 1; London: Oxford University Press, 1923), 23. This motif is not limited to Hammurabi; see, e.g., Rim-Sin I in RIME 4, E4.2.14.20:15–16.

[14] Tallay Ornan suggested that the beards were adjusted or fixed when the Elamites commandeered the Stela. "Unfinished Business," 94–104.

not static: it is not simply the evocation of the memory of a legendary figure. The interplay of elements conveys a story.[15] Hammurabi and the god exemplify action and are not merely juxtaposed. The god and Hammurabi face each other, and they make simultaneous gestures. The rhythm of the action reflects the type of relationship that exists between the two figures, and the orientation of the hands of the figures indicates emotional disposition. The god Shamash is extending his hand holding the symbols of kingship to the king, while Hammurabi, the figure worshipping the god, turns the palm of his hand toward himself, covering his mouth, as an expression of respect and submission.[16] The image is an integrated composition that promotes a message of the exaltation of Hammurabi by the god of justice, not a pell-mell juxtaposition of elements. As the exclusive image on the Stela, the representation of Shamash and Hammurabi as making simultaneous gestures symbolizes the eternity of the relationship between them.

Furthermore, just as the investiture scene at the top of the Stela differed from those commissioned by other Babylonian kings, the overall layout of the Stela of the Laws of Hammurabi differed from other royal monuments.[17] Earlier kings may have had an inscription used as a caption in an image, such as in the Victory Stela of Naram-Sin (Image 1.5), or an inscription inserted between the images, as in the Stela of the Vultures.

But no other king had an image conjoined with such a lengthy text. Apart from the investiture scene, the rest of the Stela is covered by the text of the Laws of Hammurabi. The text is separated from the relief—one is not inside the other—yet despite the division, the inscription and the image are closely juxtaposed.[18] On the obverse (front) of the Stela, the initial line of characters appears directly below the image without any space intervening. On the reverse (back) of the Stela, the inscribed characters touch the edge of the relief, again without any space intervening. The image at the top of the Stela commands attention, but its coordination with the lengthy text causes the observer to reappraise the monument. The focus is equally on both the image

[15] Schmandt-Besserat, *When Writing Met Art*, 90.

[16] A prototype for the image of Hammurabi is extant. A seal of Shamshi-Adad (1808–1776 BCE) shares elements of the depiction of Hammurabi: his pose with his hand humbly in front of his mouth, and his beard, fringed garment, and brimmed cap resemble the relief atop the Stela. See Melissa Eppihemer, "Representing Ashur: The Old Assyrian Rulers' Seals and Their Ur III Prototype," *JNES* 72 (2013), 49.

[17] See e.g., Harper, "Mesopotamian Monuments Found at Susa," pp. 169–170, fig. 110, and p. 181, fig. 117, where an element intervenes between the god and the king, obstructing their direct gaze.

[18] Schmandt-Besserat, *When Writing Met Art*, 90–91.

Image 1.5 The Victory Stela of Naram-Sin, c. 2270 BCE. Pink limestone, h. 198 cm. Found in Susa, Iran. Sb 4. Photo: Franck Raux. © RMN-Grand Palais / Art Resource, NY.

and the text. The image is not subordinate to the text, but neither is the text subordinate to the image.

The text itself is rendered artistically, drawing attention. Fifty-one columns are laid out in vertical lines, skillfully suited to the less than regular shape of the monument, with four columns for the prologue, forty-two for the statutes, and five for the epilogue. Deep horizontal lines intersect the vertical lines to form cases, and within the cases the signs appear in vertical columns. The vertical orientation of the script is archaic, not the one used in the time of Hammurabi. All this makes for an eye-catching geometric design.

The image at the top and the geometric patterning of the inscribed text reinforced the message that the Stela conveyed. This interaction was crucial because the casual passerby could not read the Stela.[19] It is debated what percentage of the population could read, and even if an observer

[19] On the extent of education and literacy, see the excursus to chapter 4.

could read, the physical dimensions of the Stela and the orientation of the script meant that a reader would have to bend and stretch to read the inscription from top to bottom. The text is inscribed in archaic ductus, the manner of writing used before the direction of writing and reading was turned ninety degrees counterclockwise, making it more difficult even for those who could read. The image at the top would have left an impression on the passerby, especially since the image is occupying so much space, one-third the height of the Stela. The extensive space and artistic quality of the text would have captured attention and respect. Even those who were illiterate could comprehend the message of the image and appreciate the intricate design.

Schmandt-Besserat argued that the designer of the Stela exploited the advantages of each medium and was using them in a sophisticated fashion not accomplished earlier.[20] The image and text were meant to blend together, and the characteristics of one were echoed in the other. They reinforced one another. The calligraphy of the inscription was inscribed with great aesthetic beauty, yielding a pattern that is both text and art. In the image, the god's triple-horned crown and the king's royal headdress act like the determinatives in writing, signaling the significance of each figure. The aesthetic valence of the relief was transferred to the text—the text became a calligraphic design. The strength of one medium counterbalanced the weakness of the other. For the illiterate, the text was unreadable and alien, but the image gave life to words. The god so impossible to see was revealed, and the king became present to his subjects. The image of the sun god and the king inspired the onlookers to feel that they were witnesses to a remarkable event.[21] The image animated the inscribed text, giving life to the words and actualizing the text. In so doing, it manifested the king's authority vividly.[22]

[20] Schmandt-Besserat, *When Writing Met Art*, 99. She also argued that it was the artistic representation, the dynamic interface of writing and art, that made the Laws of Hammurabi memorable. However, while it may be that the dynamic interaction was a decisive factor contributing to the preservation of the Stela(s) of the Laws of Hammurabi, what was copied in later texts was not the imagery but the text of the statutes.

[21] The image was placed above eye level so that the viewer would look up at the god and king.

[22] For an instructive example of the interrelationship between text and image and how they reinforced one another in presenting the same ideas, see Beate Pongratz-Leisten, "Tigridian Royal Representation: Text and Image between Tradition and Innovation," in *Text and Image Proceedings of the 61e Rencontre Assyriologique Internationale, Geneva and Bern, 22–26 June 2015* (Orbis Biblicus et Orientalis 40; ed. P Attinger, A. Cavigneaux, C. Mittermayer, and M. Novak; Leuven: Peeters, 2018), 347–354.

Not surprisingly, then, the extant Stela of the Laws of Hammurabi that was excavated at Susa was most likely only one of a number of similar or near identical stelas manufactured for display in various cities of Hammurabi's realm. The text of the Stela states that it was erected at Esagila, the temple of Marduk in Babylon:

> LH XLVII:59–78
>
> In order that the strong not wrong the weak, to provide justice for the destitute[23] girl and the widow, I have inscribed my precious pronouncements upon my stela and set it up before my statue (called) "King of Equity," in Babylon, the city which the gods Anu and Enlil have elevated, within the Esagila, the temple whose foundations are fixed as the heavens and the earth, in order to render the judgments of the land, to give the verdicts of the land, and to provide justice for the wronged.

The wording appears to indicate the Stela was erected in the Esagila temple in Babylon. However, the text of the Stela also contains a reference to the Ebabbar temple in Sippar:

> LH LI:70–83
>
> May the great gods of heaven and earth, all the Anunnaki deities together, the protective spirit (the shedu-spirit) of the temple, (and) the bricks themselves of the Ebarbar temple, curse that one, his seed, his land, his troops, his people, and his army with a terrible curse.[24]

This reference to the Ebarbar temple of the god Shamash in Sippar indicates that the Stela was erected there, and it seems likely that another stela,

[23] See CAD E 72–73 s.v. ekūtu A for the rendering "destitute" instead of "orphan."

[24] Translations published soon after the discovery of the Stela rendered lines 70–85 along the lines of "may the great gods of heaven and earth, all the Anunnaki deities together, curse with a destructive curse the protective spirit of the temple, the brickwork of this Ebarbar temple . . . ," understanding that the Stela was standing in the Ebarbar temple in Sippar (see David Gordon Lyon, "Where and When Was the Code Hammurabi Promulgated?" *JAOS* 27 [1906]: 130–134). However, the text should be construed as "may the great gods of heaven and earth, all the Anunnaki deities together, the protective spirit of the temple, (and) the brickwork of this Ebarbar temple curse with a destructive curse that aforementioned one (the one who defaces the Stela), his seed, his land, his troops. . . ." Confusion arose from determining the referent of *šuāti*, "that one," which the early translators understood as being used attributively modifying the Ebarbar temple, but which is an independent personal pronoun used anaphorically, "the aforementioned one." (See John Huehnergard, *A Grammar of Akkadian* [Harvard Semitic Studies; Winona Lake, Ind.; Eisenbrauns, 2000], 41–42.)

an earlier one, was installed at the Esagila temple in Babylon because of the reference to the Esagila temple. The Elamites took much spoil from Sippar, so that is another clue that the extant Stela of the Laws of Hammurabi was probably erected at the temple in Sippar. Most likely, it remained there in the public eye until it was looted by the Elamites and transported to Susa. We cannot be entirely sure since the Elamite dedicatory inscription was not filled in, and it is unknown whether the Elamite king reached Babylon. Hammurabi did have a palace in Sippar in which he resided from time to time, and he may have lived there near the end of his reign.[25] We can safely presume then that the extant Stela was from Sippar.

Besides the references in the text of the Laws of Hammurabi, there is evidence for other stelas in the other major cities of Hammurabi's realm. At the site in Susa where Scheil found the Stela, he also discovered three small fragments from another possible stela.[26] One fragment contained LH 60–62 and part of the section erased on the Stela. A second fragment contained more of the erased section, and a third fragment contains part of the epilogue as well as more of the erased section. These fragments most likely made up part of another stela since they are made of the same material as the Stela and are incised with the same script. Another stela containing the Laws of Hammurabi may have been set up in Enlil's temple, Ekur, in Nippur, because in a Neo-Babylonian copy, the name of the god Enlil replaces the name of the god Marduk.[27] The substitution may indicate that the copy was based on a text inscribed on a stela erected in Enlil's temple, the Ekur in Nippur.

I want to highlight here another text from Hammurabi's reign that was composed about the same time as the original edition of the Laws, a text with which it shares both language and monumental form and positioning.[28] Both

[25] See AbB 4 number 22.

[26] Victor Scheil, *Textes élamites-sémitiques, quatrième série* (Mémoires de la Délégation en Perse X; Paris: Ernest LeRoux, 1908), 81–84. The Stela of the Laws of Hammurabi was itself found in three pieces: the two pieces forming the lower part were discovered in December 1901, and the piece forming the upper part was found in January 1902. For the initial publication, see Scheil, "Code des Lois de Hammurabi (Droit Privé), roi de Babylone, vers l'an 2000 avant Jesus Christ," in *Textes élamites-sémitiques, deuxiéme série* (Mémoires de la Délégation en Perse IV; Paris: Ernest LeRoux, 1902), 11–162, plates 3–15. Scheil also published *La Loi de Hammourabi Vers Av. J.C.* (Paris: Ernest LeRoux, 1904). For an account of the Susa excavations, see Nicole Chevalier, *Une Mission en Perse 1897–1912* (Paris: Réunion des Musées Nationaux, 1997).

[27] See Avigdor Hurowitz, "Spanning the Generations: Aspects of Written and Oral Transmission in the Bible and Mesopotamia," in *Freedom and Responsibility: Exploring the Challenges of Jewish Continuity* (ed. Rela Mintz Geffen and Marcia Bryan Edelman; Hoboken, N.J.: Ktav, 1998), 15.

[28] Natan Wasserman, "'CT 21, 40–42': A Bilingual Report of an Oracle with a Royal Hymn of Hammurabi," *RA* 86 (1992), 1–18.

CT 21, 40–42 and the Laws of Hammurabi were inscribed on stone monuments, and both CT 21, 40–42 and the original edition of the Laws were composed about the time that Hammurabi conquered Larsa, in the twenty-first year of his reign and commemorated in his twenty-second year name. The phraseology they share may come from the stock phrases employed by scribes, and it may be that the scribes composing each inscription were working alongside one another.[29] The intertextual correspondence between the two texts might be the result of communication between the scribes. But equally intriguing is this: it is reported twice in the Laws of Hammurabi that it was positioned in front of another monument of Hammurabi, his statue as "King of Equity" (XLVII: 74–78 and XLVIII: 6–7), a statue erected in the Esagila temple in year 22 of Hammurabi.[30] The stone statue on which CT 21, 40–42 was inscribed might have been positioned in front of the Stela on which the Laws of Hammurabi was inscribed.[31] Just as the Stela of the Laws of Hammurabi was set up in front of the statue of Hammurabi King of Equity, the stone statue on which CT 21, 40–42 was inscribed was set up in front of the Stela of the Laws of Hammurabi. CT 21, 40–42 and the Laws of Hammurabi may have shared both language and monumental form and positioning.

As for whether previous kings displayed their law collections in a stela, that is debatable. There is little evidence that they did,[32] and whether we assert that there were others that simply have not been found depends on whether we assess the Stela of the Laws of Hammurabi as an innovation or as the sole extant example of an earlier tradition of displaying a law collection on a stela.

Whether previous kings displayed their law collections in a stela or not, it may be that the Stela served as a model for later kings to raise stelas of a law collection. Two objects with presentation scenes similar to the image on the Stela were found at the excavations at Susa, and it may be speculated that they also served as monuments for an inscribed law collection. One limestone stela features a presentation scene of the king before a seated deity at its top, similar to that at the top of the Stela of the Laws of Hammurabi. This scene

[29] Wasserman, "'CT 21, 40–42,'" 7–12.

[30] Jørgen Laessøe, "On the Fragments of the Hammurabi Code," *JCS* 4 (1950–1951), 186.

[31] Wasserman, "'CT 21, 40–42,'" 18.

[32] An inscription of the Elamite ruler Attahushu (ca. 1927 BCE) mentions that "a stela of justice" was erected in the market at Susa, but it is not clear what that stela would have included. See Victor Scheil, *Mélanges Épigraphiques* (Mémoires de la Délégation en Perse XXVIII; Paris: Ernest LeRoux, 1939), 4–7.

does incorporate a royal libation poured into a symbolic plant, representing the king's role as maintaining the fertility of the land. This presentation scene does differ from the one on the Stela by the inclusion of a date palm altar, and it is debatable whether that overly detracts from the open and spacious setting.[33] The role of maintaining fertility is mentioned in the prologue to the Laws of Ur-Nammu and may have been mentioned in the prologue to other law collections, but it is absent in the prologue to the Laws of Hammurabi.[34] If this image is from a stela of a law collection, the omission of the king's role in ensuring fertility may be why the libation and altar are omitted in the Stela of the Laws of Hammurabi. The second object with a similar presentation scene is a basalt stela with an Elamite ruler approaching a seated god and, like the Stela of the Laws of Hammurabi, it might be the top of another stela of laws.[35] Since the Stela was taken by the Elamites, it could have served as a model for an Elamite king.

It would not be surprising if later royal administrations displayed a law collection on a stela because the Stela of the Laws of Hammurabi was effective as a manifestation of political power. It is a bold assertion of royal authority because its decoration forcefully affirms Hammurabi's right to rule. The Stela's design is not banal and humdrum: it is innovative and incorporates vivid use of imagery that reinforces royal control. The blending of text and ornamentation is inventive and catches the eye of the onlooker. Its monumentality and decoration conveyed a forceful message about the authority of the king. Text and image were joined together to impress the onlooker: the decoration and text of the Stela are an integrated composition that incisively promoted the message that Hammurabi has been exalted and authorized as king by the gods.[36]

[33] Harper, "Mesopotamian Monuments Found at Susa," 169–170.

[34] Another relief, one with an image but without text, has been identified as an exemplar of the Laws of Ur-Namma (Douglas Frayne, *Ur III (2112–2004 BC)*, (RIME 3; Toronto: University of Toronto, 2008), 45). Researchers have hypothesized that it might be a piece of a monument with the law collection inscribed: it contains an image depicting Ur-Namma pouring an oblation before a seated god, a scene similar to this fragment of a stela. Like the Stela of the Laws of Hammurabi, it was found at Susa and was probably taken as booty from Sippar.

[35] Harper, "Mesopotamian Monuments Found at Susa," 182.

[36] The overall structure of the Laws of Hammurabi is an expression of the king's relationship to the divine, yet the statutes do not include any ritual law or any type of religious law that regulates human behavior toward the gods. The statutes in the Laws of Hammurabi resolve disputes of an everyday nature, disputes that often arise between members of a society. Recourse was to be made to religious acts, such as the river ordeal or oaths before a deity, but they are used to regulate society, not shape an individual's or society's relationship with the gods.

1. 2. The Role of the Gods in Justice

The appearance of a deity on the relief at the top of the Stela of the Laws of Hammurabi signals the crucial importance of divinities in justice. In the Mesopotamian worldview, the gods guided the activities of the cosmos, and particular gods had their sphere of responsibility. Justice was a concern of the gods, and a number of deities supervised it. Hammurabi is portrayed as being commissioned by the gods to establish justice, and he himself is compared to the sun god when he guarantees justice.

The primary god perceived to be the god of justice is Shamash (Sumerian Utu), and it is his figure that interacts with Hammurabi at the relief at the top of the Stela.[37] The sun god's presence was manifested in sunlight, and presumably nothing was hidden from the intense light experienced by those living in Mesopotamia. The sun god observed the activities of human beings in his journey sailing over the earth during the day. He was, therefore, in the appropriate position to judge human behavior and supervise justice. His nighttime journey through the underworld allowed him to judge the dead.[38] As one hymn pronounces,[39]

(11) In the general assembly, you are its first judge. . . .
(14) Utu, of the just man, you are his helper.
(15) Utu, to the wicked, you destroy his foothold,
(16) You apprehend the criminal in his flight. . . .
(21) Utu, the judge, Utu, (you are) the decider
(22) Utu, the judge of the gods. . . .
(26) Utu, you are the god of justice. . . .
(28) Utu, (you are) the principal judge in the land (of Sumer).
(29) Utu, to give judgment is in your power.
(30) Utu, to issue decisions is in your power.
(31) Utu, justice is in your power.

[37] For more on the sun god Shamash, see Dominique Charpin, "'I Am the Sun of Babylon': Solar Aspects of Royal Power in Old Babylonian Mesopotamia," in *Experiencing Power, Generating Authority: Cosmos, Politics, and the Ideology of Kingship in Ancient Egypt and Mesopotamia* (ed. Jane A. Hill, Philip Jones, and Antonio J. Morales; Philadelphia: University of Pennsylvania Museum of Archaeology and Anthropology, 2013), 65–96; Claudia Fischer, "Twilight of the Sun-God," *Iraq* 64 (2002), 125–134.

[38] Claus Wilcke, *Early Ancient Near Eastern Law: A History of Its Beginnings—The Early Dynastic and Sargonic Periods* (Winona Lake, Ind.; Eisenbrauns, 2007), 36.

[39] Samuel Noah Kramer, "Sumerian Theology and Ethics," *Harvard Theological Review* 49 (1956), 56–59; Kramer, "Law and Justice: Gleanings from Sumerian Literature," in *Reflets des deux fleuves: volume de melanges offerts à André Finet* (Akkadica Supplementum 6; ed. M. LeBeau and P. Talon; Leuven: Peeters, 1989), 79–80.

The god plays a preeminent role in providing justice. Even in hymns where the god's other activities, such as his appearance in sunrise from behind the mountains, is praised, a transition is swiftly made to the god's judicial role.

The Hymn to Shamash[40]

(56) Before you the wicked and just prostrate themselves.
(57) [There is none] but you who goes down to the deep,
(58) [. . .] you blaze abroad the judgments on the criminal and law-breaker.
(59) . . .
(60) It/he pours bruises upon him. . . .
(61) You dismiss (to the underworld) the rogue who is surrounded [. . .]
(62) You bring up from the underworld river the one entangled in a lawsuit [. . .]
(63) What you say in a just verdict, Shamash. . . .
(85) He who in taking an oath [. . .]
(86) Who does not fear [. . .]
(87) Your wide net is spread [. . .]

Shamash is praised in this hymn for presiding over justice in general. The hymnist then shifts the focus to particular types of offenders. The fate of an adulterer is highlighted in an elaborate description:

(88) A man who covets his neighbor's wife
(89) Will [. . .] before his appointed day.
(90) A nasty snare is prepared for him [. . .]
(91) Your weapon will strike at him, and there [will be] none to save him.
(92) [His] father will not stand for his defense,
(93) And at the judge's command, his brothers will not plead.
(94) He will be caught in a copper trap that he did not foresee.
(95) You destroy the horns of a scheming villain.
(96) A zealous . . . his foundations are undermined.

[40] BWL, 129; Erica Reiner, *Your Thwarts in Pieces, Your Mooring Rope Cut: Poetry from Babylonia and Assyria* (Michigan Studies in the Humanities 5; Ann Arbor: Horace Rackham School of Graduate Studies at the University of Michigan, 1985), 72–73, 75–76.

The corrupt judge is expressly condemned:

(97) You give the unscrupulous judge the experience of fetters.
(98) You make the one who accepts a bribe and lets justice miscarry bear his punishment.
(99) As for him who declines a bribe but nevertheless takes the part of the weak,
(100) It is pleasing to Shamash, and he will prolong his life.
(101) A circumspect judge who pronounces just verdicts
(102) Controls the palace and lives among the princes.

The hymn then proceeds to focus on the activities of the merchant, both dishonest and honest:

(103) How is the one who invests money in unscrupulous trading missions benefitted?
(104) He is disappointed in regard to profit and loses his capital.
(105) As for him who invests money in distant trading missions and pays one shekel per . . .
(106) It is pleasing to Shamash, and he will prolong his life.
(107) The merchant who practices trickery as he holds the scales,
(108) Who uses two sets of weights, thus lowering the . . .
(109) He is disappointed in the matter of profit and loses (his capital).
(110) The honest merchant who holds the scales (and gives) true weight,
(111) Everything is presented to him in good measure[. . . .]
(112) The merchant who practices trickery as he holds the grain measure,
(113) Who weighs out loans by the minimum standard but requires a large quantity in repayment,
(114) The curse of the people will overtake him before his time,
(115) If he demanded repayment before the agreed date, there will be guilt upon him.
(116) His heir will not assume control of his property,
(117) Nor will his brothers take over his estate.
(118) The honest merchant who weighs out grain by the maximum standard, thus multiplying kindness,
(119) It is pleasing to Shamash, and he will prolong his life.

(120) He will enlarge his family, gain wealth,
(121) And like the water of a never failing spring his descendants will never fail.
(122) For him who does kind deeds and knows no trickery—
(123) The man who constantly disguises his intentions with hypocrisy—his case is before you.
(124) The progeny of evildoers will [fail].
(125) Those whose mouth says no—their case is before you.
(126) In a moment you discern what they say.
(127) You hear and examine them; you determine the lawsuit of the wronged.

The hymn details the god's actions in ensuring justice by punishing specific types of malefactors, emphasizing that the sun god helps the honest and punishes the unscrupulous.

The motif about the care of widows and orphans, usually articulated in a stock formula about human kings, is employed to depict the sun god.

Shir-namshub Hymn to Utu, lines 50–56

For those who venture forth single-handed, who venture forth from a man's house, for those who venture forth from a man's house, who venture forth single-handed, Utu: you are their mother, Utu, you are their father. Utu, as for the orphans, Utu, as for the widows, Utu: the orphans look to you as their father, Utu, you succor the widows as their mother.[41]

As an extension of the concept that the sun god oversaw justice, being present in the light of the sun appears to be linked to legal activities and justice.[42] Two deities, Enlil and Ninlil, are depicted as rendering judgments while orienting themselves toward the morning appearance of the sun god:

Enlil in the Ekur, line 164[43]

You decide the fates together at the place facing the sun god.

[41] See Samuel Noah Kramer, "BM 23631: Bread for Enlil, Sex for Inanna," *Or* 54 (1985), 127; ETCSL 4.32.f <http://etcsl.orinst.ox.ac.uk/section4/tr432f.htm>

[42] Mary Shepperson, "The Rays of Šamaš: Light in Mesopotamian Architecture and Legal Practice," *Iraq* 74 (2012), 57.

[43] ETCSL 4.05.1 <http://etcsl.orinst.ox.ac.uk/section4/tr4051.htm>

Facing the sun may make a person more inclined to tell the truth. In a Neo-Babylonian letter, two sisters write to their brother:

> Lift your head and tell the truth by looking towards the sun (god).[44]

By cajoling their brother to face the light, they hope to make him admit the truth.

Legal decisions were delivered in major gateways, especially of temples. The main entrances of temples appear to be oriented toward maximizing the intensity and duration of morning sunlight.[45] Their gate-entrances served as a local site where legal transactions would take place.

While Shamash was the primary god of justice, other gods could act as judge. In Gudea Cylinder A, 10:24–26, the god Ningirsu is likened to the sun god:

> In the Ebarbar, the place where I issue orders, where I shine like Utu, I decide justly, like Ishtaran, the lawsuits of the city.[46]

The goddess Nanshe was perceived to judge humanity on New Year's Day, with the goddess Nisaba, the goddess of writing and accounting, at her side.[47]

> (20) She is concerned for the orphan and concerned for the widow.[48]
> (21) She does not forget the man who helps (?) others,
> (22) She is a mother for the orphan;
> (23) Nanše, a carer for the widow,
> (24) Who always finds advice for the debt-slave,
> (25) The lady who gives protection for refugees.
> (26) She seeks out a place for the weak.
> (27) She swells his collecting basket for him;

[44] A. Leo Oppenheim, *Letters from Mesopotamia* (Chicago: University of Chicago Press, 1967), 193.
[45] Shepperson, "The Rays of Shamash," 57–62.
[46] Dietz Otto Edzard, *Gudea and His Dynasty* (Toronto: University of Toronto Press, 1997), RIME 3/1, E3/1.1.7.CylA x 24–26; ETCSL 2.1.7.271–273 <http://etcsl.orinst.ox.ac.uk/section2/tr217.htm>; Ira M. Price, "The Relation of Certain Gods to Equity and Justice in Early Babylonia," *JAOS* 52 (1932), 175.
[47] ETCSL 4.14.1, <http://etcsl.orinst.ox.ac.uk/section4/tr4141.htm>
[48] The motif of caring for the orphan and the widow has the same content as the motif employed for human kings, but it is not articulated in the identical stock formula as in many of the texts about human kings.

(28) She makes his collecting vessel profitable for him.
(29) For the righteous maiden who has taken her path,
(30) Nanshe chooses a young man of means.
(31) Nanshe raises a secure house like a roof over the widow who could not remarry.

The goddess is also portrayed as inspecting the temple personnel on New Year's Day and discharging those who have been negligent or corrupt.[49] While the activity of the deity is mythological, it may reflect the historical practice of the yearly review of temple officials. The passage also reflects a number of procedures of Mesopotamian law: the testimony of witnesses, the notation of tablets, and the use of the river ordeal as a judicial determinant.[50]

Considering the crucial role of the gods in justice, it is not surprising, then, that the gods, especially the sun god, are portrayed as commissioning kings to guarantee justice through the promulgation of law collections. This is true for the Laws of Hammurabi. Even the earliest collection of law extant, the Laws of Ur-Namma, begins with the declaration that the king was empowered by the sun god, Shamash, and the city-god of Ur, Nanna, to dispense justice:[51]

Laws of Ur-Namma A iii 104–113
[At that time, I] Ur-Namma [mighty warrior, lord of the city of Ur, king of the lands of Sumer] and Akkad, [by the might] of the god Nanna, my lord, [by the true command of the god Utu], I established [justice in the land].

The king is depicted as fulfilling the divine mandate to institute justice.

[49] Hymn to Nanshe A, lines 94–112: "At new year, on the day of rites, the lady pours water as a libation on the holy. . . . On the day when the bowls of rations are inspected, Nanshe also inspects the servants during the appointments. Her chief scribe Nisaba places the precious tablets on her knees and takes a golden stylus in her hand. She arranges the servants in single file for Nanshe and then it will be decided whether or not a leather-clad servant can enter before her in his leather, whether or not a linen-clad servant can pass before her in his linen. Any registered and . . . hired (?) person about whom observers (?) and witnesses claim to witness his fleeing from the house will be terminated in his position. . . . The king who always cares for the faithful servants, Haia, the man in charge of registration, registers on a tablet him who is said to be a faithful servant of his lady but deletes from the tablet her who is said not to be the maidservant of her lady."

[50] The hymn also records the types of actions considered offensive, lines 137–221.

[51] The beginnings of the other law collections, the Laws of Lipit-Ishtar and the Laws of Eshnunna, are not preserved, and therefore we cannot know whether they started with the commissioning of the king by the sun god.

It is striking but not surprising that kings are compared to the sun god when they establish justice.[52] An early king who was the subject of many hymns, Gudea, is depicted as establishing justice and is likened to the sun god:

Gudea Cylinder B, 18:10–13

Days of justice had risen for him, and he set his foot on the neck of evil and complaint.

Had he not himself risen for his city from the horizon like Utu?[53]

Other kings are also likened to the sun god when issuing verdicts:[54]

Iddin-Dagan B

When, like Utu, you (Iddin-Dagan) bring forth a just light, people's eyes are indeed directed towards it.[55]

Ishme-Dagan A + V

When, like Utu, I (Ishme-Dagan) decide a just verdict, the people bring their prayers to the holy shrines (?).[56]

The judicial activity of Hammurabi is matched to the rising of the sun god in both the prologue and epilogue of the Laws of Hammurabi:

LH I:32–44

At that time, Anum and Enlil to improve the welfare of the people pronounced my name Hammurabi the pious prince who fears the gods,
to make justice prevail in the land,
to destroy evil and wickedness,
to prevent the strong from oppressing the weak,
to rise like Shamash over the black-headed people and illuminate the land.

52 See Charpin, "I Am the Sun of Babylon," 75–96; Fischer, "Twilight of the Sun-God," 130–134.

53 Edzard, *Gudea and His Dynasty*, RIME 3/1, E3/1.1.7.CylB xviii 10–13.

54 The likening of a king to the sun god may be more general in some instances. Naram-Sin is portrayed as rising like the sun god on the holy dais of Akkad in "The Curse of Akkad," lines 40–41. See <http://etcsl.orinst.ox.ac.uk/section2/tr215.htm>. Naram-Sin may also be depicted on the "Victory Stele of Naram-Sin" as the representation of the sun god when he rises. See Claudia Fischer, "The Twilight of the Sun-God," *Iraq* 64 (2002), 125–134. That the general deification of a king as a sun god may be part of the royal ideology of the Sargonic and Ur III dynasties, see Steinkeller, *History, Texts, and Art in Early Babylonia*, 138–150.

55 ETCSL 2.5.3.2, <http://etcsl.orinst.ox.ac.uk/cgi-bin/etcsl.cgi?text=t.2.5.3.2#>

56 ETCSL 2.5.4.01, <http://etcsl.orinst.ox.ac.uk/cgi-bin/etcsl.cgi?text=t.2.5.4.01#>

LH XLVII:15–21
I have sought for (the black-heade0d people) peaceful places.
I have removed difficulties.
I have spread light over them.

While it may seem far-fetched for the king to be likened to the sun god (or any god), the parallel was made because the king was portrayed as fulfilling a divine mandate to ensure justice and the sun god played a crucial role in guaranteeing justice in the cosmic order. The hyperbole is extended further on in the Laws of Hammurabi: another subsequent passage names Hammurabi as "the god of kings" (III 17–23).[57]

Hammurabi was depicted as intent on ensuring the proper regulation of society through the establishment of justice. In so doing, he emulated the gods, who were not seen as capricious but as attentively governing human society and the cosmos and guaranteeing justice. Not surprisingly, the relief at the top of the Stela of the Laws of Hammurabi portrays Hammurabi receiving the symbols of royal kingship from the god of justice.

1. 3. Monumentality: The Stela as Monument

Monumentality, the physical presence of the Stela of the Laws of Hammurabi, served the king both as an individual and as a royal personage. The physical

[57] The audacity of the epithet "the god of kings" has motivated an emendation of the text. Martha T. Roth suggested <šubat> ili šarrī, "<the dwelling of> the god of kings," and attached it to the mention of the Ezida temple so that the text would read "to the Ezida temple, <the dwelling of> the god of kings" (Roth, *Law Collections*, 140 n.1). However, considering that Hammurabi is described elsewhere in the Laws of Hammurabi as "rising like Shamash over the black-headed people" and "who illuminates the lands of Sumer and Akkad," depictions that clearly liken the king to Shamash, the sun god and the god of justice, the hyperbole of "the god of kings" does not appear out of place. Another royal inscription names him as "the god of his country" (Edmond Sollberger, "Two Old-Babylonian Royal Inscriptions," in *Essays on the Ancient Near East in Memory of Jacob Joel Finkelstein* [ed. M. de Jong Ellis; Hamden, Conn.: Archon, 1977], 197). While deification seems like sheer effrontery, it is not unique. Other hymns and inscriptions show that other kings were portrayed in such magnification, such as Shulgi and Ammi-ṣaduqa. For example, a hymn to Shulgi recounts his deification by the goddess Nin-sumun:

Shulgi Hymn P, segment C 56–59
(Nin-sumun says:) The great Anunaki gods stood up together at the place where destinies are determined,

(and) on my account, they made manifest the shepherdship of Shulgi for all time.

They caused Shulgi, the righteous one, to rise in the land like the sun-god in order to be (the people's) god. <http://etcsl.orinst.ox.ac.uk/section2/tr24216.htm>

It must be noted that terming the king as a god does not mean that the king was perceived to be of the same status as high-ranking divinities.

existence of the Stela acted as a means of preserving the king's name and existence after his death. It prevented the king from falling into oblivion. And as we have seen, the Stela also served to manifest the king's power and authority through the material existence of the Stela and through its imagery and decoration. The presentation of the king's deeds and statutes in the text inscribed served to amplify the king's dominion even further.

1. 3.1. The Preservation of the King's Name

The Mesopotamians regarded names as possessing great significance for an individual: a name was not considered arbitrary or mere convention.[58] A person's name contained the essence of a person, and like a person's genes, it encoded one's role and actions in life according to the divine plans on the Tablet of Destinies. To exist, one must have a name.[59] Exceptional personalities had more than one name, especially so among the gods and goddesses, and Marduk, raised to the acme of the pantheon in the first millennium BCE, had fifty names to embody his exaltation.[60] Preserving one's name was crucial to human beings, and the recollection of a person's name became a crucial part of the memorialization of the dead.[61]

Apprehension of falling into oblivion served as the impetus for a monarch to commission memorabilia of his reign. The epilogue of the Laws of Hammurabi avers:

> LH XLIX:2–52
> If that man heeds the words which I have inscribed on my stela,
> and does not throw out my judgments, does not change my words,
> does not alter my engraved image,
> then may the god Shamash lengthen his reign, just as he has done for me,
> the king of equity.
> May he tend his people with equity.

[58] Schmandt-Besserat, *When Writing Met Art*, 63–66.

[59] Jean Bottéro, "Le Noms de Marduk," in *Essays on the Ancient Near East in Memory of Jacob Joel Finkelstein* (Memoirs of the Connecticut Academy of Arts and Sciences 19; ed. Maria de Jong Ellis; Hamden, Conn.: Archon Books, 1977), 26.

[60] See W. G. Lambert, *Babylonian Creation Myths* (Winona Lake, Ind.; Eisenbrauns, 2013), 160–168.

[61] Schmandt-Besserat, *When Writing Met Art*, 64. There was the fear that if the dead were not memorialized, their ghosts would haunt the earth and trouble the living.

(However), if that man does not heed the words which I have inscribed on my stela,
and he disdains my curses, and does not fear the curses of the gods,
and overturns the judgments which I issued, changes my words, alters my engraved image, erases my inscribed name and inscribes his own name,
or because of those curses, has another do so—
that man, whether king, lord, governor, or any person at all,
may the great god Anum, father of the gods, who has proclaimed my reign, remove the aura of royalty from him, smash his scepter, and curse his destiny.

The later king who preserves Hammurabi's name and judgments is blessed, but the king who erases Hammurabi's name is condemned.

The Stela and its inscription served to preserve the king's name and existence after his death by the monument's physical existence. They prevented the king's name from falling into oblivion. In so doing, the purpose of the Stela and its inscription mirrored the purpose of many a royal inscription. The king's name and identity escaped the grave.[62]

1. 3.2. The Manifestation of Royal Power through the Promulgation of a Royal Monument

The physical presence of the Stela and its decoration and textual inscription served to manifest Hammurabi's rule and legitimacy. Its sheer physicality acted as a reminder of the king's actions and authority, and its material dimensions enhanced his prestige as ruler. The imagery and decoration of the Stela served to affirm his rule, as we have seen, and the inscribed text acted as another means, perhaps even more effective, of confirming his legitimacy as king.

In general, monumental art served as symbols of the ideology of a state, whether Hammurabi's or another king's.[63] It affirmed that there should be a state, with a centralized leadership under a monarch and a ruling elite, the controlling and the controlled. Obedience was due to a monarch because he

[62] Jeremy D. Smoak, "Describing Temple Space: The Ekron Dedication as Monumental Text," *JNES* 76 (2017), 319.

[63] Norman Yoffee, *Myths of the Archaic State: Evolution of the Earliest Cities, States and Civilizations* (Cambridge: Cambridge University Press, 2004), 39.

guaranteed law and order. He mediated between the gods and human society and thereby deserved to amass power and wealth, as did the elite who served him and furthered his aims.

In promulgating royal inscriptions and monuments, Hammurabi was employing two methods of convincing the public that the king has control and authority—tradition and religion, which maintained and altered tradition.[64] Tradition assured continuity and stability. Tradition gave the appearance that the king could avert disorder and the accompanying economic crisis. The ruler and his administration engaged with or rejected tradition based on whether it upheld his power. They preserved or altered tradition so long as it allowed him (and them) to continue political domination. They retained traditions that were controlled by royal needs.

At the same time, religion anchored the order of social life, and it made the role of the king and his law unassailable. It was crucial for Hammurabi as he expanded his empire that his base continued to accept his political domination. A threat to social order might come from developments internal to a society. Religion served as an essential structural element anchoring social life: it made aspects of society appear to be ordained by the gods and therefore immutable and unalterable. It justified the ruler as the guarantor of order and prosperity for the community. By using tradition and religion, Hammurabi sought to assure the public of the effectiveness of his ability to maintain control.

The Stela and the text of the Laws of Hammurabi served as political and theological propaganda to win the allegiance of the inhabitants of city-states that had been independent but were now under his rule. Hammurabi's political system no longer enriched them but channeled wealth to the capital at the expense of the conquered city-states. The Laws of Hammurabi was meant to convince the hearts and minds of the inhabitants of formerly autonomous city-states to accept royal authority. In so doing, Hammurabi was following the traditional pattern of a king in affirming his legitimacy.

Hammurabi and his regime were not unique in creating monuments and promulgating royal inscriptions. Other Mesopotamian kings and their administrations sought to legitimate their rule in monuments and royal inscriptions. It may be that Hammurabi needed no special affirmation

[64] Marlies Heinz and Marian H. Feldman, "Introduction: Representation—Tradition—Religion," in *Representations of Political Power: Case Histories from Times of Change and Dissolving Order in the Ancient Near East* (Winona Lake, Ind.: Eisenbrauns, 2007), 1.

beyond the usual circumstances common to any monarch's reign. However, it is probable that his authority required more because of the circumstances in which his empire came into being. In the power vacuum left at the beginning of the second millennium BCE, many city-states vied for domination in southern and central Mesopotamia, and the area was riven by a near-constant state of war. Kings competed violently for dominance. But it was Hammurabi who succeeded in extending his rule from the area around the city of Babylon out to the east and the west.[65] Crucially, he gained control of the heavily populated south, and his administration utilized tight regulation to exert domination over land, even if previously specific tracts of land had been owned privately. Resources from the south were shifted to the capital in the north, and local concentrations of power were sidelined. Hammurabi sought to achieve political unification by means of imperialistic policies. In this political context, he differed from most of the earlier kings, and the physical presence of his monument served as special affirmation of the legitimacy of his rule.

Dominion over other territories was not a legacy to Hammurabi from earlier members of his dynasty. The kings of Babylon prior to Hammurabi did not manage to extend their kingdom, with the modest exception of Suma-la-el, the second in the dynastic line. During his forty-five-year reign, he subdued Sippar and brought it under his control. Hammurabi's conquests, by contrast, were far more extensive.

Even so, Hammurabi's success did not last long.[66] Hammurabi's unification of the region existed only in the final dozen years of his reign and did not last beyond the reign of his son and successor. His empire was ephemeral. Pressures from the north, west, and south eventually eroded it. It may be that these stresses were already evident during his reign, and the raising of the Stela and the probable existence of other stelas were an attempt to strengthen Hammurabi's dominion over his extended kingdom.

[65] Marc Van De Mieroop, *King Hammurabi of Babylon: A Biography* (Malden, Mass.; Blackwell, 2005), 15–78; Yoffee, *Myths of the Archaic State*, 104.

[66] Hammurabi's empire was a highly centralized state: it was initially prosperous from tribute and taxes from far-flung provinces, but then collapsed. Norman Yoffee claimed that the state was too inflexible (*The Economic Role of the Crown in the Old Babylonian Period* [Malibu, Calif.: Undena, 1977], 149), but which empire of the time in that region was more long-lasting? In fact, Hammurabi's state arose as a territorial kingdom after a long period of fractured city-states. A smaller state under later monarchs of his dynasty managed to continue and did not fall victim to a foreign foe, even though it was sacked by the Hittite king, Mursilis I. The Hittites did not assume control of Babylonia. Only much later in the second millennium BCE did a new dynasty, the Kassite dynasty, rule a territorial state in Mesopotamia for four hundred years.

It was not just the unification of different regions under a single rule that posed a challenge. Mesopotamian city-states themselves were not monolithic communities. They consisted of Sumerians, Akkadians, Amorites, Kassites, Hurrians, and others.[67] How could they interact without a sense of commonality? This was even more so the case in the development of an empire in Hammurabi's time. Unifying his kingdom may have served as another reason for erecting the Stela.

There may have been an additional need for Hammurabi to affirm his legitimacy. Hammurabi as heir to an Amorite dynasty may have been aware that his dynasty differed culturally from the people over whom it ruled and that the ruler's native culture was deemed to be inferior.[68] In order to establish the legitimacy of his reign and authority, the ruler needed the bureaucratic know-how and the royal ideology promulgated by the scribes. It was vital for the ruler to adopt and foster existing cultural traditions, and the promulgation of a law collection and the raising of a stela served as a means to do so.

The Laws of Hammurabi enshrined as a royal monument served to exert the king's authority. It was more psychological and cultural than coercive: it sought to use position and prestige rather than military force or economic pressure. It should be emphasized that it was not the statutes of the Laws of Hammurabi that were being imposed but the supremacy of Hammurabi's regime. Hammurabi had compelling reasons to seek affirmation of his authority through the monumentality of the Stela and the promulgation of his law collection. He had extended his rule far beyond that of earlier Babylonian kings, and the stresses on his rule were great. Even the individual city-states over which he ruled were not monolithic communities, and he himself was a member of a dynasty that differed culturally from those he ruled.

1.4. The Taking of the Stela as Booty

Ironically, the monumentality of the Stela was employed by a king of another dynasty and territory to affirm his rule as king. The Stela containing

[67] Although these designations refer to languages, the languages most likely refer to ethnic differences.

[68] A. Leo Oppenheim argued for this phenomenon among the kings of the empire of Ur, and it may be that the kings of Isin and Larsa were as instrumental to preserving a Sumerian legacy as Charlemagne was to the classical heritage. See Oppenheim, "The Position of the Intellectual in Mesopotamian Society," *Daedalus* 104 (1975), 40–41.

the Laws of Hammurabi was excavated at Susa, the Elamite capital, hundreds of miles away from Babylonia because the Elamite king Shutruk-Nahhunte I (r. 1190–1155 BCE) had taken it to Susa as spoils of war. During his reign and the reigns of his sons and successors, Susa became the capital of the most extensive Elamite empire, regaining its prominence after being in eclipse for about a century. The Elamites were able to dominate the kingdoms southeast of Susa and the roads of the northwest foothills after relations with Kassite Mesopotamian deteriorated. This enabled the Elamites to exert control over Mesopotamia, and Shutruk-Nahhunte I conducted many campaigns in which he brought back spoils from Mesopotamia. The trophies he plundered from Mesopotamia, including such prominent items as the Victory Stela of Naram-Sin, the statue of Manishtushu, and the Stela of the Laws of Hammurabi—as well as other royal sculptures, victory monuments, and official records—were displayed in the richly adorned sanctuary of the god Inshushinak.[69] Exhibiting plunder captured in war allowed the Elamite king to present his dynasty as the legitimate successor to the Kassite kings who had ruled Mesopotamia for four centuries and his capital city, Susa, as a great city in Mesopotamian fashion.[70]

Shutruk-Nahhunte I ordered an inscription engraved on each of the most prominent items (the Victory Stela of Naram-Sin, the statue of Manishtushu, and the Stela of the Laws of Hammurabi) as a record that he was the one who had taken them as loot. The secondary inscriptions indicate the place from which the booty was carried off: the Victory Stela of Naram-Sin was taken from Sippar, and the sculpture of Manishtusha was plundered from Akkad. At the lower front of the Stela of the Laws of Hammurabi is a smoothened area, probably intended for a secondary inscription that was never inscribed.

Just as the Stela of the Laws of Hammurabi served to manifest Hammurabi's royal authority, so too did its being taken as spoil and its presentation in the Elamite capital serve to manifest the authority of Shutruk-Nahhunte and his dynasty. Ironically, the Stela was taken in modern times by French archaeologists to be displayed in the Louvre Museum in the French capital, partially to display French cultural and political power.

[69] Elizabeth Carter, "A History of Excavation at Susa: Personalities and Archaeological Methods," in *The Royal City of Susa: Ancient Near Eastern Treasures in the Louvre* (ed. Prudence O. Harper, Joan Aruz, and Françoise Tallon; New York: Metropolitan Museum of Art, 1992), 22; Béatrice André-Salvini, *Le Code de Hammurabi* (Paris: Réunion des Musées nationaux, 2000), 6–8; Roth, *Law Collections*, 73.

[70] Elizabeth Carter, "The Middle Elamite Period, circa 1500–1000 B.C.," in *The Royal City of Susa: Ancient Near Eastern Treasures in the Louvre*, (ed. Prudence O. Harper, Joan Aruz, and Francoise Tallon; New York: Metropolitan Museum of Art: Distributed by H.N. Abrams, 1992), 122.

2

Royal Legitimization through the Establishment of Justice

Hammurabi portrayed himself as the legitimate ruler by fulfilling the traditional requirement of a king to establish justice. Mesopotamian kings conducted their activities in the legal arena in three directions: resolving legal disputes, issuing social reform decrees, and promulgating law collections. We have clear evidence for Hammurabi's involvement in two of these, settling legal disputes and authorizing a law collection, but only oblique evidence for a social reform decree.

Hammurabi participated in the judicial process by resolving disputes and often acting as a judge in cases that administrators in the southern areas of his kingdom referred to him.[1] W. F. Leemans categorized the ways Hammurabi disposed of these cases: (1) the king acted as a court and rendered a judgment; (2) the king determined the law but remitted the case to local judicial authorities for the determination of the facts; and (3) the king transferred the entire case to the appropriate local authorities. In a number of instances, Hammurabi ruled against his administrators to support the contentions of locals who claimed they had long-standing rights.[2] Whether these particular acts were political or legal is debatable. They can be seen as political acts of the king constraining his officials when there were complaints about their behavior.[3] They can also be interpreted as royal interventions on the side of justice, and it may justifiably be asked whether Hammurabi's action needs to be interpreted as either political or legal. In any case, Hammurabi promoted his legitimacy as king by resolving disputes, thereby exerting his claim to be a just monarch.

[1] W. F. Leemans, "King Hammurapi as Judge," in *Symbolae iuridicae et historicae Martino David dedicatae II* (ed. J. A. Ankum, R. Feenstra, and W. F. Leemans; Leiden: Brill, 1968), 110.

[2] J. J. Finkelstein, "On Some Recent Studies in Cuneiform Law," *JAOS* 90 (1970), 243–256; Leemans, "King Hammurapi as Judge," 105–128.

[3] Norman Yoffee, "Context and Authority in Early Mesopotamian Law," in *State Formation and Political Legitimacy* (ed. Ronald Cohen and Judith D. Toland; New Brunswick, N.J.; Transaction Books, 1988), 104.

The Laws of Hammurabi. Pamela Barmash, Oxford University Press (2020). © Oxford University Press.
DOI: 10.1093/oso/9780197525401.001.0001.

Similarly, by promulgating the Laws of Hammurabi, Hammurabi followed the traditional crown pattern of legitimization through establishing justice. He commissioned the law collection to portray his mastery over the territory he inherited and the newly vanquished territories as just (and therefore justified). The prologue to the Laws of Hammurabi includes the detailed and reverential listing of twenty-one regional areas, naming their patron deity and most important shrine. Even though Hammurabi subjugated these cities and regions, at times with violence and destruction, he justified himself by echoing the traditional pattern of a legitimate monarch. The vanquishing of his enemies was vindicated, and the violence was justified by his declaration in the epilogue that he will assure prosperity and cause the people to feel safe and fear no one.

The law is portrayed in the Laws of Hammurabi as under the control of the king: the monarch and his government are depicted as having oversight of the legal system. In historical reality, most disputes were settled by local authorities, such as the elders of a city ward, the assembly of a town, or a mayor.[4] But by co-opting the legal activities of local authorities, the monarch increased his authority. Nowhere in the Laws of Hammurabi was the legal authority of local authorities invalidated. Their authority was never transferred to royal officials, but by portraying their activities as part of royal law, the monarch's dominion was affirmed and extended. The monarch appropriated the activities of local authorities, who operated by the affirmation and agreement of the people in their locality, and made it appear as if they were operating under his jurisdiction. This appropriation was an assertion of his control as king, even though the local authorities continued to operate as they always did. The local authorities continued to be independent of the crown and may have acted at times in opposition to the interests of the monarchy.[5] But the propaganda value of appropriating what they did as being under royal jurisdiction was crucial.

The Laws of Hammurabi was intended to regulate society under the control of the monarch and central government, whether in reality or by perception. It was not necessary for the monarchy to possess absolute power in every sphere of society, but it was imperative for the monarchy to be perceived to exert overall power. The state did not have a monopoly on law, but

[4] Dominique Charpin, *Mesopotamien: Die altbabylonische Zeit* (Orbis Biblicus et Orientalis 160/4; Fribourg and Göttingen: Academic Press and Vanderhoeck & Ruprecht, 2004), 305–308.

[5] Norman Yoffee, *The Economic Role of the Crown in the Old Babylonian Period* (Malibu, Calif: Undena Publications, 1977), 17, 145; Yoffee, *Myths of the Archaic State*, 110.

it utilized royal ideology to give the appearance of paramount control.[6] The state sought to portray itself as holding jurisdiction over the legal activities that affected all citizens. Nonetheless, local groups maintained their own power in the legal arena.[7]

2. 1. Social Reform Decrees and Law Collections

Presenting the king as overseeing the legal system was central to royal ideology. Kings demonstrated their fulfillment of the mandate to ensure justice through their involvement in particular disputes, and by issuing decrees of social reform and law collections bearing their name. The nature of the social reform decrees is opaque. Among the earliest texts extant are ones decreeing amnesty and promulgating social and legal equity.[8] Starting in the third millennium BCE, these decrees were aimed at promoting social peace and curbing the abuses and corrupt actions of officials. Over time, their focus shifted to debt release and economic issues. The decrees varied in scope: some specified that they applied only to citizens or to certain cities, while others were more encompassing.

These decrees are termed in modern scholarship as social reforms, but that is a misnomer. It is doubtful that they initiated long-lasting changes in society.[9] Rather, they were perceived to restore equity to distortions and imbalances in the social order. They alleviated the risks of impoverishment caused by the internal and inherent dysfunction of the social system. The decrees embodied the king's mandate to ensure justice by preventing the powerful from oppressing the weaker. They countered the wrongs done against those who could be taken advantage of. Whether they were issued when there was widespread discontent or popular protest movements is unknown to us because documentation from the nonliterate masses does not exist. The documentation we possess was commissioned by the elite, and we cannot determine whether reforms were spurred by adverse circumstances in society.

[6] Norman Yoffee, "The Decline and Rise of Mesopotamian Civilizations: An Ethnoarchaeological Perspective on the Evolution of Social Complexity," *American Antiquity* 44 (1979), 18.

[7] Andrea Seri, *Local Power in Old Babylonian Mesopotamia* (Studies in Egyptology and the Ancient Near East; Sheffield: Equinox, 2006), 2, 7, 136–137, 181–196.

[8] For a survey of the evidence for these decrees throughout the ancient Near East, see Pamela Barmash, "Amnesty and Reform Decrees," in *Oxford Encyclopedia of the Bible and Law*, 9–13.

[9] Benjamin R. Foster, "Social Reform in Ancient Mesopotamia," in *Social Justice in the Ancient World* (ed. K. D. Irani and Morris Silver; Westport, Conn.: Greenwood, 1995), 165.

The reforms are articulated as responses to economic instability and crisis, as a barometer of economic emergency. The king is presented in these texts as seeking to modify social conditions as part of the royal mandate to ensure justice. There is an undertone that the newly implemented decrees marked a contrast with what was then occurring in a society, but this may have been a literary conceit informed by royal ideology. It is possible that a decree was issued to affirm royal ideology—for example, that the king had fulfilled the divine mandate to ensure justice—rather than effectuate an actual change.[10]

The decrees were envisioned as protecting citizens who had fallen on hard times. Those who were weaker had their property and economic conditions safeguarded from those who wielded administrative or economic power. The decrees were not associated with mass movements or charismatic leaders.[11] They were not about protecting the weakest stratum of society, such as those who were born into slavery or poverty, but shielded those citizens whose normal self-sufficiency was in peril.

The evidence we have for these decrees of social reform falls into two categories, and I use two different terms for them to make the distinction clear. I also employ the term "equity" rather than "reform" in these two terms to emphasize that they were aimed at correcting a distortion in the social order. A number of them are memorialized in royal inscriptions and hymns of a number of kings, and I call them "acts of equity." We have a number of the texts of the decrees from the Old Babylonian period, and I term them "edicts of equity."

2.1.1. The Terms *kittum* and *mīsharum* as Articulating the Concept of Justice

By issuing acts and edicts of equity, the king aimed at restoring economic and social order and balance, part of his mandate to establish justice. The terms employed to articulate the notion of justice reflect this conceptualization. When Marduk is portrayed in the Laws of Hammurabi as commanding Hammurabi to furnish justice to the people, Hammurabi obeyed by instituting *kittum*, "truth," and *mīsharum*, "equity":

[10] Debt release required less involvement by the government than debt restructuring: forgiving debt was a one-time act, while restructuring would have demanded a long-term commitment on part of the monarchy.

[11] For a differing view, see Samuel Noah Kramer, "'Vox Populi' and the Sumerian Literary Documents," *RA* 58 (1964), 149–156.

LH V:14–25

When the god Marduk commanded me to provide justice for the people of the land in order to keep order, I established truth and equity as the declaration of the land.[12] I enhanced the welfare of the people.

The Laws of Hammurabi states that the god Shamash bestowed upon Hammurabi *kittum*, "truth," not statutes:

LH XLVIII:95–XLIX:1

I am Hammurabi, king of equity,
to whom Shamash has given truth.
My words are choice,
my achievements are unequalled.
Only to the unintelligent are they meaningless,
but to the wise, they are praiseworthy.

In these texts and elsewhere, these two terms—*kittum*, "truth," and *mīsharum*, "equity"—are used, often in tandem, to express both the concept and reality of justice. A deity was perceived to endow a ruler with *kittum* (or *kīnātum*), a sense of truth, not a set of specific laws. This concept refers to a cosmic, transcendental sense of natural order permeated by fairness, untainted by wrongs. It is a kind of natural law: it is justice that transcends human culture and limitations and whose ideals are those toward which human beings should strive. It should not be subverted by legal technicalities or social corruption, and this is why truth must work in tandem with the second term, *mīsharum*, "equity." The term *mīsharum* means literally "a straightening out": it refers to how justice is achieved in praxis, in the reality of a society. When *mīsharum* prevails in society, then *kittum* exists in society. *Mīsharum* rectifies injustice and restores balance, and thereby *kittum* resides in society.

Thus, the king was to be animated by an ideal of truth, and it was the king's responsibility for ensuring that equity prevailed in society. His role in justice served as the impetus for the promulgation of *mīsharum*, "equity," in the name of Mesopotamian monarchs when law collections and reform decrees were issued. When a law collection was promulgated in the king's name, the specific rules animated by the sense of truth and equity were left up to the scribe composing laws. The king was not seen as a legislator but as one who

[12] I analyze this difficult line in further detail in the next chapter.

brought human affairs into equity. When a king issued acts or decrees of social reform, he actuated *kittum*, making legal practice concur with cosmic truth so that *mīsharum* prevailed. Equity was achieved by a king when he issued decrees restoring economic balance. The king acted to restore the status quo that had been altered by injustice, a corruption of the natural order.[13]

2.1.2. Acts of Equity

Acts of equity are memorialized in royal inscriptions and hymns of a number of kings. These commemorative inscriptions employ a number of characteristic rhetorical elements: a contrast is intuited, whether explicitly or implicitly, between the previous period and present time; the current situation is portrayed as ideal; and the king's dominion is due to his selection by the divine realm. The motivation for an act of equity varied, and it is not entirely clear that it actually took place. It may be that acts of equity were more royal rhetoric than a historical event.[14]

2.1.2.1. Enmetana of Lagash

The earliest reference to an act of equity is recorded in two brief inscriptions issued by Enmetana, ruler of Lagash (early twenty-fourth century BCE).[15] In the words of the inscriptions, "He issued a release of obligations for Lagash and restored mother to child and child to mother." This may indicate that he cancelled debts and released those who were either taken as payment for

[13] Raymond Westbrook, "Social Justice in the Ancient Near East," in *Social Justice in the Ancient World* (ed. K. D. Irani and Morris Silver; Westport, Conn.: Greenwood, 1995), 155.

[14] In first-millennium BCE Mesopotamia, an act of equity was portrayed as a return to traditional values and institutions, and it was articulated in the traditional rhetoric of the oppression of the orphan and the widow by the powerful. See Foster, "Social Justice in Mesopotamia," 170; Niels Peter Lemche, "Andurārum and Mīsharum: Comments on the Problem of Social Ethics and Their Application in the Ancient Near East," *JNES* 38 (1979), 20–21 (for examples of first-millennium BCE references in royal decrees and in documents recording private transactions, where money was to be returned if real estate or slaves were affected by an edict of equity). See also "Advice to a Prince," another first-millennium BCE text protecting the rights of the citizens of Sippar, Nippur, and Babylon from judicial misbehavior by the king as well as from taxation, forced labor, and misappropriation of their property (Lambert, *BWL*, 110–115), and J. N. Postgate, "Royal Exercise of Justice under the Assyrian Empire," in *Le palais et la royauté, archéologie et civilisation: XIXe Rencontre Assyriologique Internationale* (Paris: Paul Geuthner, 1974), 417–426.

[15] Douglas R. Frayne, *Presargonic Period (2700–2350 BC)* (RIME 1; Toronto: University of Toronto Press, 2008), E1.9.5.5, E1.9.5.26; Horst Steible, *Die Altsumerischen Bau- und Weihinschriften: Teil 1, Inschriften aus 'Lagaš'* (Wiesbaden: Franz Steiner, 1982), numbers 35 and 79.

those debts or as distraint to force payment. It may also be that he released those engaged in forced labor for state projects. For the act of equity, the texts used the Sumerian term ama.r-gi_4, whose original meaning was "to return to the mother": it later became the technical term for "release, liberation, restoration to the original state."

When did this act take place? One of the Enmetana inscriptions recalled events that would have ushered in the king's accession to the throne, and therefore the inscription must have come from early in the king's reign, and it indicates that the act of equity was issued early in the king's reign. But it is not clear whether an act of equity was issued as a matter of course at a set point in a king's reign or was inspired by social inequalities. The second inscription mentioning the act is a foundation deposit recording the restoration and rebuilding of temples. Here, the cancellation of debt was extended to the citizens of three more cities, Uruk, Larsa, and Pa-tibira. The reason for this may be hinted at in the inclusion of the city of Uruk in the reform. Enmetena had an alliance with the ruler of Uruk but may have reneged on the pact of brotherhood by taking control over the city of Uruk.[16] This may indicate that a release of obligations for that city (Uruk) was a means of gaining the trust and loyalty of the inhabitants more than correcting social asymmetry. There may have been an alternative or additional impetus: the text notes that the cities for which the king issued a release were returned to the control of their city-god. This may have been a further means of earning loyalty, that of the priesthood as well as of the population. The allegiance of the priesthood was crucial in an era when a temple's wealth was considerable: arable land was concentrated in temple estates owned in the name of the city-god.

2. 1.2.2. Uruinimgina of Lagash

The act of equity most celebrated by scholarship is that of Uruinimgina,[17] ruler of Lagash in the mid-twenty-fourth-century BCE. He issued a set of reforms aiming at administrative abuses, declaring himself to be the righter of social wrongs and the defender of the weak. His historical inscriptions recounted that common citizens were mistreated by various officials and priests: their labor and goods were appropriated, and exorbitant fees,

[16] Douglas Frayne, *Presargonic Period*, RIME 1, 193. Frayne noted that the inscriptions of Enmetena's ally never mention an overlord, and therefore the possibility that Enmetena installed him as a vassal seems unlikely.

[17] The first two elements of the king's name are obscure: the name may have been Urukagina or Irikagina. See Frayne, *Presargonic Period*, RIME 1, 245–246; Piotr Steinkeller, "The Reforms of UruKAgina and an Early Sumerian Term for 'Prison,'" *Aula Orientalis* 9 (1991), 227 n.2.

especially for funerals, were demanded.[18] In response, Uruinimgina is portrayed in those inscriptions as issuing an array of reforms, regulating the actions of officials in their areas of authority, fixing the compensation for particular services, and removing corrupt officials from their posts.

Uruinimgina's acts of equity are recounted in three lengthy historical inscriptions. Like the inscriptions that mention Enmetena's act of equity, Uruinimgina's are recounted in a genre that typically names the divine favors granted to the king, the building and irrigation projects of the king, and the military conquests of the king. These texts are broken and unclear: their obscurity poses a considerable challenge for interpretation. Furthermore, each of the texts contains an overlapping but not identical set of abuses and reforms.[19] Only one text mentions friction between men and women—RIME 1, E1.9.9.3 iii 14′–24′—and it is far from clear to what it refers.[20] Even within a single text, not every abuse has a corresponding remedy (e.g., the complaint that certain professions—surveyor, chief lamentation singer, supervisor, brewer, and foreman—were forced to pay in silver rather than providing a lamb is not paralleled by a remedy in RIME 1, E1.9.9.1). Correspondingly, a number of remedies are lacking an articulated abuse. Only one of the texts mentions the rations to be given to the blind (RIME 1, E1.9.9.1 x 38–xi6) but even that text does not mention the complaint that rations were withheld from the blind. The differences between the texts make it appear that they present three different acts of equity accomplishing a number of overlapping provisions rather than a single act of equity.[21]

Uruinimgina's acts of equity address two broad areas: (1) the remedy of abuses committed by officials, articulated in detailed and elaborate

[18] Frayne, *Presargonic Period*, RIME 1, E1.9.9.1–3. It is not clear why Uruinimgina's historical inscriptions are in the form of clay cones. See Jerrold S. Cooper, "Medium and Message: Inscribed Clay Cones and Vessels from Presargonic Sumer," *RA* 79 (1985), 97–114.

[19] The individual texts have unique details about other royal acts. One version of the decree concludes with the statement that Uruinimgina made a covenant with the god Ningirsu. The king promised that he would protect the orphan and widow from the powerful. This reference to a covenant between a god and ruler is sui generis in Mesopotamian religion. It differs from the covenant between God and the Israelites depicted in the Bible in two ways: (1) the king establishes the rules in his capacity as king, and (2) the king initiates the accord, not the deity. See Jan Joosten, "Covenant," in *The Oxford Handbook of Biblical Law* (ed. Pamela Barmash; Oxford: Oxford University Press, 2019), 7–18.

[20] Scholars have disagreed on the rendering of this passage. It may be that it reads, "Women of former times each married two men, but women of today have been made to give up that crime." See Jerrold S. Cooper, *Presargonic Inscriptions* (Sumerian and Akkadian Royal Inscriptions; New Haven, Conn.: American Oriental Society, 1986), 77–78. But it may read "had to perform marital obligations to two men" because of their husband's debts. See Frayne, *Presargonic Period*, RIME 1, E1.9.9.3 20′–24′.

[21] See Wilcke, *Early Ancient Near Eastern Law*, 21 n.16.

descriptions; and (2) the transfer of land to the nominal ownership of the gods. Officials were depicted as exerting their power and manipulating transactions to their benefit, and the act of equity purportedly halted the maltreatment of citizens by officials. A telling example of exploitation is the demand of payment in silver by officials, an abuse that could yield greater profit to them: if a person did not have silver to pay, he would be forced to sell or hand over material possessions at a significant loss.[22] Actual payment in silver was likely never contemplated: valuing debt in silver was a means of forcing the payee to sell an item at a disadvantage, for less than it was worth. Uruinimgina is portrayed as ordering that payment in kind be accepted. Furthermore, officials were depicted as taking advantage by appropriating items and the labor of people over which they had authority and by levying additional fees. The king's decree(s) abolished taxes for divorce or betrothal and prohibited public officials from seeking extra compensation for their services from citizens. An individual of lower rank was given the right to refuse a request from a superior, and that superior was enjoined from striking the lower-ranking person in response.

The reform of Uruinimgina is also represented as clarifying the authority of the gods and human beings over property. It stated that specific gods held ownership of particular property, not the king or queen. In so doing, Uruinimgina is epitomized as regulating the activity of officials who had prebend rights. The officials did have the right to benefit from the materials under their jurisdiction as well as to receive gifts from their subordinates, but Uruinimgina reported that they abused their offices.[23] (One may well guess whether they would agree with this assessment.)

The nature of the broad categories of abuses remedied may shed light on a hotly debated issue, the timing and nature of Uruinimgina's act(s) of equity. It is not entirely clear that (one of) his act(s) was decreed at the start of his reign, but if it had been issued then, it might explain his accession to the throne.[24] Uruinimgina was not the son of the previous king and may have

[22] Ferris J. Stephens, "Notes on Some Economic Texts of the Time of Urukagina," *RA* 49 (1955), 132. We do have evidence for an actual occurrence of one of the abuses allegedly remedied by Uruinimgina's reform(s). See Daniel Foxvog, "A New Legal Text Bearing on Uruinimgina's Reform," *JCS* 46 (1994), 11–15.

[23] Wilcke, *Early Ancient Near Eastern Law: A History of Its Beginnings*, 23–24.

[24] D. O. Edzard, "'Soziale Reformen' im Zweistromland bis ca. 1600 v. Chr.: Realität oder literarischer Topos," *Acta Antiqua Scientiarum Hungaricae* 22 (1974): 145–156; J. J. Finkelstein, "Some New Misharum Material and Its Implications," in *Studies in Honor of Benno Landsberger on His Seventy-Fifth Birthday* (AS 16; Chicago: University of Chicago Press, 1965), 243–246; Blahoslav Hruška, "Die innere struktur de Reformtexte Urukaginas von Lagaš," *Archiv Orientalni* 41

been a usurper: he may have seized the throne, whether he or his supporters were motivated by dissatisfaction with those abuses, and, therefore, he issued the decree to seek support for his accession to the throne. It may also be that he was the legitimate heir: he may have been a member of the royal family, and upon his accession to the throne, he naturally sought the support of certain temple officials at the expense of other officials and professionals. His act of equity is depicted as terminating specific royal taxes on temple property and prohibiting the confiscation of temple property by the monarchy. Whether a usurper or not, a monarch would see the wisdom of bringing temple officials to his side by promising relief from the incursions of royal power.

What was the prevailing state of affairs in Uruinimgina's territory when he assumed power, and who had traditionally controlled the estates of arable land? If estates had been in the hands of the temples and were under the control of the priests, Uruinimgina was less a reformer and more of a reactionary. He curbed royal authority in order to restore the prerogatives of the temple.[25] However, if the lands had not traditionally been owned by the temples, Uruinimgina was more of a radical than a reactionary: he was in fact reversing established custom by making the god Ningirsu owner in name of the city's lands.[26]

It may be useful to move beyond the broad strokes of whether Uruinimgina was on the side of royal power or was manipulated by the priests. A number of the abuses were due to temple officials misappropriating goods or overstepping their authority, while others were caused by the ruler's administrators taking advantage of temple property. In the process of redressing these wrongs, Uruinimgina named his wife's household as the Bau Temple, and when he abolished the existence of the household of a number of other members of the royal family and transferred their personnel to his wife's household, he substantially increased the Bau Temple. This may indicate an outright attempt to prevent abuses by consolidating and exerting tighter royal control or a veiled attempt to gain power by the king.

(1973): 4–13, 104–132; Hruška, "Die reformtexte Urukaginas: der verspätete versuch einer konsolierung des stadtaates von Lagaš," in *Le palais et la royauté: XIXe recontre assyriologique internationale* (ed. Paul Garelli; Paris: Librairie orientaliste Paul Guethner, 1974), 151–161; F. R. Kraus, *Königliche Verfügungen in altbabylonische Zeit* (SDIOAP 11; Leiden: Brill, 1984); M. Lambert, "Les 'Reforms' Urukagina," *RA* 50 (1956): 169–184.

25 I. M. Diakonoff, "Some Remarks on the 'Reforms' of Urukagina," *RA* 52 (1958): 12–13.

26 Benjamin F. Foster, "A New Look at the Sumerian Temple State," *JESHO* 24 (1981): 236–237.

Uruinimgina's act(s) of equity included an order to release certain offenders from prison—among them, included debtors, those who defrauded by falsifying measures, thieves, and killers. This type of general amnesty, the release of all categories of offenders, appears to be unique.[27] None of the other sources from Mesopotamia mention the release of prisoners, and it is named in only one of the texts extant: RIME 1, E1.9.9.1 xii 13–22. Even if it was not put into practice and was only meant as rhetoric articulating an ideal of justice, it is striking that pardoning criminals was seen as ethical and desirable.

Of the seventy rulers from the Presargonic period from whom we have inscriptions, two issued reforms that were recounted in their inscriptions. Both of them, Enmetana and Uruinimgina, were rulers of Lagash. Is this just a coincidence? Or does this reflect an innovation in the political life of Lagash or in the rhetoric of justice in Lagash? The next king to decree an act of equity was also in Lagash but from a different dynasty.

2.1.2.3. Gudea of Lagash

Gudea, king of Lagash in the twenty-second century BCE, is also portrayed as issuing an act of equity as part of the rebuilding of the Eninnu temple in the city of Lagash. This is recounted in what arguably may be the greatest masterpiece of Sumerian poetry, the two cylinders of the Hymn to Ningirsu, patron of that temple. The earlier acts of equity, those of Enmetena and of Uruinimgina, were narrated in historical inscriptions, and we must be cognizant that both genres may reflect the rhetoric of legal ideals more than actual historical events.

The hymns narrate that Gudea restored the temple in order to guarantee the prosperity of his city and the favor of the god Ningirsu, and in the course of the renovation, the king ordered that the inhabitants of the city purify their behavior toward the god and toward each other. This act of equity was intended to restore social peace and concord in society:[28]

> <u>Hymn to Ningirsu Cylinder A</u>
>
> (xii 18–19) Ningirsu's intention (now) had become as clear as daylight to Gudea.

[27] Steinkeller, "The Reforms of UruKAgina and an Early Sumerian Term for 'Prison,'" 232.

[28] Edzard, *Gudea and His Dynasty*, RIME 3/1, E3.1.1.7 CylA and E3.1.1 CylB; Adam Falkenstein and Wolfram von Soden, *Sumerische und akkadische Hymnen und Gebete* (Die Bibliothek der Alten Welt; Zurich: Artemis-Verlag, 1953), 150, 168–169, 179–180; Thorkild Jacobsen, *The Harps That Once . . . : Sumerian Poetry in Translation* (New Haven, Conn.: Yale University Press, 1987), 403–404, 428–429, 440; Kramer, "Law and Justice," 77–82.

(xii 20) He is wise and able, too, to realize things.

(xii 21–23) The ruler issued orders to his city as to a single person, making the land of Lagash of one accord like the children of one mother.

(xii 24–25a) They (the people of Lagash) took tools in hand, weeded shrubs, raked the weeds together (?).

(xii 25b–26) (Gudea) barred (unnecessary) words and sent crime back to its "house."

(xiii 1–2) He undid the "tongue" of the whip and the goad, and (instead) he laid in its place the wool of ewes in the hands (of the overseers).

(xiii 3–5) No mother would have words with her child, and no child would disobey its mother.

(xiii 6–9) No master hit (his) slave on the head (when) he had . . . and no mistress would slap the face of the slave-woman who had misbehaved toward her.

(xiii 10–11) Nobody before the ruler building the Eninnu, before Gudea, would let fall a chance utterance.

(xiii 12–13) The ruler purified the city, let the (purifying) fire go over it.

(xiii 14–15) He banned from the city all persons ritually unclean, unpleasant to look at and. . . .

<u>Hymn to Ningirsu Cylinder B</u>

(iv 13–14) The ruler made the (whole) city kneel down, made the land prostrate itself,

(iv 15–16) He levelled what was high, refused to listen to chance utterances, "spittle" (of sorcery) was removed from the roads.

(iv 17–19) In the city (only) the mother of a sick person administered a potion—the wild animals cattle, the creatures of the steppe, all crouched together.

(iv 20–21) Lion, leopard (?), the "dragon of the steppe" (viper?), enjoyed sweet sleep.

(iv 22–24) Rites (had made) the day (go by), prayer the night, the early morning (had) the moonlight (caused to fade)—was the master of the House on his way?

(v 1) The warrior Ningirsu was entering his House. . . .

The god is depicted as conferring an idea upon the king, who comprehended it and brought it to fruition. The ideal of social concord is expressed in the unity of the people and in the peaceful behavior reigning between those often in contention, mother and child, owner and slave. The city was ritually purified, witchcraft uprooted, and vicious animals were at ease together. To what extent could this reflect an actual act of equity? The hymn contains aspects that could only be fanciful or utopian: the lion, leopard, and viper sleep side by side in peace. But whether the act of equity achieved all that is recounted or none at all, the ideal was to create such an atmosphere. It is striking that rhetoric mandated social harmony.

At the climax of the hymn, when the rebuilding of the temple-complex of Eninnu is depicted, the poem describes the remission of debts:

Hymn to Ningirsu Cylinder B

(xvii 17) (The ruler) had debts remitted, and he granted pardons.

(xvii 18–21) When his master had entered his house, for seven days, the slave-woman was allowed to be equal to her mistress, the slave was allowed to walk side by side with his master.

(xviii 1) In his city the one who appeared unclean (to someone) was permitted to sleep (only) outside.

(xviii 2–3) He has words cut off the evil-speaking tongue, and he had anything disharmonious turned away from the house.

(xviii 4–7) He paid attention to the justice (ordained) [by Nanše] and Ningirsu; he did not expose the orphan [to the wealthy person] nor did he expose the widow to the [influential] one.

(xviii 8–9) [In(?)] a house having no [male] child, the daughter [would slaughter] its sheep.

(xviii 10–11) Days of justice had risen for him, and he set his foot on the neck of evil and complaint.

(xviii 12–13) Had he not himself risen for his city from the horizon like the sun god?

Ritual purity and social justice were intertwined. Social equality prevailed, at least during the festival of dedication: master and slave walked side by side. Ritually unclean individuals had to sleep outside the city. The act of equity is portrayed as providing protection for orphans and widows from oppression by the rich and the powerful. It also incorporated the provision that for a household lacking a male heir a daughter may serve as the family member serving as heir responsible for ritual acts. We can speculate that this pronouncement is so specific and oriented to practical law that it may well be that this reflected historical practice. If this were so, this would be a sharp contrast with the other acts that appear to be more rhetoric than reality.

It must be noted that the acts of equity occupy a very minor part of the hymn, because the purpose of the hymn was the glorification of the king. The section narrating the reform concludes with highlighting the one responsible for all this, the king, acclaimed as appearing like the sun god, the god of justice. The king is presented in a way that coheres with his royal inscriptions as a whole: no political events are mentioned, and the king and his subjects reside in ritual harmony with the gods.[29]

Gudea's reform did not address the abuses of officials or the ownership of lands, as did Uruinimgina, but it did prescribe debt relief and social concord, as did Enmetena's. Gudea's reform also dealt with the relationship of the god to the people, an aspect that Uruinimgina's reform took in another direction. Lastly, as we shall see, the rhetoric of protecting orphans and widows is echoed in the earliest law collection, the Laws of Ur-Namma, which dates from a few decades after the reign of Gudea (LU A iv 162–168, C ii 30–39).

2.1.2.4. Shulgi of Ur

No reform decree was associated with Ur-Namma, the first ruler of the Third Dynasty of Ur and the ruler associated with the earliest law collection,[30] but his son, Shulgi, is presented as instituting one (r. 2094–2047 BCE). This reform, recorded in hymns ascribed to Shulgi, was intended to protect the weak from the powerful and to promote concord within families, like its predecessors:

<u>Shulgi Hymn F[31]</u>

(20) That justice cease not,

(21) That evil, though it is not a "noble" stone, be locked in the sea,

(22) That man make not his (fellow) man into a hireling—

(23) (This is why) in the well-built palace of Sumer,

(24) Shulgi seated himself on the lapis-lazuli throne of his enduring dais.

[29] Piotr Steinkeller, *History, Texts and Art in Early Babylonia* (SANER 15; Berlin: De Gruyter, 2017), 32.

[30] It has been a matter of debate whether Shulgi or his son Ur-Namma commissioned the law collection associated with Ur-Namma. See the discussion of the Laws of Ur-Namma later in this chapter.

[31] Kramer, "Law and Justice," 80–81.

(25) That the king, the Ishtaran of Sumer,
(26) Pronounce the judgment of the land, decides the decisions of the land,
(27) That Ur, the city of the *me*, raise high (its) neck,
(28) This is why his mother gave birth to the hero—Ninsun,
(29) This is why his mother gave birth to Shulgi—Ninsun.

Shulgi Hymn X[32]
(141) In the lofty palace of Ningal, he seated himself on the holy dais,
(142) He, the Ishtaran of Sumer, the omniscient one from the womb,
(143) Pronounces the judgment of the land,
(144) Decides the decisions of the land,
(145) (So that) the strong does not oppress the weak,
(146) The mother speaks kindly to her son,
(147) The son answers truthfully to his father.

Shulgi is depicted as a judge promoting social concord, an activity that shares affinities with those of earlier kings. Family harmony is mandated by both Gudea and Shulgi: Gudea—"No mother would have words with her child, and no child would disobey its mother (xiii 3–5)"—and Shulgi—"The mother speaks kindly to her son, The son answers truthfully to his father (146–147)."

Shulgi's legal wisdom is exalted in another hymn: he is portrayed as a judge able to render verdicts in multiple languages and as a jurist who instructs his officials how to deliberate:[33]

Shulgi Hymn B
(206–209) When I . . . like water gushing with the roar of a great storm, in the capture of a citadel in Elam . . . , I can understand what their spokesman answers.
By origin I am a son of Sumer; I am a warrior, a warrior of Sumer.
(210–211) Thirdly, I can conduct a conversation with a man from the black mountains.
(212–214) Fourthly, I can do service as a translator with an Amorite, a man of the mountains . . . I myself can correct his confused words in his own language.

[32] ETCSL 2.4.2.24, <http://etcsl.orinst.ox.ac.uk/section2/tr24224.htm>; Jacob Klein, *Three Šulgi Hymns: Sumerian Royal Hymns Glorifying King Šulgi of Ur* (Ramat-Gan: Bar-Ilan University Press, 1981), 145.
[33] ETCSL 2.4.2.02, <http://etcsl.orinst.ox.ac.uk/cgi-bin/etcsl.cgi?text=t.2.4.2.02#>

(215–216) Fifthly, when a man of Subir yells . . . , I can even distinguish the words in his language, although I am not a fellow-citizen of his.

(217–220) When I provide justice in the legal cases of Sumer, I give answers in all five languages. In my palace no one in conversation switches to another language as quickly as I do.

(221–229) When I pronounce a completed verdict, it is heartily welcomed, since I am wise and exalted in kingship. So that my consultative assemblies, sitting together to care for the people, inspire respect in their hearts when the chief herald sounds the horn, they should deliberate and debate; and so that the council should decide policy properly, I have taught my governors to deliberate and to debate. While the words at their dining tables flow like a river, I tackle crime, so that the foundations are securely established for my wide dominions.

(230–240) I vanquish a city with words as weapons, and my wisdom keeps it subjected just as violence with burning torches would. I have taught them the meaning of the words "I have no mother." My words can be words smooth as the finest quality oil; I know how to cool hearts which are hot as fire, and I know how to extinguish a mouth set on fire like a reed-bed. I weigh my words against those of the braggart. I am a man of the very highest standards of value. The importance of the humble is of particular value to me, and they cannot be counterproductive to any of my activities.

This royal hymn depicts the king as the ideal type of ruler, who preserves the social order by ensuring justice, in addition to protecting Mesopotamia from foreign attack. However, he is not portrayed as issuing an act of equity. In the other Shulgi hymns and in the Gudea hymns, the king is portrayed as instituting an act of equity.[34] A distinction must be drawn between claims of acts of equity and boilerplate affirmations of a king's fulfillment of the mandate for establishing justice.[35]

[34] Another text indicates that Shulgi could also pardon those convicted of capital offenses: however, the text does not give any indication of what the nature of those offenses were. See Martha T. Roth, "A Reassessment of RA 71 (1977) 125 ff," *Archiv für Orientforschung* 31 (1984), 9–14.

[35] Such as in Ishme-Dagan A + V: "Utu put justice and reliable words in my mouth. To make judgments, to reach decisions, to lead the people rightly, to excel in rectitude, to keep the righteous on the

2.1.2.5. Enlil-bani of Isin

The Babylonian king Enlil-bani (r. 1860–1837 BCE) is depicted as issuing a decree in which the king's acts of equity are extolled in vague rhetorical terms: the only specific changes recorded were reduction in taxes and corvee labor:[36]

> (v 7–vii 17) O Enlil, (this) is my destiny which you established at your temple Ekur: I established justice in Nippur. I made righteousness appear. As if for sheep, I sought out forage and fed (the people) in green pastures. I lifted the heavy yoke from their necks. I settled them in a secure abode. The righteousness which I established in Nippur made (the inhabitants of Nippur) happy. I established righteousness and justice in Isin, the city which Anum and Enlil gave to Ninisima. I made the land content. I reduced to one-tenth the grain tax that formerly was one-fifth. I made the commoner/palace dependent[37] serve (only) four days a month. The cattle of the palace which used to graze in certain fields and which were a cause for

track and to destroy the wicked, so that each man should speak justice to his brother, should make obeisance to his father, should not speak contrary words to his elder sister, and should respect his mother; so that the weak should not be handed over to the strong, so that the feeble should . . . ; so that the strong should not do just what he pleases, and so that one man should not be assigned to another (through debt); to destroy wickedness and violence, and to make righteousness flourish—all this Utu, the son born to Ningal, made my apportioned share" (ETCSL 2.5.4.01.90–99). A similar statement is made about Lipit-Ishtar: "Lipit-Eštar, Enlil's son, you have realized justice and righteousness. Lord, your goodness covers everything as far as the horizon. King Lipit-Eštar, counsellor with huge intelligence, who never tires of discussion, wise one whose decisions guide the people, amply wise, knowing everything in great detail! To decide justly the lawsuits of foreign countries, you recognize true and false even in people's thoughts. Lipit-Eštar, you . . . the wicked, but you also know how to save someone by commuting his death sentence; you know how to free someone from the severe punishment, from the jaws of destruction. The mighty do not commit robbery and the strong do not abuse the weak anymore: you have established justice in Sumer and Akkad and made the land feel content" (ETCSL 2.5.5.2.25–39).

36 Frayne, *Old Babylonian Period*, RIME 4, E4.1.10.1001.

37 The term *muškēnum* has been the subject of great debate, and this is not the place to solve the puzzle. The term is translated as "commoner / palace dependent" in this book. Marten Stol argues that it refers to someone who is not a member of the palace organization, a plain "citizen" (Stol, "Muškēnum," RLA 8.492–493). Piotr Steinkeller contends that the socioeconomic situation in Mesopotamia was such that the menial workforce that was a permanent fixture of temples and palace organizations employed in the cultivation of grain became impoverished and landless wage earners hired by agents of a palace or a wealthy landowner ("Labor in the Early States: An Early Mesopotamian Perspective," in *Labor in the Ancient World* (ed. Piotr Steinkeller and Michael Hudson; Dresden: ISLET, 2015), 26. Marc Van De Mieroop argues that we are just unable to comprehend the native terminology (*Cuneiform Texts and the Writing of History* [London: Routledge, 1999], 86, 107). Provisionally, I shall translate it as "commoner / palace dependent," who was socially subordinate to a member of the elite class. See also I. M. Diakonoff, "Socio-Economic Classes in Babylonia and the Babylonian Concept of Economic Stratification," in *Gesellschaftsklassen im Alten Zweistromland und in den angrenzenden Gebieten; XVIII. Rencontre assyriologique internationale, München, 29. Juni bis 3. Juli 1970* (Munich: Bayerischen Akademie der Wissenschaften, 1972), 41–52; I. M. Diakonoff, "On the Social Structure of Old Babylonian Society," in *Beiträge zur sozialen Struktur des alten Vorderasien* (ed. Horst Klengel; Berlin: Akademie Verlag, 1971), 26–31; F. R. Kraus,

complaint. I am a judge who loves righteousness. I abolished evil and violence. I restored (?) the just man.

The text portrays the reduction of taxes and forced labor, and the fact that only the government was required to make a sacrifice may mean that this abatement may actually have been carried out. The practice of the palace that was the cause for complaint was abolished. The rest of the text exudes with the rhetoric of ideals: a contrast is to be intuited between the previous period and present time, and the current situation is portrayed as impeccable.[38]

2.1.3. Old Babylonian Edicts of Equity

From the Old Babylonian period, we have the texts of a number of edicts of equity, to be distinguished from references to acts of equity in royal inscriptions and hymns. These texts depict a change in the nature of the decrees of equity. Old Babylonian kings regulated economic activity, especially the prices of commodities, through these edicts, rather than promoting social concord as in the earlier acts of equity. As part of their oversight of the economy, their edicts promulgated the cancellation of taxes and debts owed both to the monarchy and to private creditors, including the release of persons and property pledged, commandeered, or enslaved because of debt. The cancellations could apply to an entire country or to specific cities.

It could be surmised that the development in decrees of equity from promoting social concord to regulating economic activity may be due more to the genre of the textual evidence than a change in content: royal inscriptions and hymns may describe elements of an act of equity that an edict would not address, and vice versa. Royal inscriptions and hymns employ hyperbole that are avoided in other textual genres: the purpose of royal hymns and inscriptions is to extol the king. By contrast, the edicts come across as precisely worded texts meant for promulgation.[39]

Vom mesopotamischen Menschen der altbabylonisichen Zeit und seiner Welt: Eine Reihe Vorlesungen (Amsterdam: North Holland, 1973); J. N. Postgate, *Early Mesopotamia*, 239–240; Reuven Yaron, *The Laws of Eshnunna* (second edition; Jerusalem: Magnes Press, 1988), 133–154.

[38] A year name of Irra-Imite of Isin (1868–1861 BCE) may refer to the promulgation of an act of equity: "Year in which (Irra-imite) established justice (in the land)." But we have no further documentation. See Edward Chiera, *Legal and Administrative Texts from Nippur* (PBS VIII, part 1; Philadelphia: University Museum, 1914), 69.

[39] We do have a set of royal inscriptions from an Old Babylonian king of the city of Ur, Sin-Kashid, in which is recorded the prices in silver for barley, copper, wool, and vegetable oil. The question is

These edicts were generally issued at the start of a reign. They were also decreed at intervals later in a king's reign, whether regularly or irregularly.[40] Since a king was responsible to the gods for establishing and ensuring justice, issuing such edicts would assure the legitimacy of his reign, especially at the start of his rule. It is unclear why edicts were issued later in a king's reign. It may be that as socioeconomic imbalances were building up in a society, discontent had to be relieved by the cancellation of debts.[41] However, it may be that kings issued such decrees from time to time as part of their general mandate to ensure justice, not in response to a specific state of crisis.[42]

Evidence to solve this question is found in a letter from Hammurabi's successor explaining the reason for an edict of equity:

> TCL XVII 76
> To Etel-Marduk, speak. Thus says Samsuiluna: My father, the king, [became sick and died]. Because of his death . . . I have acceded to the throne of the house [of my father] (lit. sat on the throne), and to strengthen the bearers of tribute (i.e., state tenants), I have released the balance of . . . the farmers. . . . I have invalidated the tablets of obligation of a soldier, fisherman, or commoner / palace dependent. I have established equity in the land. In the land . . . must not dun the estate of any soldier, fisherman, or commoner/ palace dependent. When you see my tablet, you and the elders of the land you supervise will come up and meet with me.[43]

The purpose of the edict is articulated as strengthening certain classes that were economically stressed. It served as a relief valve: it prevented a too severe buildup of debt.[44] The accumulating arrears for debts and burden of debt servitude would eventually imperil the economy and jeopardize the

whether this records the regulation of prices or an expression of the abundance brought by the king's reign. See Frayne, *Old Babylonian Period*, RIME 4, E4.4.1 8–15.

[40] Finkelstein, "Some New Misharum Material and Its Implications," 243–246; Hannes Olivier, "The Effectiveness of the Old Babylonian Mēšarum Decrees," *Journal of Northwest Semitic Language* 12 (1984), 107–113; G. Komoróczy, "Zur Frage des Periodizität der altbabylonischen *mīšarum-Erlässe*," in *Societies and Languages of the Ancient Near East: Studies in Honor of I. M. Diakonoff* (ed. M. A. Dandamayev; Warminster: Aris and Phillips, 1982), 196–205.

[41] Jean Bottéro, "Désordre économique et annulation des dettes en Mèsopotamie à l'époque paléo-babylonienne," *JESHO* 4 (1961): 113–164.

[42] Klaas Veenhof, "Relationship between Royal Decree and 'Law Codes' of the Old Babylonian Period," *JEOL* 35/36 (1997), 49–83.

[43] Kraus, *Königliche Verfügungen in altbabylonischer Zeit*, 66–67.

[44] Finkelstein, "Some New Misharum Material and Its Implications," 233–246; Kraus, "Ein zentrales Problem des altmesopotamischen Rechts: Was is der Codex Hammu-rabi?" 283–296, 292; D. J. Wiseman, "The Laws of Hammurabi Again," *Journal of Semitic Studies* 7 (1962): 161–172.

stability of the social order. The edict protected citizens, not those born into slavery (or poverty, who might have been sold at a young age because of their parents' financial straits). Since an edict also incorporated the cancellation of state taxes and arrears, it may be presumed that it was designed to have maximum impact at the least expense for the royal administration.[45]

Three edicts of equity are known from the Old Babylonian period:[46] the Edict of Samsu-iluna (r. 1749–1712 BCE), the Edict of Ammi-ditana (r. 1683–1647 BCE),[47] and the Edict of Ammi-ṣaduqa (r. 1647–1626 BCE). Since each edict repeated the provisions of the previous edict while adding to them, the final edict, the Edict of Ammi-ṣaduqa, will be the focus of our discussion.

The Edict of Ammi-ṣaduqa employed a method of economic adjustment that appears designed to assist farmers, not those engaged in trade. It annulled loans of barley or silver made at interest, but sums advanced as credit in business transactions, such as goods provided as merchandise for a commercial journey or for a joint business venture, were not rescinded:

> Edict of Ammi-ṣaduqa 4
>
> Whoever has lent barley or silver to an Akkadian or an Amorite[48] for an interest-bearing loan or as a melqētum . . . and had a tablet drafted, because the king has invoked an equity (mīsharum) for the land, his document is voided. He may not collect the barley or silver on the basis of his document.
>
> Edict of Ammi-ṣaduqa 8
>
> An Akkadian or an Amorite who has received barley, silver or (other goods) either as merchandise for a commercial journey or as a joint enterprise for the purpose of profit, his document is not voided (by the edict); he must repay according to the stipulations of his agreements.

This ordinance protected farmers, the majority of the population, from debt, but those engaged in trade would not be subject to interference. Only

[45] Olivier, "The Effectiveness of the Old Babylonian Mēšarum Decree," 109.

[46] The classic works on these edicts are F. R. Kraus, *Ein Edikt des Königs Ammi-ṣaduqa von Babylon* (SDIOAP 5; Leiden: Brill, 1958); Kraus, *Königliche Verfügungen in Altbabylonischer Zeit* (SDIOAP 11; Leiden: Brill, 1984). The Edict of Ammi-ditana extended the Edict of Samsuiluna with statute I (= 22), and the Edict of Ammi-ṣaduqa added statute 15. The statutes of previous acts were incorporated and reenacted into a new edict.

[47] Kraus, *Königliche Verfügungen in Altbabylonischer Zeit*, 293. Lieberman and Jursa argued for Abi-esuḫ as the king who commissioned the edict (r. 1711–1684) (S. Lieberman, "Royal 'Reforms' of the Amurrite Dynasty," *Bibliotheca Orientalis* 46 [1989], 251; Michael Jursa, "'Als könig Abi-Ešuh gerechte ordnung hergestellt hat' eine bemerkenswerte altbabylonisch Prozessurkunde," *RA* 91 [1997]: 135–145). But it might be that this Edict is simply another copy of the Edict of Samsu-iluna.

[48] The distinction between the Akkadian and Amorite population is about an Akkadian population, which is settled and territorially organized, in contrast to an Amorite population, which is largely pastoral and organized along tribal lines.

transactions at interest were revoked. Those who lent to traders made a profit or loss from capital, and traders' debts were not voided. This principle was extended in another provision in the edict to a business advance that contained a provision imposing interest after default: the edict voided the exaction of interest, but the debt for the advance remained in force:

> Edict of Ammi-ṣaduqa 9
> Whoever has lent barley, silver or (other) goods to an Akkadian or an Amorite either (as an advance) for purchases, for a commercial journey or as a joint enterprise for the purpose of profit, and had a tablet drafted, however, in the document he had executed, the creditor stipulated in writing that at the time of the expiration of the (contract's) term, the money would accrue interest or if he had made any (other) additional stipulations, he (the debtor) shall not pay on the basis of the (additional) stipulations but shall (only) pay the barley or silver (of the original agreement).

The interest obligation upon the Akkadian and the Amorite is to be revoked. But the principal had to be repaid.

The debt assumed by a trader was only partially revoked, while farmers' debts were entirely cancelled. The reason for this may be that loans at interest to farmers could be difficult to regulate because even if excessive interest rates were restricted, the price for the crop could be adjusted to conceal a higher rate.[49] A lower rate could be offset by an increase in the price and, therefore, farmers would remain vulnerable. The entire debt burdening a farmer had to be revoked. The Edict of Ammi-ṣaduqa is unique among the social reform decrees in making this distinction between loans made at interest and commercial advances. The other decrees do not make such a distinction, and all debts and enslavements based on debt were voided.[50]

This distinction could lead unscrupulous lenders to falsify documents, and so the edict prescribed a severe remedy for this offense:

> Edict of Ammi-ṣaduqa 7
> If anyone has lent barley or silver as an interest-bearing loan and had a tablet drafted, retaining the document in his own possession, and

[49] Randolph C. Blitz and Millard F. Long, "The Economics of Usury Regulation," *Journal of Political Economy* 73 (1965), 614.

[50] Jursa, "'Als könig Abi-Ešuh gerechte ordnung hergestellt hat' eine bemerkenswerte altbabylonisch Prozessurkunde," 135–145.

> then stated: "I have not lent it to you as an interest-bearing loan or as a melqētum. The barley or silver which I have given to you, I have given (as an advance) for purchases or for the purpose of profit, or for some other objective," the person who had received the barley or the silver shall produce his witnesses to the wording of the document that the lender had denied, and they shall speak their testimony before the god. Because (the lender) had distorted his tablet and denied the transaction, he must pay six-fold to the borrower. If (the lender) cannot pay his penalty, he shall die.

Attempting to falsify a loan as a business advance was prohibited with a severe penalty. Other lenders might try to disguise a loan as another type of transaction that would not be subject to a revocation:

> Edict of Ammi-ṣaduqa 6
> Whoever has lent barley or silver to an Akkadian or an Amorite for an interest bearing loan or as a *melqētum*,[51] and in the tablet which he drew up perpetrated a deception by having it drawn up as a sale or a bailment and then persisted in taking interest, (the debtor) shall produce his witnesses, and they shall indict (the creditor) for taking interest. Because he distorted his document, his document shall be voided.

The debtor was at a disadvantage because the lender retained the tablets and could have the transaction rewritten. The lender had the advantage, and the edict, aiming at curbing abuses, restricted the lender's power.[52]

That these edicts were put into practice is documented in many contracts dating from this period that contain provisions specifically countering edicts of equity.[53] The tablets maintain that the transaction recorded occurred after the effective date of an edict or, alternatively, that the parties to the contract have agreed that the transaction was not to be covered by such an edict. Another text attests that commissions of judges and officials would scrutinize

[51] Not enough documentation of this type of loan exists to determine how it differs from an interest-bearing loan.

[52] The Edict of Samsu-iluna also decreed that if the sale of property forced by debt was made at the full price, rather than a lower price, the sale was not voided at all, and the slave or property remained with the purchaser. See Raymond Westbrook, "Hard Times: *CT* 45 37," in *Veenhof Anniversary Volume* (Leiden: Nederlands Instituut voor het Nabije Oosten, 2001), 547–551.

[53] E.g., Olivier, "The Effectiveness of the Old Babylonian Mēšarum Decree," 109–113; M. Schorr, *Urkunden des altbabylonischen Zivil- und Prozesrechts* (Leipzig: J. C. Hinrichs, 1913), no. 273.

private contracts to rule on whether a contract was affected by an edict.[54] Another text reports that an individual was not dealt with in accordance with the edict (*kīma ṣimdatim*) and the addressees of the letter are ordered to do so or to send him to Babylon to fix the matter.[55]

2.1.4. Law Collections

The law collections extant from Mesopotamia are:

Law Collection	Language	Date	Location
Laws of Ur-Namma	Sumerian	ca. 2100 BCE	Ur
Laws of Lipit-Ishtar	Sumerian	ca. 1930 BCE	Isin
Laws of Eshnunna	Akkadian	ca. 1770 BCE	Eshnunna
Laws of Hammurabi	Akkadian	ca. 1750 BCE	Babylon
Hittite Laws	Hittite (new recension, ca. 1500–1180 BCE)	ca. 1650–1500 BCE	Hattusha
Middle Assyrian Laws	Akkadian	ca. 1076 BCE	Assur
Neo-Babylonian Laws	Akkadian	ca. 700 BCE	Sippar

The genre of a law collection has three parts:

1. An introductory section, often called a prologue or preamble but which is essential, not secondary, to the overall document;
2. A collection of statutes;
3. The concluding section, consisting of imprecations against anyone defacing the king's name from the text; it is often called an epilogue, a term that makes it seem as if it is secondary to the section composed of statutes, but it is in fact integral to the work.

It is generally the second part, the statutes, that attracts the most attention. The statutes are generally articulated casuistically in conditional sentences: the specific circumstances of a case of offensive behavior are laid out in the protasis and the remedy in the apodosis.[56] The statutes manifest

[54] BM 80318. See Finkelstein, "Some New Misharum Material and Its Implications," 242.
[55] AbB VII 135 (= CT 52 135). See Lieberman, "Royal 'Reforms' of the Amurrite Dynasty," 243 n.10.
[56] The temporal value of the verb(s) in the protasis is that of an event that occurs generally (in contrast to a single occurrence in a hypothetical condition). See Eran Cohen, "Functional Value

themselves as law because they delineate offenses and prescribe punishment. They are organized organically by the subject discussed rather than subsumed under the rubric of an articulated legal principle.

The earliest law collection known to us is the Laws of Ur-Namma.[57] It predates the Laws of Hammurabi by 350 years. Since the beginning of the text is in poor condition, the name of the king promulgating the inscription is not entirely clear, and it has been debated as to whether it was promulgated by Ur-Namma[58] or his son and successor Shulgi.[59] The composition

of *iprus* Forms in Old Babylonian *šumma* Protases," in *Language and Nature: Papers Presented to John Huehnergard on the Occasion of His 60th Birthday* (Studies in Ancient Oriental Civilizations 67; Chicago: Oriental Institute, 2012), 1–11.

[57] The name has most often been read conventionally as Ur-Nammu, but Miguel Civil has argued for Ur-Namma ("On Some Texts Mentioning Ur-Namma," *Or* 54 [1985], 27 n.1). See also Esther Flückiger-Hawker, *Ur-Namma of Ur in Sumerian Literary Tradition* (Orbis Biblicus et Orientalis; Fribourg, Switzerland: University Press, 1999), 8–9.

[58] Ur-Namma was the military governor of Ur under Utuḫegal, king of Uruk, and he may have been a member of the royal family of Uruk. He threw off the domination of Uruk and founded the Third Dynasty of Ur. (In the law collection, he is termed "king of Sumer and Akkad," whereas in Hymn C, he is identified as "king of Ur." Perhaps we can safely assume that he took on the grandiose title later in his reign.) His son, Shulgi, assumed the throne after him (2093–2046 BCE). Ur-Namma may have been Utuhegal's brother or may have married his daughter. See Flückiger-Hawker, *Urnamma of Ur in Sumerian Literary Tradition*, 1. Claus Wilcke suggested that Ur-Namma was Utuhegal's brother. See Wilcke, "Die Sumerische Königsliste und erzählte Vergangenheit," in *Vergangenheit in mündlicher Überlieferung* (Colloquium Rauricum 1; ed. J. v. Ungern-Sternberg and H. Reinau; Stuttgart: B. G. Teubner, 1988), 119; Wilcke, "Genealogical and Geographic Thought in the Sumerian King List," in DUMU-E2-DUB-BA-A: *Studies in Honor of Åke W. Sjöberg* (Philadelphia: University Museum, 1989), 565–566; Wilcke, "Politik im Spiegel der Literatur, Literatur als Mittel der Politik im älteren Babylonien," in *Anfänge politischen Denkens in der Antike, die nahölichen Kulturen und die Griechen* (Schriften des Historisches Kolleg, Kolloquien 24; ed. K. Raaflaub; Munich; R. Oldenbourg, 1993), 32. Cooper suggested that Ur-Namma was Utuhegal's son-in-law ("Paradigm and Propaganda: The Dynasty of Akkade in the 21st Century," in *Akkad, the First World Empire: Structure, Ideology, and Traditions* (ed. M. Liverani; Padova: Sargon, 1993), 20–21, and 20 n.43). The textual information available does not shed light on how Ur-Namma acquired the kingship of Ur and why he claimed the title of "King of Sumer and Akkad," a title reflecting dominion over Babylonia (whether real or aspirational). Flückiger-Hawker speculated that he seized power from the legitimate heir to the kingship of Uruk and then moved the capital to Ur because he already resided there and because it was the best seaport in Sumer (*Urnamma of Ur in Sumerian Literary Tradition*, 4–5). Ur-Namma died a premature death, but whether it was during a military defeat, an assassination, or illness is unknown (Samuel Noah Kramer, "The Death of Ur-Nammu and His Descent to the Netherworld," *JCS* 21 [1967], 104–122). The territorial expansion that began during Ur-Namma's reign culminated in Shulgi's reign, when Ur became a territorial state, achieving hegemony over Babylonia and controlling the periphery, possessing an imperial bureaucracy and promoting a new conception of royalty. In so doing, it achieved the same scope of power as the previous empire, that of the Akkade dynasty(ca. 2300–2200 BCE). This achievement did not last long, and Ur III began its decline under Shulgi's son Amarsu'en (r. 2045–2037 BCE) and grandson Shūsu'en (r. 2036–2028 BCE). The empire of Ur collapsed during the reign of Ibbīsu'en (r. 2027–2003 BCE).

[59] The historical narrative includes events not known from Ur-Namma's reign, whereas Shulgi is depicted as undertaking many administrative reforms as well as a mīsharum reform, as we noted earlier in this chapter. See Piotr Michalowski and C. B. F. Walker, "A New Sumerian 'Law Code,'" in DUMU-E2-DUB-BA-A: *Studies in Honor of Åke W. Sjöberg* (Occasional Publications of the Samuel Noah Kramer Fund 11; Philadelphia: University Museum, 1989), 384–386.

as a whole is only partially preserved: not quite eight-five statutes are extant, and the continuation of the composition and its conclusion are missing.[60] We can only guess as to the complete number of statutes and the concluding content.[61] The composition begins with a pronouncement employing three motifs characteristic of law collections: (1) the claim that the gods endowed the monarch with dominion, (2) the assertion that the monarch governs according to the principles of *kittum* and *mīsharum*, and (3) the declaration that the monarch has not delivered the widow and orphan to the rich and the powerful. One paragraph, LU E3b, states explicitly that Ur-Namma modified the rule regarding slave sales.[62] Unfortunately the text is broken, and the exact details are unknown. The acknowledgment in a law collection that a law was modified is exceedingly rare: the only other instances are in the Hittite Laws.[63]

The next law collection extant comes from the reign of Lipit-Ishtar (r. 1934–1924 BCE). The cultural milieu in which the Laws of Ur-Namma was produced persisted beyond the end of the Ur III dynasty into the reign of Lipit-Ishtar, during whose dominion the long shadow of Ur III dissipated.[64] The tradition of Sumerian law, therefore, extended until the reign of Lipit-Ishtar, barely 150 years before the reign of Hammurabi. There are more than a dozen copies of the Laws of Lipit-Ishtar,[65] and they come from the city of Isin, known for the scribal schools during the Old Babylonian period, the period of the composition of the Laws of Hammurabi.

[60] The most recent critical editions are Miguel Civil, "The Law Collection of Ur-Namma," in *Cuneiform Royal Inscriptions and Related Texts in the Schøyen Collection* (Cornell University Studies in Assyriology and Sumerology 17; Bethesda, Md.: CDL, 2011), 221–310; Claus Wilcke, "Der Kodex Ur-Namma (CU): Versuch einer Rekonstruktion," in *Riches Hidden in Secret Places: Ancient Near Eastern Studies in Memory of Thorkild Jacobsen* (ed. T. Abusch; Winona Lake, Ind.; Eisenbrauns, 2002), 291–332.

[61] It is possible that the fragmentary law collection termed "Laws of X" is actually the conclusion of the Laws of Ur-Namma. See Michalowski and Walker, "A New Sumerian 'Law Code,'" 386, 395; Roth, *Law Collections*, 36–39.

[62] Civil, "The Law Collection of Ur-Namma," 252.

[63] The Hittite Laws acknowledges differences in penalties in the past and present.

[64] Isin could no longer claim the mantle of Ur III after Gungunum of Larsa broke away. (Amelie Kuhrt, *The Ancient Near East* [London: Routledge, 1995], 76–80).

[65] Whether all of the copies do in fact belong to the Laws of Lipit-Ishtar is questionable, and whether the fragments have been correctly placed together is debatable. See Roth, *Law Collections*, 24; Francis R. Steele, *The Code of Lipit-Ishtar*, Museum Monographs (Philadelphia: University Museum, 1949); Steele, "An Additional Fragment of the Lipit-Ishtar Code Tablet from Nippur," *Archiv Orientalni* 18 (1950), 489–494; G. R. Driver and John C. Miles, *The Babylonian Laws* (volume two; Ancient Codes and Laws of the Near East; Oxford: Clarendon, 1955); Émile Szlechter, "Le Code de Lipit-Ištar (I)," *RA* 51 (1957), 57–82; "Le Code de Lipit-Ištar (II)," *RA* 51 (1957), 177–196; "Le Code de Lipit-Ištar (III)," *RA* 52 (1958), 74–90.

The Laws of Lipit-Ishtar shares themes with both the Laws of Ur-Namma and the Laws of Hammurabi, demonstrating the continuity of the tradition of law collections. The Laws of Lipit-Ishtar begins with a prologue on the very same themes as the Laws of Ur-Namma, and its epilogue contains curses upon any king who would erase the king's words, just like the Laws of Hammurabi. This threat may indicate that the Laws of Lipit-Ishtar was written on a stela like the one extant for Hammurabi.

The existence and content of an Akkadian law collection slightly older than the Laws of Hammurabi, the Laws of Eshnunna, a city near Babylon, demonstrate that the tradition of a law collection, originally a genre of Sumerian literature, was taken over and transferred into Akkadian before the Laws of Hammurabi. Hammurabi's scribes did not initiate the genre of law collection in Akkadian but inherited it before advancing it to new dimensions. Three copies of the Laws of Eshnunna are extant: two are large tablets that present nearly complete copies and that might be official copies, and the third is a student exercise tablet containing excerpts from the Laws of Eshnunna.[66]

The prologue of the Laws of Eshnunna is no longer extant, and the king from the city of Eshnunna who promulgated the text is unknown. The date formula preserved at its beginning shows that it most likely promulgated during the reign of an early contemporary of Hammurabi, and the presence of a date formula itself parallels the appearance of date formulas in the reform edicts. Otherwise, only the statutes are preserved, and the beginning and ending of the composition are missing. The Laws of Eshnunna incorporates a limited number of declarative statements regulating economic matters in apodictic form, statements that mirror the language of reform edicts, a contrast to the conditional sentence format used for its other statutes.

A law collection has been found in the Hittite language with casuistic statutes in the same linguistic style of casuistic descriptions in conditional sentences as in the Sumerian and Akkadian law collections. A Neo-Hittite copy of the Hittite Laws contains revisions to the Old Hittite version of the Hittite Laws, and even the Old Hittite text includes notations that there was a difference with earlier law.

[66] Albrecht Goetze argued that the two large copies could not be official copies because of the great number of mistakes and that it was plausible that those copies were used by officials in their official duties or were produced in the training of scribes (*The Laws of Eshnunna* [AASOR 31; New Haven, Conn.: Department of Antiquities of the Government of Iraq and the American Schools of Oriental Research, 1956]), 14. See Roth, *Law Collections*, 58; Yaron, *The Laws of Eshnunna*, 30. The two large copies are from Tell Harmal (Shaduppum), and the smaller one is from Tell Haddad (Meturan).

The Middle Assyrian Laws is of a different genre from the other law collections. It appears to be a collection of laws organized topically with each grouping by topic on separate tablets, perhaps prepared as an aid to a judge in deciding cases. The unusual composition of each tablet, such as Tablet A, which deals with various offenses committed by or against women, militates against the fact that a tablet could be a section of a larger corpus since these offenses would have to be addressed repeatedly in regard to other persons. Paul Koschaker argued that the Middle Assyrian Laws (or at least Tablet A) is the product of a jurist, who has supplemented an earlier text with additional laws on a particular subject and explanations for his private use or for the use of a client.[67] Additional evidence for this is the repetition in MAL O of some but not all of the provisions in MAL B, which deals with land issues involving inheritance as well as agriculture and irrigation.

The Neo-Babylonian Laws may manifest a revival of the tradition of law collections associated with kings. It differs from the third-millennium and early-second-millennium law collections in that it is not in the textual format of a royal inscription. However, it must be noted that we have only a single poorly preserved exemplar dating from about 700 BCE, and it is damaged at the beginning and end. Only fifteen statutes dealing with free people are preserved, and their linguistic form is different from the other law collections: relative clauses in declarative sentences are employed in place of conditional sentences.

2.1.5. What Is the Date of Promulgation of the Laws of Hammurabi?

Each of the years of Hammurabi's reign was given a name, as was the style in Mesopotamia, and the second-year name, "Year in which Hammurabi established justice (equity) in the land," most likely refers to Hammurabi's promulgation of an edict of equity. The twenty-second year of his reign was called, after the raising of a statue in the temple of Esagila in Babylon, "Hammurabi, King of Equity."[68] While this may signify that the Laws of Hammurabi was promulgated during that year, the list of cities in its prologue includes those conquered by Hammurabi in later years of his reign. Therefore, it is likely that the Laws of Hammurabi was issued in two editions, the first in year

[67] Koschaker, *Quellenkritische Untersuchungen zu den 'altassyrischen Gesetzen'* (Mitteilungen der Vorderasiatisch-aegyptischen Gesellschaft 26; Leipzig: J. C. Hinrichs, 1921), 79–84.

[68] See Piotr Michalowski and M. P. Streck, "Hammurapi," in RLA, 380–383.

twenty-one of his reign (ca. 1772–1771 BCE), the year before the raising of the statue was commemorated in a royal-year name, and then a second version near the end of his reign. The second edition may have been promulgated between 1763 and 1755 BCE. There are two considerations to keep in mind for the date of the second edition. First, Hammurabi is called "warrior, who shows mercy to the city of Larsa, who renews the Ebabbar temple for the god Shamash, his helper" (II:32–36), and since Hammurabi conquered Larsa in 1763, the Laws must have been promulgated after Larsa was conquered and incorporated into his kingdom.[69] Second, since Eshnunna, the home of the main temples for both Tishpak and Ninazu, is not mentioned, the later edition of the Laws of Hammurabi may have been promulgated in 1756–1755 before Hammurabi assumed control over Eshnunna in his thirty-seventh year of rule.[70]

2.2. What Is the Relationship between the Acts of Equity, the Reform Edicts, and the Law Collections?

The nature of the relationship between the acts of equity as recorded in hymns and royal inscriptions, the edicts of equity, and the law collections requires elucidation. Two scholars, J. J. Finkelstein and Klaas Veenhof, have proposed influential theories about the correlation between these genres.

Finkelstein argued that there was a relationship between decrees of equity, whether recorded in a royal inscription, hymn, or edict, and the law collections, even though the decrees seemed to be a one-time fix, while a law collection appeared to be a set of stipulations that would be in effect permanently.[71]

[69] Hammurabi's thirty-eighth-year name commemorates his conquest of Eshnunna the prior year. However, Charpin understood the year name as meaning that Eshnunna was destroyed by a natural flood, not one intentionally caused by Hammurabi to conquer Eshnunna (Dominique Charpin, *Hammurabi of Babylon* [London: I. B. Tauris, 2012], 71). If that is the case, then Eshnunna may have been conquered in Hammurabi's thirty-first year (1762–1761), because a battle with Eshnunna was recorded in the name for his thirty-second year. However, the year name for his thirty-eighth year might or might not indicate that the destruction of Eshnunna by flooding was intentionally caused by Hammurabi. See Malcolm J. A. Horsnell, *The Year-Names of the First Dynasty of Babylon*, volume two: *The Year-Names Reconstructed and Critically Annotated in the Light of their Exemplars* (Hamilton, Ontario: McMaster University Press, 1999), 157–159; Matthew Rutz and Piotr Michalowski, "The Flooding of Ešnunna, the Fall of Mari: Hammurabi's Deeds in Babylonian Literature and History," *JCS* 68 (2016), 15–43, especially 25–28.

[70] F. R. Kraus, "Codex Ḫammu-rabi IV 32–44," *Wiener Zeitschrift für die Kunde des Morganlandes* 51 (1948), 173–177.

[71] Finkelstein, "Ammiṣaduqa's Edict and the Babylonian 'Law' Codes," 91–104.

He contended that a decree did have a long-lasting effect on certain economic circumstances, even though in general it voided a limited number of economic obligations for a fixed time period. He pointed out that there may also have been a literary relationship between the decrees and the law collections and found evidence for this in the first part of the Laws of Eshnunna, which is comprises provisions about economic matters articulated apodictically, a style thought typical of an edict. The Laws of Hammurabi contains statutes that appear to be long-lasting economic reforms as well: although the Laws of Hammurabi was not issued at the start of Hammurabi's reign but decades later, those statutes did regulate economic matters, similar to the scope of decrees issued at the beginning of a reign. Finkelstein observed,

> It might even be said that there was in Mesopotamia an early tradition for the utilization of royal *mīsharum*-acts in the drafting of the royal "apologia" inscriptions. In the development of this tradition, or genre, (the Laws of Ur-Namma) would represent a transitional phase, in which some of the characteristics of the earlier style (i.e., Urukagina's text) of the narrative recounting of the reforms were combined with the enumeration of hypothetical legal cases, the stylistic affinities of which lay probably in the "scholastic" tradition, not essentially different from the other "encyclopedic" activity of the scribal schools, such as collection and canonization of lists of objects, legal phrases, omen. etc. By the time of Lipit-Ishtar, it would appear, the change in style was more or less complete: the narrative "reform" section of the prologue (or epilogue) was reduced to the most general statements about the king's concern for social justice, while the major emphasis was placed on the "laws" themselves, as hard and fast proof of the king's conscientiousness in matters of justice. But regardless of the wide difference in format and appearance of the earliest and latest royal texts of this genre, the shadow of the mīsharum-act is to be detected in back of all of them.[72]

Finkelstein speculated on the process by which a law collection may have been compiled from an edict, and his hypothetical process consisted of a number of stages. First, decrees of equities were enacted without being

72 Finkelstein, "Ammiṣaduqa's Edict and the Babylonian 'Law Codes,'" 104.

announced in an official text. Only later were they collected together and inscribed in a single text. Even later in a king's reign, Finkelstein argued, a law collection was promulgated, and the written records of the decrees were used as a source for the law collections: at that point, the law collection was intended as a royal apologia, affirming to the gods, to the citizens of the king's realm, and to posterity that the king had fulfilled his duty to ensure justice. It should be noted that Finkelstein did not make a distinction between the differing genres recounting reforms: the royal inscriptions and hymns on the one hand, and the reform edicts on the other.

In contrast to Finkelstein, Klaas Veenhof followed a different tack: he argued that there were two types of decrees of equity, only one of which had a link to law collections.[73] At the start of a reign, royal decrees of equity were issued with great fanfare: they were originally designed to help the weak, then their content shifted to voiding debts. Those royal decrees, whether commemorated in hymns and royal inscriptions or recorded in edicts, had little relationship to the law collections. However, Veenhof surmised that kings also issued regulatory decrees, ones in which certain penalties were stipulated for breach of contract and liabilities were established for certain behavior. He found evidence for their existence in the references to *ṣimdat šarrim*, "a decree of the king." Unlike debt cancellation, which was of limited duration, these regulatory decrees were restricted only in subject matter, not in duration, and it may be that these decrees were later incorporated into law collections.

However, the difference in textual genres must be taken into account because it sheds light on the interrelationship between the acts of equity commemorated in hymns and royal inscriptions, the edicts of equity, and the law collections. I see nine conclusions to be drawn from the evidence:

A. There are affinities between the acts of equity portrayed in the royal inscriptions and hymns of Enmetena, Uruinimgina, Gudea, Shulgi, and Enlil-bani and the edicts of equity: they are all associated with the activities of a king, and they are all intended to protect a citizen who has fallen into hard times. But there are clear differences: the edicts are precisely worded texts that appear to be meant for promulgation, whereas the royal inscriptions and hymns manifest a different and less

[73] Veenhof, "The Relation between Royal Decrees and 'Law Codes' of the Old Babylonian Period," *Jaarbericht Ex Oriente Lux* 35/36 (1997), 49–83.

precisely legal scope. The edicts appear to be aimed at everyday commerce, where acts of equity memorialized in royal inscriptions and hymns seem to be aimed at curbing the behavior of government officials or modifying internal family matters. The law collections are also linked to the activities of a king, but their affinities to the acts of equity commemorated in royal inscriptions and hymns and to the edicts are divided. Their prologues and epilogues resemble the content and terminology in royal inscriptions and hymns (as we discuss further in the next chapter), but their statutes bear a literary similarity to the edicts. For example, the Laws of Ur-Namma recounts in an incomplete section in its prologue that certain individuals had seized inappropriate control of trade and commodities but that the king freed the people from the exploitation (A iii 87–124): this is similar to the removal of corrupt officials in the royal inscriptions of Uruinimgina.

B. A number of the acts of equity commemorated in royal inscriptions and hymns prescribe social concord in specific situations, between slave and master and between parent and child, a topic not addressed in the edicts. The edicts deal only with economic matters. One law collection, the Laws of Lipit-Ishtar, does refer to children supporting parents and vice versa in its prologue (LL ii 16–24, A iii 24–26, IV 106). Otherwise, it must be noted that the statutes in law collections deal with issues of slavery and of family relationships in ways distinct from the acts of equity memorialized in royal inscriptions and hymns, and the closest the statutes come to those topics is to the case of slaves denying their servitude to their masters and of parents or children denying their kinship tie. This is distinct from the prescriptions that masters not strike their slaves or that parents and children not utter nasty words to each other found in the acts of equity commemorated in hymns and royal inscriptions.

C. The edicts address debt forgiveness, a topic mentioned in the prologues of a number of the law collections and in the acts of equity commemorated in royal inscriptions and hymns. Strikingly, it is a topic not treated in the statutes of the law collections. But it must be noted that the acts of equity memorialized in royal inscriptions and hymns use the same terminology for debt forgiveness as the prologues of the law collections. The Laws of Ur-Namma declares the liberation (ama.r-gi_4) of certain cities (A iii 125–134, C i 1–10), a declaration first specified in the royal inscription of Enmetana (E19.5.4.iii.10–iv.5, v.4–8). The

Laws of Lipit-Ishtar names liberation (ama.r-gi$_4$) for the inhabitants of certain cities (ii 1–15, A iii 9–23), and it points at the king's commanding concord and mutual support within families (A iii 24–26, iv 1–6). The king is portrayed as issuing a cancellation of debt in Ur-Namma Hymn C 56, but not in the same terminology as the Laws of Ur-Namma.

> <u>Enmetana E1.9.5.4.iii.10–iv.5, v.4–8</u>
> He cancelled obligations for Lagash, restoring child to mother and mother to child. He cancelled obligations regarding interest-bearing grain loans. . . . He cancelled obligations for Uruk, Larsa, and Pa-tibira.
>
> <u>Ur-Namma Hymn C 56</u>
> The poor who went to gather fuel were exempted from their debts.
>
> <u>Laws of Ur-Namma A iii 125–134, C i 1–10</u>
> At that time, by the might of Nanna, my lord, I issued a debt cancellation for Akshak, Marad, Girkal, Kazallu, and their settlements, and Uṣarum, whatever (regions) under the subjugation of Anshan.
>
> <u>Laws of Lipit-Ishtar A iii 9–23</u>
> At that time I issued a debt cancellation for the sons and daughters of the city of Nippur, the sons and daughters of the city of Ur, the sons and daughters of the city of Isin, the sons and daughters of the lands of Sumer and Akkad, who were subjugated, and I restored order.

The acts of mīsharum recorded in hymns and royal inscriptions again show rhetorical affinities to the prologues of law collections. It is striking that the edicts do not employ this terminology, even though they address debt forgiveness.

D. The express provisions in contracts to prevent a debt from being cancelled due to an edict of equity serve as evidence that they were put into practice and enforced. There are no direct references in contracts or other records of legal activities that the statutes in the law collections were put into effect, an issue that we discuss in detail in chapter 6.

E. There is one exception to the above observation: the edicts appear to void a statute of the Laws of Hammurabi. LH 117 stipulates that free persons sold into debt-service were to be released after three years of service, but the Edict of Ammi-ṣaduqa 20 provides for their immediate release if those in debt-service were from particular towns as a result of the edict.[74] The voiding of the automatic release after three years stipulated in the Laws of Hammurabi may be a sign that it was put into practice.[75] The reason for the amendment in the Edict of Ammi-ṣaduqa lies in the realm of speculation: it may be that automatic release discouraged the extension of credit, while the edict instituted a one-time cancellation.[76] Otherwise, the statutes in the law collections share only a literary form—statutes in conditional sentences—with the edicts, not content.

> <u>LH 117</u>
> If an obligation is outstanding against a man (a financial difficulty has seized a man) and he sells or gives his wife, his son, or his daughter into debt service, they shall perform service in the house of their buyer or of the one who holds them in debt service for three years; their release shall be secured in the fourth year.

[74] This provision is paralleled in the Edict of Samsuiluna paragraph 3′ and in the Edict of X 1′. See Kraus, *Königliche Verfügungen in altbabylonischer Zeit*, 264–280; S. Lieberman, "Royal 'Reforms' of the Amurrite Dynasty," 247–250.

[75] It is possible that the edict's statutes on the woman innkeepers in paragraphs 17–18, or 14′ to 16′, were also intended to contravene the provisions on woman innkeepers in LH 108–109, but it is less clear because the statutes and the provisions of the edict do not overlap in the specific cases they adduce. Edict 16–17 considers debt, and Edict 18 is too broken for comparison. LH 108 deals with a female innkeeper raising the price of beer, and LH 109 handles the presence of criminals at an inn.

> <u>Edict of Ammi-ṣaduqa 16</u>
> A woman innkeeper of the provinces who pays out silver for the barley of the brewer to the palace—because the king has established equity for the land, the collection agent shall not dun for their (presumably the innkeeper's) the arrears.
>
> <u>Edict of Ammi-ṣaduqa 17</u>
> A woman innkeeper who has sold beer or barley on credit shall not collect for whatever she has sold on credit.
>
> <u>Edict of Ammi-ṣaduqa 18</u>
> A woman innkeeper or a merchant who by means of an untrue seal [. . .] shall die.
>
> <u>LH 108</u>
> If a woman innkeeper should refuse to accept grain for the price of beer but accepts (only) silver measured by the large weight, thereby reducing the value of beer in relation to the value of grain, they shall charge and convict the woman innkeeper and they shall cast her into the water.
>
> <u>LH 109</u>
> If there is a woman innkeeper in whose inn criminals have congregated and she does not seize those criminals and lead them off to the palace authorities, that woman innkeeper shall be killed.

[76] William W. Hallo, "Slave Release in the Biblical World in Light of a New Text," in *Solving Riddles and Untying Knots: Biblical, Epigraphic, and Semitic Studies in Honor of Jonas C. Greenfield* (ed. Ziony Zevit, Seymour Gitin, and Michael Sokoloff; Winona Lake, Ind.; Eisenbrauns, 1995), 90.

LH 118

If he gives a male or female slave into debt service, the merchant may extend the term (beyond the three years?) he may sell him; there are no grounds for a claim.

Edict of Ammi-ṣaduqa 20

If an obligation results in foreclosure against a citizen of Numhia, Emutbalum, Idamaras, Uruk, Isin, Kisurra, or Malgium (so that) he (placed) his own person, his wife, his children in debt servitude or as a pledge, because the king has invoked an act of equity for the land, he is released; his freedom is in effect.

Edict of Ammi-ṣaduqa 21

If a house-born (female) or (male) slave of a citizen of Numhia, Emutbalum, Idamaras, Uruk, Isin, Kisurra or Malgium . . . whose price . . . has been sold for silver or was given over for debt servitude or was made a pledge, his freedom shall not be effectuated.

F. The prologue of the Laws of Ur-Namma may refer to the correction of abuses by government officials, a mistreatment mentioned in the act(s) of equity recounted in the royal inscriptions of Uruinimgina. None of the edicts refers to abuse by government officials. The Laws of Hammurabi does refer to malfeasance by officials, such as military officers.

Laws of Ur-Namma A ii 87–92, 114–124

At that time, the *nisku*-people had control of the fields, the sea-captains had control of the foreign maritime trade . . . those who appropriated [the oxen] . . . those who appropriated [the sheep] . . . I returned. I established freedom for the Akkadians and foreigners in the land of Sumer and Akkad, for those conducting foreign maritime trade [free from] sea-captains, for the herdsmen (free from) those who appropriated oxen, sheep, and donkeys.

LH 33

If either a captain or a sergeant has recruited deserters [or has acquired labor conscripts] or accepted and led a hireling as a substitute on a royal campaign, that captain or sergeant shall be killed.

LH 34

If either a captain or a sergeant take a soldier's household furnishings, oppress a soldier, deliver a soldier into the power of an influential person in a law case or take a gift that the king gave to a soldier, that captain or sergeant shall be killed.

G. The acts of equity commemorated in royal inscriptions and hymns and the law collections employ the rhetoric of the king as establishing and ensuring justice using general, not parallel, language. They share the same idea but not terminology. The edicts do announce that the king has issued an edict, wording reflecting the role of the king in justice, but they do not mirror either the rhetoric of the royal inscriptions and hymns and the law collections.

<u>Ur-Namma Hymn A 139–144</u>
At the command of Ereshkigal
Soldiers, so far as they have died in action,
And sinners, so far as they have been recognized(?)
They give into the king's hands.
They . . . [Ur-Namma] there . . .
For his beloved brother Gilgamesh
He passes judgment of the netherworld and renders the decisions of the netherworld.

<u>Ur-Namma Hymn C 32–39/40</u>
I am Ur-Namma, king of Ur, the guardian-spirit of my city:
I caused offense to tremble, bodies shook there.
Thanks to the fear I have inspired. . . .
The judgments I pronounce made Sumer and Akkad hew to the one and same path.
I put my foot on the neck of thieves and oppressors.
Reaching out for malefactors as for a snake, I clasped them.
Against the fugitives I rushed forth, their hearts were set aright.
I made justice appear, subdued evil.
Like Gibil, my frown made them obedient.
My mouth/command puts. . . .

<u>Ur-Namma Hymn F 30–33</u>
He has put shackles on all (the foreign) land.
He has blocked (them) with a strong bolt. He is the king worthy of Su'en.
Evil does not pass before him.
(Rather) Urnamma has imposed justice on property matters.

Laws of Ur-Namma A i 31–42

When the gods An and Enlil turned over the kingship of the city of Ur to the god Nanna, at that time, for Ur-Namma, son born of the goddess Ninsun, for her beloved house-born slave, according to (the god Nanna's) justice and truth . . .

Laws of Ur-Namma A iii 104–113

[At that time, I], Ur-Namma, [mighty warrior, lord of the city of Ur, king of the lands of Sumer and] Akkad, [by the might] of the god Nanna, my lord, [by the true command of the god Utu], I established [justice in the land].[77]

Laws of Ur-Namma C ii 43–51

I eliminated enmity, violence, and cries for justice. I established justice in the land.

Gudea Stat B vii 41

I paid attention to the justice ordained by Nanshe and Ningirsu.

Gudea Cylinder B xviii 6–7

(xviii 4–7) He paid attention to the justice (ordained) [by Nanše] and Ningirsu.

LH I:27–49

At that time, Anum and Enlil to improve the welfare of the people ordained Hammurabi the pious prince who fears the gods, to make justice prevail in the land,

to destroy evil and wickedness,

to prevent the strong from oppressing the weak,

to rise like Shamash over the black-headed people and illuminate the land.

LH V:14–25

When the god Marduk commanded me to provide justice for the people of the land in order to keep order, I established truth and justice as the declaration of the land.[78] I enhanced the welfare of the people.

H. In contrast to the general wording about the king ensuring justice discussed immediately above, the *topos* of the care of widows and orphans, articulated in a stock formula of a single sentence, is found both in royal

[77] Reconstruction follows Roth, *Law Collections*, 15.

[78] For an analysis of what this clause signifies, see chapter 3.

inscriptions and hymns memorializing reforms and in the prologues and epilogues of law collections.[79] The stock sentence may be modeled on the phrasing of the reform of Uruinimgina. This rhetoric is not found in the edicts.

Urukagina 1.9.9.1.12:23–25
Urukagina made a binding agreement with the god Ningirsu that he would never subjugate the orphan or the widow to the powerful.

Laws of Urnamma A iv 162–165, C ii 30–39
I did not deliver the orphan to the rich. I did not deliver the widow to the strong. I did not deliver the man with but one shekel to the man with one mina (60 shekels). I did not deliver the man with but one sheep to the man with one ox.

Gudea Stat B vii 42–43
I did not expose the orphan to the rich nor did I expose the widow to the influential one.

Gudea Cyl B 18:6–7
He did not expose the orphan [to the wealthy person] nor did he expose the widow to the [influential] one.

LH XLVII:59–61
In order that the strong not wrong the weak,
to provide justice for the destitute girl and the widow.

I. The hymns and royal inscriptions exhibit *topoi* that are also found in the prologues and epilogues of the law collections: selection and designation

[79] The prologue of the Laws of Hammurabi presents the king boasting that he protects the orphan girl and the widow, the impoverished and the weak, but there may be a dissonance between that boast and the content of the statutes. Few statutes mention these categories, yet a number do seem to seek to defend those who can be taken advantage of. LH G protects a tenant who has paid the full amount of the rent from a landlord who wants to evict him. LH X sanctions a merchant who changes the weight for repayment to his advantage. LH Z allows a borrower to repay a loan with goods other than silver or barley, forestalling a premium he might otherwise have to pay if he had to convert his goods into silver or barley. LH 34 protects a private soldier from a superior officer. LH 116 prescribes punishment for the death of a distrainee from physical abuse. LH 119 protects a slave woman who has borne children to her owner. LH 177 safeguards a widow. While the last statute is the only one in the Laws of Hammurabi that specifically mentions one of those the king boasts of helping, the statutes do seek to protect those who are vulnerable to be wronged.

A number of statutes safeguard those harmed by events beyond human control. Debt is to be remitted when fields are flooded, and the government is to pay for stolen goods when the thief is not found. The statutes are meant to restore equity in society by remedying uncontrollable harm.

> as king by a god or gods, and the investiture of the king by a god. These motifs are not limited to royal inscriptions and hymns commemorating acts of equity but are common to royal inscriptions and hymns in general.

These observations demonstrate that the rhetoric employed both in acts of equity as recorded in hymns and royal inscriptions and in the prologues and epilogues of law collections displays clear affinities, but in general the edicts do not appear to intersect with them rhetorically. The edicts employ conditional sentences to articulate statutes, like the statutes in the law collections. In regard to content, the acts of equity recounted in royal inscriptions and hymns seem to be aimed at curbing the behavior of government officials or modifying internal family matters, whereas the edicts address economic issues. The acts of equity prescribe social concord in specific situations, between slave and master and between parent and child, a topic not addressed in the edicts. The statutes in law collections deal with issues of slavery and of family relationships differently than the acts of equity. The acts of equity and the edicts both address debt forgiveness, a topic mentioned in the prologues of a number of the law collections, but it is an issue not addressed in the statutes of the law collections. In sum, a number of elements are found in both the acts of equity and the prologues and epilogues of the law collections, but the overlap does not extend to the statutes. The edicts and the statutes in the law collections do share a literary form: casuistic description in conditional sentences.

The next stages of our study of the Laws of Hammurabi unfold from these observations: the similarity of the Laws of Hammurabi to royal inscriptions is explored in the following chapter, and the nature of the statutes is addressed in chapter 4. The similarities and dissimilarities, as becomes apparent, flow from the disparate streams of royal and scribal traditions that were united by the scribe who composed the Laws of Hammurabi.

3

The Laws of Hammurabi as a Royal Inscription

3.1. The Literary Genre of the Laws of Hammurabi

The Laws of Hammurabi is composed as a royal inscription, but it is far from a commonplace version of that form. It is not a stereotypical text of trite and banal reiterations of standard wording. Rather, it is inventive and subtle in its political and theological engagement, and with its robust emphasis on the king's role in upholding justice and the incorporation of an agglomeration of statutes, it structures and reconfigures the standard form of a royal inscription with great innovation. It employs a wealth of rhetorical and structural devices to achieve its aims. To identify the Laws of Hammurabi as a royal inscription is not to reduce it to a hackneyed form of textual expression but to highlight how much the genre's structure can be infused with inventiveness.

Employing the format of a royal inscription transforms a king's legal activities into an area of royal heroism. Just as a king is depicted in royal inscriptions as combating enemies and repulsing invaders, building temples and palaces, digging canals, and providing prosperity for his people, the representation of a king as guaranteeing and dispensing justice casts him into a heroic mode.[1] As the one portrayed as being bestowed personally by the gods with *kittum*, "truth," and as actualizing *mīsharum*, "equity," the king becomes a colossus bestriding the earth. Everyday legal activity, however, is quite different. The historical reality reconstructed from the primary documents of law, such as conveyances (transfers of property), contracts, administrative texts, records of court litigation, and the like diverges from the heroism of royal inscriptions: it is mundane and banal. Disputes were resolved as best they could be (or not). The day-to-day humdrum of buying and selling, of marriage and divorce, and of bureaucracy, whether efficient or creaky, is

[1] Mario Liverani, "The Deeds of Ancient Mesopotamian Kings," in *CANE*, 2353.

The Laws of Hammurabi. Pamela Barmash, Oxford University Press (2020). © Oxford University Press.
DOI: 10.1093/oso/9780197525401.001.0001.

prosaic and perhaps a bit bland. By contrast, the impression left by the king's activities in the realm of justice according to the Laws of Hammurabi is hyperbolic. The likening of Hammurabi to the sun god, the god of justice, is not accidental: it raises him beyond mere mortal. The royal inscription format has a purposeful trajectory, and it gives texture to the statutes integrated within it.

The hyperbole is aimed at the explicitly named audience of a royal inscription, the gods and future kings. It is affirmed that the gods selected the right individual as king and that he was able to successfully fulfill the tasks bestowed upon him. Future kings are cautioned on how to exercise kingship and are adjured to preserve the inscriptions of the kings of the past. This audience of the gods and future kings is named explicitly by royal inscriptions. At the same time, the implicit audience of a royal inscription is the king's contemporaries and subjects. The king's control was exerted by ideological force as much as, if not more than, the physical coerciveness of royal personnel, whether bureaucratic or military. The king exercised his dominion by impressing, frightening, and marshalling his subjects to follow his instructions and orders. He increased his control by manipulating and alarming his enemies, whether internal or external, and by nipping opposition to his rule in the bud.

These lofty and practical goals aimed at the twofold audience of royal inscriptions may have meant that royal administrators sought out scribes who were among the better of their profession.[2] It is likely that only a select group of scribes had the capacity to compose royal inscriptions, and only a minority of this set was able to compose texts that are rhetorically masterful. The most able scribes balanced the dictates of tradition and the interests of the king who commissioned them. They were able to use their literary skills and talent by combining traditional elements in inventive ways and devising new components of royal inscriptions. The scribe(s) who composed the Laws of Hammurabi possessed unusual skill and composed an inventive and vivid text in the form of a royal inscription.[3] (For most royal inscriptions, the results show the talent of their scribes to be pedestrian: those inscriptions are trite and boilerplate and probably not intended to be anything more.)

Importantly, identifying the Laws of Hammurabi as a royal inscription corrects the perception that the statutes are the essence of the text and that

[2] Liverani, "The Deeds of Ancient Mesopotamian Kings," 2355.
[3] Gerhard Ries, *Prolog und Epilog in Gesetzen des Altertum* (Munich: C. H. Beck, 1983), 18–30.

the rest of the text is secondary.[4] Even though the conventional division of the Laws of Hammurabi into three parts, with parts one and three termed "prologue" and "epilogue," makes it appear that the statutes are primary, the terms "prologue" and "epilogue" are misnomers—taking them too seriously causes a skewed perception of the whole. To apprehend the statutes as wholly independent from the rest of the text is to misconstrue the work.

Excitement over the discovery of such an extensive collection of laws has contributed to this false perception. The editio princeps, the first edition of the work, published in 1902 in Paris by its modern discoverer Victor Scheil, contained a French translation of the statutes but not the rest of the text.[5] Translations of the entire work published within a year or two divided the text into three parts and called the units before and after the statutes "prologue" and "epilogue."

Another factor prompting this tripartite division is the lopsidedness of the text, the space devoted to the agglomeration of statutes. This massiveness, with so much of the text's bulk devoted to statutes, contributes to this perception. The prologue and epilogue each take up five columns, and the statutes occupy forty-one columns. The imbalance prompts the question of whether the Laws of Hammurabi is the splicing together of a royal inscription (the prologue and the epilogue) and a set of statutes. One of the earliest scholars to put his analysis into print, D. H. Müller, argued that the prologue and epilogue were written by one author and the collection of statutes by another. Many scholars who have considered the question have upheld this understanding of separate authorship.[6]

However, scholars use the terms "prologue" and "epilogue" for elements regularly found in royal inscriptions. Many interpreters have subdivided the prologue and epilogue but rarely are the subunits named, as they might be for a royal inscription.[7] Admittedly, the terms "prologue" and "epilogue" are vague and therefore may be useful, as long as the marginality they imply is ignored.[8] They are expedient for reference, but they are inexact in denoting

[4] Victor Avigdor Hurowitz, *Inu Anum ṣīrum: Literary Structures in the Non-Juridical Sections of Codex Hammurabi* (Occasional Publications of the Samuel Noah Kramer Fund; Philadelphia: University Museum, 1994), 2.

[5] Scheil, *Textes élamites-sémitiques, seconde série*, 11–162, plates 3–15.

[6] Hurowitz, *Inu Anum ṣīrum*, 2 n.4. Hurowitz offered a concise summary of early scholarship on the Laws of Hammurabi. The question of whether the statutes and the prologue and epilogue derive from different authors is addressed later in this chapter.

[7] Hurowitz, *Inu Anum ṣīrum*, 3.

[8] Nomenclature like unit 1, unit 2, unit 3, etc., avoids the problematics of terms like "prologue" and "epilogue" but is too bland to be useful.

the essential nature of the text they describe. They do not shed light on the sections of the text that are consequential to the aims of the composition as a whole. The contents of the prologue and epilogue are intimately related and intertwined with the statutes on the level of theme, and it must be emphasized that even though the work can be partitioned into distinct sections, the Laws of Hammurabi is a single, integrated work.

The statutes have attracted the overwhelming amount of attention from scholars, but a number of scholars have focused on the prologue and epilogue. Two scholars stand out. Gerhard von Ries, in his volume *Prolog und Epilog in Gesetzen des Altertums*, compared the prologues and epilogues across the law collections. Victor Avigdor Hurowitz advanced the study of the Laws of Hammurabi magnitudes further in an array of publications, and in his book *Inu Anum ṣirum: Literary Structures in the Non-Juridical Sections of Codex Hammurabi*, he analyzed the literary stratagems and identified the literary models employed in the prologue and epilogue of the Laws of Hammurabi.

3.2. The Royal Inscriptions That Served as Models for the Laws of Hammurabi

The extent to which the Laws of Hammurabi has moved beyond the dull and banal is evident when considering Hammurabi's own royal inscriptions that may have served as models. One of Hammurabi's royal inscriptions reads as follows:

<u>RIME 4, E4.3.6.7 (= LIH 95)</u>

(1–9) Hammurabi, mighty king, king of Babylon, king who makes the four quarters (of the earth) be at peace, who achieves the victory of the god Marduk, the shepherd who pleases him (the god Marduk), am I.

(10–16) When the gods Anum and Enlil gave the land of the Sumerians and the Akkadians to me to rule, and entrusted their nose-rope into my hands,

(17–20) I dug the canal "Hammurabi is the abundance of the people," which brings abundant water to the land of Sumer and Akkad / the Sumerians and the Akkadians.

(21–37) I turned both its banks into cultivated land. I kept heaping up piles of grain. I provided perpetual water for the land of Sumer and Akkad and gathered the scattered people of the land of Sumer and Akkad and provided them with pastures and watering places. In abundance and plenty I tended them as a shepherd. I settled them in peaceful abodes.

(38–49) At that time, I, Hammurabi, mighty king, favorite of the great gods, with the mighty strength which the god Marduk gave to me, I raised high a tall fortress with great (mounds of) earth, whose tops were like a mountain. I built (it) at the intake of the canal "Hammurabi is the abundance of the people."

(50–57) I named that fortress "Fort Sin-muballit, father who engendered me." (In such a manner) I made the name of Sin-muballit, the father who engendered me, pre-eminent throughout the (four) quarters (of the world).

The commonalities between RIME 4, E4.3.6.7 and the Laws of Hammurabi are as follows:[9]

A. RIME 4, E4.3.6.7:1–9 has the royal title in the syntactic form of "royal name + title + I (*anāku*)," a characteristic shared by LH I:50–V:13, in which the amount of titles is greatly expanded:

RIME 4, E4.3.6.7:1–9

Hammurabi, mighty king, king of Babylon, king who makes the four quarters (of the earth) be at peace, who achieves the victory of the god Marduk, the shepherd who pleases him (the god Marduk), am I.

LH I:50–V:13

Hammurabi,
the shepherd chosen by Enlil,
who heaps up plenty and abundance,
who perfects every possible thing for Nippur, where heaven and earth meet,
the pious provider for the Ekur-temple (extensive exposition of titles) . . . am I.

[9] Hurowitz, *Inu Anum ṣīrum*, 15–16.

B. Both texts have the divine commission of the king in a temporal clause, "when (*inu*) + divine name + subordinate verbs":

RIME 4, E4.3.6.7:10–16
When the gods Anum and Enlil gave the Sumerians and the Akkadians to me to rule, and entrusted their nose-rope into my hands . . .

LH V:14–19
When the god Marduk commanded me to provide justice for the people of the land in order to keep order . . .

C. Both texts contain a listing of royal deeds in the form "object + verb in preterite indicative":

RIME 4, E4.3.6.7:17–37
I dug the canal "Hammurabi is the abundance of the people," which brings abundant water to the land of Sumer and Akkad / the Sumerians and the Akkadians. I turned both its banks into cultivated land. I kept heaping up piles of grain. I provided perpetual water for the land of Sumer and Akkad and gathered the scattered people of the land of Sumer and Akkad and provided them with pastures and watering places. In abundance and plenty I tended them as a shepherd. I settled them in peaceful abodes.

LH V:20–24
I established truth and justice as the declaration of the land. I enhanced the welfare of the people.

D. Both texts preface the fulfillment of the divine commission with the phrase "at that time (*inūmīšu*)":

RIME 4, E4.3.6.7:38
At that time . . .

LH V:25
At that time . . .

E. Both texts contain a second expression of the king's royal title in the syntax of "Hammurabi + titles + I (*anāku*)":

RIME 4, E4.3.6.7:39–41

Hammurabi, mighty king, favorite of the great gods, (am) I.

LH XLVII:9–10

Hammurabi, the perfect king, (am) I.

F. Both texts use the phrase "with the X the god Y gave to me, I accomplished Z":

RIME 4, E4.3.6.7:36–38

with the mighty strength which the god Marduk gave to me,
I raised high a tall fortress . . . ,

LH XLVII:22–29

with the mighty weapon which the gods Zababa and Ishtar bestowed upon me,
with the wisdom which the god Ea allotted to me,
with the ability which the god Marduk gave me,
I annihilated enemies everywhere.

G. Both texts name the accomplishment for which it was written: RIME 4, E4.3.6.7:44–55, the building of the wall of Sippar, and LH XLVII:11–77, the pacification of the land and the raising up of the Stela.

RIME 4, E4.3.6.7:44–55

I raised high a tall fortress with great (mounds of) earth, whose tops were like a mountain. I built (it) at the intake of the canal "Hammurabi is the abundance of the people." I named that fortress "Fort Sin-muballit, father who engendered me." (In such a manner) I made the name of Sin-muballit, the father who engendered me.

LH XLVII:11–77

I have not been neglectful nor lazy toward the black-headed people, handed over to my care by the god Enlil and whose governance the god Marduk has given me.
I have sought for them peaceful places.
I have removed difficulties.
I have spread light over them.
With the mighty weapon that the gods Zababa and Ishtar have bestowed upon me, with the wisdom that the god Ea has

apportioned to me, with the capability that the god Marduk has given me, I annihilated enemies from north to south.

I put an end to strife. I improved the well-being of the people. I made the people of the inhabited world lie down in safe pastures. I did not tolerate villains.

The great gods have selected me, and I am the shepherd who brings peace and whose scepter is just.

My benevolent shade is stretched out over my city. I hold the people of the lands of the Sumerians and the Akkadians in my bosom. They have prospered under my protective spirit. I have maintained them in peace. I have protected them in my wisdom.

In order that the strong not wrong the weak,

to provide justice for the orphan girl and the widow,

I have inscribed my precious pronouncements upon my Stela and set it up before my statue (called) "King of Equity."

It is striking that the Laws of Hammurabi and this royal inscription bear such a strong resemblance: seven elements appear in identical order.

The Laws of Hammurabi bears a similarity to another royal inscription of Hammurabi:

<u>RIME 4, E4.3.6.2</u>

(1–12) When the god Shamash, great lord of heaven and earth, with his shining face looked joyfully upon me, Hammurabi, the prince, his favorite, granted to me everlasting kingship and a reign of long days,

(13–27) made firm for me the foundation of the land which he had given me to rule, spoke to me by his pure word which cannot be changed to settle the people of Sippar and Babylon in peaceful abodes, and bestowed upon me the great commission to build the wall of Sippar and to raise its head,

(28–35) at that time, I, Hammurabi, mighty king, king of Babylon, reverent one, who obeys the god Shamash, beloved of the goddess Ayya, who pleases the god Marduk, his lord,

(36–45) by the supreme might that the god Shamash gave to me, with the levy of the army of my land, I raised the top of the foundation of the wall of Sippar with earth like a great mountain. I built (that) high wall.

(46–50) That which no king among the kings in the past had built, I grandly built for the god Shamash, my lord.

(51–55) The name of that wall is "By the decree of the god Shamash, may Hammurabi have no rival."

(56–61) In my gracious reign which the god Shamash called, I cancelled corvée duty for the people of Sippar, the ancient city of the god Shamash.

(62–69) I dug its canal and provided perpetual water for its land. I heaped up plenty and abundance. I established joy for the people of Sippar.

(70–81) They pray for my life. I did what was pleasing to the god Shamash, my lord, and the goddess Ayya, my lady. I put my good name in the mouths of the people (in order) that they proclaim it daily like (the name of) a god and that it not ever be forgotten.

The elements from this inscription, RIME 4, E4.3.6.2, that are shared with the Laws of Hammurabi are as follows:

A. RIME 4, E4.3.6.2:1–9 depicts the sun god Shamash looking upon the king joyfully, an image depicted in three dimensions in high relief at the apex of the Stela:[10]

> RIME 4, E4.3.6.2:1–9
>
> When the god Shamash, great lord of heaven and earth, with his shining face looked joyfully upon me, Hammurabi, the prince, his favorite . . . .

B. Both this inscription and the Laws of Hammurabi begin with a god endowing the king with royal authority and commissioning the king. RIME 4, E4.3.6.2:1–27 puts the emphasis on the task of securing peace by the building of a wall for the city of Sippar, while LH I:1–49 delineates the background to the divine commission to ensure justice. The two texts share an elaborate section conveying the relationship of the king to the god: in so doing, the texts highlight the bestowal of the task upon the king by the god.

[10] This description of the sun god looking joyfully upon Hammurabi is found elsewhere in Hammurabi's royal inscriptions. See chapter 1.

RIME 4, E4.3.6.2:1–27

When the god Shamash, great lord of heaven and earth, with his shining face looked joyfully upon me, Hammurabi, the prince, his favorite, granted to me everlasting kingship and a reign of long days, made firm for me the foundation of the land which he had given me to rule, spoke to me by his pure word which cannot be changed to settle the people of Sippar and Babylon in peaceful abodes, and bestowed upon me the great commission to build the wall of Sippar and to raise its head. . . .

LH I:1–49

When august Anum, king of the Annunaku-gods, and Enlil, lord of heaven and earth, who determines the destinies of the land, allotted to Marduk, first-born son of Ea, lordship over all people, they exalted him among the Igigi-gods, gave Babylon its august name, made it pre-eminent among the regions of the world; they established for him within it an eternal reign, whose foundations are as secure as heaven and earth.

At that time, Anum and Enlil to improve the welfare of the people ordained Hammurabi the pious prince who fears the gods, to make justice prevail in the land,

to destroy evil and wickedness,

to prevent the strong from oppressing the weak,

to rise like Shamash over the black-headed people and illuminate the land.

C. Both texts use the adverb *inūmīšu*, "at that time," to usher in the fulfillment of the divine command. RIME 4, E4.3.6.2:28, 36–45 depicts the fulfillment of the task by the king commissioned by the god, and LH V:25 demonstrates that Hammurabi has fulfilled the divine command by introducing the statutes.

RIME 4, E4.3.6.2:28, 36–45

At that time . . . with the supreme might that the god Shamash gave to me, with the levy of the army of my land, I raised the top of the foundation of the wall of Sippar with earth like a great mountain. I built that high wall.

LH V:25

At that time (statutes)

D. RIME 4, E4.3.6.2:29–35 includes a royal titulary (as does the royal inscription treated earlier, RIME 4, E4.3.6.7:39–41). The Laws of Hammurabi has a second titulary in XLVII:9–10.

> <u>RIME 4, E4.3.6.2:29–35</u>
> I, Hammurabi, mighty king, king of Babylon, pious one, who obeys the god Shamash, beloved of the goddess Ayya, who pleased the god Marduk his lord . . .
>
> <u>LH XLVII:9–10</u>
> I am Hammurabi, the perfect king.

E. Both texts use the phrase "with the X the god Y has given to me, I accomplished Z." This is true as well for RIME 4, E4.3.6.7:36–38 ("with the mighty strength which the god Marduk gave to me, I raised high a tall fortress . . .").

> <u>RIME 4, E4.3.6.2</u>
> with the supreme might which the god Shamash gave to me
>
> <u>LH XLVII:22–29</u>
> with the mighty weapon which the gods Zababa and Ishtar bestowed upon me, with the wisdom which the god Ea allotted to me, with the ability which the god Marduk gave me, I annihilated enemies everywhere

F. RIME 4, E4.3.6.7:51–55 uses a nominal sentence to name the wall that is the fulfillment of the divine command of securing peace. LH XLVII:1–8 also uses a nominal sentence to link the statutes to Hammurabi complying with the divine injunction of ensuring justice.

> <u>RIME 4, E4.3.6.7:51–55</u>
> The name of that wall is "By the decree of the god Shamash, may Hammurabi have no rival."
>
> <u>LH XLVII:1–8</u>
> These are the just decisions that Hammurabi, the able king, has established and thereby has enabled the land to follow upright practices and correct behavior.

G. RIME 4, E4.3.6.2:70–81 portrays the people adoring Hammurabi by mentioning his name on a daily basis and that they do so like the mentioning of the name of a deity. LH XLVIII:3–58 even puts words of prayer into the mouth of a supplicant.

<u>RIME 4, E4.3.6.2:70–81</u>

They pray for my life. I did what was pleasing to the god Shamash, my lord, and the goddess Ayya, my lady. I put my good name in the mouths of the people (in order) that they proclaim it daily like (the name of) a god and that it not ever be forgotten.

<u>LH XLVIII:3–58</u>

May any wronged man who has a legal dispute come before my statue, "King of Equity,"
and may he read aloud my inscribed stela so that he hear my precious pronouncements,
and may my stela explain his dispute, and may he calm his heart (and praise me by saying):
Hammurabi, the lord, who is like a father and begetter to his people, who was obedient to the command of Marduk, his lord, and fulfilled the battle wish of the god Marduk north and south. He gladdened the heart of Marduk, his lord, and he secured the eternal well-being of the people and provided just ways for the land.
May he say thus,
and may he bless me with his entire heart before Marduk, my lord, and Sarpanitum, my lady.
May the spirit (the *shedu*-spirit) and the protector (the *lamassu*-spirit), the gods who enter the Esagila temple, and the very brickwork of the Esagila temple make my daily portents auspicious before the god Marduk, my lord, and Sarpanitum, my lady.

Victor Avigdor Hurowitz argued that the correspondence between RIME 4, E4.3.6.7 and the Laws of Hammurabi in seven elements in consecutive order indicates strongly that they follow the same literary pattern.[11] Hurowitz also contended that elements of RIME 4, E4.3.6.2 were incorporated and integrated into the overall pattern represented by the other inscription. A question remains: Were RIME 4, E4.3.6.7 and RIME 4, E4.3.6.2 themselves the

[11] Hurowitz, *Inu Anum ṣīrum*, 16, 91.

model for the Laws of Hammurabi or did another text serve as the model for both? This question may be unanswerable.

Hurowitz argued further that the absence of statutes in RIME 4, E4.3.6.7 shows that the statutes are a foreign element extrinsic to the literary pattern: their insertion interrupts the syntactic pattern awkwardly. The statutes may have originally been an independent composition with a concluding line after them:

> *dīnāt mīšarim ša Ḫammurapi šarrum lēʾûm ukinnu-ma mātam ussam kīnam u rīdam damqam ušaṣbitu*
> (These are) the just decisions that Hammurabi, the able king, has established and thereby has enabled the land to follow upright practices and correct behavior.

Hurowitz speculated that the original conclusion may have been shorter and was rewritten in order to echo the wording of the earlier part of the royal inscription framework but that it was not successful because of the grammatical inconsistency.

However, it seems to me that structures of both royal inscriptions have been spliced together to form a literary pattern for the Laws of Hammurabi that includes a double commission and that the double commission was employed to tie together the entire composition because of the sheer length of the section devoted to statutes. The author shaped the text so that LH V:14–24 articulates the fulfillment of the divine task of ensuring justice, switching the position of *inūmīšu* to be the introduction to the statutes. Both royal inscriptions provided a commissioning statement—RIME 4, E4.3.6.2.1–27 and RIME 4, E4.3.6.7.10–16—and both commissioning statements were retained in the Laws of Hammurabi (LH I:1–49; V:1–49). Furthermore, the Laws of Hammurabi is a royal inscription in which the king's activities in the legal realm are emphasized in addition to the usual emphasis on a king's building activities.[12] The statutes are the literary expression of the king's legal activities, and the adverb *inūmīšu*, "at that time" is used to introduce the fulfillment of a divine command in other royal inscriptions:

[12] Finkelstein, "Ammiṣaduqa's Edict and the Babylonian 'Law Code,'" 103 (although Finkelstein, "A Late Old Babylonian Copy of the Laws of Hammurapi," *JCS* 21 [1967], 42 n.2, calls the prologue "an adaptation of a royal hymn"); Hurowitz, *Inu Anum ṣīrum*, 4.

RIME 4, E4.3.6.1:13–19—"at that time, in order to increase (the amount of food), I piled up a dike in the flooded field (and) built the wall of the cloister upon it"
RIME 4, E4.3.6.3:20–23—"at that time, I built a storehouse which pleases (Enlil) in Babylon, his beloved city"[13]

That both royal inscriptions served as models for the Laws of Hammurabi is established by the repeated commission laid upon the king by the gods in LH I:1–49 and V:14–19. The double commission was inspired by the splicing together of literary structures. It is unusual for a text to have a double commission, but I think that the melding of two literary models with the insertion of a massive collection of legal provisions makes the duplication comprehensible. It may even have been needed to foster a sense of unity between the usual features of a royal inscription and the lengthy set of statutes The so-called prologue and epilogue along with the statutes form a single composition, not two separate works. The Laws of Hammurabi is a unified text.

The prologue and epilogue do employ language distinct from that of the collection of statutes. They share language whose timbre and tone cannot quite be captured in translation. The language is poetic and contains stylistic elements commonly found in Old Babylonian hymns and epics.[14] This is in sharp distinction to the statutes, written in the Old Babylonian dialect contemporary to the time in which the statutes were written and containing typical legal terminology. The distinct language of the statutes is not to be taken necessarily a sign of multiple authors: the same scribe may use one style for the elements common to royal inscriptions, while using legal language for the statutes.[15]

The two royal inscriptions RIME 4, E4.3.6.2.1–27 and RIME 4, E4.3.6.7.10–16 served as models for the overall structure of the Laws of Hammurabi. Other royal inscriptions served as models for specific sections of the Laws of Hammurabi, and I analyze those texts in the appendix to this chapter.

[13] These two examples are from Hammurabi's own royal inscriptions, but the same linguistic phenomenon is found in the royal inscriptions of other kings, e.g., Warad-Sin, RIME 4, E4.2.13.3:20–29 and Rim-Sin I, RIME 4, E4.2.14.20:34.

[14] Driver and Miles, *The Babylonian Laws*, 1.40; Wolfram von Soden, "Der hymnisch-epische Dialekt des Akkadischen," *ZA* 40 (1931), 163–227; continued in *ZA* 41 (1933), 90–183.

[15] Cf. the source criticism of the Pentateuch, which utilizes doublets of narratives and laws and divergent vocabulary to identify discrete sources. See R. N. Whybray, *The Making of the Pentateuch: A Methodological Study* (Journal for the Study of the Old Testament Supplement Series 53; Sheffield: JSOT Press, 1987). Our analysis reveals across discrepancies between statutes that may indicate that more than one scribe had a hand in composing them.

3.3. The Prologue

The prologue begins with the commissioning of the king. The gods Anu and Enlil, the heads of the pantheon, are portrayed as exalting Babylon and its city-god, Marduk, and then commissioning Hammurabi. The emphasis is on Hammurabi's authority:

LH I:1–49

When august Anum, king of the Annunaku-gods, and Enlil, lord of heaven and earth, who determines the destinies of the land, allotted to Marduk, firstborn son of Ea, lordship over all people. They exalted him among the Igigi-gods, gave Babylon its august name, made it preeminent among the regions of the world; they established for him within it an eternal reign, whose foundations are as secure as heaven and earth. At that time, Anum and Enlil to improve the welfare of the people ordained Hammurabi the pious prince who fears the gods,
(in order) to make justice prevail in the land,
to destroy evil and wickedness,
to prevent the strong from oppressing the weak,
to rise like Shamash over the black-headed people and illuminate the land.

The gods are depicted as playing an active role in this commission, and Hammurabi is the subject of their actions. Hammurabi is portrayed as passive, yet at the same time the text makes a near equivalence between Hammurabi and the god Shamash: Hammurabi ascends like Shamash over the people. The elevation of Hammurabi embodies the relief at the top of the Stela with its dual nature, both subordinating and equalizing the human king to the god.

Another text tradition, manuscript B, is a variant that highlights the selection of Hammurabi even more intensely and applies the focus on the selection of Hammurabi as king even more sharply:

When Anum . . . Enlil [ ] humanity
gave just shepherding as a gift to Hammurabi, the son of Sīn-muballit, the shepherd created by their hands,
and presented to him the measuring rod and coil of rope befitting his kingship,

and called the exalted name of Nippur, and made it preeminent among the quarters of the world, and established for him (Hammurabi) in its (Nippur's) midst eternal kingship whose foundations are made firm as the heavens and the earth.
Anum and Enlil to improve the welfare of the people pronounced my name/ordained
Hammurabi, the just king, the pious prince who fears the gods, me,
(in order) to make justice prevail in the land,
to destroy evil and wickedness,
to prevent the strong from oppressing the weak,
to rise like Shamash over the black-headed people and illuminate the land.[16]

In this version, the gods Anu and Enlil select Hammurabi and elevate the city of Nippur as the site of his eternal kingship, omitting the elevation of Marduk and the city of Babylon. The emblems of kingship are explicitly granted to Hammurabi, and he is linked to the preeminent city of Nippur. In so doing, the text confers both religious and political legitimacy, if not also supremacy, to Hammurabi. The explicit granting of the measuring rod and coil of rope more closely adheres to the image atop the Stela. Yet it differs as well: unlike the image, which depicts the god Shamash, the text of the Stela invokes Anu and Enlil, and the text specifies that it is Marduk who has commissioned Hammurabi to establish justice, not Shamash.

Both versions of this opening section announce the main theme of the Laws of Hammurabi as a whole: the legitimacy of Hammurabi's status as king and the mandate issued to him by the gods to ensure justice. The next section highlights the piety of the king, implicitly affirming that the gods selected the appropriate mortal. It lists (at exhaustive length) deeds that he performed throughout his reign, including the ones that occurred in the final part of his reign, after the initial publication of the Laws of Hammurabi. But rather than presenting these deeds in a chronology of events occurring over the course of the king's reign, it presents them as if the king promulgated the laws immediately after he was

[16] Borger, BAL, I.1, 8–9; Hurowitz, *Inu Anum ṣīrum*, 18–19, 22; Ries, *Prolog und Epilog*, 22–23; Wiseman, "The Laws of Hammurabi Again," 161–172. Hurowitz argued that this tradition was original because rhetorical components employed in this section to integrate the clauses are found only in this text. However, one could question how the other tradition developed if it is rhetorically less developed. In my opinion, manuscript B was more likely a later improvement, rather than the original text.

bestowed with kingship by divine appointment.[17] Strikingly, the use of participles and titles distances the king's actions from their contingency at a particular time and in a specific place—it wraps them in timelessness:

> LH I:50–62
>
> Hammurabi, the shepherd, chosen by Enlil, who heaps up plenty and abundance, who perfects every possible thing for Nippur, where heaven and earth meet, the pious provider for the Ekur-temple . . .

The listing of Hammurabi's pious deeds contains one or two epithets for the king, the deed undertaken by the king for a specific city, and the deed undertaken by the king for the temple or god of that city, but no chronology and no date on which the deed took place. The activity of the king has a timelessness because it is not tied to a specific year, nor it is part of a narrative listing royal activities one after another.[18] The register of pious deeds presents the king in eternal and unassailable achievement, as a success in all ventures, in unwavering piety.

In this catalog, theological and political concerns serve as the ordering principle of the first seven passages. First mentioned are the cities of Enlil, Ea, and Marduk, whose temples were among the most prominent of the time. The cities of the major heavenly deities follow, Sin and Shamash, with those of the astral deities Anum and Ishtar concluding the set:

> ***Prominent temples***
>
> P1 = I:50–62
>
> Hammurabi,
>
> the shepherd chosen by Enlil,

[17] Hurowitz, *Inu Anum ṣīrum*, 22. It is correct, as Hurowitz noted, that this section, either in whole or in part, could be deleted without affecting the flow of the text, but just because it can be deleted does not mean that it is extraneous.

[18] The Laws of Eshnunna, a law collection that is an older contemporary of the Laws of Hammurabi, is preceded by a date formula:

> . . . 21st day . . . of the gods Enlil and Ninazu [when Dadusha ascended to] the kingship of the city of Eshnunna [and entered] into the house of his father, [when] he conquered with powerful weapons within a single year the cities of Supur-Shamash [and . . . on] the far bank of the Tigris river . . .

Unfortunately, the two copies of the Laws of Eshnunna are broken and do not preserve the conclusion.

There is a third witness to the Laws of Eshnunna, an extract of a number of statutes, which does not include either the start or end of the composition.) A look at the road not taken is revealing. The Laws of Eshnunna is tied to a date. The Laws of Hammurabi, by contrast, presents a timeless pattern, a pattern that sharply focuses on the command from the deity to establish justice and on the king's reliable obedience to that command.

who heaps up plenty and abundance,
who perfects every possible thing for Nippur, where heaven and earth meet,
the pious provider for the Ekur-temple.

<u>P2 = I:63–II:1</u>
the capable king,
the restorer of the city Eridu,
the cleanser of the Eabzu temple,
<u>P3 = II:2–12</u>
the assailant of the four regions (of the world),
the one who exalts the reputation of Babylon,
who gladdens the heart of his lord Marduk
whose days are devoted to the Esagila temple,

Heavenly deities
<u>P4 = II:13–21</u>
royal seed whom the god Sin created,
enricher of the city of Ur,
humble and talented,
who provides abundance for the Egishnugal temple,
<u>P5 = II:22–31</u>
sagacious king,
obedient to the god Shamash,
the mighty one,
who establishes the foundation of the city of Sippar,
who decorates the shrine of the goddess Ayya with greenery,
who made famous the temple Ebabbar which is like the abode of heaven,

<u>P6 = II:32–36</u>
warrior,
who shows mercy to the city of Larsa,
who renews the Ebabbar temple for the god Shamash, his helper,

Astral deities
<u>P7 = II:37–47</u>
the lord,
who revitalizes the city of Uruk,
who provides an abundance of water for its people,
who raises the summit of the Eanna temple,
who heaps up bountiful produce for the gods Anum and Ishtar,

By inaugurating the listing of pious deeds with the major deities and the most venerable cities and temples, Hammurabi's preeminence is affirmed: Hammurabi is associated with the cities of significance and is linked to the major deities. As a consequence of the emphasis on Hammurabi's glorification, two curiosities are to be noted in this listing: the god Ea is not mentioned at all in P2, even though his major temple is, and the god Shamash is named twice in P5 and P6. The omission of Ea may be to strengthen the naming of Marduk, the city-god of Babylon, Hammurabi's capital. Ea's city, Eridu, is named in antediluvian traditions, such as the Sumerian King List as the first city, so it may be speculated that Eridu is diminished by the omission of the god's name in favor of the ascension of Babylon. Hammurabi was "the one who exalts the reputation of Babylon," as the text notes in P3, and the inclusion of Marduk among the major deities marks his elevation because of his status as the city god of Babylon, Hammurabi's capital. The other curiosity, the twofold mention of Shamash and the inclusion of his consort in P5 and P6, has a more obvious reason, laying emphasis on the god of justice whom Hammurabi is emulating. Hammurabi's stature is elevated by the tie to the cities of Sippar and Larsa, sites of Shamash's most prominent temples (even if Sippar ought to belong in the next section in the listing of pious deeds by virtue of its location). Furthering the emphasis are the multiple epithets for the king in the passage about his deeds for Shamash: "sagacious king, obedient to the god Shamash, the mighty one."

The descriptions employed in the initial position of each passage are selected to highlight the qualities of the king. The passages about the three major temple-cities denote the king as "the shepherd chosen by Enlil," "the capable king," and "the assailant of the four regions (of the world)," portraying the king as having the qualities of divine selection, ability, and military prowess.[19] The following passages depict these qualities in the same order: "royal seed whom the god Sin created," "sagacious king," and "warrior." The section concludes with a general epithet, "the lord," marking Hammurabi's authority.[20]

[19] Hurowitz, *Inu Anum ṣīrum*, 76–77.

[20] A number of key words in a chiastic chain tie the section of the listing of pious deed together: *mukammer*, "who heaps up," in P1 and P7; "plenty" in P1 and P7 (and its root in verbal form in P4, "who enriches"); "the capable king" in P2 and "the sagacious king" in P5; and "to the Esagil temple" in P3 and "for the Egishnugal temple" in P4. The word "plenty" is used five times in the prologue.

The septet begins and ends with the mention of a god. It names two gods at the end for the sake of closure, and it may be that the position of the god in each passage varies, eventually reversing in radial order, so as to emphasize the dominant position of the god.

P1	god Enlil			
	city of Nippur			
	temple Ekur			
P2	city of Eridu			
	temple Eabzu			
P3		city of Babylon		
		god Marduk		
		temple Esagila		
P4			god Sin	
			city of Ur	
			temple Egishnugal	
P5				god Shamash
				city of Sippar
				goddess Ayya
				temple Ebabbat
P6			city of Larsa	
			temple Ebabbar	
			god Shamash	
P7		city of Uruk		
		temple Eanna		
		god Anum		
		god Ishtar		

The passage begins and ends with the naming of divinities, apropos for a register of pious deeds.

After the theologically ordered section of the listing of pious deeds, the following sections are ordered geographically in groups of six. This maps verbally Hammurabi's domination of the region. It is listing of territories and cities conquered and incorporated piece by piece into a kingdom that did have an amount of lasting power, political integration, and social order for the first time in Mesopotamian history.[21] The first group follows a circular route through central Babylonia, as shown in Map 1:

21 Bottéro, "The 'Code' of Hammurabi," 167.

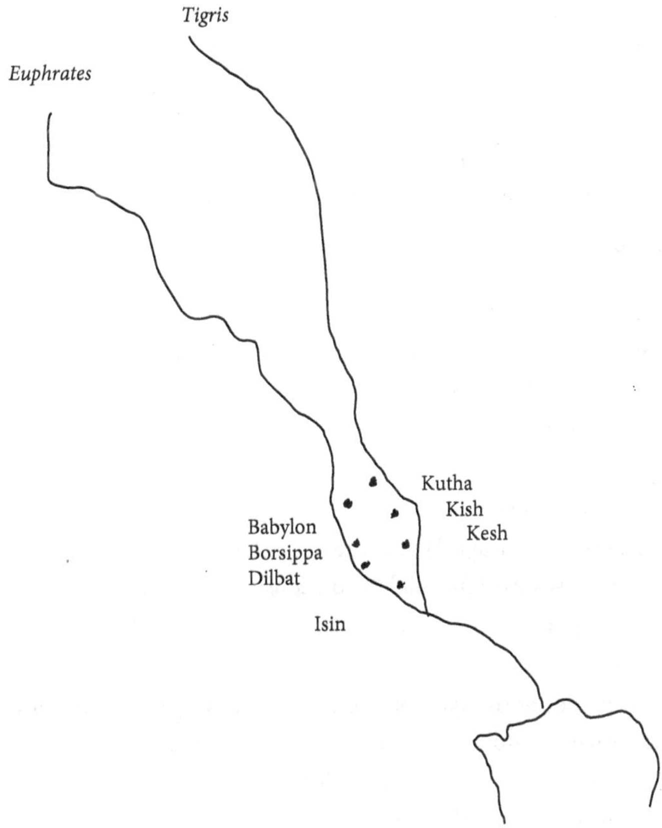

Map 1 Central cities of Babylonia

P8 = II:48–54
the protecting canopy of the land,
who gathers together the scattered people of the city of Isin,
who supplies abundance for the temple Egalmah,[22]

P9 = II:55–67
dragon among kings,
favorite brother of the god Zababa,
provider of the foundation of the settlement of Kish,
who surrounds the Emeteursag temple with splendor,
who arranges the great rites for the goddess Ishtar,
who takes charge of the temple Hursagkalamma,

[22] Curiously, the god Ninurta is not mentioned in the section on Isin and his temple Egalmah.

P10 = II:68– III:6

the enemy-ensnaring net,
whose companion, the god Erra, has allowed him to obtain his heart's desire,
who makes excellent the city of Kutha,
who augments everything for the Emeshlam temple,

P11 = III:7–16

the aggressive wild bull who gores the enemy,
beloved of the god Tutu,
the one who brings pleasure to the city of Borsippa,
the pious one who is not negligent in his duties to the Ezida temple,

P12 = III:17–23

the god of kings,[23]
the one who is omniscient,
who develops the arable land of the city of Dilbat,
who fills the stores of the mighty god Urash,

P13 = III:24–35

the lord,
worthy holder of the symbolic scepter and crown which the wise goddess Mama bestowed to him,
who devised the plans of the city of Kesh,
who provides the pure food for the goddess Nintu,

The emphasis is placed on the king's prowess, both military and administrative. The initial passage depicts Hammurabi as military protector.[24] Three of the six initial epithets used here—"dragon among kings" (P9), "the enemy-ensnaring net" (P10), and "the aggressive wild bull who gores the enemy" (P11)—occupying the central passages in this sextet exemplify Hammurabi's military might. Passages 8 and 10 specify the encompassing nature of Hammurabi's rule—"the protecting canopy of the land" (P8) and "the enemy-ensnaring net" (P10)—and passages 9 and 11 focus on his violence: "dragon among kings" (P9) and "the aggressive wild bull who gores the enemy" (P11). P12 references Hammurabi's wisdom and capability, and P13 names Hammurabi's jurisdiction and divine selection. This order—military

[23] See chapter 2 for a discussion of this passage.
[24] See CAD Ṣ 243 s.v. ṣulūlu A mng. 2b.

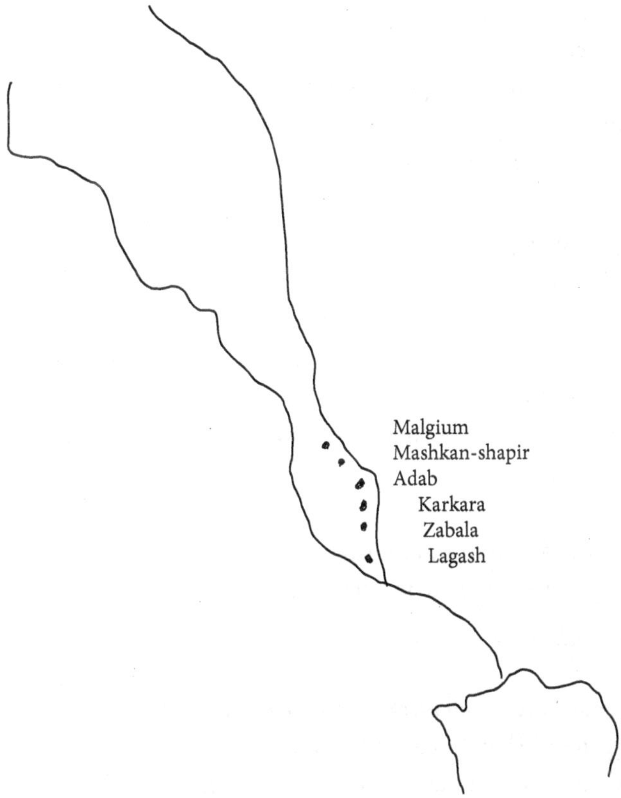

Map 2 Peripheral Cities to the East

prowess, intellect, domination, and divine selection—may refer in reverse to the same qualities as passages 1–7.[25]

The following group follows a linear tour of the cities on the periphery of the country to the east, mapping Hammurabi's authority over the region, as shown in Map 2:

P14 = III:36–46
the perfect arbitrator,
the noble one,
who allots pasture and watering place for the cities of Lagash and Girsu,
who provides plentiful offerings for the Eninnu temple,

[25] Hurowitz, *Inu Anum ṣīrum*, 79.

P15 = III:47–54
the apprehender of enemies,
favorite of Telitum (the goddess Ishtar),
the able one,
who perfects the oracles of the city of Zabala,
who gladdens the heart of the goddess Ishtar,

P16 = III:55–64
the pure prince,
whose prayers the god Adad acknowledges,
appeaser of the heart of the god Adad,
the hero in the city of Karkara,
who installs the proper appointments in the Eudgalgal temple,

P17 = III:65–69
the king,
who gives life to the city of Adab,
who organizes the Emaḫ temple,

P18 = III:70–IV:6
lord of kings,
warrior against whom no one can contest,
who granted life to the city of Mashkan-shapir,
who gives abundant waters to the Emeslan temple,

P19 = IV:7–22
wise one,
leader,
he who has mastered knowledge,
who protects the people of Malgium from catastrophe,[26]
who establishes their settlements in abundance,
who decreed eternal pure offerings for the gods Enki and Damkina who magnify his kingship,[27]

In this mapping of the cities on the eastern periphery under Hammurabi's jurisdiction, the epithets for the king are arranged chiastically, a means of

[26] Lines 9–15, "who protects the people of Malgium from catastrophe, who establishes their settlements in abundance," appear to be an interpolation since their syntactic structure disrupts the pattern of IV:9–22 (Borger, BAL, 7; Martin Worthington, *Principles of Akkadian Textual Criticism* [SANER; Berlin: De Gruyter, 2012], 113).

[27] The Stela and manuscript B both have the honorific nominative *mušarbû* in place of *mušarbî* (Borger, BAL, 9; Worthington, *Principles of Akkadian Textual Criticism*, 190–193).

accentuation: the king's qualities of ability, "the perfect arbitrator," in P14; military prowess, "the apprehender of enemies," in P15; and of dominion, "the pure prince," in P16, are echoed in reverse order by "the king" in P17; "lord of kings, warrior against whom no one can contest," in P18; and "wise one, leader, he who has mastered wisdom" in P19.[28] Both P15 and P16 have a verbal link depicting Hammurabi's relationship to a god: "who gladdens the heart of the goddess Ishtar" in P15, and "appeaser of the heart of the god Adad" in P16. The following couplet, P17 and P18, shifts the emphasis to Hammurabi's care for cities under his control: "who gives life to the city of Adab" in P17 and "who gives life to the city of Adab" in P18. Perhaps this explains the omission of the divine names in P17 and P18. P19 contains verbal links to the end of the previous section, P13, both using the word "pure," and to the next section, P20, both using the word "people." It is notable that in P14, the god Ningirsu is absent, yet the town, Girsu, that was his center of worship is designated. The town of Girsu was a town dependent on the city of Lagash, capital of the city-state of Larsa, and so both are named. In P17 and P18, the gods are omitted as well. The Emah temple was devoted to the goddess Ninmah, and the Emeslam temple was devoted to the god Erra. It is not clear why three divine names are omitted but their temples are included.

The third group of cities follows a route looping through cities to the north, plotting Hammurabi's jurisdiction afresh, this time over more distant territories, as indicated in Map 3:

> P20 = IV:23–31
> chief of kings,
> who subdues the settlements along the Euphrates river by the command of Dagan, his creator,
> who showed mercy[29] to people of the cities of Mari and Tuttul,
>
> P21 = IV:32–44
> the pious prince,
> who brightens the face of the god Tishpak,

[28] Hurowitz, *Inu Anum ṣīrum*, 80.

[29] J.-M. Durand suggested that the reading *ikmilu* is to be preferred over the standard reading *igmilu* so that the line should be rendered "who was angry at the people of the cities of Mari and Tuttul" ("Dagan et la fin du Mari," *NABU* 2004/51). While both are plausible, the verb *kamālu* usually occurs with the preposition *itti*, not with the direct object. See Rutz and Michalowski, "The Flooding of Eshnunna," 21.

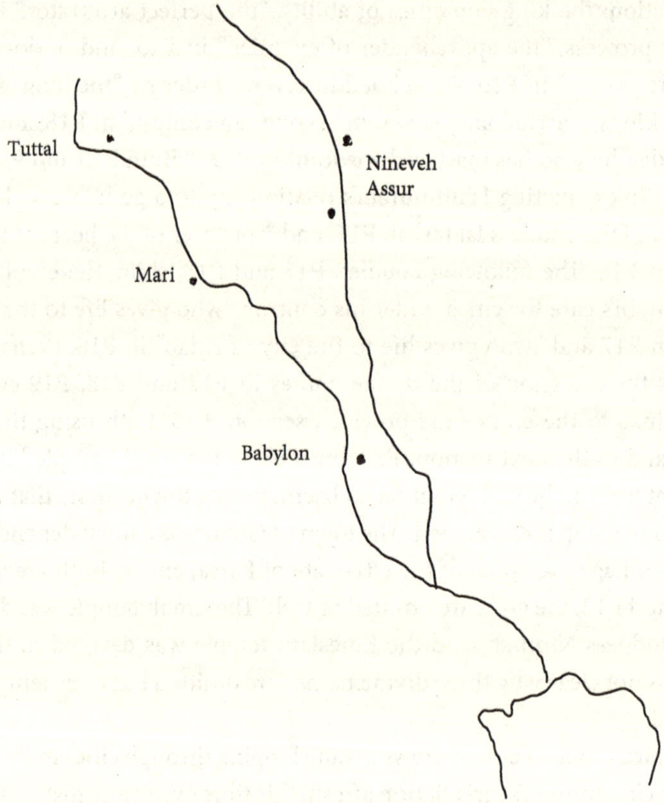

Map 3 Cities to the North

who provides pure food for the goddess Ninazu,
who preserves his people in distress,[30]
who establishes their foundations in the midst of Babylon in peace,

P22 = IV:45–52
shepherd of the people,
whose deeds are pleasing to the goddess Ishtar,
who establishes Ishtar in the Eulmash temple in the midst of central Akkad,

P23 = IV:53–58
who proclaims truth,

[30] Lines 38–47 are omitted in some exempla and may be an interpolation since line 38 contains a suffix without a referent, "who preserves his people in distress" (Borger, BAL, 1.7; Worthington, *Principles of Akkadian Textual Criticism*, 113).

who guides the people properly,
who restores the protective spirit to the city of Assur,

P24 = IV:59–63

who silences the rebels,
the king,
who proclaimed the rites for the goddess Ishtar in Nineveh in the Emeshmesh temple,

P25 = IV:64–66

the pious one,
who prays ceaselessly to the great gods . . .

The patterning of the passages in this set is asymmetric compared to the previous sets, reflecting that Hammurabi's activity in the northern region was more limited. P20 does not name a temple. P21 mentions gods but no temple.[31] P22, P23, and P24 address Hammurabi's activities in Assyria and are shorter. P23 has "a protective spirit" in place of a named god. The royal year formulas that mention the cities of Malgium, Mari, and Assur (Subir in the date formulas) do not contain references to any cult offerings or building activities.[32] It is possible that the scribe(s) writing this text did not have sources with which to expand the description. But more probably, Hammurabi did not devote the same resources to these areas, either because they were of less concern or because he had less control or wanted to devote more resources to more central regions. The fact that the gods are mentioned six times but few temples are may indicate the lack of resources devoted to this region.

The mention of the city of Akkad is striking because at this time the ancient capital city was nearly deserted or at best in sharp decline. Nonetheless, dominion over Akkad had great symbolic value because it was the capital for the first Mesopotamian empire. As Bottéro wrote,

> This was the city around which Sargon I and his successors had assembled the first and largest Mesopotamian empire (ca. 2340–2150), an empire

[31] This passage may include the mention of the city of Eshnunna, as Kraus suggested regarding the insertion of the city name (Kraus, "Codex Ḫammu-rabi IV 32–44," 175). The exclusion of Eshnunna may mean that Hammurabi had less control over it. See the discussion of the date of the promulgation of the Laws of Hammurabi in chapter 2.

[32] Hurowitz, *Inu Anum ṣīrum*, 81.

> which joined into one entity the territory between the two seas: the Persian Gulf and the Mediterranean. An ambiguous memory had been preserved about this old adventure in Mesopotamia: people knew that such an exceptional political rise had been paid for with unending sufferings, violence, revolts, wars, misery and bad luck. I wonder if Hammurabi did not want to subtly contrast his own achievements and his own glory to that of the most famous of his predecessors by evoking Akkad, which undoubtedly had not the least importance at the time, unless as a symbol. This he did by suggesting that, if in the time of Hammurabi the country had become again almost as powerful and extensive as before, it had however remained in prosperity and well-being.[33]

Hammurabi's success as king is symbolized in his dominion over the old capital Akkad and in the political and social climate sketched in his inscription—he is an able ruler.

The qualities mentioned in the text serve as culmination of Hammurabi's exaltation as king:[34]

> dominion "chief of kings," in P20;
> divine selection, "who subdues the settlements along the Euphrates river by the command of Dagan, his creator," in P20;
> ability, "shepherd of the people," in P22, and "who proclaims truth, who guides the people properly," in P23;
> military prowess, "who silences the rebels," in P24;
> dominion "the king," in P24.

The nature of the qualities and deeds recorded is striking: they are a mix of the martial and the pacific, with the peaceful ones of temple-building and providing for the people in the majority. Even violence is often camouflaged in terms of protection and benevolence; in P6, for example, the conquest of Larsa is described as "who shows mercy to the city of Larsa." The emphasis on the peaceful and the protective is made manifest in the relief atop the Stela of the sun god handing the symbols of kingship to Hammurabi in the form

[33] Bottéro, "The 'Code' of Hammurabi," 167–168.

[34] The verb "to proclaim as excellent" is used twice, once to depict Hammurabi's city (at the start of the text) and once to depict Hammurabi (XLVII:79–83).

of a measuring rod and coil of rope, items used for building, not weapons of war.[35]

The passage concludes by stating that Hammurabi worshipped all the great gods, a fitting summation to the listing of pious deeds.[36] It is also the transition to the next section, on Hammurabi's lineage.

P 25 = IV:67–V:13
descendant of Sumu-la-el,
mighty heir of Sin-muballit,
eternal seed of royalty,
solar disk of the city of Babylon,
who illuminates the lands of Sumer and Akkad,
the king who makes the four quarters (of the world) obedient,
favorite of the goddess Ishtar,
am I.

Here, Hammurabi is no longer the passive recipient of the gods' commission, as he is at the beginning of the prologue. He is depicted as speaking in the first person, aiming the vector of the text toward the king's actions. It is rare for Old Babylonian inscriptions to present a king's genealogy, and the major emphasis of the Laws of Hammurabi is on Hammurabi's individual legitimacy as king, rather than through the antiquity of his royal lineage.[37] The king is likened to Shamash, the sun god and the god of justice, in the image of illuminating the lands. The means by which Hammurabi fulfills his role in the arena of justice is soon made clear.

[35] In CT 21, 40–42, a text composed at the same time as the original edition of the Laws of Hammurabi, the martial spirit is not obscured in any way. E.g. "En[lil] has given you [lordship—[Y]ou, whom are you waiting for?! Sîn has given you supremacy—You, whom are you waiting for?! Ninurta has given you a noble weapon—You, whom are you waiting for?! Istar has given you fight and warfare (Sumerian: warfare and fight)—You, whom are you waiting for?! Samas and Adad are your sheriffs—You, whom are you waiting for?!" See Wasserman, "'CT 21, 40–42,'" 5.

[36] In addition, the adjective "devout" is employed five times for Hammurabi (P3, P4, P11, P17, and P20).

[37] The text termed the Genealogy of the Hammurabi Dynasty testifies to the private cult of royal ancestors and was not written to justify a claim to the throne. See Jacob J. Finkelstein, "The Genealogy of the Hammurapi Dynasty," *JCS* 20 (1966), 95–118.

3.4. Hammurabi's Fulfillment of the Divine Command for Equity: The Naming of Statutes

The next section, composed of five units, adroitly presents the promulgation of the statutes in a concentric pattern.[38] The first unit, a narrative, depicts Hammurabi's fulfillment of the divine commission: it is a first-person narrative that acts as a bridge from the so-called prologue to epilogue. The issuance of the statutes is echoed at the other end of this section, in Unit 5, and the inside units depict the king protecting his people in a concentric pattern:

Unit 1 = V:14–25, XLVII:1–8

When the god Marduk commanded me to provide justice for the people of the land in order to keep order, I placed truth and equity in the mouth of the land.[39] I enhanced the welfare of the people. At that time:

[corpus of statutes]

These are the just decisions that Hammurabi, the able king, has established and thereby has enabled the land to follow upright practices and correct behavior.

[38] Hurowitz, *Inu Anum ṣīrum*, 27.

[39] The meaning of *kittam u mīšaram ina pī mātim aškun*, "I placed truth and equity in the mouth of the land," is not clear. Martha T. Roth construed it as, "I established truth and justice as the declaration of the land" (*Law Collections*, 81). CAD Š/I 124 s. v. šakānu mng. 2′ translated it as "I caused loyalty to be professed in (my) country." T. J. Meek rendered it as "I wrote them in the vernacular Akkadian rather than in Sumerian," suggesting that there was significance in the fact that the Laws of Hammurabi was issued in Akkadian, rather than Sumerian: that it was composed in Akkadian was a substantive change from the Sumerian law collections (ANET, 165). In this case, the Laws of Eshnunna, it may be surmised, was either unknown or considered inconsequential to the promulgation of the Laws of Hammurabi. It is also unclear just how innovative a leap it was for the language of a genre to be changed: to a significant extent in Mesopotamian literate culture, Sumerian and Akkadian were interchangeable languages. See Marc Van De Mieroop, *Philosophy before the Greeks: The Pursuit of Truth in Ancient Babylonia* (Princeton, N.J.: Princeton University Press, 2016), 12–13. But it is striking that the Laws of Hammurabi veers from other Akkadian texts in the lack of Sumerograms and in the overall use of syllabograms, making it an easier text to read for those with a weaker grasp of Akkadian, whether people in antiquity or modern students of Akkadian, who often encounter the Laws of Hammurabi for the first time in an elementary course in Akkadian for this reason.

Victor Avigdor Hurowitz translated the line "I taught the (people of the) land," and argued that the Laws of Hammurabi were promulgated both in oral form and written form and that the oral promulgation was intended to teach the masses (*Inu Anum ṣīrum*, 27 n.40, and "Spanning the Generations," 12–19). That there was a means of teaching the masses the Laws of Hammurabi orally is an attractive idea, and CAD P 465 s.v. pû A mng. 5b notes that the prepositional phrase *ina pī* may mean "orally." Hurowitz pointed to two levels of education that may be reflected in the colophon to Enuma Elish:

145 May (the fifty names of Marduk) be learned, may the teacher expound them.
146 May the wise and the knowledgeable take counsel together.
147 May the father repeat them and make the children learn.
148 May the ears of the shepherd and the herdsman be opened.

Unit 2 = XLVII:9–21

I am Hammurabi, the perfect king. I have not been neglectful nor lazy toward the black-headed people, handed over to my care by the god Enlil and whose governance the god Marduk has given me.
I have sought for them peaceful places.
I have removed difficulties.
I have spread light over them.

Unit 3 = XLVII:22–39

With the mighty weapon that the gods Zababa and Ishtar have bestowed upon me, with the wisdom that the god Ea has apportioned to me, with the capability that the god Marduk has given me, I annihilated enemies from north to south.

I put an end to strife. I improved the well-being of the people. I made the people of the inhabited world lie down in safe pastures. I did not tolerate villains.

Unit 4 = XLVII:40–58

The great gods have selected me, and I am the shepherd who brings peace and whose scepter is just.

My benevolent shade is stretched out over my city. I hold the people of the lands of the Sumerians and the Akkadians in my bosom. They have prospered under my protective spirit. I have maintained them in peace. I have protected them in my wisdom.

Unit 5 = XLVII:59–78

In order that the strong not wrong the weak,
to provide justice for the orphan girl and the widow,
I have inscribed my precious pronouncements upon my stela and set it up before my statue (called) "King of Equity"
in Babylon, the city which Anum and Enlil have elevated, in Esagila, the temple whose foundations are as fixed as heaven and earth,
in order to render decisions for the land,

Two modes of learning are described, reflecting a class divide. The educated class—teachers and their students—are depicted as learning and studying written documents—but more than just reciting or copying them, they elucidate, interpret, and analyze them. By contrast, the last two lines describe fathers teaching their children, while shepherds and herdsmen hear about the fifty names of Marduk. In this mode of education, fathers repeat to their children what they themselves learned, perhaps doing so word for word. Shepherds and herdsmen do not interpret but are recipients of oral knowledge, passed from person to person. They learn what they heard and repeat it themselves. This mode of education is conceived to be without any elucidation, interpretation, or analysis. However, more extensive evidence for the knowledge of the Laws of Hammurabi among the masses is lacking.

to give the verdicts of the land,
to provide vindication for the wronged.

In this concentric pattern, the first and last units depict Hammurabi issuing his laws. The second and fourth units portray Hammurabi as protecting his people, and the central unit pictures Hammurabi pacifying the inhabited world by force. The units on Hammurabi protecting his people represent him as diligently making life easier for them, seeking their comfort, illuminating them, protecting them with his shadow, holding them in his bosom, and so on. By contrast, Hammurabi is portrayed as providing for the people of the inhabited world initially by force, subduing enemies everywhere and ending warfare, and only thereafter by causing them to prosper and other behavior appropriate to the image of the king as shepherd of his people. A striking deviation from the standard formula in royal inscriptions about protecting the orphan and widow is the substitution of "orphan girl" in unit five: "to provide justice for the orphan girl and the widow."[40]

Many of the terms employed in the first unit reappear in the final unit: "truth and equity" (*kittam u mīšaram*) in unit one // "I set it up before my statue (called) 'King of Equity' " (*mīšarim ukīn*) in unit five, where the root of "truth" is the same as the root of the verb "to set up"; "to provide justice" (*šutēšur*) in unit one // "to provide justice" (*šutēšurim*) in unit five; "the king has established" (*šarrum . . . ukinnu*) in unit one // "I set it up before my statue (called) 'King of Justice (equity)' " (*šar mīšarim ukīn*) in unit five, using the same verb. These inclusios are employed to emphasize Hammurabi's fulfillment of the mandate of justice.[41]

The concentric pattern of this section depicts Hammurabi's fulfillment of the divine command to establish justice. It articulates the purpose of inscribing laws on the Stela and has named the statutes. It places the emphasis on Hammurabi as a military leader who brings peace, protecting his people.

[40] The god Shamash is called the father of the orphaned girl in "A Prayer to the Gods of the Night," line 12, and in the incantation Shamash 73, the terms "orphan girl" and "widow" are placed side by side as beneficiaries of the god. See Jeffrey L. Cooley, "An OB Prayer to the Gods of the Night," in *Reading Akkadian Prayers and Hymns: An Introduction* (Ancient Near Eastern Monographs; ed. Alan Lenzi; Atlanta: Society of Biblical Literature, 2011), 76; and Duane Smith, "A Ritual and Incantation-Prayer against Ghost-Induced Illness," in Lenzi, *Reading Akkadian Prayers and Hymns*, 206. For manuscript A of this text, see Wayne Horowitz, "Astral Tablets in the Hermitage, Saint Petersburg," *ZA* 90 (2000), 194–206; Wolfram von Soden, "Schwer zugängliche russische Veröffentlichungen altbabylonischer Texte—1. Ein Opfershaugebet bei Nacht," *ZA* 43 (1936), 305–308. For manuscript B, see G. Dossin, "Prières aux 'Dieux de la nuit,' (AO 6769)," *RA* 32 (1935), 179–187.

[41] Hurowitz also noted that the word "land" is repeated as well (*Inu Anum ṣīrum*, 27–28).

In the following sections, Hammurabi's fulfillment of the divine command is echoed in the voices of other human beings, by those who derive benefit from his legacy.

3.5. A Prayer on Behalf of Hammurabi

A prayer uttered by an individual is the climax of a section affirming Hammurabi's ability as king and his fulfillment of the divine mandate. This section opens with a hymn praising the king and emphasizes his wisdom by focusing on his verbal utterances and skill. An invocation calls upon Shamash, the god of justice, and moves quickly to Marduk and the temple of Esagila, located in Babylon, the center of Hammurabi's power. Then, a party to a lawsuit who feels he has been wronged is prompted to pray on behalf of Hammurabi, the centerpiece of this section.

Hymn praising the king

XLVII:79–83

I am the king proclaimed as preeminent among kings.
My words/utterances are choice.
My capability is unparalleled.

Invocation of the gods

XLVII:84–XLVIII:2

By the command of the god Shamash, the great judge of heaven and earth, may my justice prevail in my land.
By the order of the god Marduk, my lord, may my engraved image not have any defacer.
May my name always be mentioned favorably in the temple Esagila, which I love.

Prayer of the wronged man

XLVIII:3–19

May any wronged man who has a legal dispute come before my statue, "King of Equity,"
and may he read aloud my inscribed stela so that he may hear my precious pronouncements,
and may my stela explain his dispute, and may he calm his heart (and praise me by saying):

<u>XLVIII:20–38</u>

Hammurabi, the lord, who is like a father and begetter to his people, who was obedient to the command of Marduk, his lord, and fulfilled the battle wish of the god Marduk north and south. He gladdened the heart of Marduk, his lord, and he secured the eternal well-being of the people and provided just ways for the land.

<u>XLVIII:39–58</u>

May he say thus, and may he bless me with his entire heart before Marduk, my lord, and Ṣarpanitum, my lady.

May the protective spirit, the gods who enter the Esagila temple, and the very brickwork of the Esagila temple make my daily portents auspicious before the god Marduk, my lord, and Ṣarpanitum, my lady.

Strikingly, it is a wronged man who comes before Hammurabi's statue, consults the statutes, and then feels relief and is prompted to recite a prayer. Three questions arise from this tableau: (1) Is the wronged man supposed to read the Stela himself? (2) Why is a wronged man, not a vindicated man, depicted as praying on Hammurabi's behalf? and (3) What is the wronged man supposed to do with the knowledge that he is in the right? In regard to the first question, whether the wronged man has the Stela read aloud to him or reads it aloud himself, it is to be noted that the text inscribed in the Stela of the Laws of Hammurabi was spelled using syllabic signs, rather than logograms derived from Sumerian, making it easier to read, and that could serve as evidence that the text was meant to be read by those with weaker reading skills. (At the same time, the signs were archaic and oriented in a different direction than was the norm in Hammurabi's time.) Nonetheless, most translations follow the first option, including the CAD, that the stela is to be read aloud to the wronged man, but curiously CAD Š/II 165–166 s.v. šasû mng. 10b translates all the other examples as "to read something oneself."[42] One Old Babylonian text, ARM II. 132:5ff., contains the instruction from the king that the letter's addressee was the only person allowed to read it and that no one else was permitted. However, the letter itself begins with a command to a scribe to read it to the addressee![43] The assumption is that the addressee

[42] See CAD Š/II 166 s v. šasû mng. 10b. Meek translated, "and then read carefully my inscribed stela" (ANET, 178). Roth translated, "Let him have my inscribed stela read aloud to him" (*Law Collections*, 134).

[43] Charles-F. Jean, *Lettres Diverses* (ARM II; Paris: Imprimerie nationale, 1950), 218–219.

could not have even read the letter by himself. It was as if the scribe was present but considered to be like an automaton or loudspeaker. Even the gods require a scribe to read a text to them:

> In the House of Dust that I entered . . .
> there sat Erishkegal, the Queen of the Netherworld,
> Beletseri, the scribe of the underworld, knelt before her,
> she was holding the Tablet (of Destinies) and was reading it out to her. . . .[44]

The conclusion we must draw is that most likely the text was read to the oppressed man but that there was no meaningful difference between reading a text oneself and having a letter read to oneself. It must also be noted that the assumption is that reading meant pronouncing aloud, so that whether the wronged man was read to or was reading himself, it was done audibly.

It is a wronged person who has lost in a lawsuit who comes before the Stela with a troubled heart; a vindicated person would hardly be interested in doubting a favorable result. The scribe's artistry depicts a poignant tableau of an oppressed man seeking relief. But contrary to what might be expected, the reading of the Stela is not designed for him to use the law that he learns to gain the upper hand in his case and win a favorable ruling but in order to prompt him to pray on behalf of the (deceased) king.[45] The Stela served as a place to turn in prayer, thereby finding solace in a moral victory, not in a successful lawsuit. It may still be that the wronged man can use what he learned to litigate his case again,[46] but in the thought-world of the Laws of Hammurabi, what is essential is the entreaty on behalf of the king and promoting the king's name and fame.

The prayer addresses four points:

1. How Hammurabi has protected his land like a father.
2. How Hammurabi obeyed the command of Marduk and wreaked victory.

[44] Epic of Gilgamesh, VII:193, 203–205. See A. R. George, *The Babylonian Gilgamesh Epic: Introduction, Critical Edition, and Cuneiform Texts* (Oxford: Oxford University Press, 2003), 1.645.

[45] Roth, "Hammurabi's Wronged Man," *JAOS* 122 (2002), 38–45. For an analysis of whom a wronged person could actually have turned to for assistance in the Old Babylonian period, see Shirley Graetz, "To Whom Does a Wronged Man Turn for Help? The Agent in Old Babylonian Letters," Ph.D. dissertation, Ben-Gurion University of the Negev, March 2012.

[46] A party to a lawsuit may contest the result. See CT 29 42, where a dispute is litigated three times, as cited in Pamela Barmash, *Homicide in the Biblical World* (New York: Cambridge University Press, 2005), 37–39.

3. How Hammurabi gladdened Marduk's heart and brought prosperity to his people.[47]
4. How Hammurabi ensured justice.[48]

It is striking how little the prayer is about law: only a single clause is devoted to justice. It might be expected that the entreaty of a wronged man might concentrate on how a statute from the Laws of Hammurabi has vindicated him or provided him with solace. But this prayer is similar to other prayers recited on behalf of a king. Prayers on behalf of a king usually name military victory, prosperity, the length and stability of the king's reign, and a peaceful succession—and the first two are mentioned. This prayer is extremely truncated, and the brevity scarcely leaves space for the wronged man to utter anything more than a general mention that Hammurabi provided justice for the land: strikingly, the wronged man makes no mention of the relief that the Stela has conferred upon him. This prayer hardly resonates with the legal themes of the text as a whole.[49]

The tableau of the wronged man seeking relief at the Stela does make a connection between the first two sections of the epilogue and the statutes. The focus on the oppressed and downtrodden is more than a rhetorical flourish of a royal inscription. As Martha Roth observed,

> Hammurabi's focus in the epilogue on the downtrodden and powerless is mirrored in the law provisions themselves. When we ask, Who is protected by the law provision? we find that an overwhelming number of law provisions protect the downtrodden and powerless in Babylonian society who are largely dependent on the whims and good-will of the empowered: the falsely accused, the soldier away on a tour of duty, the depositor, the unwary victim of poorly trained physicians, boat builders and construction workers, the small-time renter of oxen and agricultural tools, and especially women and children whose property rights (in marriage,

[47] Points 2 and 3 may be different sides of the same coin and therefore should not be separated.

[48] An inclusio operates between the third line of the prayer and the last, an invocation of favor for Hammurabi in the Esagila temple, the major temple of his city-god and the site in which the Stela was erected and his statue as "King of Equity" stands.

> May my name always be mentioned favorably in the Esagila temple, which I love. . . .
> May the spirit (the *shedu*-spirit) and the protector (the *lamassu*-spirit), the gods who enter the Esagila temple, and the very brickwork of the Esagila temple make my daily portents auspicious before the god Marduk, my lord, and Sarpanitum, my lady.

[49] Contra Hurowitz, *Inu Anum ṣīrum*, 33.

adoption, and inheritance) are most easily usurped by the adult free males.[50]

While the scenario of the oppressed man may offer him only a moral victory and a prayer, the statutes themselves provide a countermeasure to those who may suffer a legal outrage.

In this section, the focus switches from Hammurabi's actions in accomplishing his mission to a prayer on behalf of the king. Hammurabi is no longer the actor: the gods are invoked to act on his behalf. In the next section, Hammurabi's fulfillment of the divine command serves as a model for future rulers.

3.6. Prayer about the Behavior of a Future King

Like the prayer of the wronged man, the prayer about the behavior of a future king is about preserving Hammurabi's establishment of justice. It integrates the usual plea against erasing the royal name and altering the inscription with an exhortation that the future king should preserve Hammurabi's words of justice. This second prayer then employs the same casuistic style as the statutes to express the wish that a wise king will heed what is written on the Stela and provide justice for his people. This prayer is presented in Hammurabi's voice.

XLVIII:59–74

In the future at any time, may the king who will appear in my land guard my words of justice which I have inscribed on my stela.

May he not alter the judgments of the land that I issued and the verdicts that I rendered.

May he not remove my engraved image.

XLVIII:75–85

If that man has discernment and is able to provide just ways for his land, may he heed the words which I have inscribed on my stela.

May that stela explain to him the traditional customs and rules of the land, the judgments of the land which I issued and the verdicts of the land that I rendered,

[50] Roth, "The Law Collection of King Hammurabi," 21.

XLVIII:86–94

and may he provide just ways for the blackheaded people.
May he issue their judgments,
may he render their verdicts,
may he eradicate the wicked and the evil from his land.
May he enhance the well-being of his people.

The future king is exhorted to preserve Hammurabi's legal decisions, not altering or removing them. Moreover, the king is to learn how to govern justly from the Stela and, thereby, issue fair decisions, purging injustice, and promoting prosperity and success. It is crucial to note that it is the future king who is to use the Stela as a model, not judges. It is striking that not a word in the epilogue is directed at judges.

3.7. Blessing and Curses

The Laws of Hammurabi end with an elaborate series of blessings and curses. The prayer about the behavior of the future serves as the transition to this section, which is introduced by a hymnic transition or prelude. It highlights Hammurabi's wisdom, an emphasis seen in the sections just before it, in the introduction to the prayer of the wronged man and the admonition to a future king to learn from Hammurabi's words.

XLVIII:95–XLIX:1

I am Hammurabi, king of equity,
whom Shamash has entrusted with truth.
My words are choice,
my achievements are unequaled.
Only to the unintelligent are they meaningless, but to the wise, they are praiseworthy.

The usual grant that a god bestows upon a king in a royal inscription is long life, prosperity, and victory, but here the gift that the god Shamash is depicted as granting to Hammurabi is truth, part of the oft-cited pair *kittum* and *mīsharum*, "truth and equity." Not surprisingly, Hammurabi's words and deeds are exceptional. Highlighting that the wise and the foolish will have differing reactions to them marks the transition to blessings and curses.

The typical exhortation for royal inscriptions against erasing the royal name and altering the inscription is modified here to include a warning about not discarding Hammurabi's judgments, and the customary reward of victory and a stable reign is transformed to a promise that the respectful king would be able to dispense justice during a long reign. The stereotypical grant has been subtly transformed to highlight Hammurabi's role in justice, and so too has the charge to the worthy and unworthy king.

XLIX:2–17
If that man heeds the words which I have inscribed on my stela,
and does not throw out my judgments,
does not change my words,
does not alter my engraved image,
then may the god Shamash lengthen his reign, just as he has done for me, the king of equity.
May he tend his people with justice.

This invocation employs recurrent language: it reiterates much of the prayer about the behavior of a future king, but it does so to mark a distinction—between the respectful king and the disrespectful king.

XLIX:18–52
(However), if that man does not heed the words which I have inscribed on my stela,
and he disdains my curses,
and does not fear the curses of the gods,
and overturns the judgments which I issued,
changes my words,
alters my engraved image,
erases my inscribed name and inscribes his own name—or because of those curses, has another do so—
that man, whether king, lord, governor, or any person at all,
may the great god Anum, father of the gods, who has proclaimed my reign, remove the aura of royalty from him,
smash his scepter,
and curse his destiny.

The invocation uses different wording for the respectful and disrespectful successor king: "may the king who will appear in my land guard my words of justice which I have inscribed on my stela" (*šarrum ša ina mātim ibbaššû awât mīšarim ša ina narîya ašṭuru liṣṣur*), and, "if that man who heeds the words which I have inscribed on my stela" (*šumma awīlum šû ana awâtīya ša ina narîya ašṭuru iqūl*). But then it employs nearly the same wording to develop the contrast between the rewards of preserving and heeding Hammurabi's words and the curses that would befall the king who would not:

> does not throw out my judgments // overturns the judgments which I issued,
> does not change my words // changes my words,
> does not alter my engraved image // alters my engraved image.

The repetition intensifies the antithesis between the respectful and disrespectful kings.

The curses that conclude the Laws of Hammurabi are fourteen in number, an intentional doubling of seven intensifying the potency of the curses. The supreme god Anum is mentioned first, and the god Enlil, who replaced him as head of the divine polity, is invoked twice, in the second curse and the concluding curse. The order of the gods has significance. The gods Anum and Enlil were successive heads of the pantheon, and in the Laws of Hammurabi, they were highlighted as the ones conferring kingship upon Hammurabi at the beginning of the Laws. Enlil is followed by his consort, Ninlil. The god Ea, a god whose level of power was near Enlil's and whose city, Eridu, was considered as the oldest by the Mesopotamians, follows. The trio of Anum, Enlil, and Ea rule over the three regions of the cosmos: heaven, earth, and the waters. Shamash, the sun god, and Sin, the moon god—the major astral deities—are invoked next. The gods of war follow: Adad, Zababa, Ishtar, and Nergal. The list of twelve deities end with two more named deities: the mother goddess, Nintu, and the goddess of healing, Ninkarrak. A blanket invocation of all gods follows, probably to avoid missing any divine power that could be used in a curse. The sequence concludes with a call to Enlil to enforce the sum total of the curses. The god are arranged in order of importance, not geographically as in the prologue. Strikingly, the god in whose temple the stela was erected, Marduk, is not invoked in the curses; while he is raised to be the Enlil of all people in the prologue (I:11–12), he does not yet possess cosmic oversight, a limitation that future developments in Mesopotamian religion will surmount.[51]

Curse 1 = XLIX:45–52

May the great god Anum, father of the gods, who has proclaimed my reign, remove the aura of royalty from him,
smash his scepter,
and curse his destiny.

Curse 2 = XLIX:53–80

May the god Enlil, who sets destinies, whose utterance cannot be countermanded, who magnifies my kingship,
incite turmoil that cannot be quelled and trouble that will end in his annihilation even in his own residence,
may he cast as his fate a reign of weariness, of few days, of years of famine, of darkness without illumination, and of sudden death.
May he declare with serious speech the obliteration of his city, the dispersion of his people, the overturning of his dynasty, and the blotting out of his name and his memory from the land.

Curse 3 = XLIX:81–97

May Ninlil, the great mother, whose utterance is important in the Ekur temple, the lady who makes my portents auspicious, spoil his case before the god Enlil in the place of litigation and judgment,
may she induce the god Enlil, the king, to pronounce the defilement of his land, the obliteration of his people, and the pouring out of his life force like water.

Curse 4 = XLIX:98–L:13

May the god Ea, the great prince, whose destinies take precedence, the sage among the gods, the omniscient, who lengthens my days, remove knowledge and wisdom from him,
may he lead him into confusion,
may he dam up his rivers,
may he not allow any life-sustaining grain (for his) people.

[51] See Lambert, *Babylonian Creation Myths*, 248–277; T. Oshima, "The Babylonian God Marduk," in *The Babylonian World* (ed. G. Leick; London: Routledge, 2007), 348–360. In the Laws of Hammurabi, he is given authority over human beings, but he is eventually raised to be Enlil of the gods.

Curse 5 = L:14–40

May the god Shamash, the great judge of heaven and earth, who provides just ways for all living creatures, the lord, my trust, overturn his kingship, may he not issue his judgments, may he confuse his path and cause his army to slip,
when an oracle is sought for him, may he provide an inauspicious omen portending the uprooting of the foundations of his kingdom and the obliteration of his land,
may the evil word of the god Shamash quickly overtake him,
may he uproot him from among the living above and make his shade thirst for water below in the underworld.

Curse 6 = L:41–63

May the god Sin, the lord of heaven, my creator, whose oracle prevails among the gods, take away from him the crown and throne of kingship,
impose upon him terrible punishment,
a great condemnation, which will not depart from his body,
may he conclude every day, month and year of his reign with groaning and moaning,
may he raise a rival for him for his kingship,
may he decree a life for him that is equal to death.

Curse 7 = L:64–80

May the god Adad, lord of abundance, canal inspector of heaven and earth, my helper, deprive from him rain from heaven and overflow from springs,
may he obliterate his land, with poverty and famine,
may he thunder fiercely over his city,
and may he turn his land into ruins from (the time of) the Flood.

Curse 8 = L:81–91

May Zababa, the great warrior, firstborn son of the Ekur Temple, who walks at my right side, smash his weapon in the midst of battle,
may he turn day into night,
may he make his enemy infuriated by him.

Curse 9 = L:92–LI:23

May the goddess Ishtar, lady of conflict and battle, who makes my weapon effective, my benevolent protective spirit, who loves my reign, with her angry heart and great fury curse his kingship,
may she turn his auspicious omens into disasters,
may she smash his weapons on the field of battle,
may she throw him into confusion and anarchy,

may she strike down his warriors,
may drench the earth with their blood,
may she make a heap of the corpses of his warriors upon the field,
and may she show his warriors no mercy.
As for him, may she deliver him into the hand of his enemy,
and may she lead him bound captive to the land of his enemy.

Curse 10 = LI:24–39

May the god Nergal, the mighty one among the gods, the irresistable onslaught, who enables me to achieve my victories, burn his people with his supernatural power like a raging fire in a reed bed,
may he strike him with his mighty weapon,
may he shatter his limbs like a clay figurine.

Curse 11 = LI:40–49

May the goddess Nintu, august mistress of the lands, the mother, my creator, deprive him of an heir and give him no offspring,
and may she not allow a human child to be born among his people.

Curse 12 = LI:50–69

May the goddess Ninkarrat, daughter of Anum, who promotes my favor in the Ekur temple, cause a terrible disease to break out, an evil demonic disease, an awful wound that cannot be soothed, which a physician cannot diagnose, which cannot be bandaged, cannot be stopped,
may he mourn his lost virility until his life comes to an end.

Curse 13 = LI:70–83

May the great gods of heaven and earth, all the Anunnaki deities together, the protective spirit (the shedu-spirit) of the temple, (and) the bricks themselves of the Ebarbar temple, curse that one, his seed, his land, his troops, his people, and his army with a terrible curse.

Curse 14 = LI:84–91

May the god Enlil, whose command cannot be countermanded, curse him with these curses,
and may they swiftly overtake him.

The deliberate doubling of seven intensifies the curses, and the order of the gods, from highest on down, serves to heighten them further. The final curse, returning to Enlil, the highest god active in the divine pantheon, specifies that his command cannot be countermanded, giving a final affirmation to the curses.

The entire composition concludes with an elaborate series of blessings and curses, one of the longest curse series known in Mesopotamian literature. The usual adjuration found in royal inscriptions not to erase the king's name and alter the inscription is modified to include an admonition not to discard Hammurabi's judgments, and the boilerplate reward is modified to a promise that a respectful king would be able to dispense justice during a long reign. Fourteen curses, a deliberate doubling of seven, end the composition on a powerful note.

3.8. Is the Laws of Hammurabi a Unified Composition?

An adroit chiastic pattern ties the entire composition together. Verbal echoes before and after the statutes create a sense of unity. The sentence before the statutes reads as follows:

V:14–25

inūma Marduk ana šutēšur nišī mātim ūsim šūḫuzim uwa'eranni ***kittam*** *u* ***mīšaram ina pī mātim aškun***

šīr nišī uṭīb

inūmišu

When the god Marduk commanded me to provide justice for the people of the land in order to keep order, I established truth and justice as the declaration of the land. I enhanced the welfare of the people.

This sentence is matched after the statutes by the following sentence:

XLVII:1–8

dīnāt ***mīšarim*** *ša Ḫammurapi šarrum lē'ûm ukinnu-ma* ***mātam ussam kīnam*** *u rīdam damqam* ***ušaṣbitu***

These are the just decisions that Hammurabi, the able king, has established and thereby has enabled the land to follow upright practices and correct behavior.

Words are repeated (*mīsharum*, "justice/equity"); the roots of a key word, *kittum*, are echoed (he has extablished *ukinnu*, upright *kīnam*); and a pivotal concept is echoed ("the declaration of the land" // "enabled the land to follow practices").

Other echoes between the beginning and conclusion of this long composition produce a sense of unity:

a. I:14–26 "proclaim Babylon pre-eminent," in the "prologue" // XLVII:79–83 Hammurabi proclaimed as pre-eminent in the "epilogue"
b. I:14–26 gods designated Babylon with an exalted name // I:27–49 gods designated Hammurabi to improve the welfare of the people, in the "prologue" // XLVII:40–45 gods designated me // XLIX:18–52 Anum designated my reign, in the "epilogue"
c. I:27–49; I:50–62; III:7–16; IV:32–44; IV:60–66 Hammurabi designated as pious in the "prologue" and the "epilogue"
d. I:27–49 "justice" in the "prologue" and XLVII:84–XLVIII:2 "to display justice in the land, to make justice prevail in the land" in the "epilogue"
e. verb "to display" used also in L:41–63 of Sin's oracle and in IV:60–66 of Ishtar's shrine
f. I:27–49 "to destroy evil and wickedness" in the "prologue" // XLVIII:86–94 "to eradicate evil and wickedness from the land" in the "epilogue"
g. I:27–49 "to prevent the strong from oppressing the weak" in the "prologue" // XLVII:59–78 "in order to prevent the strong from oppressing the weak" in the "epilogue"
h. I:27–49 "to improve the welfare of the people" // V:14–25 "I enhanced the welfare of the people" in the "prologue" // XLVII:32–39 "I enhanced the welfare of the people" // XLVIII:20–39 "he enhanced the welfare of the people" // XLVIII:86–94 "may he enhance the welfare of his people" in the "epilogue"

These echoes are used skillfully to provide structure and unity to a long, almost unwieldy, inscription. The verbal reflections unify the composition.

3.9. Conclusion

The Laws of Hammurabi is structured in the format of a royal inscription. It employs a rich treasury of rhetorical and structural devices to achieve its aims. It is in the form of a royal inscription, but it is not an ordinary agglomeration of hackneyed bromides repeating standard wording. It transforms the typical structure of a royal inscription with inventiveness in order to emphasize the king's role in upholding justice and to incorporate a collection of statutes. The scribe managed to enlarge the size of the composition while preserving the textual structure of a royal inscription.

It may be that the earlier law collections are themselves based on royal inscriptions. One obstacle to determining this is that the prologue of the Laws of Ur-Namma is preserved poorly and the epilogue is missing entirely. Until more complete copies are discovered, it is difficult to define more clearly how the Laws of Ur-Namma follows a royal inscription model. The fact that the Laws of Lipit-Ishtar has a similar structure to the Laws of Hammurabi may be evidence that the structure of the Laws of Hammurabi was based on the antecedent pattern of a law collection. This itself was structured on the long-established pattern of a royal inscription. The Laws of Hammurabi is also influenced by Hammurabi's own royal inscriptions.

The Laws of Hammurabi were part of an elaborate and extensive project of the exaltation of the king, presumably to extend and cement his authority. The Laws of Hammurabi and Hammurabi's royal inscriptions—both those from which elements of the Laws derive and those to which they share affinities—are part of a robust effort on the part of the royal scribes to exploit the textual patterns of royal inscriptions.[52]

The collection of statutes gives meaning to the royal inscription. The statutes affirm the contention of the royal inscription that the king's authority is justified. The statutes ground and give meaning to the royal inscription. At the same time, the royal inscription format gives authority to the statutes by affirming that they are exempla of truth and equity. By so doing, the royal inscription format makes law and justice central aspects of its cultural construct. It builds a depiction of law that is richer and more essential than mere rules. It shapes a master textual structure that frames the statutes.[53] The statutes incorporated in the Laws of Hammurabi flow from another scribal domain, one of law and legal matters, and it is to that domain that we turn in the next chapter.

[52] It is beyond the scope of this volume to provide a more in-depth analysis of the extant royal inscriptions of Hammurabi beyond those with a more direct relationship with the Laws of Hammurabi. See Rutz and Michalowski, "The Flooding of Eshnunna," 17–20; Å. W. Sjöberg, "Prayers for King Ḫammurabi of Babylon," in *Ex orbe religionum. Studia Geo Widengren* (Leiden: Brill, 1972), 58–71.

[53] For a parallel phenomenon, see Robert Cover, "Nomos and Narrative," in *Narrative, Violence, and the Law* (Ann Arbor: University of Michigan Press, 1993), 95–172; Jane Kanarek, *Biblical Narrative and the Formation of Rabbinic Law* (New York: Cambridge University Press, 2014), 174–175.

Appendix
Other Royal Inscriptions That Served as a Source for the Laws of Hammurabi

Additional royal inscriptions of Hammurabi served as sources for the prologue and epilogue of the Laws of Hammurabi beyond the three treated earlier in this chapter:[54]

1. Other royal inscriptions are likely the source for Hammurabi's genealogy:

   LH IV:64–V:5
   the pious one,
   who prays ceaselessly to the great gods,
   descendant of Sumu-la-el,
   mighty heir of Sin-muballit,
   eternal seed of royalty

This is based upon a number of royal inscriptions,[55] among which is

> Hammurabi,
> the god of his country,
> whom An has covered with royal splendor,
> whose great fate Enlil has decreed,
> who reveres, who fervently prays to the great gods,
> the scion of Sumu-la-ilum,
> the mighty heir of Sin-muballit . . . [56]

2. Epithets for Hammurabi are included in the lineage section:

   LH V:3–12
   mighty king,
   solar disk/god of the city of Babylon,
   who illuminates the lands of Sumer and Akkad,
   the king who makes the four quarters (of the world) obedient,
   favorite of the goddess Ishtar

These are paralleled in the typical list of epithets included in a number of his royal inscriptions:

> [Hammurabi, mighty king, king of Babylon,
> king of all] the Amorite land,
> [king] of the land of Sumer and Akkad,
> who makes the four quarters (of the world) be at peace[57]

The only epithet that appears to lack a parallel in the Laws of Hammurabi is the title "king of the Amorite lands."[58] The term "king" has been replaced with words that better reflect

[54] Driver and Miles, *Babylonian Laws*, 1.40–41; Ries, *Prologue und Epilogue*, 60–62; Hurowitz, *Inu Anum ṣīrum*, 92–103.
[55] See also Edmond Sollberger and Christopher Walker, "Hammu-rāpī à Mari et à Sippar," in *Miscellanea Babylonica: mélanges offerts à Maurice Birot* (ed. J.-R. Kupper and J.-M. Durand; Paris: Editions Recherche sur les civilisations, 1985), 257–264.
[56] Sollberger, "Two Old-Babylonian Royal Inscriptions," 197.
[57] RIME E4.3.6.9, 343–344.
[58] M. Stol, *Studies in Old Babylonian History* (Leiden: Brill, 1976), 84–85.

the legal aspect of the Laws of Hammurabi: "king of the city of Babylon" has become "solar disk/god of the city of Babylon," and "king of the lands of Sumer and Akkad" has become "the one who illuminates the lands of Sumer and Akkad."

3. The epilogue depicts Hammurabi as the king who pacified the land by defeating enemies and bringing peace:

   LH XLVII:15–21
   I have sought for them peaceful places.
   I have removed difficulties.
   I have spread light over them.

   LH XLVII:22–39
   With the mighty weapon that the gods Zababa and Ishtar have bestowed upon me,
   with the wisdom that the god Ea has apportioned to me,
   with the capability that the god Marduk has given me,
   I annihilated enemies from north to south,
   I put an end to strife.
   I improved the well-being of the people.
   I made the people lie down in safe pastures.
   I did not tolerate villains.

In the Akkadian version of the bilingual hymn LIH 95, Hammurabi is depicted as

> Hammurabi, the king, the mighty warrior,
> the slayer of enemies, deluge of war,
> who topples the land of foes, who extinguishes war,
> quiets turmoil,
> destroys warriors like a clay figurine,
> who opens up hard places [in the mountains . . .]

The pacification is referenced in a Sumerian hymn of self-praise, in which Hammurabi is portrayed as boasting,

> I am the king who has fulfilled the battle wish of Marduk,
> who has sent destructive might against his enemies.
> I have driven out the hostile,
> I have uprooted the wicked,
> I have made (the people) of my land lie down in bounteous pastures,
> I have not let anyone make my people afraid.[59]

The prayer uttered by the wronged man echoes the theme of military victory and peace:

LH XLVIII:20–38
"Hammurabi, the lord, who is like a father and begetter to his people, who was obedient to the command of Marduk, his lord, and fulfilled the battle wish of the god Marduk north and south. He gladdened the heart of Marduk, his lord, and he secured the eternal well-being of the people and provided just ways for the land."

It is striking that the wronged man does not praise the king's justice.

[59] Åke Sjöberg, "Ein Selbstpreis des Königs Ḫammurabi von Babylon," *ZA* 54 (1961), 52, lines 21–23.

4. The use of curses against those who would deface a monument is shared by RIME 4, E4.3.6.11:46–70: "[as for the man who gives orders to do ev]il (against it), has my [handiwork destroyed] or [erases] its inscription and writes his own name, or because of this curse incites an evil man to do so . . . may the god Meslamtea. . . . If he does this, may he break out in sighs of woe. May (the god) pronounce the time he has to live (to be) one day. May he rip out his foundation and destroy his seed.

4
Scribes and Statutes

The scribes who composed the statutes in the law collections improvised on a repertoire of standard cases, which they learned during their education. They were trained in legal terms, phrases, textual models, and concepts, and many of the copies we have of law collections were inscribed by students. After their training, many scribes were employed in legal matters, and their education and experience shaped the way they drafted statutes for the law collections. They had the freedom and prerogative to compose statutes as they thought the statutes should be. But the scribe who composed the statutes in the Laws of Hammurabi went beyond the scope of the earlier law collections. He deftly created incremental sets of statutes in order to formulate a more comprehensive treatment of a legal topic. The scribe associated cases that were independent and not connected in earlier law collections, created sets of statutes clustered around a major theme, incorporated explanations, and employed specific types of punishment across varying cases. With these innovative methods of composition, he adroitly cultivated systematization and conceptualization in the statutes in the Laws of Hammurabi.

Previous scholars have generally followed two approaches in analyzing the statutes in the Mesopotamian law collections, either focusing on studying specific types of disputes or trying to discern the principles of composition that have shaped the statutes in general. In this chapter, I also seek to advance our understanding of the principles of composition and systematization employed in the Laws of Hammurabi. I contrast the method of composition applied in the Laws of Eshnunna—maximal variations and polar variants—with the use of incremental variants in the Laws of Hammurabi. I also identify other methods of composition used in the Laws of Hammurabi that foster classification and conceptualization. In so doing, I analyze the generative dynamics of the statutes and their organizational framework. I also examine why the statutes were articulated in casuistic form and how the casuistic formulation in sets of statutes prompts casuistic reasoning, a type of thinking that stimulates further conceptualizing.

The Laws of Hammurabi. Pamela Barmash, Oxford University Press (2020). © Oxford University Press.
DOI: 10.1093/oso/9780197525401.001.0001.

4.1. The Statutes as Part of a Repertoire of Standard Cases

Two types of sources serve as evidence for the repertoire of standard cases that scribes learned. First, the law collections reflect the polished compositions of scribes, and indeed many of their exempla are found in copies inscribed by students. Second, there are also legal exercises written by, and for, scribal students. The statutes in the law collections and student exercises exhibit certain characteristics that are evidence for their being part of scribal tradition, even though they originate in varied times and places. The statutes share much material, but how they do so is instructive:

(1) There are statutes whose content and word choice are exactly or nearly exactly the same in a number of law collections:[1]

LL 10 // (parallel to) LH 59

(LL 10) If a man cuts down a tree in another man's orchard, he shall pay 20 shekels of silver.

(LH 59) If a man cuts down a tree in another man's date orchard without permission of the owner of the orchard, he shall pay 30 shekels of silver.

(2) There are statutes whose content is nearly the same but whose word choice is substantially different across the law collections:[2]

LL 24 // LH 167

(LL 24) If the second wife whom he marries bears him a child, the dowry which she brought from her paternal home shall belong only to her children. The children of the first-ranking wife and the children of the second wife shall divide the property of their father equally.

(LH 167) If a man marries a wife and she bears him children, and later that woman goes to her fate, and after her death he marries another woman and she bears him children, after which the father then goes to his fate, the children will not divide the estate according to the

[1] Another example of this phenomenon may be found in LL d,e,f // SLEx 1′–2′ // LH 209, 210, 213.
[2] Another example may be found in LL 28 // LH 148.

mothers. They shall take the dowries of their respective mothers and then equally divide the property of the paternal estate.

(3) There are statutes treating the same topic but whose content is substantially different in at least one other law collection:[3]

LL 25 // LH 170–171

(LL 25) If a man marries a wife and she bears him a child and the child lives and a slave woman also bears a child to her master, the father shall free the slave woman and her children. The children of the slave woman will not divide the estate with the children of the master.

(LH 170). If the wife of a man bore him children and his slave-woman bore him children, and during his lifetime the father said "my children" to the children that the slave-woman bore him—after he has passed on, the children of the wife and the children of the slave shall divide the property of the paternal estate equally. The primary heir of the wife shall take first choice of the inheritance.

(LH 171). But if during his lifetime the father did not say "my children" to the children that the slave-woman bore him—after he has passed on, the children of the wife and the children of the slave will not share in the property of the paternal estate. The freedom of the slave-woman and her children will be affirmed, and the children of the wife may not claim the children of the slave-woman for slavery. The wife shall take her dowry and the wedding gift [marriage settlement] that her husband gave her and registered in a document and shall live in her husband's residence. She may use it as long as she is alive but may not sell it. Her own estate is her children's only.

(4) The sequence of a set of statutes on a specific legal topic is the same in a number of law collections:[4]

LL 31–32 // LH 165–166

(LL 31) If a father during his lifetime gives his favored son a gift for which he writes a sealed document, after the father has died, the heirs

[3] Another example is LL 9 // LE 12, 13 // LH 21 // HL 93.
[4] Another example is LE 53–55 // LH 250–252.

shall divide the (remaining) paternal estate. They will not contest the share that was allotted. They will not repudiate their father's word.

(LL 32) If a father during his lifetime designates a betrothal gift for his eldest son, and (the son) marries while the father is still alive, after the father's death, the heirs [shall . . .] the estate [. . .] from the paternal estate the betrothal gift they shall [. . .] the betrothal gift.

(LH 165) If a man gave a field, orchard, or house to his heir who pleased him and wrote out a sealed document for him, when the brothers divide the estate after the father has gone to his fate, he will take the bequest his father gave him, and in addition to that bequest they will divide the property of the father's estate equally.

(LH 166) If a man provided wives for the sons he had[5] but did not provide a wife to his youngest son, when the brothers take shares after the father has gone to his fate, they will set up as a betrothal gift silver as an additional inheritance for their younger brother who does not have a wife and thereby enable him to obtain a wife for him.

(5) The order of the parallel statutes is the same in two law collections, but in another law collection, a variant is added or the cases are combined with a variant:[6]

<u>LL 35–37 // LOx 3,1,2,4 // LH 247–248</u>

(LL 35) If a man rents an ox and destroys its eye, he shall pay half its value in silver.

(LL 36) If a man rents an ox and breaks its horn, he shall pay one-quarter of its value.

(LL 37) If a man rents an ox and breaks its tail, he shall pay one-quarter of its value.

(LOx 1) If (the renter) destroys the eye of an ox, he shall pay half its value.

(LOx 2) If (the renter) cuts off the horn of an ox, he shall pay one-third of its value.

[5] Roth clarified this phrase by rendering it as "eligible sons" (*Law Collections*, 112). There is also a variant *irbû*, which can be understood as "for his sons who are grown," in contrast to "for his young son" in the following clause (Martha T. Roth, private communication).

[6] A second example is LU 18–22 // LE 42–46 // LH 196–201 // HL 7, 11–16.

> (LOx 3) If (the renter) severs the hoof tendon of the ox, he shall pay one-quarter of its value.
>
> (LOx 4) If (the renter) cuts off the tail of the ox, [he shall pay . . . of its value].
>
> (LH 247) If a man has hired an ox and puts out its eye, he shall give half its price to the owner of the ox.
>
> (LH 248) If a man has hired an ox and has broken its horn, injures its tail, or gashes (?) its shoulder, he shall give one-fifth of its price.

Throughout the law collections and scribal exercises, particular cases occur again and again, identical or near-identical word choice occurs again and again, and equivalent ordering of statutes occurs again and again. At the same time, there is substantial variation. These characteristics occur in law collections and scribal exercises varied in language and origin. They recur in statutes addressing a variety of cases. It is not simply that the statutes share word choice: if material were shared in only that way, it could be argued that it is merely because the Mesopotamian scribes were trained in the use of a distinct set of phrases and technical terms. It is not simply that the statutes address the same cases: if material were shared in only that way, it could be argued that the similarities originate in the fact that similar areas of conflict occur in societies of similar socioeconomic character in Mesopotamia. It is not simply that the statutes in the law collections and student exercises share the cases in the same order: if material were shared in only that way, it could be argued that it is merely an instance of word-for-word copying. The parallels in ordering shared by a number of law collections and student exercises but not by all indicate a common tradition. The dissimilarities in content, order, and word choice for identical or similar cases indicate that they did not draw on a memorized canonical text. Rather, I argue that they share a common tradition in which a scribe improvised on a repertoire of typical cases in composing the statutes in the law collections and had the freedom to shape them as he thought they should be.

A scribal tradition prevailed in Mesopotamia in which a scribe would demonstrate his legal talent and skills by revising, reworking, redrafting, and revamping the shared repertoire of standard cases. During his education, a scribe studied legal texts, not for the sake of learning them by rote, but for becoming familiar with legal concepts and institutions, acquiring legal terminology and textual patterns, and absorbing their worldview in order to use them in legal activities. A scribe would employ his legal knowledge when called upon to draft legal documents and administrative texts. He may have advised the parties to a legal transaction or a dispute. Therefore, when a scribe composed statutes for a law collection or student exercise, he would have utilized the repertoire of standard cases and would have had the ability to reshape them, applying his education and experience. The resulting statutes mirrored both law as it was practiced and law as it should be, according to the scribe's viewpoint.[7]

4.2. A Scribe's Ability to Improvise

How a scribe could fluidly reformulate a standard case can be seen in the example of the jilted bridegroom, which is found in four of the law collections: the Laws of Ur-Namma, the Laws of Lipit-Ishtar, the Laws of Eshnunna, and the Laws of Hammurabi.

In the Laws of Ur-Namma, the earliest law collection, the case appears as follows:

> <u>LU 15</u>
> If a son-in-law [enters] the household of his father-in-law but subsequently the father-in-law [gives his wife to his (son-in-law's) comrade], he (the father-in-law) shall [pay him (the jilted son-in-law)] twofold (the value of) the betrothal gift [which he (the son-in-law) brought (when he entered the house)].

A couple has entered into what scholars have termed an inchoate marriage. Inchoate marriage was a problematic time period when the relationship between the groom and the bride has reached a level of formality and permanence but is not yet a fully complete relationship of marriage.[8] The couple has proceeded forward in a series of acts through which their bonds have become more permanent. In the case in the Laws of Ur-Namma, the future

[7] It must be emphasized that a drafter of laws who is influenced by prior formulations is the one who has taken the proactive stance. The theory of influence, in which an earlier writer influences a later writer, needs to be turned on its head, for the later author who has drawn on, resorted to, appropriated from, adapted, referred to, taken on, engaged with, and reacted to is the one who has taken action. The later author is not a passive recipient. See Jay Clayton and Eric Rothstein, "Figures in the Corpus: Theories of Influence and Intertextuality," in *Influence and Intertextuality in Literary History* (ed. Jay Clayton and Eric Rothstein; Madison: University of Wisconsin Press, 1991), 6–7.

[8] Driver and Miles, *The Babylonian Laws*, 1.248–250, 322–324; Samuel Greengus, *Laws in the Bible and in Early Rabbinic Collections: The Legal Legacy of the Ancient Near East* (Eugene, Or.: Cascade Books, 2011), 40–42; Samuel Greengus, "Redefining 'Inchoate Marriage' in Old Babylonian Contexts," in *Riches Hidden in Secret Places: Ancient Near Eastern Studies in Memory of Thorkild Jacobsen*, (ed. Tzvi Abusch; Winona Lake, Ind.: Eisenbrauns, 2002), 123–125.

groom has joined his father-in-law's household and has given the betrothal gift. However, the bride has been married off to another man, and therefore the father-in-law must pay a penalty to the rejected groom. He must compensate the jilted groom with twice the value of his betrothal gift.

The same case appears in another Sumerian law collection, the Laws of Lipit-Ishtar, but with a twist:

> <u>LL 29</u>
> If a son-in-law enters the household of his father-in-law and performs the betrothal gift presentation, but later they evict him and give his wife to his comrade, they shall restore to him twofold (the value of the) betrothal gift which he brought, and his comrade will not marry his wife.[9]

Here, the draftsman has added, "and performs the betrothal gift presentation, but later they evict him and give his wife to his comrade, they shall restore," a different scenario than in the Laws of Ur-Namma. The prospective bridegroom suffers the same result, the loss of his intended wife, and enjoys the same remedy, receiving twice the value of the betrothal gift he gave. The guilty party is left vague, but we can safely assume that the father-in-law or others in the father-in-law's household wronged the groom. They are the ones who must pay the jilted groom, as in the previous case. The comrade who would have married the woman is punished as well: he might not even be the perpetrator of the wrong and may not have taken an active part in expelling the first groom. Nonetheless, the scribe drafting the text has introduced a penalty for him, the restriction that he may not marry the bride.

The Laws of Lipit-Ishtar addresses a case in which the groom, having taken up residence in his father-in-law's household, formally presents a betrothal gift. By contrast, the statutes in the Laws of Eshnunna and the Laws of Hammurabi address a situation in which the betrothal gift has been presented,[10] but the groom does not reside in his father-in-law's house. It is possible that this variation reflects a difference between Sumerian society and Old Babylonian society: in Sumer, the prospective groom moves to his father-in-law's home, but not in Babylonia. In the Laws of Hammurabi, the bridegroom has sent the betrothal gift by a messenger, and it may be that the groom has never been present at the bride's home.

[9] See the revised text in Daria Di Tullio, "Un articulo del codice di Lipit-Ištar," *NABU* 2004/43.

[10] While LE 25 does not explicitly state that the betrothal gift was presented, the wording that the man has come to claim his bride indicates that the betrothal was in effect.

LE 25

If a man comes to claim (his bride) at the house of his father-in-law, but his father-in-law wrongs(?)[11] him and then gives his daughter to [another], the father of the daughter shall return twofold the betrothal gift which he received.

LH 161

If a man has the ceremonial betrothal gift brought to the house of his father-in-law and gives the betrothal gift, then his comrade slanders him [with the result that] his father-in-law declares to the one entitled to the wife, "You will not marry my daughter," he shall return twofold everything that has been brought to him. Moreover, his comrade will not marry his (intended) wife.

Both the Laws of Lipit-Ishtar and the Laws of Eshnunna place the blame on the bride's family for the failed inchoate marriage: the Laws of Lipit-Ishtar leaves the motive vague and states that the bride's family has evicted the groom, while the Laws of Eshnunna puts the focus on the father-in-law without offering a reason for his treachery. The Laws of Hammurabi puts the blame on the bridegroom's comrade and envisions a scenario in which the c omrade slanders the bridegroom, provoking the father-in-law to reject the original suitor. The penalty on the comrade in the Laws of Hammurabi seems well-deserved, but less so in the Laws of Lipit-Ishtar because the statute in the Laws of Hammurabi explicitly mentions the comrade's perfidy and the Laws of Lipit-Ishtar does not. The comrade in LL 29 has obtained the wife by chance: the eviction of the prospective son-in-law is caused by the independent action of the members of the bride's family, not by a comrade's slander. It is not prompted by the negative influence of the other man. The comrade in the Laws of Lipit-Ishtar might be entirely innocent of an intentional offense. The remedy is the same in both statutes: double indemnification and the prohibition of the other man from marrying the woman involved.

With the possible exception of the differing residence of the groom during inchoate marriage in Sumerian and Old Babylonian society, the similarities

[11] The reading here is uncertain. A number of scholars have identified the verb as *kašûm* (CAD K 294 s.v. *kašû* A mng. 2; Roth, *Law Collections*, 63; von Soden, AHw, 463b). Goetze read it as a form of the verb *kalāmum*, "to take into bondage" (*The Laws of Eshnunna* [New Haven, Conn.: American Schools of Oriental Research, 1956], 77). Finkelstein suggested the verb *nakārum*, "to deny," ("The Laws of Ur-Nammu" *JCS* 22 [1969], 76). See Yaron, *The Laws of Eshnunna*, 58.

and differences in the statutes demonstrate the freedom of the scribe to modify and improvise on a standard case. The variety in expressing the circumstances of the case while positing the identical or nearly identical penalty indicates that this is a typical case by which a scribe would demonstrate his legal flair.

However, J. J. Finkelstein argued that the scribe writing on the jilted groom in the Laws of Hammurabi knew the text of the Laws of Lipit-Ishtar.[12] He suggested that the omission in LE 25 of the prohibition of the comrade's marriage is primarily due to the Laws of Eshnunna's general terseness and that the prohibition of the comrade's marriage is not necessary to the essential point of the statute. Finkelstein further argued that the irrelevant detail brought into the situation by LL 29, the woman's subsequent marriage to the comrade, became an independent *topos* in LH 161, otherwise identical to the rule in LH 160. This would suggest that the scribe of the Laws of Hammurabi actually knew the text of LL 29. However, it is debatable as to whether the omitted prohibition of the comrade's marriage in the Laws of Eshnunna is irrelevant (certainly not to the comrade!). The statute in LH 160 contains more differences than similarities to LL 29: the circumstances of the inchoate marriage and the offense against the groom are different. Only the sanction is the same. The comrade's marriage after his friend has been rejected seems reason enough for him to be punished and is insufficient to prove dependency.

The statute on the jilted groom in the Laws of Hammurabi is part of a set, LH 159–161, that illustrates a characteristic compositional maneuver of the Laws of Hammurabi, the creation of a series of statutes in which incremental variants are applied to a situation. This method of composition generates a more comprehensive treatment of a legal situation. A series of possibilities in which the official presentation of the marriage gift by the groom does not result in his marriage is presented: in LH 159, the *groom* refuses to go through with the marriage, and the marriage is obstructed; in LH 160, the *father of the bride* refuses to go through with the marriage, and the marriage is obstructed; in LH 161, an *outsider*, not the bridegroom nor the father of the bride, impedes the marriage, and the marriage is obstructed.[13] The scribe has

[12] Finkelstein, "The Laws of Ur-Nammu," 75–76.

[13] The penalty is adjusted so that the party at fault loses the amount of the betrothal gift. The groom in LH 159 loses the betrothal gift, and the father in LH 160–161 must give twice the amount of the betrothal gift received.

devised a series of statutes exploring a variable: the individuals who could obstruct a marriage.[14]

While we can imagine many more variants that could have been composed, the appropriate comparison is to other Mesopotamian law collections. The Laws of Hammurabi is far more comprehensive and systematic than its predecessors.[15] It may not contain the more complete exposition on the laws of marriage found in later non-Mesopotamian legal texts, yet it develops the laws of marriage further than any other Mesopotamian law collection. It must be acknowledged that every law collection or code, ancient or modern, cannot cover every possibility, and that the Laws of Hammurabi covers some possibilities and not others does not leave it open to criticism on that account. Without a doubt, it is far more methodical and comprehensive than its predecessors.[16] The scribe who composed the Laws of Hammurabi had the freedom to improvise on a repertoire of traditional cases, like earlier scribes, but he composed a collection of statutes far more comprehensive and elaborate than his predecessors.

4.3. Contrasting Methods of Composition

In the example of the groom whose marriage fails to come to pass, we have identified one method of composition, the technique of incremental variants, by which the scribe of the Laws of Hammurabi accomplishes greater systematization and conceptualization than his predecessors.[17] In order to probe deeper into the nature of this technique, we can contrast it with

[14] The one party that could not prevent or obstruct a marriage was the bride herself.

[15] See Martha T. Roth's analysis of the internal logic and comprehensiveness and omitted variants in the laws on bodily assault in the Laws of Hammurabi: "On Persons in the Old Babylonian Law Collections: The Case of *mār awīlim* in Bodily Injury Provisions," in *Extraction & Control: Studies in Honor of Matthew W. Stolper* (Studies in Ancient Oriental Civilization; ed. Michael Kozuh, Wouter F. M. Henkelman, Charles E. Jones, and Christopher Woods; Chicago: Oriental Institute, 2014), 219–227.

[16] Nonetheless, there are still significant lacunae in the Laws of Hammurabi: there are only two statutes on shepherds, LH 57–58, and there is little on animal husbandry, otherwise one of the bases of the Mesopotamian economy.

[17] I have deliberately chosen the term "incremental variants" in order to contrast them with the method of "maximal variants." Finkelstein identified the method as a principle of gradation (*The Ox That Gored*, 34). The method has also been called "pointillism," based on the similar phenomenon found in omen literature. See Jean-Jacques Glassner, "Pour un lexique des termes et figures analogiques en usage dan la divination mésopotamienne," *RA* 77 (1983), 3–10; Abraham Winitzer, "The Generative Paradigm in Old Babylonian Divination," and *Early Mesopotamian Divination Literature*. Raymond Westbrook argued that the Laws of Hammurabi and the Laws of Eshnunna used the same technique of maximal variants. See Westbrook, "Codex Hammurabi and the Ends of the

another technique of generating statutes, one that does not generate comprehensiveness, used in another law collection.

The scribe of the Laws of Hammurabi employed the technique of incremental variants, in which multiple statutes are grouped together, and incorporated minimal variations on a case in order to express legal principles.[18] By contrast, the scribe of the Laws of Eshnunna used a technique of juxtaposition of statutes in order to express a legal concept through maximal variation and polar variants.[19] Both law collections comprise topical groupings, but their scribes employed differing principles of arrangement. The contrast between the techniques is striking. The Laws of Hammurabi conveys legal ideas through a series of three or more laws, and the Laws of Eshnunna is focused on the counterpoint between two statutes. The scribe of the Laws of Hammurabi composed a series of statutes in which the variants change incrementally by fine modifications. The incremental variants sketch a clear statement in a continuum defined by the parameters of the permutations. By contrast, the scribe of the Laws of Eshnunna placed side-by-side paired statutes in which the variants are maximal. These polar cases articulate a clear statement of the just laws in extreme cases, but they leave a gray area in the middle where some but not all of the criteria are fulfilled. By employing maximal variants, the scribe of the Laws of Eshnunna sought to illuminate a legal principle by placing one legal case next to another. The cases are shaped as binary opposites, and the relationship between one case and the neighboring case, its binary opposite, shapes the conceptual context in which the cases ought to be understood. By contrast, the scribe of the Laws of Hammurabi

Earth," in *Law from the Tigris to the Tiber: The Writings of Raymond Westbrook* (ed. Bruce Wells and Rachel Magdalene; Winona Lake, Ind.: Eisenbrauns, 2009), 136–139.

[18] This principle of arrangement is significantly different from the principle of arrangement of other legal texts. For example, a chapter of the Mishnah appears to be intentionally arranged in such a way as to explore the gray areas in the middle, where the variations between cases are minimal. See Jacob Neusner, *Judaism: The Evidence of the Mishnah* (Chicago: University of Chicago Press, 1981), 257–261.

[19] Barry L. Eichler, "Literary Structure in the Laws of Eshnunna," in *Language, Literature, and History: Philological and Historical Studies Presented to Erica Reiner* (AOS 67; ed. Francesca Rochberg-Halton; New Haven, Conn.: American Oriental Society, 1987), 71–84; Eichler, "Exodus 21:22–25 Revisited: Methodological Considerations," in *Birkat Shalom: Studies in the Bible, Ancient Near Eastern Literature, and Postbiblical Judaism Presented to Shalom M. Paul* (Winona Lake, Ind.: Eisenbrauns, 2008), 11–29; Eichler, "Examples of Restatement in the Laws of Hammurabi," in *Mishneh Todah: Studies in Deuteronomy and Its Cultural Environment: In Honor of Jeffrey H. Tigay* (ed. Nili Sacher Fox, David A. Glatt-Gilad, and Michael J. Williams; Winona Lake, Ind.: Eisenbrauns, 2009), 365–400. See also J. J. Finkelstein, "Sex Offenses in Sumerian Law," *JAOS* 86 (1966), 368, and Kraus, "Ein zentrales Problem des altmesopotamischen Rechtes," 286.

elucidated legal principles by modifying a number of variants in a set of statutes. The scribe created a paradigm in which a factor is modified to construct the conceptual context for the set of statutes.

The statutes on the death of a spouse in the Laws of Eshnunna and the Laws of Hammurabi veer in different directions due to these distinct techniques. LE 17 addresses the situation in which a bridegroom has offered the betrothal gift but has not yet completed the marriage process. The bride or bridegroom, alas, has in the meantime passed away, and therefore the ruling is that her family must return the betrothal gift:

> LE 17
> (In the case of) a son of a free man bringing the betrothal gift to the house of his father-in-law—if either (the bride or the groom) should go to his fate, the silver shall return to its original owner (the widower or his heir).

The finances are equalized: the groom receives back what he gave, and the bride's family reverts to its financial state before the betrothal. The maximal variant, found in the next statute, LE 18, deals with a death after the marriage process has been completed:

> LE 18
> If (the groom) marries (the bride) and she enters his house and then either the bride or the groom goes to his fate, (the surviving spouse) will not take out all that he had brought but only its excess (of the betrothal gifts in relation to the dowry) shall he take.[20]

The finances are to be equalized once again: the party that put more financial resources into the marriage regains the excess. But the wrinkle is that after the marriage had taken place, the situation of a widower and a widow was vastly different.[21] The financial possibilities in a future marriage were far scantier for a woman who was no longer a virgin. This was recognized in the law of the chronological period in which the Laws of Eshnunna was written. Old Babylonian law recognized that widows and other women with disrupted marriages found themselves in a problematic financial situation, and statutes and legal records both reflected ways in which their

[20] There are a number of textual difficulties in these statutes. See Roth, *Law Collections*, 69 n.6; Yaron, *The Laws of Eshnunna*, 179–190.
[21] Yaron, *The Laws of Eshnunna*, 188–190.

plight was to be alleviated.[22] The Laws of Hammurabi provides for women whose husbands had been captured but whose household did not contain sufficient provisions to be allowed to remarry (LH 134). A widow possessed the right to remain in the residence she lived in with her late husband and to retain the marriage gift her late husband gave her (LH 171). If she had not received a marriage gift, she was to receive her dowry as well as a share equivalent to that of an heir in her late husband's estate (LH 172). Even the Laws of Eshnunna itself protects a woman whose husband is absent (LE 29–30), as well as a divorcee with children (LE 59). But this is not the case in LE 17–18. The counterpositioning of LE 17–18 due to maximal variants illustrates a legal principle, the equalization of finances after the death of a marriage partner. The principle mandating that each party return to the same financial state before the marriage leads to a grave inequality: the status of each side was not the same after the marriage. This leads to a problematic remedy, one that otherwise is rejected in Old Babylonian law and even elsewhere in the Laws of Eshnunna. The use of polar variants in the Laws of Eshnunna leads to statutes whose remedies are in stark contradiction to the law practiced in its own time period and to other statutes in the Laws of Eshnunna.

By contrast, the laws on the death of a spouse in the Laws of Hammurabi address a different issue. The set focuses on the dowry given by the bride's family:

> <u>LH 162</u>
> If a man married a wife, she bore him children, and then that woman passed away, her father will not lay claim to her dowry. Her dowry belongs to her children.
>
> <u>LH 163</u>
> If a man married a wife but she did not cause him to have children, and then that woman passed away, if his father-in-law has returned to him the betrothal gift that the man brought to his father-in-law's house, her husband will not lay claim to the dowry of that woman. Her dowry belongs to her father.

[22] Herbert Petschow, "Zur Systematik und Gesetzestechnik im Codex Hammurabis," *ZA* 57 (1965), 137; Petschow, "Zur 'Systematik' in den Gesetzen von Eschnunna," in *Symbolae iuridicae et historicae Martino David dedicatae II* (ed. J. A. Ankum, R. Feenstra, and W. F. Leemans; Leiden: Brill, 1968), 160–161; Westbrook, *Old Babylonian Marriage Law*, 86–88.

LH 164
If the father-in-law should not return to him the betrothal gift, (the widower) shall deduct the value of the betrothal gift from her dowry and return (the remainder) of her dowry to her father's house.

The varying possibilities are expressed in incremental variants. If the wife dies after having children, her children are to receive the amount she brought into the marriage as her dowry since they should be the ones to be her heirs. If she dies without having children, the betrothal gift and dowry return to those who gave them: the betrothal gift returns to her husband and the dowry to her father. If her father refuses to return the betrothal gift, the widower deducts the amount from the dowry and returns the excess to her father.[23] The consequence of the technique of incremental variants is that only the death of the wife after the marriage has been completed is addressed. The variables are then adjusted: death of the wife who bore children, death of the wife who did not bear children, and the recalcitrant father of the deceased wife. What is omitted is instructive: death during the inchoate period of the marriage is not addressed, and the death of the husband is not considered at all. The Laws of Eshnunna offers the example of death during inchoate marriage because naming that variable and adjusting it create a polar opposite, distinct from the glacial variants of the Laws of Hammurabi.[24] The technique employed in the Laws of Hammurabi results in a series of statutes on a more focused set of parameters that define the law more precisely.

Both law collections address the case of an adulterous couple but in different contexts, illustrating how the two distinct methods of composition at work in the Laws of Hammurabi and the Laws of Eshununna yield diverse statutes. In LE 28, the case of a wife who is discovered in flagrante delicto, the statute decrees her fate but omits the penalty for the man with whom she was found. By contrast, the parallel law in LH 129 (as well as the statutes in other law collections: MAL A 15 and HL 198) conveys the penalties for both guilty parties, the wife and her paramour. The scribe who wrote LE 28 has omitted the penalty for the lover because he juxtaposed it with LE 27, the case of a man who marries a woman without the consent of her parents and the proper legal formalities.

[23] The dowry is assumed to be larger than the betrothal gift, which may reflect historical reality.
[24] Why the drafter of the Laws of Hammurabi did not devise a set of statutes dealing with death during inchoate marriage as an incremental variant is anyone's guess.

LE 27

If a man marries the minor daughter of a free man without the consent of her father and her mother, and does not settle the nuptial feast and the contract with her father and her mother, even if she resides in his house for a year, she is not a wife.

LE 28

If he completes the contract and nuptial feast with her father and her mother and marries her, she is a wife. On the day she is seized in the lap of another man, she shall die. She will not live.

The focus of LE 27 is on the woman, and correspondingly the ruling of LE 28 deals with the fate of the woman and does not bother with naming the fate of the paramour. By contrast, LH 128–129 address the same situation, but a penalty for the male lover is included in addition to the penalty for the woman:

LH 128

If a man married a wife but did not establish an agreement concerning her,[25] that woman is not a wife.

LH 129

If a man's wife has been caught in flagrante delicto with another man, they shall bind them and throw them into the water; if the wife's husband allows his wife to live, then the king shall allow his servant (the other man) to live.

The penalty for the paramour is included because the adjacent laws in the set mention men who have committed offenses. The previous statute, LH 127, deals with a rumor-mongering man, and the following statute, LH 130, addresses the wife and her paramour when they are not caught in the act.

LH 127

If a man has caused a finger to be pointed in accusation against an *ugbabtu*-priestess or against a man's wife but cannot bring proof, they shall beat that man before the judges and shall shave off half his hair.

[intervening statutes LH 128–129]

[25] Scholars have disagreed on whether the agreement needed to be a written contract, as Koschaker argued (*Rechtsvergleichende Studien zur gesetzgebung Hammurapis: Königs von Babylon*, 111–113). But Samuel Greengus proved this was not the case ("The Old Babylonian Marriage Contract," *JAOS* 89 [1969], 506–514). See also Westbrook, *Old Babylonian Marriage Law*, 31.

LH 130

If a man has pinned down another man's virgin wife who was (still) residing in her father's house and has intercourse with her, and they have seized him, that man shall be killed; that woman shall be released (from culpability).

A rule is provided for the case of a man who spreads rumors, slandering the innocent priestess or wife through gossip, and the remedy is designed to stop the rumors by publicly humiliating the rumor-mongering man (LH 127).[26] The death penalty is provided for the rape of the bride in an inchoate marriage, and the bride is declared innocent (LH 130).[27] This set of statutes addresses the behavior of both men and women, and therefore the statute on adultery placed in this set in the Laws of Hammurabi includes the punishment of the paramour in addition to that of the nefarious wife. By contrast, the couplet in the Laws of Eshnunna focuses on the wife, and no punishment for the paramour is included.[28] The technique of maximal variants utilized in the Laws of Eshnunna omits situations in the middle, and it focuses so narrowly that the fate of other actors in the drama is omitted. The scribe of the Laws of Hammurabi, by using the technique of incremental variants, employs a wider vantage point.

Similarly, the situation of the absent husband receives distinct treatments in the Laws of Eshnunna and the Laws of Hammurabi. LE 29 and 30 are placed in the context of a series of laws about personal status and the legal rights that one individual has to another. They address the issue of an absent husband, involuntarily and voluntarily. The absent husband willfully loses

[26] LH 126 and 127 act as a bridge between two distinct sets of statutes because both address unsubstantiated claims: LH 126 deals with a false claim about deposited property, while LH 127 addresses a false claim about a woman's fidelity to her husband. See Eichler, "Exodus 21:22–25 Revisited," 14.

[27] The two techniques dictate a different placement for the statute on the rape of a betrothed woman, even though adjacent statutes deal with similar situations. In the Laws of Eshnunna, LE 25–26 form a couplet in which innocent parties in an inchoate marriage are harmed, and LE 27 and 28 are shaped into a couplet on breached marriage:

LE 25 betrothed man jilted
LE 26 *betrothed woman raped*
LE 27 marriage without legal formalities
LE 28 **married woman caught in flagrante delicto with another man**
But the order of the topics in the Laws of Hammurabi is transposed:
LH 128 marriage without legal formalities
LH 129 **married woman caught in flagrante delicto with another man**
LH 130 *betrothed woman raped*

The law on the betrothed woman raped is placed after the other two cases in the Laws of Hammurabi because it serves as a link to a set of cases in LH 131–132 on suspicion that a married woman has a lover.

[28] This is also the case for LE 26: the fate of the innocent betrothed woman is omitted.

his rights to his wife, but if he were missing due to circumstances beyond his control, the woman is to return to him as his wife, even if she married another man.

> LE 29
>
> If a man should be captured or kidnapped during a military expedition or while on patrol, even if he resides in a foreign land for a long time, and another has married his wife and she has borne a child, whenever he returns, he shall take back his wife.
>
> LE 30
>
> If a man repudiates his city and his lord and flees, and another marries his wife, whenever he returns, he will have no right to his wife.

These cases are maximal variants, and the distance between them leaves issues unresolved: the example of involuntary absence specifies that he left on military orders, but what if he left in order to attend to business matters?[29] Even her circumstances are expressed in maximal variants: either she remains a wife to her new husband or returns to her old husband, but what if she had a child by her new husband? The Laws of Eshnunna is silent because the binary opposition does not allow for a case in the middle, but the technique of incremental variants in the Laws of Hammurabi provides an answer. LH 135 specifies that while the wife returns to her absent husband, the child is the heir to his own father. It is part of a set of statutes on absent husbands, LH 133a–136, as expressed in incremental variants:

133a	absent husband; *wife has sufficient provisions*
133b	absent husband; wife has sufficient provisions *but is intimate with another*
134	absent husband; *wife does not have sufficient provisions*; may she remarry?
135	absent husband; wife does not have sufficient provisions; she remarries, *but husband returns*; what happens to wife?
136	absent husband; wife does not have sufficient provisions; she remarries and *bears a child to new husband*, but husband returns; what happens to child?

[29] Yaron, *The Laws of Eshnunna*, 133–134.

The scribe of the Laws of Hammurabi has sought to sketch all variants rather than offering a pair of maximal variants. He shaped the cases to address the decisive variables as he envisioned them to be and has created a paradigm in which the variables are modified.

Even when the Laws of Eshnunna moves beyond a pair of statutes in a rare shift to a triplet, ostensibly operating in a mode more like that of the Laws of Hammurabi, the method of polar opposites implemented by the Laws of Eshnunna still results in lacunae. LE 22–24 address the issue of distraint, a case in which a loan was due to be repaid but the debtor failed to pay it back: the creditor has seized a person from the debtor's household in order to force payment.

> <u>LE 22</u>
> If a man had no claim against a free man yet distrained the man's slave woman, the owner of the slave woman will swear by a god, "You have no claim upon me," he shall weigh out as much silver as the value (?) of the slave woman.
>
> <u>LE 23</u>
> If a man had no claim against a free man yet distrained the man's slave woman, detained the distrainee in his house and caused (her) to die, he shall replace 2 slave women to the owner of the slave.
>
> <u>LE 24</u>
> If he had no claim against him yet distrained the wife of a commoner / palace dependent or the son of a commoner / palace dependent, detained the distrainee in his house and caused him/her to die, it is a case of life; the distrainer who distrained shall die.

LE 22 deals with illegal distraint in which the distrainee was not harmed. By contrast, the second and third statutes, LE 23–24, address illegal distraint in which the creditor has caused the death of the distrainee. LE 23 treats the seizure of a slave belonging to a member of the free class, while LE 24 treats the seizure of a member of the commoner / palace dependent class. But what is omitted are statutes dealing with cases that are not polar opposites: (1) illegal distraint in which the creditor has caused the death of the wife or son of a free person; (2) illegal distraint in which the creditor has severely injured but not killed the distrainee, whether free, commoner / palace dependent, or slave; or (3) the creditor has seized the person of the creditor of any class, rather than his slave, his wife, or his son. These lacunae, prompted by polar variants, make it impossible to extrapolate the legal principles that should be applied in these middle cases.[30]

For the scribe of the Laws of Hammurabi, employing incremental variants was the means by which to present the full gamut of statutes on a demarcated area of law. The set of slave laws in LH 15–19 are far from exhaustive when viewed from the perspective of the totality of possibilities of the circumstances of escaped slaves. However, the set deals exhaustively with a few possibilities. Two cases about a slave belonging to the palace or a commoner / palace dependent are addressed:

> LH 15
> If a man should enable a slave or slave woman belonging to the palace or a commoner / palace dependent to leave through the gate,[31] he shall be killed.
>
> LH 16
> If a man should harbor a fugitive slave or slave woman of either the palace or a commoner / palace dependent in his house and not bring him out at the herald's proclamation, that master of the house shall be killed.

A man, perhaps pretending to be the owner, guides the slave through the city gate or hides the slave in his home. The focus shifts to a slave found outside a city, in open country:

> LH 17
> If a man seized a fugitive male or female slave in the hinterland and has conducted him back to his owner, the slave owner shall give him 2 shekels of silver.[32]
>
> LH 18
> If a slave should refuse to identify his owner,[33] he shall lead him to the palace; his circumstances shall be investigated, and they will return him to his owner.

[30] By contrast, LH 115–116 address legal distraint in which the distrainee from the debtor's house dies a natural death or an unnatural death, and if the latter were the case, the scribe indicates the differing penalties for the death of a son or the death of a slave.

[31] This refers to the city gate. See CAD A 86 s.v. *abullam šūdû* "to confine to the city." There are far fewer references in the lexicon to the entrance gate of a building, and they are mostly from the neo-Assyrian period.

[32] The payment is comparable to other expenses incurred by a slave owner. In LH 217 and 223, a slave's healing at the hands of a physician incurs a fee of two shekels.

[33] Slaves who were habitual runaways were inscribed with a tattoo. See Erica Reiner, "Runaway—Seize Him," in *Assyria and Beyond: Studies Presented to Mogen Trolle Larsen* (ed. J. G. Dercksen; Leiden: Nederlands Instituut voor het nabije Oosten, 2004), 475–482.

LH 19
If he has detained that slave in his own house and afterwards the slave is discovered in his possession, that man shall be killed.

LH 20
If the slave has escaped the custody of the one who has seized him, that man shall swear an oath by the god to the owner of the slave and he shall be released (from liability).

A slave belonging to an individual[34] is found in the hinterland and is returned to the city. Incremental variants are dealt with: the slave is returned to his master; the slave refuses to identify his master; the slave escapes again. The scribe has produced the decisive minimal variants in order to convey what he deemed the totality of the law of escaped slaves.

By means of the technique of incremental variants, the scribe of the Laws of Hammurabi assembled multiple statutes together in order to express legal principles. He did not express them through formal, abstract articulation. He treated a case standard to the repertoire of scribal learning more comprehensively in a set of statutes, rather than in a single example or in a pair of polar opposites. By employing incremental variants and creating a paradigm, he highlighted the decisive elements in a dispute and, in so doing, presented a clearly delineated exposition of the law. He encapsulated legal principles in concrete situations. By contrast, the technique of maximum variation and polar opposites employed in the Laws of Eshnunna served to obscure the law by leaving gaps.

4.4. Casuistic Formulation and Casuistic Reasoning

The statutes in the Laws of Hammurabi do not expressly articulate legal principles in abstract form, yet their linguistic form and the method of composition work together to convey legal concepts. This may seem counterintuitive. The sets of incremental variants in the Laws of Hammurabi are articulated in casuistic formulation, as case law, with the details of a situation conveyed. They address mundane matters, such as irrigation, slaves, and betrothal, and they do not articulate abstract principles or broad concepts. They do

[34] It is not clear whether a slave belonging to a commoner / palace dependent falls into this category. This may be a sign of compositional weakness.

not contain explicit legal conceptualization. They do not name or define legal concepts, such as intention or negligence. The statutes in the Laws of Hammurabi address specific cases and deal with realia—mundane physical actions and objects. Nonetheless, casuistically expressed statutes in sets of incremental variants do demonstrate legal principles, even if legal principles are not articulated in direct, abstract form.

While the absence of articulated legal principles in the Laws of Hammurabi may be seen as negative, and perhaps even a sign of primitiveness in legal development, their usefulness in law is limited. Leib Moscovitz observed,

> Principles are so broad and vague, and consequentially incapable of precise, mechanical application, that they are essentially meaningless until the relevant interpretive gaps are filled in through the discretionary interpretation and hence casuistic application of these notions. Indeed, this is presumably why such rulings were formulated casuistically: mention of the broad principles which apparently underlie these rulings would be of no practical use to the jurist.[35]

Concepts may be expressed too vaguely to be applicable, and hard and fast principles may not take into account the variety of factors affecting a case. By contrast, casuistic formulation supplies the factors that need to be taken into account in adjudicating a case. The use of casuistic formulation in the Laws of Hammurabi is an asset, not an obstacle, to legal reasoning.

A number of scholars have surmised that casuistic formulation derives from the initial origin of law in individual cases: a dispute arose, a verdict was rendered, and the decision was remembered in casuistic form.[36] A casuistically formulated statute is a narrative in miniature in its protasis, accompanied by its consequences in its apodosis.[37] The decision enshrined in the casuistic statute may have been made on an ad hoc basis, but it may also have been an expression of a new legal principle. Alternatively, it may have also been an extrapolation from a similar case or the implementation of an already established legal principle.

[35] Leib Moscovitz, *Talmudic Reasoning: From Casuistics to Conceptualization* (Texte und Studien zum antiken Judentum; Tübingen: Mohr Siebeck, 2002), 48.

[36] E.g., Boaz Cohen, *Jewish and Roman Law: A Comparative Study* (New York: Jewish Theological Seminary of America, 1966), 2:481.

[37] For an investigation of casuistic law as narratives, see Assnat Bartor, *Reading Law as Narrative: A Study of the Casuistic Laws of the Pentateuch* (Ancient Israel and Its Literature 5; Atlanta: Society of Biblical Literature, 2010).

In the Laws of Hammurabi, the casuistic statutes are not articulated as records of a prior decision, even though the epilogue names them as Hammurabi's judicial decisions (XLVII:1). They are not presented as registers of historical events—that is, as "King Hammurabi ruled on date A that the incident B perpetrated by person C on date D was met with punishment E." They are presented as generalized rulings about situations that recur. The way the statutes are formulated invites inferring legal principles.

Some scholars have argued that the propensity for casuistic law is linked to what can be derived from history: in general, conceptual thought is a later development.[38] Only when a legal system has evolved to a higher level of intellectual sophistication does it articulate and employ legal concepts. However, Roman law, arguably the most highly developed legal system in antiquity, is highly casuistic, and Justinian's *Digest* issued a warning, quoting Lucius Javolenus Priscus: "Every definition in civil law is dangerous, for rare is the one that cannot be overthrown."[39] Reasoning by principles may be inflexible, and case law may have the pliability to respond better to the social and moral dimensions of a situation.[40] It is more effective to examine the features of a legal domain—for example, sale and debt—in concrete examples than to propose a definition.[41]

The casuistic form is used in many other ancient legal systems, and its regular and widespread use may mean that it has cognitive appeal. The near-universality of the form may reflect its psychological fit rather than being created in a court case.[42] It cannot be assumed that it necessarily derives from adjudication.

[38] Moscovitz, *Talmudic Reasoning*, 93.

[39] Digest, 50.17.202. See Moscovitz, *Talmudic Reasoning*, 102; Alan Watson, *The Spirit of Roman Law* (Athens: University of Georgia Press, 1995), 146–157.

[40] This assumes that the scribes were motivated by functionalist goals or had an alternative to casuistic formulation. See Moscovitz, *Talmudic Reasoning*, 92; Cass R. Sunstein, *Legal Reasoning and Political Conflict* (New York: Oxford University Press, 1996), 121–128.

[41] Watson, *Spirit of Roman Law*, 146. Watson remarked that it is remarkable that Roman law failed to systematize: there were repeated failures to arrange legal rules and procedures in a systematic manner. The praetorian Edict exhibited an organization based on linguistic attraction, where the actio Serviana is placed next in the section dealing with the interdictum Salvianum (Watson, *Spirit of Roman Law*, 121). There was no prestige in systematizing, most likely because it had not been sought in the past and therefore it lacked prestige (Watson, *Spirit of Roman Law*, 146). Gaius's *Institutes*, an attempt at systematization, was unique in Roman law: Gaius attempted to set out the law in a methodical way, but his attempt was ignored by other jurists (Watson, *Spirit of Roman Law*, 201–203). Only one Roman jurist, Pomponius, ever referred to him. His book, however, became an esteemed teaching tool, and more fragments of his work survive than any other classical law book. It was a major factor in the influence of Roman law upon Western law.

[42] Bernard S. Jackson, "Historical Aspects of Legal Drafting in the Light of Modern Theories of Cognitive Development," *International Journal of Law and Psychiatry* 3 (1980), 354–355, 359–361; Jackson, *Law, Fact, and Narrative Coherence* (Liverpool: Deborah Charles Publications, 1988), 98–99.

At the same time that law in casuistic form makes sense in general, two characteristics specific to Mesopotamian thinking flowed together in composing the statutes of the Laws of Hammurabi: the disposition to organize knowledge into lists, and the propensity to articulate knowledge in casuistic form.[43] The list was *the* method of scholarly presentation, and the compilation and transmission of such lists was a leading activity of Mesopotamian education and scholarship. Lists were used as part of the basic curriculum of scribal education, and their purpose was to lay out an orderly and systematic rendering of the world.

The Mesopotamian lists do not offer any explicit articulation of their goal, but a late Egyptian list provides an explanation. Mogen Trolle Larsen observed,

> When writing first appeared . . . at the end of the fourth millennium, it was used for two purposes: bureaucracy and lists. It is easy to understand these lists of signs as designed to facilitate the training of scribes, so that they form elements in the wider literate system of bureaucratisation which needed uniformity and standardisation. There is no doubt that the lists did function within the scribal world as part of the basic curriculum, but it is likewise possible to understand the lists as serving another purpose, to present a systematic and ordered picture of the world. It is this aspect, the placc of the lexical tradition in the cognitive scheme of the ancient Mesopotamians, which concerns us here. It is interesting to note that lists of signs are not necessary for the scribal training within systems of logographic or mixed logographic and syllabic scripts; such lists are known from Egypt, to be sure, but they appear quite late—perhaps under influence from Mesopotamia—and the most famous such text states in the introduction that it had clearly defined philosophical aims:
>
>> Beginning of the teaching for clearing the mind, for instruction of the ignorant and for learning all things that exist.[44]

[43] Benno Landsberger was the first to suggest that the Mesopotamian law collections were part of a scholastic tradition ("Die babylonischen Termini für Gesetz und Recht," in *Symbolae Paulo Koschaker dedicatae* [SDIOAP; ed. J. Friedrich, J. G. Lautner, and J. Miles; Leiden: Brill, 1939], 219–234. See also Kraus, "Ein zentrales Problem des altmesopotamischen Rechtes," 283–296.

[44] Mogens Trolle Larsen, "The Babylonian Lukewarm Mind: Reflections on Science, Divination, and Literacy," in *Language, Literature, and History: Philological and Historical Studies Presented to Erica Reiner* (ed. Francesca Rochberg-Halton; New Haven, Conn.: American Oriental Society, 1987), 208–209.

The lists had a philosophic goal, placing phenomena into an order. The early Mesopotamian lists may seem opaque: they are catalogs of nouns arranged in columns placed side by side. The scribes played with the various possibilities for words and created lists.[45] But the lists are arranged by category and types of object. These ordering principles are never articulated, but the agglomerations of nouns display an implicit categorization. As these texts were recopied over the millennia, they were augmented and expanded. The logic enshrined within was not a logic that operated by subordination, abstraction, and analysis, but a logic that operated by addition and accumulation.

The lexical lists, the elementary form of the lists, were not only a method for learning the cuneiform script but also served to inculcate a way of seeing the world and understanding the written word. The lists shaped the mentality of Mesopotamian scribes. It must be emphasized that lexical lists appear very rarely in other systems of scribal education, yet they are one of the most characteristic features of Mesopotamian culture and learning.[46] Mesopotamian scribes composed them and employed them extensively.

The propensity toward lexical lists prompted Mesopotamian scribes to organize other forms of knowledge in lists, and these lists were articulated in casuistic formulation. Knowledge about omens, for example, were conveyed in lists of phenomena formulated casuistically in conditional sentences, and this method of composition and reasoning shaped the statutes in the law collections.[47]

The casuistic formulation of the statutes in the Laws of Hammurabi originates in the tendency of Mesopotamian scribes to articulate knowledge in lists of casuistically formulated statements. They conveyed law in the form of detailed cases, not as general principles. The method of incremental variants employed in the Laws of Hammurabi to generate lists prompts casuistic reasoning, where concepts are made by reasoning from analogy, from case to case.[48] Casuistic formulation expresses the specific, and casuistic reasoning

[45] Van De Mieroop, *Philosophy before the Greeks*, 73–74.

[46] Steinkeller, *History, Texts, and Art in Early Babylonia*, 51.

[47] Because a Mesopotamian catalog refers to a tablet beginning "if," the word that begins the conditional sentences in both omens and statutes, it is possible that both genres were known collectively as "if" (*šumma*) texts. See Ulla Koch, *Mesopotamian Divination Texts: Conversing with the Gods, Sources from the First Millennium* BCE (GMTR 7; Münster: Ugarit Verlag, 2015), 5; and Aaron Shaffer, "A New Look at Some Old Catalogues," in *Wisdom, Gods, and Literature: Studies in Assyriology in Honor of W. G. Lambert* (ed. A. R. George and I. L. Finkel; Winona Lake, Ind.: Eisenbrauns, 2000), 433.

[48] Casuistic formulation and casuistic reasoning are to be distinguished from the casuistic conception of law, in which legal decisions are rendered based on ad hoc considerations specific to the circumstances of a particular dispute. See Edward H. Levi, *An Introduction to Legal Reasoning* (Chicago: University of Chicago Press, 1949), 1–2; Moscovitz, *Talmudic Reasoning*, 1; Sunstein, *Legal*

moves from the specific elements in one example to those in another example. From which details in a case should an analogy be drawn? Casuistic reasoning works through this question and analyzes the extent to which a specific ruling should be extended to a similar case. It identifies which elements in a specific ruling are the pertinent ones that should be applied in another case. The statutes in the Laws of Hammurabi use casuistic formulation and thereby have the capacity to stimulate casuistic reasoning.

The technique of incremental variants employed by the scribe in the Laws of Hammurabi generates a set of casuistically formulated statutes that prompt casuistic reasoning. An isolated casuistic ruling may leave its pertinent point obscure: its specificity may make it too narrow. The aspects of the phenomena associated in a case that proved decisive are left obscure, and determining the legal basis of an isolated ruling is therefore problematic. However, a series of casuistic rulings overcomes the problems generated by the specificity of case law.[49] A series carefully formulated by a scribe highlights the relevant variables. It brings to light the conceptual underpinnings. Through a set of statutes, how far the ruling should be extended is delineated through the variables and, therefore, which other cases should be related by analogy to the casuistic ruling. A set highlights the similar characteristics that need to be identified in another situation for them to be connected. We can then infer a ruling or legal principle because it appears self-evident. Even when a derived principle may seem to be too broad and therefore difficult to apply, the casuistic formulation makes its scope more clear and its application more logical.

A series of casuistic rulings clarifies that the specific examples used is a particular instance of a general case because of the implicit conceptualization and reasoning embodied in a series. The shape of a series can define the boundaries of the actions or objects addressed in a statute. Its contours prompt the inferences that should be drawn from a ruling, and what a series delineates influences how inferences should be applied to other cases. The scope of a series can place boundaries around and define the legal concepts that are to be derived from a ruling or set of rulings. Casuistic formulation articulates the conceptualization implied by the specifics given and the

Reasoning and Political Conflict, 32. The term "casuistics" has also been used to denote a methodological approach to ethics as well as being used as a term of opprobrium.

[49] Moscovitz, *Talmudic Reasoning*, 2–3.

remedy offered. Casuistic reasoning from case to case and focusing on the key similarities and differences allow a rule to emerge.[50]

Detecting implicit conceptualization requires three stages: (1) close reading of a particular statute to determine which legally significant details it presents; (2) comparing statutes in a series, identifying the elements that serve as variables between them; and (3) inducing the common principle.[51] One characteristic of the Laws of Hammurabi, its sparse formulation, aids in determining the legally significant elements of a case and isolating the variable(s) in a set of statutes. The lack of excess verbiage is an advantage: the statutes mention only a few details. The relevant factors and principles underlying them are more readily discernible. The wording and selection of terminology of the Laws of Hammurabi have been done with great skill: the statutes are concise and straightforward. Each clause has significance and adds meaning, and there is little or no excess verbiage. Reading a statute in the Laws of Hammurabi closely and determining which legally significant details it presents is easily accomplished. Making a comparison among statutes in a set aids in identifying the elements that serve as variables between them.

Inferring the implicit concept, the final step, utilizes the variable and commonality in a set of statutes. It affirms the existence of a common principle and identifies its content. Isolating the pertinent variables in a case and identifying conceptualization is aided by a second characteristic of the Laws of Hammurabi: the grouping of the statutes in a series whose demarcation is generally clear. The side-by-side placement of casuistically formulated statutes prompts their association, justifying the linkage. The grouping of statutes aids in identifying a discrete set of statutes that organically link together to embody an implicit concept.

A number of methodological caveats must be kept in mind when deriving a legal principle from the Laws of Hammurabi:

(1) It may be that a legal principle was not applied uniformly across the entire corpus of the statutes of the Laws of Hammurabi. A legal principle may be limited to a single set of statutes and a single domain of law (i.e. just to the laws of theft) and not across legal domains, and the method by which a concept was applied may not have been uniform in that single set or domain of law. A legal principle may have ramifications

[50] Levi, *An Introduction to Legal Reasoning*, 3–8.

[51] This is comparable to the process of legal reasoning articulated by Levi, *An Introduction to Legal Reasoning*, 1–2.

across legal domains and may even operate across a gamut of otherwise unconnected statutes.

(2) The implicit conceptual basis of some sets of statutes is transparent. However, the legal principles demonstrated in a set of statutes may be obscure. They may be isolated only with difficulty, and the generalization may be relative or subjective at times.

(3) A set of statutes may actualize a number of legal principles; others may illustrate fewer.

(4) One may ask whether it is even possible to determine the conceptual basis (or in legal terminology, the ratio decidendi) because any number of rationales underlying a ruling may be extrapolated.

5) It must be acknowledged that, for us, figuring out the implicit conceptualization of a series of ancient casuistic statutes is fraught with pitfalls. Other plausible explanations may exist based on realia of which modern scholars are not aware. What we may devise as logically plausible may be far from what the ancient authors intended.

Inferring a principle does bring an amount of uncertainty into the process.[52] Identifying an implicit legal axiom can be done only with a certain amount of confidence, not complete confidence. Certainty is a matter of degree. Any derived principle must be tested against other explanations. Reconstructing the implicit rules and principles must be done with modesty and awareness of the methodological problems. A reconstruction must be tentative.

The use of casuistic formulation seems to be characteristic of ancient law in general, not only in the Laws of Hammurabi and other Mesopotamian law collections. The formulation of law in general principles and apodictic rules is exceedingly rare. Added to this general tendency to express law in casuistic terms was an intellectual characteristic of Mesopotamian culture: the tendency to express knowledge in casuistic form in lists. Therefore, what was prestigious to the Mesopotamians was developing to the nth degree what earlier scribes had done—formulating new casuistic statutes on a repertoire of traditional cases. Scribes did not start with legal principles and then create casuistic statutes. They started with standard cases that were part of a scribe's repertoire and used them to convey a rule or principle, as a demonstration of a scribe's flair in legal reasoning and decision-making. But the scribe drafting

[52] Moscovitz, *Talmudic Reasoning*, 75–84.

the statutes in the Laws of Hammurabi advanced beyond the earlier law collections. Statutes were traditionally articulated in casuistic formulation in Mesopotamian law collections, but the scribe of the Laws of Hammurabi employed the technique of incremental variants to create sets of statutes. The variants within those sets prompt casuistic reasoning and stimulate and amplify the intuitive detection of legal principles.

The distinction between law as a set of rules and as a system of rules is a helpful way to understand the Laws of Hammurabi. We can see an attempt at making systematic sets of rules in the use of incremental variants so that eventually they will cohere and constitute a system of rules. While these cases derive from the tendency toward lists, this is not the outcome of a scholastic tradition entirely divorced from the realities of a legal system. Scribes were educated both in the scholastic tradition of lists and in legal terminology, model contracts, and exercises that enabled them to be employed in legal matters. To posit a strict dichotomy between those with scholastic knowledge and those involved in the legal system is false. Moreover, an essential point is that the Laws of Hammurabi exhibits legal thinking even though it stems from a society that did not have philosophical or jurisprudential writing about law. The tendency toward systematization and conceptualization embodies reasoning about law, even if developed arguments are absent.

4.5. Other Methods of Conceptualization and Systematization

The scribe of the Laws of Hammurabi employed the technique of incremental variants to convey legal principles concretely in a paradigmatic set of statutes. Other methods of composition the scribe used in drafting the Laws of Hammurabi manifest conceptualization and systematization. Cases that share an implicit connection in the mind of the scribe are classed together. Diverse situations are integrated and in the process are themselves reshaped and transformed. Sets of statutes were clustered around a major theme of law, such as land tenure or commercial transactions. Rarely, the scribe added an explanation as to clarify a remedy or to provide a rationale for a punishment. The scribe also employed certain types of punishment as a means of systematization. By means of these techniques, the scribe advanced toward conceptualizing and creating a more encompassing compilation.

4.5.1. Linking Cases by Theme

One trajectory of conceptualization, the linking of cases heretofore independent, is employed in the opening set of statutes in the Laws of Hammurabi. Mesopotamian law collections generally open with a provision on homicide, and what is striking is that all but one of the cuneiform law collections for which the beginning of the statute section is preserved start with a statute on some aspect of homicide:[53]

LU 1

If a man commits a homicide, they shall kill that man.

HL 1

[If] anyone kills [a man] or a woman in a [quarr]el, he shall [bring him] (for burial) and give 4 persons (lit. heads), male or female respectively, and he shall look [to his house for it].

LH 1

If a man accuses another man and charges him with homicide but then cannot bring proof against him, his accuser shall be killed.

A homicide statute is placed at the beginning of the Laws of Ur-Namma, the Laws of Hammurabi, and the Hittite Laws, but not the Laws of Eshnunna.[54] Each of these is different: LU 1 is a more general rule than the others, HL 1 addresses a specific type of homicide, and LH 1 deals with an accusation of homicide.

The scribe drafting the Laws of Hammurabi has transformed that tradition of starting with homicide by coupling it with cases of false accusation and unproven testimony. He adopted the tradition but modified the case to one of false accusation. The scribe created a series of laws addressing falsehoods in the legal process, starting with sham accusations and concluding with judicial malfeasance:

[53] Roth, *Law Collection*, 72.

[54] In the Laws of Lipit-Ishtar, regrettably, there is a sizable gap between the preamble and statute section. The beginning of the statute section of the Laws of Lipit-Ishtar is missing, and therefore we cannot know whether the Laws of Lipit-Ishtar inaugurated its set of statutes with one on homicide.

No regulation on homicide appears at the beginning of the Middle Assyrian Laws. However, it is not part of the same tradition as the other law collections. It is not a unified composition in the form of a royal inscription with the incorporation of statutes but appears to be more of a private collection made for the use of a legal professional. See the discussion in chapter 2.

LH 1

If a man accused another man and charged him with homicide but then cannot bring proof against him, his accuser shall be killed.

LH 2

If a man accused another man of witchcraft but cannot bring proof, the one against whom witchcraft is charged will go down to the River and will dive in the water. If the River has overcome him, his accuser will carry away his estate. If the River has cleared that man and he has survived, the one who accused him of witchcraft shall be killed; the one who dove into the River will carry away the estate of his accuser.

LH 3

If a man came forward in a legal case to (present) false testimony and has not proved the word(s) he spoke,[55] if that case is a capital case, that man shall be killed.

LH 4

If he came forward for testimony about grain or silver, he shall continue to bear the penalty of that case.[56]

[55] What is entailed by failing to prove his word is unclear. There are a number of possibilities: the witness came forward but could not provide valid or pertinent testimony, the witness could not provide any testimony, the witness could not supply other witnesses to confirm his testimony, or the witness was dishonest and provided false testimony.

[56] The reading with an iterative verb, *ittanašši*, is found on the Stela and all but one of the other manuscripts: it envisions the situation through the perspective of the judiciary. In a case involving property, an individual who could not confirm his testimony cannot later bring proof, whether witnesses or a written record to prove his deposition or agree to take an oath after his initial refusal to take one. He failed to offer verification at the appropriate time, and therefore he always remained liable. Even though his claim might be true, he missed his chance to confirm it and therefore the dismissal of his claim stood. He was permanently deemed as someone who could not produce witnesses. See I. Tzvi Abusch, "'He Should Continue to Bear the Penalty of that Case': Some Observations on *Codex Ḫammurabi* 3-4 and 13," in *From Ancient Israel to Modern Judaism: Intellect in Quest of Understanding—Essays in Honor of Marvin Fox* (ed. Jacob Neusner; Ernest S. Frerichs; Nahum M. Sarna; Atlanta: Scholars, 1989), 81.

The variant in manuscript r reads *šum-ma a-na ši-bu-ut še-e ù KUG.BABBAR ú-ṣí-am ru-gu-um-ma-ne-é [di-nim šu-a-]ti i-ip-pa-al*, "If he came forward in a case involving grain or silver (but then cannot substantiate the statement that he made), he shall pay the claims in this case" (Manuscript r = J. J. Finkelstein, "A Late Old Babylonian Copy of the Laws of Hammurapi," *JCS* 21 [1967], 39–48). This reading, with a different verb and tense, changes the viewpoint of the statute—the perspective of the litigants determines the penalty. The remedy is transformed from one of permanent liability to that of satisfying claims. The parties are concerned with the issue of who must pay, the issue of immediate concern to the litigants at the time of the dispute, rather than the judicial question of whether the case could be reopened.

The reading of the Stela seems more original because it is in accordance with the larger issues of jurisprudence and legal procedure addressed in LH 1, 2, 3, and 5. Capital punishment in LH 3 and the removal of a judge from office in LH 5 both deal with permanent penalties for offenses, as does statute 4 according to the reading in the Stela. In this case, the witness may be telling the truth, but the judicial system cannot operate if a case can be reopened indefinitely. Manuscript r revises the statute: the

LH 5

If a judge adjudicated a decision, rendered a verdict, issued a document, but later altered his judgment, they shall charge and convict that judge of changing the decision he adjudicated; he shall give twelve times the fine which occurred in that judgment, and they shall remove him from his judicial seat in the assembly and he shall no longer sit with the judges (in deciding cases).

The earlier law collections began with a statute on homicide, but the scribe drafting the Laws of Hammurabi modified the tradition and composed a statute on false accusation of homicide. Then he applied the issue of falsehood in legal matters to other cases. In the initial statutes of the Laws of Hammurabi, he addressed legal procedures and how they can be impeded by mendacity. The scribe offered a comprehensive review of fabrication in legal procedures: the statutes are ordered in the chronological sequence of initial accusation, trial, verdict.[57] The first two statutes deal with false accusation, the second two with unproven testimony, and the last with judicial duplicity.

The earlier law collections do not have statutes on procedure, and it is unusual for an archaic code of laws to have any statutes on legal procedure at all. The earlier Mesopotamian collections lack statutes on procedure, and this is true for other archaic laws as well. The laws promulgated by the early kings of Britain, for example, lack statutes on administration.[58] An exception is one ancient law code that does deal with legal procedure: the Roman XII Tables begins with a statute on how to summon a party to court. It may be that the administration of law and the process of law occupy greater attention as societies develop. It may also be that by placing laws on legal procedures at the start of a set of statutes, the scribe of the Laws of Hammurabi has shown an awareness of the need to make sure that people accept legal rules and verdicts. The integrity of a system of law depends on the truthfulness of those

one who offers testimony that cannot be corroborated must pay. While this may seem to be an unfair penalty, the witness was the one who initiated the case. The witness was not called to testify in a case initiated by another. See Barmash, "Scribal Initiative in the Clarification and Interpretation of Mesopotamian Law Collections," 556.

[57] Raymond Westbrook, "Codification and Canonization," in *La Codification des Lois dans l'Antiquité* [ed. Ed. Lévy; Paris: De Boccard, 2000], 37.

[58] See F. L. Attenborough, ed. and trans., *The Laws of the Earliest English Kings* (Cambridge: Cambridge University Press, 1922), passim.

who testify and on whether the parties to a dispute believe in the trustworthiness of a trial.

Prior Mesopotamian law collections contained regulations on unproven accusations (LU 28–29; LL 17), but the scribe of the Laws of Hammurabi has placed the topic at the beginning of the statutes section, integrating them with other laws on procedure and trials. He has linked together cases that were independent of each other in other law collections. He followed the tradition of drafting the initial statute on homicide but transformed it to a case of an unsubstantiated accusation. He has preserved tradition while innovating on it.

By modifying the nature of the homicide statute, the scribe countered the chaos posed by the specter of unwarranted accusations. We can only speculate whether the Old Babylonian period, either in reality or only in the mind of the scribe, was rent by economic or social stress, spurring a rising tide of false accusations,[59] or whether the scribe recognized that greater havoc can come from false accusations than from acts of homicide and witchcraft themselves without there necessarily being a spate of false accusations.

The first two statutes treat the instance of an accuser who cannot prove his assertion that another person has committed an offense of the utmost seriousness.[60] The accuser has made an accusation before legal authorities.[61] This is not a happenstance to be taken lightly. The Fable of the Fox paints a vivid scene of a forlorn animal being formally charged before Shamash, the god of justice, with a capital crime.[62] The Dog, claiming that he was tormented by the Fox, has implored Shamash to bring the Fox to judgment, and in turn the weeping Fox pleads not to be arraigned in court:

[59] In one case, a father and son were engaged in hostilities toward one another, with the son being at fault, but the father blamed his daughter-in-law and her mother, shifting the blame on the more vulnerable women. See Stanley D. Walters, "The Sorceress and her Apprentice: A Case Study of an Accusation," *JCS* 23 (1970), 38; Kuhrt, *The Ancient Near East*, 113–114.

[60] The accuser is charged with not being able to do an action described by the verb *kânum*. See CAD K 168–169 s.v. *kânum* A mng. 4: "to prove by means of testimony" or "to establish as true by means of witnesses."

[61] Does the verb *ubburum*, used in LH 1–2, mean to defame publicly, as in informal conversation and gossip, or to prosecute the person in a court of law formally or making a formal charge before an official? The usage in the Fable of the Fox does offer evidence that the verb refers to a formal accusation in a legal context by the aggrieved party. (See H. L. J. Vanstiphout, "The Importance of 'The Tale of the Fox,'" *Acta Sumerologica* 10 [1988], 203.) This activity is to be distinguished from that of the professional *munaggirum*, who was not punished if his accusation was not upheld. See Benno Landsberger, "Remarks on the Archive of the Soldier Ubarum," *JCS* 9 (1955), 124.

[62] Enrique Jimenez, *The Babylonian Disputation Poems* (Culture and History of the Ancient Near East 87; Leiden: Brill, 2017), 39–54; W. G. Lambert, *Babylonian Wisdom Literature* (Winona Lake, Ind.: Eisenbrauns, 1996), 186–209, esp. 200–201; Vanstiphout, "The Importance of 'The Tale of the Fox,'" 191–227.

> When the Fox heard this, he lifted his head, weeping to Shamash,
> His tears came before the ray of Shamash,
> "Do not arraign me, Shamash, in this lawsuit."

This fable reflects the emotional turmoil of being called to court: falling into the clutches of a lawsuit is a calamity. The far more common subject of Mesopotamian fables, a debate over which plant or animal is of greater benefit to humanity,[63] lacks the heightened emotions, the panicked reaction and hysteria, of the Fox in this fable. The Fable of the Fox depicts a creature haunted by the specter of a trial for a capital crime before the god of justice. A false accusation was a catastrophe.

Making false accusations might have been easy enough to do. The right to make an accusation about a homicide appears to be fairly general in Mesopotamia: it is not limited to a member of the victim's family or an eyewitness.[64] An accusation mentioned to an official would set the machinery of investigation into play, and one could well imagine that a number of unproven or unprovable charges could harm many individuals. Accusation could also bind the royal administration into knots and prevent any other official business from being accomplished. False accusations could cause great unrest and even plunge a society into chaos. This is not an unwarranted fear: in an Akkadian prophecy text, adverse times are marked by rampant denunciations.[65] A specious accusation of homicide was a calamity.

False accusations of witchcraft were equally incendiary. Other Mesopotamian law collections open with statutes on homicide, but only the Laws of Hammurabi follows it with a statute on witchcraft. Placing witchcraft on a par with homicide signals the seriousness with which it is, or should be, taken. As witchcraft developed in Mesopotamia, it was transformed from the activities of a local practitioner, who could be employed legitimately, to the destructive acts of an antisocial individual, motivated only by evil intentions.[66] Initially, whether the local practitioner's skills were deemed licit or

[63] Examples are a debate between the tamarisk and the palm tree or the horse and the ox, a debate resolved by the decision of a god.

[64] See Barmash, *Homicide in the Biblical World*, 27.

[65] Robert D. Biggs, "Babylonian Prophecies, Astrology, and a New Source for "Prophecy Text B," in *Language, Literature, and History: Philological and Historical Studies Presented to Erica Reiner* (AOS 67; ed. Francesca Rochberg-Halton; New Haven, Conn.: American Oriental Society, 1987), 8 line 38.

[66] I. Tzvi Abusch argued that despite the fact that the texts he analyzed are from the first millennium BCE, the demonization of witchcraft should be dated earlier due to a number of factors, such as the development of exorcism in the Old Babylonian period and the incantation against demons from the third millennium BCE. See I. Tzvi Abusch, "The Demonic Image of the Witch in

illicit depended on the point of view of the interpreter: if witchcraft was of benefit to him, then it was viewed positively; if it harmed him, then it was deemed unlawful. However, when the witch was regarded as the adversary of the *āšipu*, the exorcist or incantation priest, with powers to control demons, as it may have already been in the Old Babylonian period, then the witch was reckoned as operating with exclusively hostile intentions. Setting witchcraft next to homicide, therefore, is not surprising, because it is so grave an offense.

The statute on witchcraft differs from the other statutes dealing with administration of justice because those statutes stipulate punishment of the false accuser once the false accuser cannot bring testimony to prove his accusation. The charge of witchcraft, however, is not withdrawn if the accuser cannot prove the charge. Rather, another form of proof, the ordeal, is to be employed.[67] This deviation is due to the insidiousness of witchcraft, acts performed in secret and difficult to prove.

Witchcraft could be investigated by means other than ordeal: MAL A 47 requires a hearsay witness to report witchcraft activity, and an eyewitness who denies seeing witchcraft is forced to swear an oath affirming his obligation to testify to the commission of a crime. The Laws of Hammurabi, earlier than the Middle Assyrian Laws, prescribes a river ordeal—a suprarational and cultic means of investigation—while the later law collection demands a forensic investigation of the people involved directly and indirectly.[68] The

Standard Babylonian Literature: The Reworking of Popular Conceptions by Learned Exorcists," in *Mesopotamian Witchcraft: Toward a History of Understanding of Babylonian Witchcraft Beliefs and Literature* (Ancient Magic and Divination V; Leiden: Brill-Styx, 2002 <1989>), 7–8, 14; Abusch, "Witchcraft and the Anger of the Personal God," in *Mesopotamian Witchcraft: Textual, Historical, and Interpretative Perspectives* (Ancient Magic and Divination I; ed. Tzvi Abusch and Karel van der Toorn; Gröningen: Styx, 1999), 51–57. See also Greengus, *Laws in the Bible and in Early Rabbinic Collections*, 269–273; Erica Reiner, *Astral Magic in Babylon* (Transactions of the American Philosophical Society, vol. 85/4; Philadelphia: American Philosophical Society, 1995), 101.

[67] The river ordeal described is one in which the innocent party floats and the guilty party sinks. There is a Mari letter that describes this procedure (ARM 26.249; see Jean Bottéro, "L'ordalie en la Mésopotamie ancienne," in *Annali della Scuola Normale Superiore di Pisa. Classe de Lettere e Filosofia* serie III, vol. XI, 4 (1981), 1017; Cahit Günbatti, "The River Ordeal in Ancient Anatolia," in *Veenhof Anniversary Volume* (Leiden: Nederlands Instituut voor het Nabije Oosten, 2001), 151–160; Driver and Miles, *Babylonian Laws*, 1.64); and Middle Assyrian ritual text from Assur (Driver and Miles, *The Babylonian Laws*, 1.65). See Wolfgang Heimpel, "The River Ordeal in Hit," *RA* 90 (1996), 7–18; Kuhrt, *The Ancient Near East*, 106–107, 117; Bertrand Lafont, "The Ordeal," in *Everyday Life in Ancient Mesopotamia* (Edinburgh: Edinburgh University Press, 2001), 199–210; Wolfram von Soden, "Ein neues Bruchstück des assyrischen Kommentars zum Marduk-Ordal," *RA* 52 (1957), 224–234.

[68] The terminology "cultic" and "forensic" is suggested by Bruce Wells, "The Cultic versus the Forensic: Biblical and Mesopotamian Judicial Procedures in the First Millennium BCE," *JAOS* 128 (2008), 205–232.

river ordeal was not limited to accusations of witchcraft or adultery. The law collections mention its use only in those cases, but Mesopotamian court records indicate that parties would undergo the river ordeal in disputes over lesser matters, such as the ownership of a field, slave, or sheep. A party could refuse to undergo the river ordeal and would have to renounce his claim. One text recounts a dispute between father and son over barley that devolved into accusations of witchcraft; while the river ordeal might have been imposed in this case because of the charge of witchcraft, it is possible that witchcraft was tangential to the dispute over ownership.[69] An angry party smeared the other party to the dispute with allegations of witchcraft, and the other side returned the slur.

The scribe of the Laws of Hammurabi provided two statutes on false accusations of homicide and witchcraft (LH 1 and 2) and then added two more on unproven testimony in a capital case and in a noncapital case (LH 3 and 4). The redundancy of the statutes manifests the gravity of false accusation and testimony. The problem of false accusations and unproven testimony derives in part from the assumption in Mesopotamia that serious offenses had to be reported. While a requirement that every offense had to be reported does not seem to be in evidence,[70] those with knowledge of serious offenses had to report them. The wife of the victim was deemed as culpable as the killers in the Nippur Murder Trial.[71] The female innkeeper was required to seize criminals and lead them off to the authorities (LH 109). A person who has seized runaway slaves who refuse to identify themselves must take them to the palace (LH 18). A man who sees a veiled prostitute must bring her to the palace entrance and enlist witnesses (MAL A 40). A person who comes across an eyewitness to witchcraft must report it to the king (MAL A 47). The reason these offenses had to be reported is that otherwise the offenders were difficult to catch. The wife knew of her husband's murder in the Nippur Murder Trial, and with intimate access to her husband, she could have betrayed him to his murderers. The female innkeeper, a woman with independence rare in society, could use her autonomy to provide a safe haven for criminals. The one who seized runaway slaves who refused to identify their owner could

[69] Marie-Louise Thomsen, "Witchcraft and Magic in Ancient Mesopotamia," in *Witchcraft and Magic in Europe: Biblical and Pagan Societies* (ed. Bengt Ankarloo and Stuart Clark; Philadelphia: University of Pennsylvania Press, 2001), 25–28.

[70] Contra F. R. Kraus, "Ein Sittenkanon in Omenform," *ZA* 43 (1938), 107–108; Landsberger, "Remarks on the Archive of the Soldier Ubarum," 124.

[71] Barmash, *Homicide in the Biblical World*, 151–153, 206.

take them for his own (since they already have the general slave mark but not the particular brand of their owner). A veiled prostitute was subverting the social structure, and the one who recognizes her as a prostitute despite her veil cannot be permitted to let her escape. An act of witchcraft was difficult to prosecute, and in order to force eyewitnesses to come forward, those who heard them tell of it had to report the eyewitnesses, even if the eyewitnesses were reluctant. Mandatory reporting of serious crime can be corrupted by dishonesty, and the statutes on false accusation of homicide and witchcraft and on unproven testimony in a capital case are a response.

The statute on unproven testimony in a capital case generates the statute on unproven testimony in a noncapital case, the logical next situation that needs to be addressed. The scope of falsehood in the legal process is completed by addressing mendacity in a judicial verdict in the final statute in the set (LH 5). The fifth and final statute addresses the case of a judge who has issued a verdict and then altered it. The set of five statutes address falsehood in the legal process, from accusation to testimony in a trial to verdict, and is generated by the technique of linking cases by theme.

Besides associating homicide, witchcraft, and mendacity in legal procedures in the initial set of statutes, the scribe has also linked together cases on dishonesty that were independent in other law collections. We have already analyzed how the technique of incremental variants used in the Laws of Hammurabi and the technique of polar variants employed in the Laws of Eshnunna shaped LH 127–130 differently than LE 27–28. Now we are going to investigate how LH 127–130 is part of a longer set in which the scribe linked previously independent cases. A lengthy series of statutes, LH 122–132 is based on the theme of misusing and circumventing legal relationships (LH 122, 123, 124, 127): two of them, LH 126 and 131, refer to a formal denunciation, and one, LH 132, addresses an informal accusation.[72] Both types of accusations are perilous to the accused: the evildoer inveighed against in a didactic hymn[73] and in a Sumerian literary disputation[74] is depicted as slandering the innocent through gossip, indicated by the term "pointing the

[72] If it is correct to posit a distinction between *ubburum* and *ubānam šuṭruṣum*, assuming the drafter(s) of the Laws of Hammurabi were attempting to describe two different actions, then the distinction to be drawn is between formally accusing and defaming through gossip and informal talk. See CAD T 211 s.v. *tarāṣum* mng. 3c for references to the act of pointing a finger with both positive and negative intentions.

[73] BWL 119:7–9.

[74] Jana Matuszak, "'Und du, du bist eine Frau?!'—Untersuchungen zu sumerischen literarischen Frauenstreitgesprächen nebst einer editio princeps von Zwei Frauen B,": Ph.D. dissertation, University of Tübingen, 2017.

finger," and through a formal legal denunciation by presenting a malicious charge formally. The statutes on dishonesty do not concern the grave accusations of homicide or witchcraft but start with the lesser issue of bailment:

> <u>LH 122</u>
> If a man intends to give silver, gold, or anything else to another man for safekeeping, he shall exhibit before witnesses anything which he intends to give, draw up a written contract and (with this procedure) he shall give the goods for safekeeping.
>
> <u>LH 123</u>
> If he has given goods for safekeeping without witnesses or an agreement and they have denied that he gave anything, that case has no basis for a claim.
>
> <u>LH 124</u>
> If a man gave silver, gold, or anything else before witnesses to another man for safekeeping but (the other man) has denied it, they shall convict that man, and he shall give twice that which he denied.
>
> <u>LH 125</u>
> If a man gave his property for safekeeping and his property together with the householder's property has become missing either through (theft gained through) a breach or by scaling over a wall, the householder who was careless shall make restitution and shall restore to the owner of the property whatever was given to him for safekeeping that he allowed to be lost; the householder shall continue to search for his lost property and shall take it from his thief.
>
> <u>LH 126</u>
> If a man whose property was not missing should declare, "My property is lost," and accuse his city quarter, his city quarter/district shall establish against him before the god that no property of his is lost, and he shall give to his city quarter twice whatever he claimed.

The topic of bailment is explored through incremental variants. LH 122 prescribes the need for a contract and witnesses to confer legitimacy on the transfer of custody over goods. LH 123 sanctions the depositor for claiming a deposit that lacks the legal safeguards of witnesses and a contract, a deposit that was most likely false, while LH 124 sanctions the safekeeper for denying a deposit, presumably one that was witnessed and recorded in a contract. LH 125 prevents a safekeeper from easily claiming theft. In LH 126, a property owner falsely accuses his city quarter/district of losing his property when in fact his property is not lost at all. These statutes all deal with honesty and mendacity in regard to chattels: the initial statute presents the legal necessities for deposit, and the others unfold the possible falsehoods that can ensue in depositing goods in another person's custody. This set contrasts sharply with LE 36–37, where the safekeeper claims that the goods were lost due to theft: his claim is accepted only when his personal goods were purloined along with the deposited chattels. The underlying issue in the treatment of deposit in the Laws of Hammurabi is falsehood, and therefore the statutes are placed side by side with other false claims.

The scribe of the Laws of Hammurabi develops the set further with another dispute stemming from dishonesty:

> LH 127
> If a man caused a finger to be pointed in accusation against an *ugbabtu*-priestess or against a man's wife but cannot bring proof, they shall beat that man before the judges and shall shave off half his hair.

In LH 127, a person spreads falsehoods and causes rumor-mongering against a woman. Then either the woman or her husband initiated formal proceedings, but the person spreading rumors could not substantiate his words.[75] The punishment is a beating and the shaving of half his hair. The latter penalty was used as part of the penalty for those bringing suit when they should not, as it is explained in a court record, "since he had made out tablets renouncing further claims but did make claims again, they led him around the city with half his hair shaved off, his nose pierced, (and) his arms twisted."[76]

The scribe proceeded forward with the theme of falsehood and dealt with dishonesty in marriage, first with a counterfeit marriage and then with other dishonest transgressions in licit marriages. Like the statutes on falsehoods in depositing chattels, he started with an illegal transaction, then moved on to misuse of legal relationships. In so doing, the scribe defines a legal marriage through highlighting what is illegal. As we saw in our earlier analysis, the scribe dealt initially with a woman found in flagrante delicto (LH 129), and then in LH 130, he addressed the case of a woman forced upon in possibly

[75] Koschaker argued that this statute is in a strange location, that the combination of high priestess and ordinary married woman is surprising, and that a strange man, not the husband, has brought the proceedings (Koschaker, *Rechtsvergleichende Studien zur gesetzgebung Hammurapis*, 210–214).
[76] CT 45, 18:16.

incriminating circumstances: she is in an inchoate marriage and is still living in her father's house. Her intimacy with another man could easily be seen as akin to adultery. The next step in the paradigm is that of a woman under a cloud of false accusation, suspected of adultery. A court of law applies the remedy based on whether the accusation is formally made by the husband or is the result of gossip:

> LH 131
> If her husband has accused his own wife[77] (of adultery), even though she has not been seized lying with a man, she shall swear an oath (about her innocence) to the god and return to her house.
>
> LH 132
> If a man's wife has a finger pointed against her in an accusation involving another male, even though she has not been seized lying with another male, she shall submit to the river ordeal[78] for her husband.

In LH 131, the woman's husband is the source of the accusation, and the woman is acquitted by an oath. In LH 132, a rumor arises about this woman, and somehow it has arrived to legal proceedings.[79] Here, the woman is acquitted by the river ordeal, a form of trial that appears to give more credence to the possible truthfulness of the accusation. A woman who is the subject of gossip must be proven innocent by evidence made in public so that the rumors end. All the woman who has been accused directly by her husband has to do is take an oath, perhaps to prevent the husband from tormenting his wife with a river ordeal again and again by making accusations.[80] General gossip might have more credence to it, or at least it is more pernicious and difficult to stop, and therefore she must undergo the river ordeal, a test performed in public, so that her guilt or innocence is proven in public.

Dishonesty in depositing goods and transgressions against marriage (LH 122–132) are not associated in other law collections. The Laws of Eshnunna does not link adultery (LE 26–28) with dishonesty in bailment (LE 36–37).

[77] Literally, "If her husband accuses the wife of a man (his own wife) . . ."

[78] The apodosis of LH 132 reads *ana mutīša Id išalli*. The verb *šalûm*, "to dive," refers to the river ordeal. See CAD Š 273 s.v. *šalûm* B mng. 1.

[79] Driver and Miles argued that there is nothing to suggest that the accuser brought court proceedings, so he may have failed to prove his accusation in proceedings he has brought himself or the accused woman has brought or those acting on her behalf (*The Babylonian Laws*, 1.278).

[80] It is not clear whether the river ordeal or taking an oath by the gods would have been less frightening. In both cases, the accuser and accused were putting their life at risk.

Adultery is an independent *topos* in the Hittite Laws (197–198), as are rape (LU 6) and accusations of adultery (LU 14) in the Laws of Ur-Namma. The scribe who has drafted the statutes in the Laws of Hammurabi has linked them, prompted by the theme of mendacity. This theme serves as a transitional link between the cluster of statutes addressing commercial transactions (LH fragments L–CC; 100–126) and the cluster of statutes addressing family law (LH 127–194).

The scribe has organized the statutes by linking cases that were formerly independent. The scribe has taken the tradition of starting a law collection with a statute on homicide and transformed the initial statute into one about a false accusation of homicide (LH 1), innovating on tradition. The scribe composed a systematic set of statutes on legal processes that have been obstructed by various means: false and unproven accusations, charges of witchcraft, and judicial malfeasance (LH 2–5). The scribe also linked together statutes about transgressions in the deposit of chattels (LH 122–126) with transgressions in marriage (LH 127–132) by rooting them in dishonest behavior.[81] By placing side by side statutes about cases that were independent in earlier law collections, the scribe advanced toward systematization and conceptualization.

4.5.2. Organization of Laws in Clusters

The statutes are not in a random jumble but are organized in elaborate clusters made up of sets of statutes. Their organization manifests a drift toward systematization and conceptualization. The scribe of the Laws of Hammurabi was unwilling, or perhaps even unable, to articulate principles, but his organizing of the statutes by broad clusters and narrower sets projects an intrinsic sense of implicit concepts.

An outline of the Laws of Hammurabi demonstrates that the statutes are assembled in extensive clusters on a major topic of law:

[81] One might wonder if these two sections were written by the same scribe, who included two statutes on the procedure to be followed in case of unfounded accusation as well as two adjoining statutes that use the language "a finger be pointed against someone in accusation" (LH 127 and 132). Does this mean that the same scribe drafted these two statues and another scribe LH 1 and 2? Or did the proximity of LH 1 and 2 to each other and of LH 127 and 132 prompt the scribe to use the same expression in nearby statutes?

1–5	Legal procedure, including perjury and corruption
6–25	Theft and robbery of property, including slaves
26–65; fragments A–H	Land tenure
fragments L–CC; 100–126	Commercial transactions
127–194	Family law
195–214	Assault
215–277	Professional rates of hire and responsibilities
278–282	More on slaves

The clusters reflect a tendency to articulate as many laws as possible governing a major legal topic. For example, of the approximately three hundred statutes in the Laws of Hammurabi, fifty-eight deal with issues of marriage and divorce, especially inchoate marriage, the between and betwixt time when the groom has a relationship with the wife-to-be that confers specific restrictions and obligations but that is not yet fully constituted marriage. Marriage represented the formation of a new personal status for the wife: she was no longer under the authority of her parents but in the jurisdiction of her husband. She was not a chattel, an item to be bought or sold. Nonetheless, she did not possess complete freedom of action—her husband retained control over her actions and property. During inchoate marriage, the parents have relinquished authority, but the groom has not yet acquired complete official standing in the marriage relationship. This betwixt-and-between state propels inchoate marriage to be a topic addressed at length in the Laws of Hammurabi.

At the same time, there is a limit to the methodical investigation of a major topic of law. Marriage occupies more than a sixth of the statutes in the Laws of Hammurabi, but what is striking is that the Laws of Hammurabi never tells us directly how to form a marriage. The tendency toward systematic analysis is temperate and mild.[82]

[82] Marc Van De Mieroop argued that the length of the Laws of Hammurabi may have been a consequence of its presentation upon a stela (Van De Mieroop, *Philosophy before the Greeks*, 167–168). He observed that a much longer text than the one extant for the Laws of Hammurabi could have been composed. In comparison to the other genres that stemmed from the lexical tradition, the lexical lists and the omen texts, the Laws of Hammurabi is short. It may be that the length of the law collection was limited by the size of the stela upon which it was inscribed. Thus, there may have been a practical limit on the text of the Laws of Hammurabi. However, this claim rests on a shaky foundation: the signs could have been made smaller, and other parts pertaining to the overarching royal inscription structure could have been curtailed to allow for a longer composition.

Within the elaborate clusters in the statutes in the Laws of Hammurabi, there are sets that address specific topics within a legal domain, and the statutes within each set are generated by the method of incremental variants. The opening set of regulations on procedure, LH 1–5, is followed by a series of statutes addressing theft and the illegal acquisition of property, LH 6–13. We can only speculate on the placement and implicit connection between the one set and the next, but the clustering of statutes on theft (LH 6–25) versus procedure (LH 1–5) demonstrates that a sense of systematization and concomitant generalization is employed in the Laws of Hammurabi, even if it is not expressly articulated.

The series on theft is composed of sets of statutes that organize thefts into types. The series LH 6–13 first distinguishes theft based on the means of acquisition and type of chattel (LH 6–8) and then second on deceitful claims by supposed owners, sellers, and buyers (LH 9–13). The series LH 14–20 treats the willful loss of human property, in a sense, beginning with the kidnapping of a young child[83] and then with runaway slaves, and the last series in this cluster, LH 21–25, addresses robbery.

If we focus on the first two sets, we can gain a sense of how the elaborate cluster is built from sets of statutes.

<u>LH 6</u>

If a man steals valuables belonging to a god or the palace, that man shall be killed, and the one who received the stolen items shall be killed.

<u>LH 7</u>

If a man should purchase silver, gold, a male slave, a female slave, an ox, a sheep, a donkey, or anything else whatsoever, from the minor son of a free man[84] or from the slave of a man without witnesses or a contract, or if he accepts the goods for safekeeping, that man is a thief; he shall be killed.

[83] LH 14 most probably deals with the kidnapping of a young child for slavery: older children could identify themselves and their parents, but a young child would have great difficulty in doing so.

[84] The question is whether the phrase *mār awīlim* refers to anyone in the free class or specifically to a minor child of a free man. If the terminology "*mār* (social class)" in LH 203, 205, and 208 is being used to denote a member of that class rather than a minor, and assuming that the terminology is the same across the statutes, then LH 7 is addressing the case of sale or deposit in general. But then we must ask why the statute includes the specific terminology about the child of a free man as well as the specification that it applies when the seller is a slave. Scholarly opinion is mixed. Koschaker argued that the statute does not deal with the case of a minor but with the free class in general (*Rechtsvergleichende Studien zur gesetzgebung Hammurapis*, 73–84). Driver and Miles, however, argued that LH 7 is inconsistent with LH 122–123, which demands that the depositor provide witnesses or a document, and with LH 9–13, which requires that witnesses (but no document) be

LH 8

If a man steals an ox, a sheep, a donkey, a pig, or a boat, if it belongs either to a god or to the palace, he shall give thirty-fold; if it belongs to a *muškēnum*, he shall replace it tenfold; if the thief has nothing to give, he shall be killed.

In LH 6, a person has encroached into protected areas, perhaps an insider granted special access who has stolen the valuable property belonging to a temple or palace.[85] In LH 7, an insider, a minor or a slave, who by virtue of his position has special access to a parent's or owner's property, has taken advantage of that position and stolen goods through an irregular purchase or deposit.[86] In LH 8, property usually left outside, such as an animal or boat, has been taken: it is accessible to any passerby and is vulnerable to theft. The draftsman has omitted any general law forbidding theft but has focused on situations where chattels are prone to theft: an individual gains access to the protected valuables of a temple or palace; a son or slave tries to pass his father's or owner's property as his own, and a buyer purchases or a bailee accepts the property without witnesses and a contract; or a person steals property left outside.

At first glance, the statutes in this set, LH 6–8, seem to be out of order: the statute in the middle, LH 7, addressing a sale from a minor or a slave, appears to interfere with the progression from LH 6 to LH 8. LH 6 deals with items stored inside a palace or belonging to a shrine, whose ownership by the king or a temple must be obvious, as opposed to the property mentioned in LH

produced to prove ownership or sale (*The Babylonian Laws*, 83–86). It makes more sense for this statute to address the special case of buying from a minor or a slave, who were dependent people and whose property (assuming that they can own property) can easily be mixed up with their parent's or owner's, and require special precautions. Slaves and minors had special access to their parent's or owner's property and could have had a special opportunity to abscond with it.

It must be noted that the terminology "*mār* (social class)" indicates that the individual is a dependent member of a household headed by either a (free) man or a commoner / palace dependent. See Martha T. Roth, "On *mār awīlim* in the Old Babylonian Law Collections," *JNES* 72 (2013), 267–272; Roth, "On Persons in the Old Babylonian Law Collections: The Case of *mār awīlim* in Bodily Injury Provisions," in *Extraction & Control: Studies in Honor of Matthew W. Stolper* (ed. Michael Kozuh, et al., Studies in Ancient Oriental Civilization; Chicago: Oriental Institute, 2014), 219–227; and Raymond Westbrook, "LH §§ 7 and 123—A Contradiction?" *NABU* 2007/27.

[85] The word *makkūru* refers to valuables, not ordinary property. See CAD M/I 133–136 s.v. *makkūrum*. The term *makkūrum* is used for the valuables of ordinary individuals in LH 125, 172, 232, and 235, and the valuables owned by the palace and temple are protected by the death penalty without exception.

[86] It should be noted that the statute prescribes a penalty for the purchaser. The penalty for the child and the slave is omitted: presumably the parent/owner would make that determination. There are no statutes in the Laws of Hammurabi about an owner abusing his own slave, only about maltreating another's slave.

8—ox, sheep, goat, donkey, or boat—which would be stored outside.[87] While the emphasis of LH 7 on the witnesses and documents necessary for a transaction interrupts the logical flow from LH 6 to 8 and perhaps would have been better placed after LH 8 as an introduction to LH 9–13, this illustrates how the Laws of Hammurabi is focused on incremental variants, not maximal variants: the close access a minor or slave has to a father's or owner's property enables that person to abscond with it and seems to be the logical next step. The placement of LH 7 fits in well with the movement by incremental variants from LH 6 to LH 7: special precautions must be taken to protect property from insiders who have access to it.

The next subset LH 9–11 illustrates how the scribe drafting the statutes of the Laws of Hammurabi created a series exploring a continuum of incremental variants. In each statute, one party is suspect:

> LH 9
>
> If a man who has lost property has seized his lost property in another man's possession, but the man in whose possession the lost property was discovered declares, "A seller sold it to me; I purchased it before witnesses," and the owner of the lost property declares, "I can bring witnesses who can identify my lost property," and the buyer produces the seller who sold it to him and the witnesses in whose presence he purchased it, and the owner of the lost property produces witnesses who can identify his lost property, the judges shall examine their case and if the witnesses in whose presence the purchase was made and the witnesses who can identify the lost property state what is known to them before the god, then it is the seller who is the thief; he shall be killed; the owner of the lost property shall take his lost property, and the buyer shall take from the seller's estate the amount of silver he paid.

[87] One could speculate that the theft of property of the palace or a god would involve the theft of sacred property and therefore merit the death penalty. (See Driver and Miles, *The Babylonian Laws*, 1.81; and Greengus, *Laws in the Bible and in Early Rabbinic Collections*, 228–230.) However, we do not have any indication that palace property would be deemed sacred (or even every item of temple property), but perhaps the offense merits death because the thief has stolen items while they are located in the palace or temple, places that should be secure but that have suffered infiltration. In the case of property held outside, the penalty is death only when the thief cannot pay, even for the theft of temple and palace property, and death is also only the penalty when the thief has stolen the property of a *muškēnum* but cannot pay. The theft of agricultural implements, by contrast, is remedied with mildness: LH 259–260 prescribes the penalty of three to five shekels. The items were not on the owner's property and were left in the common irrigated area, so the offense may have been considered to be either illegal use or theft from an unattended area.

LH 10

If the buyer could not produce the seller who sold the lost property and the witnesses before whom he made the purchase but the owner of the lost property could produce witnesses who can identify his lost property, then it is the buyer who is the thief; he shall be killed; the owner of the lost property shall take his lost property.

LH 11

If the owner of the lost property could not produce witnesses who can identify his lost property, he is a liar; he has spread slander; he shall be killed.[88]

One person in the chain of seller-buyer-owner lacks the documentation for a valid sale.

LH 9—seller
LH 10—buyer
LH 11—owner

The impetus to fill out statutes incrementally is apparent in this series. By contrast, the Laws of Eshnunna has a single case on this topic, only the case of a purchaser who cannot prove the identity of the person who sold the property to him (LE 40).[89] LH 9–12 provide a neat array of the variants for the guilty parties.

[88] LH 11 treats disputes over ownership. The protasis reads, "If the owner of the lost property cannot produce witnesses who can identify his lost property . . . " The apodosis in the Stela and other manuscripts read, *sà-ar tu-uš-ša-am-ma id-ke id-da-ak*, "he is a liar, he has stirred up corruption, he shall be killed," but one text, manuscript r, reads *iqbī*, "he has uttered (corruption)," in place of *idke*, "he has stirred up (corruption)" (Manuscript r = Finkelstein, "A Late Old Babylonian Copy of the Laws of Hammurapi," 39–48). CAD, Borger, and Roth changed the text to *id-di* to render it as "he has spread malicious charges" (CAD D 125 s.v. *dekû* mng. 2b; Borger, BAL, 1.12; Roth, *Law Collections*, 83–85, 140 n.3). Finkelstein argued that *iqbī* is the correct reading since *tušša(m) qabû* is the better idiomatic expression, but he remained ambiguous whether it was the original reading. The use of the verb *dekû* with *tuššam* is not attested, whereas the verb *nadû* is attested in the clause *awīlum tuššam elīya ittadi*. This variant is an improvement because the statute involves an individual who has claimed that the property belongs to him but cannot bring witnesses to prove it. He has cast aspersions upon the ownership of property and made a situation doubtful. It is his *statement* that the property belongs to him that causes doubt to enter the proceedings. The problem is that he cannot prove his statement. He has not brought witnesses whose testimony is false nor has he forged tablets, circumstances that would be included by reading *id-ke*, "he has stirred up (corruption)." His utterance is the cause for dispute and, therefore, manuscript r reads *iqbi*, "he has uttered corruption." Commerce cannot occur if ownership is to be doubted because of a statement without witnesses or tablet as proof. See Barmash, "Scribal Initiative in the Clarification and Interpretation of Mesopotamian Law Collections," 555–556.

[89] The other law collections barely mention theft. It is not mentioned in the Laws of Ur-Namma or the Laws of Lipit-Ishtar. LE 40 is the only law in the Laws of Eshnunna to deal with theft. MAL A 3–6 deal with theft. In comparison to SLHF iii 10–15, the closest in content to the Laws of Hammurabi,

LH 9 addresses the case where the original owner and purchaser can produce witnesses, and therefore the seller is the thief. In LH 10, the purchaser is the thief because he cannot produce witnesses to prove he made a legal purchase. In LH 11, the guilty party is the one who claimed to be the original owner. The variants of the guilty party, whether seller, purchaser, or owner, fill out the possibilities of who could be the thief. The set of cases is schematic, which is why LH 12 does not immediately follow LH 9, even if both deal with the instance when the seller is the guilty party.

However, the question of who is lying becomes an acute quandary when all three parties can bring proof. That is when the judges have a hard case to solve. Perhaps one party's evidence is tainted or the seller can produce witnesses that he purchased the property from another individual. The set of cases presented may be too neat and too schematic, but no collection of law can include every possibility. The laying out of the possibilities in each statute does implicitly articulate a principle of law, and perhaps that is sufficient. The drafter has presented the variants sufficient in his mind to illustrate the law. Westbrook and Wilcke argued that the seller must have disappeared, and therefore the law is merely academic,[90] but it is likely that another factor is at work—the seller is a receiver of stolen goods, a "fence" whose business is otherwise legitimate, who runs (part of) his business in such a manner, habitually buying and selling goods. This is why the buyer had a normal process of sale with witnesses present.

The two statutes that follow reflect what the scribe felt was necessary to fully convey the adjudication of duplicitous acquisition.

<u>LH 12</u>

If the seller has died, the buyer shall take up to fivefold the claim for that case from the estate of the seller.

<u>LH 13</u>

If that man's witnesses are not available (nearby/in the vicinity), the judges shall grant him a continuance until the sixth month, but if he does not bring his witnesses by the sixth month, that man is a liar; he shall continue to bear the penalty for that case.

we can see that the Laws of Hammurabi prescribes a huge increase in penalty, effectively a death penalty since it is unlikely that anyone will buy a debt slave for such a large amount.

[90] Raymond Westbrook and Claus Wilcke, "The Liability of an Innocent Purchaser of Stolen Goods in Early Mesopotamian Law," *Archiv für Orientforschung* 25 (1974), 119.

The first statute specifies that if the seller has died, a buyer can claim compensation from the seller's estate: the circumstances are not specified, but it would seem likely that this would be the case if an individual claiming to be the original owner could produce witnesses proving that it was his lost or stolen property. The second provides one of the parties with a six-month extension to find his missing witnesses, and if he still cannot produce them afterward, he will be permanently designated as someone who could not produce witnesses and thereby be prohibited or greatly restricted from engaging in commerce.[91] This penalty, it can be surmised, was designed to prevent anyone from falsely claiming that he has witnesses: it would be easy enough to assert that they are not around and conveniently will never be around. The death penalty was imposed on false claimants in LH 9–11 so there is a strong impetus to claim that one's witnesses are absent. Here by adding LH 12 and 13 to LH 9–11, the scribe has provided a fuller exposition of duplicitous acquisition in a set of statutes.

The statutes in the Laws of Hammurabi are not in a random agglomeration but consist of statutes in extensive clusters on a broad area of law. They are then built up from sets addressing specific legal topics. This organization shows a drift toward conceptualization and systematization. The scribes were unwilling or unable to articulate principles or abstract concepts, but they projected onto the statutes an innate sense of the systematic analysis of legal issues.

4.5.3. Statutes with Explanation

The two means of composition we have analyzed so far, linking cases previously independent and the organization of the statutes in elaborate clusters and smaller sets, operate by placing statutes side by side. Another method of conceptualization and systematization that the scribe employed is the use of explanatory comments, one that unites statutes from across clusters and sets.[92] There are only rare examples of this approach in the Laws of Hammurabi. In some instances, the explanation serves to clarify the remedy,

[91] Abusch, "'He Should Continue to Bear the Penalty of That Case,'" 81.

[92] For other discussions of this phenomenon in the Laws of Hammurabi and other Old Babylonian legal texts, see Driver and Miles, *The Babylonian Laws*, 1.286–287, and Martha T. Roth, "The Because Clause: Punishment Rationalizations in Mesopotamian Laws," in *Veenhof Anniversary Volume* (Leiden: Nederlands Instituut voor het Nabije Oosten, 2001), 407–412.

and in others, the clarification explains why the offense committed is severe and, therefore, why the remedy is deservedly harsh.

The set of statutes we just discussed in the previous section contains statements that David Daube termed a diagnosis, the designation of the circumstances of an offense so that the offender is deemed to be in a certain category.[93] A declaration is made in each statute:

LH 7 "that man is the thief"
LH 9 "it is the seller who is the thief"
LH 10 "it is the buyer who is the thief"
LH 11 "he is a liar; he has indeed spread malicious charges"
LH 13 "it is that man who is a liar"

The legal consequences for the offender are viewed as deriving from that category. The articulation of diagnoses embodies a move toward conceptualization.

In LH 163–164, the scribe has drafted two verbose statutes, rare in the laconic style of the Laws of Hammurabi:

<u>LH 163</u>
If a man married a wife but she did not cause him to have children, and then that woman passed away, if his father-in-law has returned to him the bride-price that the man brought to his father-in-law's house, her husband will not lay claim to the dowry of that woman. Her dowry belongs to her father's estate.

<u>LH 164</u>
If the father-in-law should not return to him the betrothal gift, (the widower) shall deduct the value of the betrothal gift from her dowry and return (the remainder) of her dowry to her father's house.

These statutes contain an explanation, with LH 163 stating, "Her dowry belongs to her father's estate." This wording is not a ruling because if it were, it would be expressed along these lines: "the husband shall return the dowry to her father's estate." The explanation clarifies the directive that the husband

[93] David Daube, "Some Forms of Old Testament Legislation," *Proceedings of the Oxford Society of Historical Theology* (1944–1945): 39–42; Jackson, "Historical Aspects of Legal Drafting in the Light of Modern Theories of Cognitive Development," 355–356.

may not lay claim to his deceased wife's dowry: it spells out that the deceased wife's father still has the right to the dowry of his daughter if she has died without issue.[94] The estates of the husband and the wife's father are returned to the condition they were in before the marriage. This is in sharp contrast to the ruling in the case that a man wished to divorce a wife who had not borne him children: both the betrothal gift and the dowry belong to her (LH 138).[95] The explanation in LH 164 is needed, in the mind of the scribe, to clarify the remedy. Perhaps the scribe decided to incorporate a clarification because the remedy is unusual in some way.

An explanation clarifying the nature of the offense is employed as a rationale for the punishment in LH 194:

> If a man has given his child to a wet nurse to be suckled and then that child died under the care of the nurse, if the nurse then has taken another child to her breast without (the consent/knowledge of) its father or mother, they shall convict her, and because she has taken another child without (the consent/knowledge of) its father or its mother, they shall cut off her breast.

An infant died while in the care of a wet nurse, and the wet nurse has taken on another infant. The wet nurse has not informed the parents of the child, but which child is left obscure. The parents in question might be those of the first child: they contracted with her, and even though their child died, their permission to nurse another child had to be secured. Alternatively, the parents might be those of the second child, who were not informed that the previous

[94] Koschaker argued that there is superfluity in the wording and that the verbiage could easily have been pruned. He believed that LH 164 was the addition made in Hammurabi's time but what it stated was already included in LH 163 (*Rechtsvergleichende Studien zur gesetzgebung Hammurapis*, 87 n.6). Yaron argued that a new custom, that the husband gains the right to the betrothal gift which he gave to the bride's family once the marriage is fully complete and is no longer inchoate, found in LH 164, served as the basis of the statutes and that it did not matter whether it had been returned or not to the husband at the time of the wife's death. Both statutes, LH 163–164, were required, according to Yaron, to make clear that a mutual refund should occur (*The Laws of Eshnunna*, 177–178). With regard to LH 163–164, Yaron correctly noted the effectiveness of this literary feature. However, Yaron argued that the clarifying clause in LH 136 was excess verbiage that did not add value and resulted from a characteristic way that the scribe of the Laws of Hammurabi rewrote statutes from the Laws of Eshnunna. Martha T. Roth correctly notes that clarifying clauses beginning with "because" are found in reform edicts and court records, not only in the Laws of Hammurabi, and therefore they are not the result of the scribe of the Laws of Hammurabi rewriting the earlier law collection. The clarifying clauses were a means of indicating the decisive element in a case that prompts a specific penalty. See Roth, "The Because Clause," 407–408.

[95] Driver and Miles suggested that the reason the betrothal gift was to be returned to the husband in LH 164 is that he had the expense of supporting a woman who did not do her part by providing him with children (*The Babylonian Laws*, 1.252–253). But that same reasoning could be applied in the case of divorce from a woman who did not bear children.

child suckled by the wet nurse had died.[96] The second possibility seems more likely. In any case, the punishment would severely compromise the ability of the wet nurse to work in her profession. The scribe incorporated a rationale for the punishment, perhaps a sign that the punishment is unusual and unexpected and may even be met with objection. The scribe has highlighted in the explanation what was wrong with the offense, not informing the parents of the previous death.

The wet nurse in whose care a child has died was not to be punished for the death of the child, perhaps reflecting the incidence of child mortality in Old Babylonian society. However, there are consequences for her due to the death of a child in her care: she must disclose to the parents of a new child of the death of the previous child. Presumably, then, they decide whether to hire her in light of that information. If she fails to inform them, the body part that was the peccant member is removed: her breast is cut off.[97] Poetic justice and bodily mutilation are characteristic modes of punishment for the Laws of Hammurabi. Yet at the same time, the scribe appeared to be aware of social reality. The wet nurse was not held responsible for the death of the first child. Her offense was in failing to disclose the earlier death of a child to new client parents.

Similarly, LH 108 contains an explanation of the offense:

> If a woman innkeeper should refuse to accept grain for the price of beer but accepts (only) silver measured by the large weight, thereby reducing the value of beer in relation to the value of grain, they shall prove the woman innkeeper guilty and they shall cast her into the water.[98]

[96] Driver and Miles, *The Babylonian Laws*, 1.406; V. Scheil, "Les Nourrices en Babylonie et le § 194 du Code," *RA* 11 (1914): 175–182.

[97] Or perhaps both her breasts were to be cut off. It may be wondered whether the wet nurse would survive such punishment.

[98] It must be noted that the Stela and other manuscripts read *ú-ka-an-nu-ši-ma*, "they shall prove that female innkeeper guilty (and then throw her in the river)", while manuscript S reads *i-ka-[a]s-s[ú]-ši-i-m[a]*, "they shall bind her (and then throw her into the river)" (Arno Poebel, *Historical and Grammatical Texts* [Publications of the Babylonian Section 5; Philadelphia: University Museum, 1914], number 93, plates xxxix, xl, cviii, cix). This variant appears to be a clarification. In LH 129 and 155, the guilty are bound before being thrown into the water in order to clarify that they are being executed and are not being tested by the river ordeal. The reading of LH 108, "they shall prove that female innkeeper guilty (and then throw her in the river)," found in the Stela and the other manuscripts, is another means of clarifying that casting the woman is a punishment, not a test by river ordeal. The reading in manuscript S is another way of making that clarification, in line with LH 129 and 155. The penalty of throwing a woman into the water is also found in LH 133b and 143, but unfortunately the tablet of manuscript S is broken in those places so that it remains unknown whether the wording of those statutes was changed as well. See Barmash, "Scribal Initiative in the Clarification and Interpretation of Mesopotamian Law Collections," 557.

The explanation, "thereby reducing the value of beer in relation to the value of grain," clarifies how insisting on payment in silver and refusing to accept grain results in the lowering the price of beer relative to grain.[99] Other statutes in the Laws of Hammurabi prescribe that a person who needs to pay can do so either in grain or silver or even in other forms of property if he has neither grain nor silver (LH 51, U, Z). However, the female innkeeper would be able to manipulate the transaction to her benefit if she could insist on payment in silver, and her client would have no choice except to agree to the female innkeeper's terms.[100]

The explanation sets out the reason for the severe penalty in an offense that might seem minor. The penalty of drowning for a female innkeeper is harsh, even in comparison to the often severe punishments of the Laws of Hammurabi. It is prescribed as the penalty for an adulterous couple caught in flagrante delicto (LH 129), for a groom's father who is sexually intimate with his son's wife after his son has been intimate with her (LH 155), for the wife of a captured man who has sufficient provisions to sustain her household but who enters another man's house for marriage (LH 133), and for a wastrel wife (LH 143).[101] In the mind of the scribe drafting the statute, the punishment of the female innkeeper needed a rationale for why an offense that might seem minor was severe.

In the Laws of Hammurabi, explanatory comments are offered rarely. In the examples we have analyzed, one comment clarifies the remedy, and two others highlight the severity of the offense committed and provide a rationale for the remedy. The effect, if not the intended purpose, of an explanatory comment is to include that ruling in a principle of greater generality than the decision itself.[102] Casuistic laws in general infrequently divulge the reason for their ruling, and including explanatory comments is another means by

[99] For more on the female innkeeper, see Marten Stol, *Women in the Ancient Near East* (trans. Helen and Mervyn Richardson; Berlin: de Gruyter, 2016), 363–367.

[100] The Laws of Hammurabi includes a provision (LH 111) setting the interest rate in barley for a loan extended by the female innkeeper. The Laws of Eshnunna also contains a provision, LE 41, that regulates the sale of beer by the female innkeeper for three types of people who are outside the common social protective networks. See Sophie Démare-Lafont, "Women at Work in Mesopotamia: An Attempt at a Legal Perspective," in *The Role of Women in Work and Society in the Ancient Near East* (ed. Brigitte Lion and Cécile Michel; Boston: De Gruyter, 2016), 313–319; Roth, *Law Collections*, 70 n.20, and Raymond Westbrook, "The Old Babylonian Term *napṭārum*," *JCS* 46 (1994), 41–46.

[101] It may be that the wife had to commit only one of three offenses (being wayward, squandering household goods, and disparaging her husband) to face the severe penalty. It may also be that "being wayward" is the category, being expressed in the verbal adjective, and "squandering household goods" and "disparaging her husband" are examples of that category, articulated in the durative.

[102] Frederick Schauer, "Giving Reasons," *Stanford Law Review* 47 (1994–1995), 641.

which the scribe drafting the Laws of Hammurabi was advancing toward the articulation of legal principles. The rare clarifying comments manifest the legal reasoning of the scribe drafting the statutes in the Laws of Hammurabi.

4.5.4. Types of Punishment as a Means of Systematization and Conceptualization

The scribe applied identical and similar penalties as another method of systematization and conceptualization. Certain types of punishment—the death penalty, vicarious punishment, poetic justice, and bodily mutilation—operate across clusters and sets of statutes as well as within a set in which statutes are adjacent to one another. The death penalty is employed as the remedy for serious offenses, even if it is more an expression of what appeared just than what was historically applied, and at times it is to be inflicted on an innocent person. Bodily mutilation appears as a penalty only in the Laws of Hammurabi, not in the other law collections, and was an expression of poetic justice. Poetic justice informed other types of remedies, such as throwing into the fire a person who came to help put out a fire in a house but steals household items. These modes of punishment are applied across cases leading to seemingly bizarre and alarming sanctions.

The Laws of Hammurabi as a whole is characterized by the frequent recourse to the death penalty: LH 1, 2, 3, 6, 7, 8, 9, 10, 11, 14, 15, 16, 19, 21, 22, 25, 26, 33, 34, M, N, BB, 108, 109, 110, 116, 129, 130, 133b, 143, 153, 155, 157, 210, 229, and 230. If we survey the use of the death penalty across the Mesopotamian law collections, we discover a number of striking characteristics:[103]

(1) In regard to the prevalence of the death penalty, it appears only once in the Laws of Ur-Namma and not at all in the Laws of Lipit-Ishtar or in the scribal exercises. It is possible that this is due to the truncated condition of these Sumerian texts. By contrast, seven out of sixty-one statutes in the Laws of Eshnunna prescribe the death penalty, about 11.5 percent,[104] and 36 out of 277 statutes in the Laws of

[103] I am omitting the Neo-Babylonian Laws because it is too fragmentary, as well as the Middle Assyrian Laws because it is not of the same genre as the other law collections. Its remedies are distinctive because they consist of multiple punishments.

[104] The death penalty appears in LE 12, 13, 24, 26, 28, 58, and 60.

Hammurabi, about 13 percent.[105] The Laws of Eshnunna and the Laws of Hammurabi share a proclivity for the death penalty.

(2) If we focus on statutes in which the death penalty is prescribed, we discover that there are two statutes in which the injured party has been killed in the Laws of Eshnunna and five in the Laws of Hammurabi, and five in the Laws of Eshnunna in which the injured party was not killed and twenty-eight in the Laws of Hammurabi.[106]

Death penalty statutes in which the injured party dies

LE 24—causes death of a wrongly distrained wife or child

LE 58—wall owner notified that wall is buckling but does not reinforce it, causes death of a child of a free man

LH 116—causes death of a legally distrained child

LH 153—wife causes death of her husband because of another man

LH 210—free man causes death of the daughter of a free man

LH 229—builder constructs shoddy house, causing death of homeowner

LH 230—builder constructs shoddy house, causing death of home-owner's son

Death penalty statutes in which the injured party does not die

LE 12—probable robber seized in field at night

LE 13—probably robber (and potential killer) seized in house at night

LE 26—rapes betrothed bride

LE 28—married woman seized in lap of a man not her husband

LE 60—negligent guard of a burglarized house[107]

LH 1—accuses another of homicide but cannot prove it

LH 2—accuses another of witchcraft but cannot prove it

LH 3—accuses another of a capital crime but cannot prove it

105 The percentage for the prevalence of the death penalty is only a rough guide, since at times the division into statutes is debatable. The number of statutes for the Laws of Eshnunna includes a significant number of statutes prescribing prices, lowering the density of the death penalty. It seems, then, that the difference between the Laws of Eshnunna and the Laws of Hammurabi in regard to the death penalty in general is negligible.

106 The cases in three statutes that prescribe death in the Laws of Hammurabi are unclear, LH M, N, BB.

107 The text is incomplete. See Benno Landsberger, "Jungfräulichkeit," in *Symbolae iuridicae et historicae Martino David dedicatae* (ed. J. A. Ankum et al.; Leiden: Brill, 1968), 2.102.

LH 6—steals or accepts goods belonging to palace
LH 7—purchases from minor son or slave of a free man without contract or witness
LH 8—steals from the palace or temple
LH 9—seller is a fence
LH 10—buyer is a thief
LH 11—owner is a thief
LH 14—kidnaps minor child of a free man
LH 15—enables slave to escape
LH 16—harbors fugitive slave
LH 19—detains slave in own household
LH 21—robber breaks into house
LH 22—robber
LH 25—the one who comes to put out a fire steals goods
LH 26—soldier sends a substitute
LH 33—officer recruits deserters or leads substitutes
LH 34—officer oppresses subordinate
LH 108—female innkeeper accepts only silver
LH 109—female innkeeper does not arrest or report criminals
LH 110—priestess opens tavern or enters tavern
LH 129—wife commits adultery
LH 130—rapes betrothed bride
LH 133b—wife of captured man enters another man's house
LH 143—wife behaves wayward
LH 155—father-in-law engages in sexual intimacy with daughter-in-law
LH 157—son engages in sexual intimacy with mother after father's death

The percentage of the cases in which no one is killed but the penalty is death is roughly the same in both law collections. Thus, both law collections impose death when no one is killed when the offense is deemed serious.

(3) However, where the Laws of Hammurabi differs from the Laws of Eshnunna and other law collections is that it prescribes the death penalty for an innocent person. In LH 116, a lender causes the death of a legally distrained child, but it is the lender's child who pays the ultimate price. In LH 210, a free man causes the death of the daughter of a free man, and it is his daughter who is executed. In LH 230, a builder

constructs a shoddy house, causing death of the homeowner's son, and the builder's son is the one who is put to death. The death penalty for an innocent person is most likely a distinctive viewpoint of the scribe who wrote the statutes of the Laws of Hammurabi: it seemed clear to him that the appropriate penalty was death of the corresponding family member of the offender, not the offender himself. It is less likely to have been a characteristic thought-pattern of Hammurabi since this is not reflected in his letters dealing with legal and administrative matters. The appearance of the vicarious death penalty in the Laws of Hammurabi is more an expression of what seemed just to the scribe authoring the statutes than what was historically applied as a remedy. It is poetic justice.

(4) Recourse to the death penalty leads to what may seem to be a bizarre and alarming increase in the severity of punishment:

> LH 8
> If a man steals an ox, a sheep, a donkey, a pig, or a boat, if it belongs either to a god or to the palace, he shall give thirtyfold; if it belongs to a commoner / palace dependent, he shall replace it tenfold; if the thief has nothing to give, he shall be killed.

The death penalty for offenders who could not pay in the case of theft reflects the idiosyncracies of employing the death penalty in the case of serious offenses.[108] This is in stark contrast to other provisions in the Laws of Hammurabi on theft. The penalty in LH 259–260 for stealing agricultural items is reasonably close to the value of those items. Yet in the statute under discussion, LH 8, even the penalty for stealing the animals mentioned or a boat is many times the value of the item stolen. The compensation scheme seems illogical,[109] but the reason for the cognitive disjunction is that property of a temple or palace and those dependent on the protection of the palace ought to be protected with an outsize punishment, whether compensation or death. This principle is mirrored in LH 6:

> If a man steals valuables belonging to a god or the palace, that man shall be killed, and the one who received the stolen items shall be killed.

[108] Perhaps the cognitive disjunction reflects the hand of more than one scribe in the Laws of Hammurabi.

[109] Bottéro, "The 'Code' of Hammurabi," 162–163.

The intervening statute prescribes death for what is likely theft:

> LH 7
>
> If a man should purchase silver, gold, a male slave, a female slave, an ox, a sheep, a donkey, or anything else whatsoever, from a minor son of a free man or from the slave of a free man without witnesses or a contract, or if he accepts goods for safekeeping, that man is a thief; he shall be killed.

The severe penalty is applied to those who have access to their father's or master's property and who can easily commit theft.[110]

Prescribing the death penalty for innocent people is characteristic of the Laws of Hammurabi, and its parameters are revealed in the case of the faulty builder, who is to suffer the same type of harm from the perspective of the male head of the household:

> LH 229
>
> If a builder constructs a house for a free man but does not make his work sound and the house that he constructs collapses and causes the death of the householder, that builder shall be killed.
>
> LH 230
>
> If it causes the death of a son of the householder, they shall kill a son of that builder.

The punishment was deemed proportional to the offense by the scribe composing the statutes.[111] The severe penalty of the son's death is meted out to those in our eyes who do not deserve it but to the eyes of the scribe did.[112]

[110] LE 15 also prohibits purchasing goods or accepting silver from a slave, but no penalty is prescribed.

[111] Westbrook argued that the imposition of the penalty on the builder's son is a mitigation of the penalty: the penalty is limited to the son and does not encompass the builder himself (*Studies in Biblical and Cuneiform Law* [Paris: Gabalda, 1988], 56–57). It is a step in the direction of leniency only from the viewpoint of the head of the family, the builder, and Yaron observed that the penalty seems odd to us because we assume that liability falls upon the individual who committed the offense ("The Nature of the Early Mesopotamian Collections of Law: Another Approach," in *La Codification des Lois dans l'Antiquité* [ed. Ed. Lévy; Paris: De Boccard, 2000], 69). In general, vicarious punishment is an outlier in Mesopotamian law. Even in the Laws of Hammurabi, punishment falls upon the offender most of the time.

[112] In LE 58, the case of the owner of a buckling wall that fell and caused a death is deemed a capital case, but a warning to the owner is mandated. This is, therefore, a somewhat different case from that of the builder, who is a professional, like the physician, and who should have careful not to err in his work.

Correction was inflicted on those who deserved it, even if the one harmed was not necessarily the offender.

Of course, many scenarios presenting problems for the application of this remedy can be imagined. If the law stipulates that the builder's son must be killed if the homeowner's son is killed in the collapse of the house, what happens if the builder has no sons? What if the homeowner is killed in the collapse but the builder has already died—and so on and so forth? The cases addressed fill out a limited continuum of variants. Other considerations could have been applied in these statutes. LH 232, about the damage to property and compensation for it, could have been included in LH 229–230 since it would be a strange collapse of a house that killed a person but did not damage property. LH 9 shows that damages could be assessed from a dead man's estate, so it is possible that the same remedy could have been applied if the builder were dead. But poetic justice was how the remedy was articulated.

The punishment inflicted on the son of the builder employs legal analogy and reveals how the scribe conceived of the cases he was articulating, even though he never articulated the concept informing such cases. Analogously, in LH 116, a lender causes the death of a legally distrained child, but it is the lender's child who pays the ultimate price. In LH 210, a free man causes the death of the daughter of a free man, and it is his daughter who is executed. The implicit analogy between cases reflects the scribe's thinking.[113] It is the intellectual precursor of explicit and ordinary application of legal concepts and principles. The law is based on a common rationale. What applies to all members of one class is applied to all the members of another class. These analogies seem for the most part to be straightforward and even plausible. But an analogy may lead to startling consequences. The use of analogy for vicarious punishment is clear, yet it leads to a punishment that is bizarre and alarming: How is the builder's son at fault for his father's malfeasance?

Poetic justice informs other remedies in the Laws of Hammurabi. It is reflected in the odd means of employing the death penalty in LH 25: a person who has ostensibly come to help put out a fire in a house but steals household items is to be thrown in that fire. The way the statute is articulated makes it appear as if there is no trial—How else could the thief be arrested on the spot

[113] Other instances of poetic justice are found in LH 253, where the tenant farmer who steals grain is to have his hand cut off, and LH 256, where the tenant farmer who hires out the plow team or steals seed and then cannot pay the proper rental is to be dragged around in the field by the plow team.

and thrown into the fire?[114] But the penalty is an expression of what was perceived to be just.[115]

Poetic justice also informs another type of penalty, mutilation, characteristic of the Laws of Hammurabi among the cuneiform law collections. In the set of statutes on the physician,[116] malpractice is to be remedied with compensation in LH 215–220, except in one situation. The physician who blinds a free man is to have his hand cut off; the hand that did the faulty surgery is punished (LH 218).[117]

LH 215

If a physician has made a deep incision in a free man with a lancet of bronze and has saved the man's life or has opened the temple of a free man with a lancet of bronze and has saved his eye, he shall take 10 shekels of silver.

LH 216

If (the patient is) a commoner / palace dependent, he shall take 5 shekels of silver.

LH 217

If (the patient is) a slave of a free man, the master of the slave shall give 2 shekels of silver to the surgeon.

LH 218

If a surgeon has made a deep incision in a free man with a lancet of bronze and has caused the man's death or has opened the temple of a free man with a lancet of bronze and so has destroyed his eye, they shall cut off his forearm.

LH 219

If a surgeon has made a deep incision in a slave of a commoner / palace dependent and causes his death, he shall replace slave for slave.[118]

114 Driver and Miles, *The Babylonian Laws*, 1.111.

115 In the same vein, the barber who removes a slave mark is to lose his own hand (LH 226).

116 While there were magical experts who performed healings, there is no hint of this with the statutes on the physician.

117 The nature of the eye surgery addressed in this series is explored by M. Stol, "Old Babylonian Ophthalmology," in *Reflets des deux fleuves, Volume de Mélanges offerts à André Finet* (ed. M. LeBeau and P. Talon; Leuven: Peeters, 1989), 163–166.

118 A scribal error has crept into the Laws of Hammurabi in this section. LH 217 addresses the surgery performed successfully on a free man's slave, while LH 219 addresses the failure of surgery performed on the slave of a commoner / palace dependent, a status to which no reference had been made before in the medical statutes. We would have expected LH 219 to have dealt with the parallel case to LH 217, the failure of surgery on a free man's slave rather than the commoner / palace dependent's slave. Moreover, there is no parallel to LH 216, surgery on a commoner / palace dependent. It is reasonable to suppose that the copyist/engraver had a text that included statutes on the failed surgery on a commoner/palace dependent and on the free man's slave and accidentally conflated the two,

LH 220
If he has opened the carbuncle with a lancet of bronze and has destroyed his eye, he shall pay half his price in silver.

Two cases of surgery are mentioned: (1) the deep incision, a case of serious surgery, and (2) the eye operation, mentioned specifically because of the prevalence of eye diseases or because it is an operation that consists of a shallow incision that can have severe consequences. The penalty by mutilation of the surgeon in LH 218 is an expression of the drafter's conception of justice. It could not invariably be inflicted in actual legal proceedings because it would have to be proven in court that death or loss of an eye was due to the physician's error rather than to demons or the ill-will of a god, and even if it was deemed to be the surgeon's fault, presumably the parties could resort to an agreement on compensation.[119] Most crucially, such a penalty, even the remote possibility of such a penalty, would deter many physicians from attempting serious surgery or even from practicing medicine and reflects the distance of the Laws of Hammurabi from actual practice. The penalty flows from the principle that the errant body part must be punished by removal: the physician erred with his hand, so his hand must be cut off. Mutilation is more a literary utterance expressing poetic justice rather than a prescription for actual punishment.

The case of faulty surgery is not found in other law collections. but the offense of personal injury is. The Laws of Hammurabi differs from its predecessors in charting its own course by ordaining mutilation for bodily injuries. The Laws of Ur-Namma (LU 16–22) and the Laws of Eshnunna (LE 42–47A) prescribe compensation for personal injury. Monetary amounts are considered just reparation—and to an extent, this is also the case for the Laws of Hammurabi. However, the Laws of Hammurabi prescribes that in certain circumstances, mutilation is the proper remedy. What is striking about the deviation from other law collections is that the more severe penalty, mutilation, is imposed on the more privileged class.[120] In LH 196, a free man destroys a free man's eye, and therefore his eye is to be destroyed. In LH 197,

creating a statute on the commoner / palace dependent's slave. See Driver and Miles, *The Babylonian Laws*, 1.419.

[119] Driver and Miles, *The Babylonian Laws*, 1.420.
[120] John Sassoon, *Ancient Laws and Modern Problems: The Balance between Justice and a Legal System* (London: Third Millennium, 2001), 130–142.

a free man breaks a free man's bone, and therefore his bone is to be broken. In LH 200, a free man knocks out a free man's tooth, and therefore his tooth is to be knocked out, and in LH 202, a free man slaps the cheek of a free man of higher status, and therefore he is punished with sixty strokes of a whip in the assembly. While other statutes, not surprisingly, ordain compensation for a free man inflicting bodily assault on those of lower rank, the severe penalty of mutilation is imposed on a man of privileged rank assaulting those of his own class. We might expect mutilation emphasized as the penalty for those of lower rank assaulting those of higher rank, but that is not highlighted in statutes on bodily assault. We would not be surprised if lower-ranked offenders are to be mutilated, and this is sometimes the case.[121] The scribe departs from compensation for bodily injuries and dictates mutilation upon those of higher class. Strikingly, the more severe penalty is to be applied to those of higher rank.

Mutilation for higher-ranked offenders is also the case in other instances. The free man who is hired to take care of another free man's field but steals the seed or fodder is to have his hand cut off (LH 253). If the field remains uncultivated and the free man cannot deliver the expected amount of grain, he is to be dragged around the field by the ox team (LH 256). The free man who casts aspersions upon an *ugbabtu*, a priestess of high rank, or against another man's wife but cannot prove them is to be flogged and shaven (LH 127). We might expect leniency before the law for the privileged class, but here the opposite is the case.

The application of identical and similar penalties is another method of systematization and conceptualization. It operates within adjacent statutes within a set and across clusters and sets of statutes. The scribe applied the vicarious death penalty as the remedy for serious offenses, and he employed poetic justice as a means of shaping the appropriate penalty, even in alarming ways. He prescribed mutilation, especially on the privileged class, as the just sanction.

[121] A son who strikes his father is to lose his hand (LH 195). A slave of a free man who strikes the son of a free man (LH 205) or who denies his owner (LH 282) is to lose his ear. LH 192–194 addresses adoptees who try to repudiate an adoption or a wet nurse who fails to inform her employers that an infant had died under her care.

4.5.5. Other Methods of Systematization and Conceptualization

Other methods of composition are employed infrequently by the scribe to produce systematization and conceptualization in the Laws of Hammurabi. Matters not addressed in earlier law collections and scribal exercises are tackled. Statutes deal with a group of variables that are treated in separate statutes in other law collections. And finally, a few copies of the Laws of Hammurabi contain rubric titles.

The scribe addressed issues that were completely omitted in prior law collections—military matters, for example. Statutes address conscription, military discipline, misuse of authority by officers, and soldiers' families, not conduct on the battlefield or illicit activities in war. Prior law collections were not concerned at all about these issues.

Another means of systematization is found in statutes that combine variables:

> <u>LH 8</u>
> If a man steals an ox, a sheep, a donkey, a pig, or a boat, if it belongs either to a god or to the palace, he shall give thirtyfold; if it belongs to a commoner / palace dependent, he shall replace it tenfold; if the thief has nothing to give, he shall be killed.

By contrast, other law collections have separate statutes on the same offense, even though the offense and the remedy are otherwise the same:

> <u>HL 57</u>
> If anyone steals a bull—if it is a weanling calf, it is not a "bull"; if it is a yearling calf, it is not a "bull"; if it is a two-year-old bovine, that is a "bull." Formerly, they gave 30 cattle. But now he shall give 15 cattle, 5 two-year-olds, 5 yearlings, and 5 weanlings. He shall look to his house for it.
>
> <u>HL 58</u>
> If anyone steals a stallion—if it is a weanling, it is not a "stallion"; if it is a yearling, it is not a "stallion"; if it is a two-year-old, that is a "stallion." Formerly, they gave 30 horses. But now he shall give 15 horses, 5 two-year-olds, 5 yearlings, and 5 weanlings. He shall look to his house for it.

HL 59

If anyone steals a ram, they used to give 30 sheep. Now he shall give [15] sheep; he shall give 5 ewes, 5 wethers, and 5 lambs. He shall look to his house for it.[122]

The scribe drafting the Hittite Laws articulated only one variable at a time and therefore had to repeat himself in order to express the options. By contrast, the statute in the Laws of Hammurabi combines variables. This method is employed sparingly in the Laws of Hammurabi.

Explicit conceptualization is expressed in three Old Babylonian copies of the Laws of Hammurabi that contain rubric titles for a statute or a set of statutes, manuscripts S, r, and t.[123] The rubric titles use the Sumerian term for "legal decision, ordinance," then state the topic. Manuscript S has the title for LH 113 as DI.DAB$_5$.BA NÍG É ZIG^{ga}, "ordinance concerning property taken from a house," and for LH 120–121 as DI.DAB$_5$.BA É NI.[DUB], "ordinance concerning storage." Manuscript r introduces LH 26 as DI.DAB$_5$.BA AGA.US ù ŠU.KU$_6$, "ordinance concerning soldier and fisherman," and LH 36 as DI.DAB$_5$.BA A.ŠÀ ^{giš}KIRI ù É, "ordinance concerning field, orchard, and house." Manuscript t places [DI.DAB$_5$.BA KA.KEŠDA]$^{\underline{hi.a}}$ [ù NÌ.SA$_{10}$].MA, "ordinance concerning [contracts of hire and acquis]ition," in the gap before LH H.[124] It may also have a title to LH 117–119 that may be restored as [DI.DAB$_5$.BA] ki-iš-ša-a-[tim], "ordinance concerning distraint."[125] If so, it has a similar title to what manuscript S has before LH 120, "ordinance concerning . . . and storage," and manuscripts S and t might be related, either as copies of a shared text or as texts produced in the same scribal workshop.

The logic of the rubric titles in manuscript r are telling because we may quibble with the reasoning:[126] that a new title given before LH 36 would seem to indicate a change in topic, but LH 36 still deals with offenses against a soldier or fisherman. Moreover, even though modern editions separate LH 35 from LH 36 in numbering, LH 36 appears to be a clarification of LH 35. But

[122] Translation by Hoffner, in Roth, *Law Collections*, 226.

[123] Manuscript S is found in E. Bergmann, *Codex Hammurabi textus primigenius* (Rome: Pontificium Institutum Biblicum, 1953), 41. Manuscript r is Finkelstein, "A Late Old Babylonian Copy of the Laws of Hammurapi," 40–43. Manuscript t is V. Donbaz and H. Sauren, "NI 2553 + 2565: A Missing Link of the Hammurabi Law Code," *Or* NS 22 (1991), 5–28; Finkelstein, "A Late Old Babylonian Copy of the Laws of Hammurapi," 39 n.2 and 48.

[124] Reconstruction follows Sauren and Donbaz, "NI 2553 + 2565," 8.

[125] Driver and Miles, *The Babylonian Laws*, 17 n.6, but Sauren and Donbaz believed that the text was too broken and analyzed only the words that were clear and uncontestable ("NI 2553 + 2565," 15).

[126] Van De Mieroop, *Philosophy before the Greeks*, 164.

it is true that the issues facing the soldier and fisherman in LH 36 concern a field, orchard, and house. So the reasoning does make sense, even if we might divide it differently.[127]

Our discussion of lesser-used methods of systematization and conceptualization is the place to discuss the road not taken, that is, methods of composition not employed in the statutes. Another major genre of Mesopotamian literature, omen texts, contains omens expressed casuistically in conditional sentences. Some omens were based on empirical observation, but the vast majority of omens were generated by scribal reasoning.[128] This is similar to the statutes in the Laws of Hammurabi in that a scribe drew from his experience in composing statutes from a standard repertoire of cases. The principles of composition, however, are generally distinct. Omens varied based on spatial orientation, numbers, colors, and other variables that are not elaborated upon in statutes, and we can assume that they were not considered relevant in legal matters. Alternative apodoses occur in omens but not in statutes. The only example that is a remote parallel is the proviso in LH 129 after the directive in the apodosis that if a husband allows his adulterous wife to live, the king will allow her paramour to live. Otherwise, secondary remedies do not occur in statutes the way alternative forecasts appear in omens. Furthermore, casuistic law lends itself to the expression of principles since legal disputes that actually arise present more variables, and it is the task of the person(s) adjudicating the dispute to decide which are the decisive elements that prompt the remedy. By contrast, the details of a phenomenon portrayed in the protasis of an omen seem less subject to conceptualization: the specific elements directly lead to the forecast in the apodosis, and variation would lead to a different forecast. Nonetheless, the hermeneutics of omen literature is a meaningful analog to the law collections, even if applying the methods of composition of omen literature to statutes was not employed.

[127] Joachim Oelsner argued that the internal structure was known from the time of composition of the Laws of Hammurabi, even if the rubric titles only appear later, and was preserved in the manuscript tradition ("Zur Einteilung des Kodex Ḫammu-rāpi im Altertum," 79–125).

[128] The most significant advance in the analysis of the methods of composition of omen literature is Winitzer, *Early Mesopotamian Divination Literature*. See also J. C. Fincke, "Omina, die göttlichen 'Gesetze' der Divination," *JEOL* 40 (2006–2007), 131–147; A. Guinan, "Laws and Omens: Obverse and Inverse," in *Divination in the Ancient Near East: A Workshop on Divination Conducted during the 54th Rencontre Internationale, Würzburg 2008* (ed. J. C. Fincke), 105–121; Koch, *Mesopotamian Divination Texts*.

4.6. Conclusion

The scribe who drafted the statutes in the Laws of Hammurabi advanced toward the systematic analysis of legal issues. This may be described as a bland drift because Mesopotamian scribes articulated law in concrete terms, and they did not formulate abstract concepts or articulate legal principles. They expressed law in casuistic formulation, a type of literary expression that prompts conceptual reasoning. This was true as well for the scribe who drafted the statutes in the Laws of Hammurabi. He did advance his composition beyond earlier law collections by employing a number of innovative methods of composition. He aspired toward greater systematization and conceptualization. He organized the statutes into extensive clusters on a major theme and composed sets of statutes built on incremental variants. The scribe integrated diverse disputes that were independent in earlier law collections, and in the process the scribe reshaped and transformed them. He added explanations to clarify the remedy or to provide a rationale for the penalty. He applied identical and similar types of punishments across varied cases to create a sense of logical unity and systematic logic.

The scribe had the ability to advance toward systematization and conceptualization because of a scribal tradition prevailing in Mesopotamia. A scribe would demonstrate his legal talent and skills by revising and revamping a repertoire of standard cases. During his education, a scribe studied legal concepts and institutions, acquired legal terminology and textual patterns, and absorbed their worldview. Later on, he employed his legal knowledge when called upon to draft legal documents and administrative texts. When composing statutes for a law collection or student exercise, he applied his education and experience. The resulting statutes mirrored both law as it was practiced and law as it should be according to the scribe's viewpoint.

Flowing together in the Laws of Hammurabi are proclivities of the human intellect in general and of Mesopotamian knowledge in particular. Law in casuistic form makes sense in general. At the same time, characteristics specific to Mesopotamian thinking flowed together in the composing of the statutes of the Laws of Hammurabi: the disposition to organize knowledge into lists, and the propensity to articulate knowledge in casuistic form. The casuistic formulation of the statutes in the Laws of Hammurabi originates in the tendency of Mesopotamian scribes to articulate knowledge in lists of casuistically formulated statements. They conveyed law in the form of detailed cases, not as general principles.

With the Laws of Hammurabi, the scribe manifested legal thinking even though he lived in a society that did not have philosophical or jurisprudential writing about law. His predilection toward systematization and conceptualization is informed by his reasoning about law, even if developed arguments are absent. Principles and generalizations are implicitly presented, and in rare instances, the scribe offered explanatory comments to clarify the remedy or to highlight the severity of the offense and the need for deservedly harsh punishment.

Excursus

Scribes and Scribal Education

The way Mesopotamian scribes composed the statutes of the Laws of Hammurabi, by improvising on a traditional repertoire of cases, developed out of the system in which they were educated. The mode of education that scribes received instilled a process of composition in which scribes composed later works partially out of the web of the memorized words of earlier works. Scribes mastered a rich store of standard texts and absorbed their elements. This means of learning had a profound influence on the way Mesopotamian scribes wrote legal texts: when they created their own legal texts, they recalled legal terminology and textual structures and recombined and transformed them in their own compositions. Scribes were trained to recall textual forms and vocabulary, and in so doing, they were able to recall their components and allude, echo, and otherwise reshape them in their own writing.

E.1. The Purpose of Scribal Education: Mastery of Material

Scribes studied a standard set of texts, and while a primary purpose was to learn the writing system, there was a larger goal. Budding scribes were inspired to assimilate wording and phraseology.[1] The curriculum incorporated exercises in legal writing as well as typical legal cases so that students absorbed legal terminology and concepts.

It is crucial to recognize that scribes learned legal phrases, forms, topics, cases, practices, and concepts in order to use them as a repertoire from which they could draft appropriate wording. Mastery of material meant keeping it in memory, and this enabled fluid use of material in writing out a text for future

[1] David M. Carr, *Writing on the Tablet of the Heart: Origins of Scripture and Literature* (Oxford: Oxford University Press, 2005), 35–36.

The Laws of Hammurabi. Pamela Barmash, Oxford University Press (2020). © Oxford University Press.
DOI: 10.1093/oso/9780197525401.001.0001.

clients' needs. By dint of their knowledge, scribes solidified their hold on the legal arena. Scribes would rely on the stock of legal phrases and concepts in their memory in order to write out a document for a client. Legal texts of all kinds and listings of legal terminology that scribes copied, learned, and kept in their memory served as a cistern from which scribes could draw legal locutions and mechanisms as needed. It is crucial to move away from the image of scribes mindlessly copying a text. Rather, in their schooling, they copied text in order to know them, as an aid to memorization. Later on, they created texts out of the compositional elements they had learned. Scribes were able to express themselves through recalling quotations of earlier works.[2] They articulated new works through similar language, motifs, and concepts. Scribes who mastered the tradition used it as building blocks, whether of phraseology, topics, or textual structures in composing a new work.

While it may be no surprise that a text was as much a part of mental memory as a physical reality, it is crucial to recognize that the physical challenge of reading a text contributed to the knowledge of its contents through approximate memorization. The signs were small, and reading tablets may have required bright sunlight. Information retrieval increased as the reader possessed greater familiarity with the possible contents of the text. It is useful to recall an analysis of the ways a scribe would have operated:

> The primary function of a scribe . . . is that of one whose work consists in transcribing a text by his own hand. I use the word transcribe deliberately. The scribe may, in effect, perform his professional work in one of three ways, or by a combination of one or two or all three of them. He may, on the one hand, copy out his text by eye having beside him the exemplar to be transcribed. This method relies on the purely visual medium and the regular split-second effort of memory with or without oral repetition of what he is transcribing. On the other hand, he may transcribe his text from dictation. This method relies on the purely aural medium and aural memory with perhaps again some oral repetition of what has just been read to him for transcription. Or, as a third way, he may transcribe his text from memory. And here we must remark that our modern conception of memory has been modelled and seriously affected by the advent, diffusion, general use and plenty of the printed word.[3]

[2] Carr, *Writing on the Tablet of the Heart*, 162.

[3] Malachi Martin, *The Scribal Character of the Dead Sea Scrolls* (Bibliothèque du Muséon 44–45; Louvain: Publications universitaires, 1958), 1.6.

This third way accords with the ways Mesopotamian scribes were educated. It is no surprise, therefore, that in composing a new text, scribes drew from their verbatim memory of other texts and quoted, revised, alluded to, borrowed from, and transformed their wording. Of course, it was only the more talented (and fortunate and ambitious) scribes who became men (and women) of letters who had the opportunity to write down their own thoughts and compose their own works, rather than only boilerplate documents.

In an arresting statement from a later period, Babylonian scribes from the Neo-Assyrian period attest to their competence by declaring in a letter that they have stored the entire corpus of scribal learning (*kullat ṭupšarrūtu*) in their mind like goods in a repository.[4] They claim to have memorized the entire corpus of texts they have read and collated. While this may have been an exaggeration, the claim exemplified the qualifications of the best scribes. They have not merely gone through a text—they have absorbed its contents.

Scribal education served to shape the thought patterns of those who were educated. So while memorizing legal terminology, concepts, and devices for quick access was part of the process of professionalization for scribes, at the same time it became part of the enculturation of an elite, those who knew how to read. Those who went through scribal education possessed an oral and written mastery of a body of cultural knowledge as well as of a set of phraseology, concepts, and textual structures, and that cultural knowledge included law.

E.2. Curriculum

Although tablets produced by students were meant to be ephemeral, a number of those tablets have fortunately been preserved, allowing us to reconstruct the curriculum. These tablets were created as part of the process of training and memorization, and only by chance were they saved rather than recycled.[5] The providential existence of these school tablets permits us to re-create the scribal curriculum from its most elementary level to more advanced stages.

Clumsy writing on a number of tablets reflects the awkward efforts of students just beginning to learn writing, and preparatory exercises trained

[4] Grant Frame and A. R. George, "The Royal Libraries of Nineveh: New Evidence for King Ashurbanipal's Tablet Collecting," *Iraq* 67 (2005), 272, 275.

[5] Jeremy Black, *The Literature of Ancient Sumer* (Oxford: Oxford University Press, 2004), 275.

students in the basic mechanics of inscribing wedges.[6] After they learned the basics of forming wedges in varying orientations, they began to study lexical lists, compositions consisting of lists of words in Sumerian with their Akkadian equivalents. The extant lexical lists are more advanced compositionally than the ones students learned, but we can extrapolate the more elementary lists from them. The lexical list HAR-ra originally began with the list of trees, tablet III of the canonical composition.[7] The other lexical lists contained the names of objects made of reed, leather, and metal; names of towns, rivers, and canals; and professions, and the main purpose of these catalogs of signs was to enable students to learn how to write the signs. It is debatable as to whether this was the sole purpose of the lexical lists: the oral explanation that teachers most likely supplied along with the texts has been lost.[8]

It is crucial to note that the lexical lists introduced students to the writing of Sumerian, a language they did not speak or know: as one scholar puts it, "To learn to write is to learn Sumerian."[9] The students in the scribal schools of the late third and second millennia BCE learned how to write their native language by learning how to write a dead language.

As students progressed beyond the lexical lists, the first stage of their elementary education, they started to learn lists of legal terminology. They studied tablets I and II of HAR-ra, which apparently is derived from multiple sources, such as a list of legal terms, phrases from the old collections of model contracts, and excerpts from Proto-Izi, and was compiled in Old Babylonian times, with the oldest dated version from the first year of Samsuiluna.[10] Another school text of legal phrases, *ana ittišu*, derives from the contract literature of Neo-Sumerian and Old Babylonian times: it is an anthology

[6] Steven Tinney, "Texts, Tablets, and Teaching," *Expedition* 40/2 (1998), 40–52; Karel van der Toorn, *Scribal Culture and the Making of the Hebrew Bible* (Cambridge, Mass.: Harvard University Press, 2007), 54–67.

[7] See William W. Hallo, "Notes from the Babylonian Collection, II: Old Babylonian HAR-ra," *JCS* 34 (1982), 86–88.

[8] Samuel Noah Kramer, *The Sumerians: Their History, Culture, and Character* (Chicago: University of Chicago Press, 1963), 234–235. The lexical list format may have continued as part of advanced education. In TIN.TIR, a set of scholastic lists of the topography and monuments of the city of Babylon, mutually exclusive explanations are listed side by side without any analysis or evaluation. Niek Veldhuis argued that scholarly argument and rivalry were surely present in Mesopotamia, but new ideas were shaped by the power of traditional textual formats and therefore were set in lists without methodological argument ("TIN.TIR = Babylon, the Question of Canonization and the Production of Meaning," *JCS* 50 [1998], 83–84).

[9] H. L. J. Vanstiphout, "On the Old Babylonian Eduba Curriculum," in *Centres of Learning: Learning and Location in Pre-Modern Europe and the Near East* (ed. Jan Willem Drijvers and Alasdair MacDonald; Leiden: Brill, 1995), 5.

[10] Miguel Civil, "Lexicography," in *Sumerological Studies in Honor of Thorkild Jacobsen* (ed. Åke Sjöberg; AS 20; Chicago: University of Chicago Press, 1970), 127–128. There appears to be some disagreement as to the date of an unpublished tablet of HAR-ra from the Louvre: Civil argued that

of statutes, legal phraseology, and administrative terminology, consisting of Sumerian with a translation into Akkadian.[11] The lists that make up *ana ittišu* and HAR-ra are intended to teach legalese more than they were to teach Sumerian.[12]

Beyond the lexical lists, students were gradually introduced to writing model contracts,[13] court records, and administrative documents toward the end of their elementary education as scribes.[14] Contracts and court records were compiled into collections. An apparently famous homicide case became

the oldest forerunner is from the fifteenth year of Samsuiluna reign, while Hallo dated the unpublished tablet to the first year of his reign, noting that Stephen Lieberman, who promised to publish an edition of HAR-ra I–II but did not, dated it to the fifteenth year. Hallo observed that is possible that HAR-ra I and II may have derived from the standard ledger entries from account texts (John E. Curtis and William W. Hallo, "Money and Merchants in Ur III," *HUCA* 30 (1959), 136; "Notes from the Babylonian Collection II," 85). The schools of Neo-Babylonia and Late Babylonia utilized tablets 1 and 2 of HAR-RA = *ḫubullu* as part of the most elementary level of education. See Petra D. Gesche, *Schulunterricht in Babylonien im ersten Jahrtausend v. Chr.* (AOAT; Münster: Ugarit-Verlag, 2000), 66–80; Niek Veldhuis, "On the Curriculum of the Neo-Babylonian School," *JAOS* 123 (2003), 627–633.

[11] While the copy of the text we have does not date back to the Old Babylonian period, Åke Sjöberg argues that it probably was composed during the Isin dynasty ("The Old Babylonian Eduba," in *Sumerological Studies in Honor of Thorkild Jacobsen* [ed. Åke Sjöberg; AS 20; Chicago: University of Chicago Press, 1970], 164).

[12] Whether the lexical lists were intended to teach students Sumerian is debatable since it would be difficult to learn a language from a list, without instruction in constructing sentences (H. L. J. Vanstiphout, "How Did They Learn Sumerian?," *JCS* 31 [1979], 119). It may be critical to understand that oral instruction accompanied the memorization and copying of the lexical lists, perhaps along the lines of the way vocabulary lists might be used in contemporary schools, when a lexical item is explained with a sentence illustrating its use.

[13] Model contracts in Sumerian have been published in Walter Bodine, *How Mesopotamian Scribes Learned to Write Legal Documents* (Lewiston, Maine: Edwin Mellen, 2014); William W. Hallo, "A Model Court Case Concerning Inheritance," in *Riches Hidden in Secret Places: Ancient Near Eastern Studies in Memory of Thorkild Jacobsen* (ed. Tsvi Abusch; Winona Lake, Ind.: Eisenbrauns, 2002), 141–154; Jacob Klein and Tonia Sharlach, "A Collection of Model Court Cases from Old Babylonian Nippur (CBS 11324)," ZA 97 (2007), 1–25; Martha T. Roth, "Scholastic Tradition and Mesopotamian Law: A Study of FLP 1287, a Prism in the Collection of the Free Library of Philadelphia" (Ph.D. dissertation, University of Pennsylvania, 1979); Roth, "She Will Die by the Iron Dagger," *JESHO* 31 (1988), 195–196 (including two model court cases in Sumerian from the Old Babylonian period concerning adultery); Gabriella Spada, "A Handbook from the Eduba'a: An Old Babylonian Collection of Model Contracts," *ZA* 101 (2011), 204–245; Spada, "Two Old Babylonian Model Contracts," *Cuneiform Digital Library Journal* 2 (2014), 1–13; Spada, *Sumerian Model Contracts from the Old Babylonian Period in the Hilprecht Collection Jena* (Texte und Materialien der Hilprecht Collection 11; Wiesbaden: Harrassowitz, 2018). See also the Old Babylonian Model Contracts project, <http:// oracc.org/obmc>. A. R. George and Gabriella Spada have recently published *Old Babylonian Texts in the Schøyen Collection,* part two: *School Letters, Model Contracts, and Related Texts* (CUSAS: Cornell University Studies in Assyriology and Sumerology; University Park; Pennsylvania State University Press, 2019), which contains twenty-six Sumerian legal texts from the Old Babylonian period.

[14] See Eleanor Robson, "The Tablet House: A Scribal School in Old Babylonian Nippur," *RA* 95 (2001), 39–66. Model contracts and proverbs, the most advanced stage of elementary education, is predominant among the remains from schools in the Old Babylonian period. Generally, half the school texts found are tablets of these genres. Even the "Tablet House," a domicile with many

part of a collection of trials copied by students.[15] The law collections were also incorporated into the curriculum. Parts of the Laws of Lipit-Ishtar were inscribed on small round tablets (so-called lentils) meant for practice.[16] The Sumerian Laws Exercise Tablet (YBC 2177) is a student exercise in legal phraseology, and it is not surprising then that it is dedicated to Nisaba and Haya, gods associated with the scribal arts, not gods of justice. Even model letters addressed legal matters, such as an announcement about a lost seal,[17] business expenses,[18] and legal problems regarding a field.[19]

Among the very first literary compositions that students learned was a hymn to Lipit-Ishtar, king of Isin (1934–1924 BCE), and it extols the link between the scribal arts and justice.[20] It is a hymn exhibiting grammatical simplicity, appropriate as one of the first literary texts for learners, and it is preserved on single-column tablets typical of school compositions. Its sixty-three lines were spread over six 10-line columns, an arrangement suited for the large, inexperienced handwriting of students. This hymn is one of the four compositions of the group termed by scholars as the Tetrad, a collection of four texts that was the first group of literary texts encountered by students entering the advanced level of education beyond the elementary level.[21] The king's fame is described as enduring because of his renown as a scribe, and his training as a scribe is highlighted as the source of his skill as a legislator:

Lipit-Ishtar Hymn B 18–32

Nisaba, the woman radiant with joy,
The true woman scribe, the lady of all knowledge,
Guided your fingers on the clay,

tablets embedded in the building material, which has the least number of such tablets, does have 107 such tablets in a total pool of 558 tablets. The high ratio demonstrates the prevalence of these model contracts and proverbs collections.

[15] See the Nippur Murder Trial in Barmash, *Homicide in the Biblical World*, 151–152, 205–206, 208–209.
[16] Tinney, "On the Curricular Setting of Sumerian Literature," *Iraq* 61 (1999), 167.
[17] Alexandra Kleinerman, *Education in Early 2nd Millennium BC Babylonia: The Sumerian Epistolary Miscellany* (Cuneiform Monographs 42; Leiden: Brill, 2011)
[18] Kleinerman, *Education in Early Second Millennium BC Babylonia*, 161–166.
[19] Kleinerman, *Education in Early Second Millennium BC Babylonia*, 199–200.
[20] Vanstiphout, "Lipit-Eštar's Praise in the Edubba," *JCS* 30 (1978), 33–61; "How Did They Learn Sumerian?" 121–123.
[21] At least as evidenced in Old Babylonian Nippur. See Civil, "Ancient Mediterranean Lexicography," *CANE* 2308; Paul Delnero, "Variation in Sumerian Literary Compositions: A Case Study Based on the Decad" (Ph.D. dissertation, University of Pennsylvania, 2006), 95–97; Kleinerman, *Education in Early Second Millennium BC Babylonia*, 75–81; Tinney, "On the Curricular Setting of Sumerian Literature," 160.

Embellished the writing on the tablets,
Made the hand resplendent with a golden stylus.
The measuring rod, the gleaming surveyor's line,
The cubit ruler which gives wisdom,
Nisaba lavishly bestowed upon you.
Lipit-Ishtar, you are Enlil's son.
Truth and justice you make manifest;
Lord, your goodness covers even the horizon.
King Lipit-Ishtar, counsellor of great judgment,
(Whose) word never falters, wise one (whose) decision provides justice for the people;
Great mind, knowing all things deeply,
In order to lay down the law for all foreign countries,
You perceive falsehood and truth even from the words hidden in the heart.

The king's scribal wisdom informs his knowledge of justice. The section extolling scribal education is followed by praise of Lipit-Ishtar's legislative work. Presumably, students writing out this hymn absorbed the lesson that their education in the scribal arts leads to expertise in the legal realm.

A number of key details about the everyday life of schooling emerge that demonstrate how students acquired a mastery of material, including legal material.[22] Students in Nippur at least took their tablets

[22] It is debated whether schools were run by the state or privately. The evidence is that schools in the Ur III period existed on the grand institutional scale, while they were privately run in the Old Babylonian period. A. R. George argues that the eduba—a formal school with a large teaching staff (i.e., a door monitor, a jug monitor, a Sumerian monitor, etc., in addition to teachers), a large number of students, and a sophisticated and varied curriculum including surveying and music—existed only in the Ur III period: the buildings in which school texts were found in Nippur and Ur from the Old Babylonian period were modest constructions, more characteristic of private dwellings than large-scale academic institutions. See A. R. George, "In Search of the e. d u b. b a: the Ancient Mesopotamian School in Literature and Reality," in *"An Experienced Scribe Who Neglects Nothing": Ancient Near Eastern Studies in Honor of Jacob Klein* (ed. Yitschak Sefati and et al.Bethesda, MD: CDL Press, 2005), 127–137. Contra Sjöberg, "The Old Babylonian Eduba," 176. See also Donald E. McCown and Richard C. Haines, *Nippur I: Temple of Enlil, Scribal Quarter, and Soundings* (Oriental Institute Publications 78; Chicago: University of Chicago Press, 1967), 147–149. One of the Ur III kings, Shulgi, boasted of his connection with the scribal academies, and the terminology used by Shulgi for the academies—é. g é š t u g. ^{d} n i s s a b a. m u l, "House of Wisdom of Starry Nisaba," and k i. ú m u n, "Place of Learning"—are reminiscent of the ceremonial names given to temples. It is surmised that the eduba as an educational institution supported by the state, occupied substantial quarters planned for education, whether entire buildings or a compound of rooms. The formal and institutional character of schools was limited to the period of Ur III alone, when the great demand for scribes for the bureaucracy could not be fulfilled by small-scale operations of the private sector.

home.[23] In Old Babylonian Nippur, three homes close to one another had concentrations of tablets: this could reflect that children from the families who lived there all went to scribal school or that each home had a scribal school, with the scribes living near each other in a scribal quarter.[24] Concentrations of tablets containing school texts in palaces have been found in Old Babylonian remains: at Uruk, lexical lists, syllabaries, multiplication tables, a text containing a dialogue between a dog and another animal, possibly a fox, and an excerpt from a hymn were excavated in the palace of Sînkāšid; at Šaduppûm, lexical texts, geographic lists, and literary texts were discovered in the temple dedicated to Nisaba and her consort Haja, patrons of scribes; and at Larsa, texts with excerpts from literary texts, presumably used for training scribes, were found in the palace of Nūradad. School texts in private homes have been uncovered at Uruk, with large concentrations of many genres found in homes in Ur and Kish, probably indicating the presence of a school at a scribe's house.

The scribal curriculum as evidence in archaeological remains and as described in cuneiform texts is vast, from administrative and legal

(George "In Search of," 131; Hartmut Waetzoldt, "Die Entwicklung der Naturwissenschaften und des Naturwissenschaftlichen Unterrichts in Mesopotamien," in *Naturwissenschaftlicher Unterricht und Wissenskumulation: geschichtliche Entwicklung und gesellschaftliche Auswirkungen* [ed. Johann Georg Hohenzollern and Max Liedtke; Bad Heilbrunn: J. Klinkhardt, 1988], 39). Schooling in the Old Babylonian period was on the small scale, with students learning the scribal craft in the home workshop of a master scribe. Nonetheless, while the formal, state-supported educational system no longer existed, the Sumerian literary corpus had become part of the standard curriculum: the freelance scribes teaching their sons and other boys inducted them in centuries old literature that included texts set in the formal educational institutions of long before. Similar to the traditional training for other crafts, scribal education was run by private individuals. The teacher and students probably sat outside in the courtyard, where the light was strong enabling them to read texts easily. The tablets written by the students were recycled or used as building materials. A box filled with fragments of exercise tablets has been excavated in a home occupied by gala-mah priests in Sippar (Hermann Gasche, *La Babylonia au 17e siecle avant notre ere: Approche archeologique, problemes et perspectives* [Ghent: University of Ghent, 1989], 19, pl. 9), and another box made itself of tablets plastered over and filled with tablet fragments and clay was discovered in a home in Nippur (Robson, "The Tablet House," 44). In Susa, a large jar was found containing both raw clay and exercise tablets (Roman Ghirshman, "Suse au temps des sukkalmah. Campagne des fouilles 1963–1964: Rapport preliminaire," *Arts Asiatiques* 11 [1965], 3–21). Most likely, they were used to store the materials used for making exercise tablets, and those exercise tablets that have survived until today escaped by mere chance the fate of being recycled. Exercise tablets were repeatedly used and erased. They were recycled by softening the clay in water, then twisted and kneaded, and they were destroyed in the course of normal school activities except when events were brought to a sudden end (Civil, *Ea A = naqû, Aa A = naqû, with their Forerunners and Related Texts* [Materials for the Sumerian Lexicon 14; Rome: Ponficium Institutum Biblicum, 1979], 7).

[23] McCown, *Nippur*, 1.148–149.

[24] Sjöberg refers to an intriguing school letter in which the scribal school, eduba, at Nippur is described as unique ("The Old Babylonian Eduba," 176). How the eduba at Nippur was unique is provocative, but what exactly that qualification means is obscure.

documents to mathematics and surveying, and from music and music theory to literature. A student in general was not expected to master all of it. The scribal curriculum surpassed what was necessary in the daily life of a professional scribe. While it is likely that only a few scribes mastered the entirety of the curriculum, its very complexity and scope demonstrate the value placed on absorbing the cultural norms espoused by the texts and on advancing the intellectual abilities of students with challenging material. At the same time, the study of advanced mathematical skills, lists of obscure terms, music theory, and the extinct language Sumerian, even as the language of instruction,[25] developed the intellectual abilities of scribes, perhaps much in the same way that contemporary curricula include many topics beyond students' vocational needs.

It may be worthwhile to understand the Mesopotamian canon as all the compositions that a man of letters is supposed to have read and to which he can relate in a meaningful way.[26] It is a phenomenon of reception, in which new texts are composed to consciously draw on prior ones or to avoid their influences.[27]

Those more advanced in scribal training and proficiency and those higher up in the scribal hierarchy exhibited literary creativity by adapting traditions. Scribes of the Old Babylonian period were committed to the Sumerian tradition. But at the same time they focused on the transmission of Sumerian texts, they created new Akkadian texts, often based on prior Sumerian prototypes. In the invention of the Epic of Gilgamesh, scribes tailored independent stories about Gilgamesh into an integrated larger narrative: independent works in Sumerian were transformed into components of a new Akkadian composition on the same theme.[28] Old Babylonian scribes felt especially free to innovate new traditions when they were making a switch from a Sumerian tradition to an Akkadian recrystallization of that tradition.[29]

A critical aspect of the educational system must be noted. Students were indoctrinated as part of a scribal class that owed allegiance to both itself

[25] One can only speculate whether this means that students were in an immersion method from the onset of their schooling or were slowly eased into speaking Sumerian. See Å. W. (Åke) Sjöberg, "CBS 11319+: An Old Babylonian Schooltext from Nippur," *ZA* 83 (1993), 1.

[26] Veldhuis, "TIN.TIR = Babylon, the Question of Canonization," 79.

[27] There may have been differences in canon between different social groups and geographical areas and in the position a particular text has vis-à-vis the other texts in a canon.

[28] William W. Hallo, "Toward a History of Sumerian Literature," in *Sumerological Studies in Honor of Thorkild Jacobsen* [ed. Åke Sjöberg; AS 20; Chicago: University of Chicago Press, 1970], 189.

[29] Carr, *Writing on the Tablet of the Heart*, 35. See also Jeffery H. Tigay, *The Evolution of the Gilgamesh Epic* (Philadelphia: University of Pennsylvania Press, 1982).

and the king.[30] Royal inscriptions and literary texts about kings, successful and unsuccessful, shaped the way students viewed the relationship between monarchy and the bureaucracy to which they might aspire. The model letters and the law collections that students learned taught them about the role of the king in the legal realm and that he could be appealed to in the case of injustice.[31] Not surprisingly, the format of royal inscriptions was also employed as the textual pattern for law collections.

The contours of Mesopotamian scribal education meant that legal concepts, terminology, textual structures, and institutional procedures were instilled in scribes. They employed this knowledge as needed for composing everyday legal texts and administrative documents. On occasion, they utilized their knowledge to compose statutes on a repertoire of traditional cases and to employ the textual pattern of royal inscriptions for law collections.

E.3. How Were Scribes Employed?

Writing was used for diverse legal and economic functions in a variety of social strata. The occupational titles of scribes in the Old Babylonian period testify to the wide variety of roles they played: *mu.sar*, "name writer," a notary who inscribes seals ad hoc; *kab.sar*, "writer," inscriber of stone of other materials; *dub.sar a.ri.a*, "district scribe"; *dub.sar a-šà.ga*, "field scribe," land registrar; *dub.sar eme kiengira*, professor of Sumerian; *dub.sar erin.na*, scribe for laborer groups; *dub.sar geštu.la*, "deaf writer," probably served as a copyist; *dub.sar gurum.ak*, "administrator"; *dub.sar im.ma*, ordinary clerk; *dub.sar ki.lu-úb.gar.ra*, "military scribe"; *dub.sar NIG.ŠID*, "mathematician."[32]

An examination of the activities of scribes in Old Babylonian Sippar reveals that scribes could work in more than one position at a time: a scribe might be employed at times by an institution, and at other times a scribe would work freelance for private individuals. Many scribes appear to have worked freelance rather than having a permanent position. They could

[30] Piotr Michalowski, "Charisma and Control: On Continuity and Change in Early Mesopotamian Bureaucratic Systems," in *The Organization of Power* (ed. McGuire Gibson and Robert D. Biggs; Studies in Ancient Oriental Civilization 46; Chicago: Oriental Institute of the University of Chicago, 1991), 48.

[31] Kleinerman, *Education in Early Second Millennium BC Babylonia*, 127–140.

[32] These are attested for the Old Babylonian period. See Benno Landsberger, "Babylonian Scribal Craft and Its Terminology," *Proceedings of the Twenty-Third International Congress of Orientalists* (ed. Denis Sinor; London: Royal Asiatic Society, 1954), 123–127.

compose whatever legal document a client wanted since they were trained in legal terminology and textual forms. A person who hired a scribe might often have had a favorite scribe but might also employ other scribes if their favorite was unable to take on the task or charged a fee higher than they were willing to accept.[33] A scribe might work for a number of private individuals on a single day, and even a private household that employed a scribe on a particular day for a particular task might have to summon another scribe if the first one was called away or was otherwise unavailable. A private household might also engage a scribe to provide instruction if the household was wealthy enough. A household that required the services of a scribe might also have a reserve of purified clay that a scribe could use as needed.

Scribal training was advantageous for senior positions in government, probably for most higher ones, and perhaps for the lower ones.[34] The title *dub.sar* held by government officials often did not refer to a specific rank but denoted that an individual had graduated from a scribal school.[35] Royal and temple bureaucracy (as well as private households and commercial firms) required literate personnel in order to function and keep the books.[36] Many served only or primarily as scribes, but a number of those with scribal education served as priests and other members of cult personnel. Scribal education prepared scribes for assisting a judge or eventually to serve as a judge themselves.[37] Royal and state officials included (but not exclusively) those who were literate. The majority of those who were educated in the scribal arts

[33] Michel Tanret, "The Works and the Days . . . : On Scribal Activity in Old Babylonian Sippar-Amnānum," *RA* 98 (2004), 33–62.

[34] A. Leo Oppenheim, "A Note on the Scribes in Mesopotamia," in *Studies in Honor of Benno Landsberger on His Seventy-Fifth Birthday* (AS 16; Chicago, University of Chicago Press, 1965), 253–256. While the overt goal of Oppenheim's article is to demonstrate the political power of scribes, the evidence Oppenheim amassed also sketches how those in close proximity to a king utilized their scribal training. See also Michalowski, "Charisma and Control," 62.

[35] Benno Landsberger, "Scribal Concepts of Education," in *City Invincible* (ed. Carl Kraeling and Robert McC. Adams; Chicago: Oriental Institute, 1967), 99, 118.

[36] Vanstiphout, "Memory and Literacy in Ancient Western Asia," *CANE* 1.2188. While Vanstiphout argued that it is clear from the mass of documents that almost every aspect of social and economic life was managed and supervised, much of this documented in written form, Marc Van De Mieroop has cautioned about falling prey to the massive amount of documentation and assuming that it represents the totality of what was happening (Van De Mieroop, *Cuneiform Texts and the Writing of History*, 86–89). The masses of people were basically left undocumented unless they had some connection with the institutional administration of temples and palaces or had interaction with a private enterprise. Moreover, this documentation was almost entirely concerned with business. Even the documentation from periods for which we have a huge number of texts appears less impressive when we realize the long time span from which they originate. Most importantly, we must keep in mind that documents were drafted only when there was a need. Perhaps one or both parties had suspicions of the other, or they wanted to make a private agreement that skirted the law.

[37] Sjöberg, "The Old Babylonian Eduba," 164–165.

occupied the median of the profession, but a number reached the top levels of administration, where the ability to write and read on one's own would be a benefit. Whether they reached the top due to their literacy alone is doubtful, since it can be assumed that family connections, administrative ability, or luck may have played a decisive part.[38]

The path from scribe to official is also attested in Rome.[39] Those skilled in writing progressed to the profession of law as administrators, secretaries, and notaries. By the fourth century CE, a number had entered the Roman Senate, and one senator complained that the sons of sausage-makers were becoming senators based only on their skills in taking dictation.

E.4. Who Could Read?

The question of literacy in Mesopotamia is critical. The scholarly consensus for a long time was that the ability to read was greatly limited, but in recent decades the question has been reconsidered. Literacy is now considered to have spread beyond a scribal elite to others whose professional duties would have been greatly enhanced by an ability to read and write. Nonetheless, it should be noted that the overwhelming majority of Mesopotamians were illiterate. Mesopotamia was not a bookish society, akin to that which has existed since the development of mass-produced texts in the modern period.[40] The segment of society that had the ability to compose and read the contents of written works was very modest. It is crucial to note that the ability to decipher a contract does not necessarily correlate to a person's capacity to write, copy, or read a text, either of the same literary register or higher. It may be that a person who could read a contract might not have been able to write one, or even that someone who could write a contract might not be capable of writing a text of greater complexity.

[38] A study of an Old Babylonian official, Utul-Ishtar, demonstrates that he held the title of scribe while advancing through the bureaucracy to the superior status of being in charge of crown lands. See Yoffee, *The Economic Role of the Crown*, 18–76. The career of another scribe, Ile''i-Marduk, from the Neo-Babylonian period demonstrates that he began work as a member of a limited group of scribes who recorded legal proceedings supervised by royal judges and later served as a royal judge in Uruk. His earlier career as a scribe prepared him for advancement in the legal profession. See Shalom E. Holtz, "The Career of a Neo-Babylonian Court Scribe," *JCS* 60 (2008), 81–85.

[39] Hillel Schwartz, *The Culture of the Copy: Striking Likenesses, Unreasonable Facsimiles* (New York: Zone Books, 1996), 214.

[40] See the comparable situation in a society with somewhat wider literacy, Martin Jaffee, *Torah in the Mouth: Written and Oral Tradition in Palestinian Judaism, 200 BCE–400 CE* (Oxford: Oxford University Press, 2001), 15.

It has been argued that the mixture of phonetic and logographic writing in the cuneiform system made scribal education long and complex and severely limited literacy: therefore, the ability to read was limited to an elite.[41] Piotr Michalowski argued that literacy was greatly limited in general in the ancient Near East and that only scribes and some government and temple officials could read and write.[42] However, those who used cuneiform for business documents and letters employed a less expansive and less complex set of signs. A number of scholars have noted the pervasiveness of written documents in Mesopotamian society and emphasized that literacy must have been more widespread than generally assumed. Herman Vanstiphout highlighted the importance of written documents and suggested that even though the spread and rate of literacy are uncertain, it must have been more widespread.[43] J. N. Postgate flagged the existence of private correspondence of a trivial nature and of the frequent use of inscribed clay labels, testifying to the use of writing in the far from momentous activities of society.[44] Claus Wilcke observed that (1) documents have been excavated from so many private residences and (2) a number of documents show in their first-person wording and their deviations from scribal norms that they were written by laypeople, not professional scribes.[45] Others have argued for a middle position: more literacy than assumed in the past yet with reservations. Marc Van De Mieroop has emphasized that there were different levels of literacy and that those who had a modest understanding of cuneiform would not have been able to comprehend complex texts.[46] Dominique Charpin has argued that merchants, accountants, and military officers had an interest in being literate and that there was a chronological increase in the writing down of texts, perhaps in competition with the spread of alphabetic writing systems.[47]

[41] Oppenheim, "The Position of the Intellectual in Mesopotamian Society," 39.

[42] Michalowski, "Sumerian Literature: An Overview," *CANE*, 2279.

[43] Vanstiphout, "Memory and Literacy in Ancient Western Asia," *CANE*, 2181–2196.

[44] Postgate, *Early Mesopotamia*, 69.

[45] Claus Wilcke, *Wer las und schrieb in Babylonien und Assyrien: Überlegungen zur Literalität im Alten Zweistromland* (Munich: C. H. Beck, 2000), 34–49.

[46] Van De Mieroop, *Philosophy before the Greeks*, 10.

[47] Dominique Charpin, *Writing, Law, and Kingship in Old Babylonian Mesopotamia* (Chicago: University of Chicago Press, 2010), 7–24. It must be emphasized that our knowledge of Sumerian from the Old Babylonian period consists entirely of the discarded exercises of schoolboys and a few schoolgirls. We lack any evidence for the existence of libraries—either private, temple, or royal—in this period. In contrast, first-millennium BCE Mesopotamia attests to the existence of libraries: private ones belonging to scribes, diviners, priests, and high government officials, and royal ones belonging to the king. This may reflect the increasing spread of literacy from the second to the first millennium BCE.

Scribal training may have been beneficial and practical for a number of occupations. The skills of reading and writing were beneficial in attaining many governmental offices.[48] Scribes did not serve only as scribes for officials: they often *were* those officials.[49]

Certain priests may have found it beneficial to be able to read and write. Excavations of the homes of certain priests in Ur have yielded school exercise tablets.[50] One house in Sippar had close to one hundred school tablets: the teacher may have been a scribe who worked regularly for the temple official—a chief lamenter, who lived in the house, probably teaching the official's son and successor in the temple post.[51] Notably, none of these school texts were of a religious nature: the chief lamenter must have taught his son the texts recited in the temple orally, entrusting his son's general training in reading and writing to the scribe. The level of proficiency in these school texts was not particularly high: probably a youngster meant for work as a temple official need not reach the same level of skill as one whose intended vocation would be scribal employment.

That a number of merchants would have been literate has been widely accepted among scholars in the past few decades. It would have been advantageous for a merchant to be able to read his business documents and perhaps to write them himself on occasion. Johannes Renger and Mogens T. Larsen recognized that in the case of Assyrian merchants, the number of signs was limited and simplified, that learning how to read and write was not

[48] Literacy may have been almost indispensable for certain administrative positions. See Hans J. Nissen, "The Education and Profession of the Scribe," in *Archaic Bookkeeping* (ed. Hans J. Nissen, Peter Damerow, and Robert K. England; trans. Paul Larsen; Chicago: University of Chicago Press, 1993), 104.

[49] The extensive royal archives of Mari show that the high officials—whether kings, administrators, military leaders, or diviners—were able to read and write letters on their own. See Charpin, *Writing, Law, and Kingship in Old Babylonian Mesopotamia*, 13. Hamatil, the highest palace administrator during the reign of the king Yahdun-Lim, was denoted as scribe on his seal. Under the following king, the chief bookkeeper had an earlier seal on which his title was scribe. Others were called scribe in one text and called by an administrative title in another. Others may have been able to read and write administrative texts, which required less proficiency than letters. This is so because many administrative texts contain only proper names, numbers, and logograms. A number of letters clearly state that the sender or recipient will write a letter transmitting news.

A first-millennium BCE example reveals that the son of the governor of Nippur, who presumably was intentionally educated by his father to follow in his footsteps and become part of the upper-level bureaucracy, was able to copy tablets, and in fact he was used by his captors to do so. Frame and George, "The Royal Libraries of Nineveh," 278–279. For Hittite court officials, army officers, and temple personnel who also held the title of scribe, see Shai Gordin, *Hittite Scribal Circles* (Studien zu Den Bogazköy-Texten; Wiesbaden: Harrassowitz Verlag, 2015), 229–237.

[50] Charpin, *Writing, Law, and Kingship in Old Babylonian Mesopotamia*, 11.

[51] M. Tanret, *Per aspera ad astra: L'apprentissage du cunéiforme à Sippar-Amnānum pendant la période paléobabylonienne tardive* (Mesopotamian History and Environment Texts 1/2; Gand: Université de Gand, 2002).

so difficult.[52] Larsen drew attention to the far from professional writing of private documents: the hideous nature of the writing in these documents definitively attests to the amateurishness of the authors.

Certain professions would have found it advantageous to be literate. It is possible that Mesopotamian physicians had to be literate. Asher Finkel argued that during scribal training, weaker students would have been discouraged from pursuing medical knowledge and would have been guided toward a vocation in writing commercial documents, rather than the complexities of divination or medicine.[53] The script of the medical tablets resembles that of commercial documents, and a trove of Late Babylonian tablets reflects the clumsy attempts of medical students to learn their craft.

Senior military officers were literate as well: it is not as surprising as it would seem that high-ranking officers might need literacy skills. How would a king be certain that he could dispatch secret orders to a general? Charpin argued that it makes sense for reasons of security for a general to be able to read without requiring the assistance of a scribe.[54] King Zimri-Lim of Mari sent a secret tablet to one of his generals, enjoining the general to read it himself and then to read it aloud to another person. In another tablet, the sender, worried that the tablet he received from abroad might be seen as suspicious, noted that a general read the tablet at the same time he did: presumably the general's loyalty would not be questioned.

It must be emphasized that skills in reading and writing most likely varied greatly and that there were differing levels of literacy.[55] An individual who

[52] Johannes Renger, "Überlegungen zum akkadischen syllabar," *ZA* 61 (1971), 33; Mogens T. Larsen, *The Old-Assyrian City-State and Its Colonies* (Mesopotamia 4; Copenhagen: Akademisk Forlag, 1976), 305.

[53] Irving L. Finkel, "On Late Babylonian Medical Training," in *Wisdom, Gods, and Literature: Studies in Assyriology in Honor of W. G. Lambert* (ed. A. R. George and I. L. Finkel; Winona Lake, Ind.: Eisenbrauns, 2000), 141.

[54] Charpin, *Writing, Law, and Kingship in Old Babylonian Mesopotamia*, 15.

[55] Claus Wilcke argued that beyond these social groups, literacy in fact spread to many others (*Wer las und schrieb in Babylonien und Assyrien*, 7–22). He argued that the excavation of private residences from every era have yielded texts (more than half in Ur, one-quarter to one-third in Assur) and that this is evidence that (a number of) the inhabitants of these homes were able to read and write. (By contrast, Charpin noted that those residences are mainly in the neighborhoods of the elite—who knows the situation of the majority?—and that safeguarding property and financial records may have been important to those who could not read them. See Charpin, *Writing, Law, and Kingship in Old Babylonian Mesopotamia*, 12.) Wilcke finds evidence for literacy in a number of documents, that are expressed in the first person; these texts indicate that the writer has read a text, "upon seeing my current tablet," in contrast to "in listening to my current tablet." Knowing how to read, a passive knowledge of writing, was more widespread than knowing how to write, an active knowledge. This has been true in many societies until modernity.

could read a letter may have had difficulty in reading literary texts.[56] An individual who could have read a contract may not have read much else (or had any desire to read much else). And even if a person read texts on a certain level of difficulty, that person's writing skills may have been more modest. Those who habitually read business records may very well have not been able to write them well. Those who read letters may have not been able to write them well.

Lastly, it must be noted that a few Mesopotamian kings and an Achaemenid ruling in Mesopotamia (Shulgi, Assurbanipal, and Darius) claimed to be literate, but does this mean that many kings were literate or that only a few were? Scholars have greeted those claims with the same skepticism with which they have evaluated the other extravagant claims of a monarch. The paucity of claims of literacy by monarchs may reflect the restricted ranks of the literate and the great dependency of the government on professional scribes.[57]

[56] Texts from the city of Shemshara, a less-known city, show a clear distinction in education between scribes who wrote letters and those who were bookkeepers. See J. Eidem, *The Shemshara Archives 2: The Administrative Texts* (Historikfilsofiske Skrifter 15; Copenhagen: Kongelige Danske Videnskabernes Selskab, 1992), 21–24.

[57] Landsberger, "Scribal Conceptions of Education," 111.

5

Adoption in the Laws of Hammurabi

The laws on adoption illustrate the methods of composition that manifest systematization and conceptualization discussed in the previous chapter. It is useful to start by comparing adoption in legal records to adoption in the Laws of Hammurabi. The comparison reveals how the drafter of the Laws of Hammurabi composed statutes to reflect his flair in legal reasoning and his conception of justice more than the historical reality of adoption in his time.

Adoption, which abrogates blood ties and creates new ones based on fictitious blood ties, became a prominent institution in Mesopotamian society.[1] Contrary to the way adoption generally operates in contemporary Western societies, the majority of adoptions in Mesopotamia were of adults, not humanitarian adoptions of minor children. One may object that this is a mistaken impression because of the nature of the sources: adult adoption was more problematic and needed confirmation preserved in written form, and therefore it appears more often in the texts extant from Mesopotamia. But if that is so, that demonstrates even more so the artificiality of the statutes in the Laws of Hammurabi. The problematic cases of adoption were those of adults, not children. The cases of adult adoption were the ones that would require attention and explication, yet the scribe drafting the statutes in the Laws of Hammurabi focused on the adoption of minor children, not adults. The scribe did not address other forms of adoption of adults, such as the adoption of a

[1] See Barmash, "Adoption," *OEBL*, 1–9; Martino David, *Die Adoption im altbabylonischen Recht* (Leipzig: Weicher, 1927); Kristine Garroway, *Children in the Ancient Near Eastern Household* (Winona Lake, Ind.; Eisenbrauns, 2014), 48–108; Elizabeth C. Stone and David Owen, *Adoption in Old Babylonian Nippur and the Archive of Mannum-mešu-liṣṣur* (Mesopotamian Civilization 3; Winona Lake, Ind.; Eisenbrauns, 1991); Émile Szlechter, "Des droits successoraux dérivés de l'adoption en droit babylonien," *RIDA* 14 (1967), 79–106; Raymond Westbrook, "The Adoption Laws of Codex Hammurabi," in *Kinnattutu ša darâti: Raphael Kutscher Memorial Volume* (ed. Anson F. Rainey; Tel Aviv: Institute of Archaeology, 1997), 195–204.

The historical development of adoption is complex and often counterintuitive. Adoption was allowed in the United States only starting in the 1850s, and the Adoption Act, allowing full adoption to take place in Britain, was passed in 1926. See Hugh Lindsay, *Adoption in the Roman World* (Cambridge: Cambridge University Press, 2009), 23–25. The modern form of adoption, an institution protecting orphaned and abandoned children, developed in the context of the protective structures of twentieth-century Western societies. See Ellen Herman, *Kinship by Design: A History of Adoption in the Modern United States* (Chicago: University of Chicago Press, 2008).

The Laws of Hammurabi. Pamela Barmash, Oxford University Press (2020). © Oxford University Press.
DOI: 10.1093/oso/9780197525401.001.0001.

trusted slave as a form of manumission and a way of obtaining elder care. The focus in the Laws of Hammurabi is solely on the adoption of minor children.

In general in Mesopotamia, adoption was used as a flexible legal tool: it was a legal device employed to obtain a wide array of goals, such as promoting financial security and fulfilling emotional needs for both the adopter and adoptee, providing maintenance in old age and upholding a line of succession for property, continuing commercial ventures, conveying commercial assets and real estate, and securing burial and mortuary rites.[2] While there were cases of goodwill in the adoption of a foundling, even when the adopter already had children, adoption as extant in legal records was mostly of adults.

The outlines of adoption in Mesopotamian society in general were true for the Old Babylonian period, the period in which the Laws of Hammurabi was composed.[3] The legal documents from the Old Babylonian period demonstrate the widespread adoption of adults by adults. This was utilized even when a couple had a son who could support them: adopting an adult whose responsibility it would be to support the elderly parents was apparently more convenient. The adoptee was himself a party to the adoption contract.[4] The desirability and usefulness of adoption are manifested in the adoption of a slave: while a slave would have had to serve his owner as a slave, a slave would be manumitted and adopted for the purpose of supporting his or her former masters in their old age.[5] The ties formed by an adoption contract strengthened the obligation of the adoptee by binding him with both contractual and filial obligations, and the adoption of a slave shows that contractual and filial obligations were perceived to be stronger than a relationship of servitude. An adoption contract seemed to be the natural institution for an individual who would take care of the elderly and in return would receive an inheritance. It exceeded the obligations that were enshrined in commercial contracts. Adoption was also used to facilitate marriage arrangements: in one Old Babylonian text, a woman adopted a young woman from her parents, giving her parents the betrothal gift that a groom would give, acquiring the right and responsibility to marry her off, perhaps to her son.[6]

[2] Driver and Miles claimed the main purpose for adoption was to acquire a son to perpetuate the family and to perform the religion rites for the adopter after his death, but admitted that the religious rites are rarely mentioned in the sources (Driver and Miles, *The Babylonian Laws*, 1.383, 385).

[3] Peter Raymond Obermark, "Adoption in the Old Babylonian Period," Ph.D. dissertation, Hebrew Union College–Jewish Institute of Religion, Cincinnati, Ohio, 1992, 1–94; Stone and Owen, *Adoption in Old Babylonian Nippur*, passim.

[4] BIN 2 75:2 (= Dominique Charpin, *Le clergé d'Ur au siècle d'Hammurabi* [Hautes études orientales 22; Geneva: Droz, 1986], 162–164); TJA 28:1 (= Charpin, *Clergé*, 5–7); YOS 8: 120:2.

[5] CT 4 42a = UAZP 23.

[6] Westbrook, *Old Babylonian Marriage Law*, 38–39. Documentation from other time periods shows that adoption was employed for other reasons as well: adoption was employed for property transfer or for social advancement, and adoption into brotherhood would facilitate joint ownership.

By contrast, the series of statutes on adoption in the Laws of Hammurabi addresses an unrepresentative cross-section of adoption, the adoption of minors. In particular, it deals with the risks inherent in the adoption of minors: Does a relationship persist between the adoptee and the adoptee's birth parents? May the birth parent(s) try to reclaim the child, and may the child return to the birth parents and disavow the adoption? May the adoptive parents treat the adoptive child differently than a biological child? These issues are more acute in the adoption of children than in the adoption of an adult because an adult adoptee is more likely to have knowingly and willingly accepted the formation of a new relationship. The nature of the responsibility for, and the authority over, a child requires even greater clarification when the child is adopted.

The series of statutes on the adoption of minors also addresses a situation that may be akin to adoption: a craftsman's taking on of a child as an apprentice. By placing statutes on this situation adjacent to the statutes on adoption, the conceptual linkage between adoption and apprenticeship is amplified.

The series of statutes in the Laws of Hammurabi focuses on an adopted or apprenticed minor, far from the historical reality of adoption in the Old Babylonian period, but it was the usual way for apprenticeship to operate, with a craftsman taking on a child to train. It presents a detailed investigation of one area of adoption law, not an exhaustive analysis of the full gamut of adoption, and the statutes are formulated in a series of incremental variants, forming a paradigm with a variable modified:

<u>LH 185</u>

If a man takes in adoption a young child at birth (literally, in its amniotic fluid)[7] and then rears him, that rearling will not be reclaimed.[8]

[7] See the example of an abandoned infant in UET 5 260 and the discussion in Garroway, *Children in the Ancient Near Eastern Household*, 51–53, 100–101. Garroway noted the vividness of the expression *ina mêšu*, "in its amniotic fluid," instead of an expression more plainly stating that the adoption took place at birth. But Meir Malul argued that the expression refers to an unwanted child being exposed. See Malul, "Adoption of Foundlings in the Bible and Mesopotamia Documents: A Study of Some Legal Metaphors in Ezekiel 16:1–7," *Journal for the Study of the Old Testament* 46 (1990), 97–126. The series *ana ittišu* III 21–67 addresses the case of an adopted foundling (Benno Landsberger, *Die serie* ana ittišu. Materials for the Sumerian Lexicon [Rome: Pontificii instituti biblici, 1937], 44–46). While the text of *ana ittišu* is from the library of Assurbanipal, its original appears to date from Nippur in the dynasty of Isin, from the Old Babylonian period. It is a bilingual Sumerian-Akkadian text meant as a school text. In the case of adoption addressed in *ana ittišu*, the child was exposed and abandoned: "He has no father or mother. No one knows his father or mother. He was found in a well. He was brought in from the street. He was rescued from the mouth of a dog. What fell from the mouth of a raven was his." The series *ana ittišu* prescribes that a wet nurse was to be appointed for a specific period, three years, and paid a specific salary to rear him, and then the child would be adopted and trained as a scribe.

[8] A major interpretive puzzle encountered when analyzing this series on adoption is whether the statutes apply equally to male and female adoptees. While certain statutes clearly apply to male

LH 186

If a man takes in adoption a young child, and when he takes him, the child is searching for his father and mother, that rearling shall return to his father's house.[9]

LH 187

A child reared by a courtier who is a palace attendant or a child reared by a *sekretu* will not be reclaimed.

LH 188

If a craftsman takes a young child to rear and then teaches him his craft, he will not be reclaimed.

LH 189

If he should not teach him his trade, that rearling shall return to his father's house.

LH 190

If a man should not reckon the young child whom he took and raised in adoption as equal with his children, that rearling shall return to his father's house.

LH 185–190 address the possibility of the adoption being nullified in statutes that proceed by incremental variants:

LH 185: Child is an *abandoned infant*—birth parents may not reclaim.
LH 186: Child is a *young child seeking parents*—birth parents may reclaim.
LH 187: Young child *adopted by palace officials*—birth parents may not reclaim.
LH 188: Young child reared by *a craftsman who teaches the child a trade*—birth parents may not reclaim.

adoptees (LH 188–189 on apprentices, who presumably are male, and LH 191, on inheritance), a number of the statutes refer to a male adoptee in the protasis and a female adoptee in the apodosis. Nothing regarding equal treatment can be derived from this because the statutes refer to *ṣeḫrum*, "child," a male (or unmarked) noun, before the adoption, and to *tarbītum*, "rearling," a feminine (or marked) noun, after the adoption.

[9] LH 186 contains one of the few humanitarian statutes in the law collection. An adoptee who is longing for his birth parents may return to their house: here the legist has recognized the natural longing of a child for his parents and even mentions the mother in addition to the father, unusual in these statutes, as the focus of a child's yearning. See Garroway, *Children in the Ancient Near Eastern Household*, 59–60.

LH 189: Young child reared by *a craftsman who fails to teach the child his trade*—child returns to birth parents and is reclaimed.

LH 190: Young child adopted by *parent who does not treat him equally with other children*—child returns to birth parents and is reclaimed.

Each statute deals with an incremental variant in the adoption of a young child, and the statutes form a paradigm in which one factor is modified. In LH 185–186, a distinction is drawn between an infant and a young child: an infant's adoption cannot be abrogated by the birth parent(s), but a young child who still wishes to be reunited with his or her birth parents can be reclaimed. The young child is presumed to be lost, not abandoned. Such a distinction does not hold for the adoption by a courtier or *sekretu* (LH 187): in light of the implicit comparison with the two earlier statutes, that type of adoption cannot be nullified, no matter the age or desire of the adoptee. The status of the adopter as a courtier or *sekretu* meant that the adoption was irreversible, and this statute is marked off from the other statutes by being articulated in noncasuistic form. The privileged status of these two classes is highlighted by a literary difference in the formulation of the statute.

Casuistic formulation resumes when the series continues: it addresses a situation that is analogous to adoption, the taking on of a child as an apprentice by a craftsman. The standing of a child adopted by a craftsman depends on the behavior of the craftsman (LH 188–189): if the child is taught the craft, the adoption remains in force, but if not, the adoption is invalidated. The criterion of appropriate conduct toward the child prompts the next variant. If an adopted child is not treated the same as the parents' biological children, the adoption is abrogated (LH 190). This series explores the parameters of whether the birth parents retained a default relationship with the adoptee: under specific circumstances, they do, but under others, the adoption was not reversible. The incremental variants clarify the pertinent elements in a situation of adoption. They define the boundaries and implicitly define the legal concepts that are at work. The casuistic reasoning prompted by the variants in each case depicted in the statutes focuses on the key similarities and differences that allow the rules on adoption to emerge.

Incorporating statutes on apprenticeship in a series of statutes on adoption prompts a new perspective, one that evaluates the relationship to the child based on the behavior of the adult. LH 190 is also informed by the same concerns, and in so being, it serves as a transition between the set of statutes in LH 185–190 and the next set in LH 190–193: like the craftsman, an adopter must treat an adopted child in certain ways. In the case of a craftsman, this means teaching the child his trade. In the case of an adult, it means treating the child as equal to biological children. The ruling in LH 190 is modified by its placement as a transition to LH 191:

LH 190

If a man should not reckon the young child whom he took and raised in adoption as equal with his children, that rearling shall return to his father's house.[10]

[10] LH 190–191 present a number of interpretive issues:

(1) In LH 190, the significance of *itti marišu la imtanušu*, "If a man should not reckon the young child as equal with his children," must be determined. In other statutes, such as LH 170–171, the father has legitimated his sons by a slave-girl by declaring formally that they are his sons and counting them among his (natural-born) sons, but the opposite action, his refusal to legitimate them by a formal declaration, does not include the mention that he has refused to count them among his sons. Does this omission mean that the two actions—the formal declaration that the sons by a slave girl are officially his sons and counting them among his sons—are distinct? We must add the additional evidence of the phrasing in LH 191, where a formal declaration signals the desire to negate adoptive ties. So the act of not counting among one's sons in LH 170–171 is not an attempt to nullify the adoption, as Driver and Miles rightly claim (*The Babylonian Laws*, 1.395). Whether this is an indirect method of mistreating the adoptee and thereby not treating him as equal to the other sons is debatable. Note that the adoptee in LH 190 was not a foundling because there was a father's house for the disavowed adoptee to return to.

(2) LH 191 addresses the situation in which an adoptive father has brought up his adopted son and has provided him with a house (Koschaker, *Rechtsvergleichende Studien zur gesetzgebung Hammurapis*, 1.25–26). He has provided him with a separate establishment, perhaps on the occasion of his marriage. The series *ana ittišu* mentions the case of a father marrying an adopted son off to a natural daughter and providing him with a house and furniture (Landsberger, 49.35–36, 100.18–101.21). So after raising the adoptee and providing him with the means to be an independent householder, the adopter has had sons and can exclude the adoptee from having an inheritance share among them. Since the adoptee now has his own means, he does not return to his father's house like the youth in LH 190 but remains on his own.

(3) In LH 191, the compensation that the adopter gives is one-third of his property but not from the field, grove, or house. The discharged adoptee retains the right to inherit, but not from landed property, which would most likely be the ancestral property of the family that otherwise would be divided among the heirs at the father's death (Driver and Miles, *The Babylonian Laws*, 1.399). Here, the discharged adoptee is excluded because he has been set up as independent from the family.

(4) When does the discharged adoptee receive his compensation? Does he receive it immediately or only after the death of his adopter? There is no indication in the text that the adoptee must wait, unlike the indication regarding others with claims in LH 165 and 171. Driver and Miles argued that the property outside the patrimonial estate is probably not large and could be paid easily when the adoptee is discharged (*The Babylonian Laws*, 1.401). This might be so, even though a successful man might have a great deal more, but nonetheless, this property is easily paid, unlike the division of real estate. Most likely, it was paid at the time of the discharge of the adoptee.

LH 191

If a man establishes his household (by reckoning as equal with any future children) the young child whom he took and raised in adoption but afterwards he has children (of his own) and then decides to disinherit that rearling, that child will not depart empty-handed; the father who raised him shall give him a one-third share of his property as his inheritance and he shall depart; he will not give him any property from field, orchard, or house.

The ruling is qualified by implicit analogy: the one who adopts is obligated to treat the adoptee equally with biological children, if the adopter had children at the time of the adoption. But if the adopter did not have biological children at the time, he has the right to revoke the adoption. In order to do so, the adopter is obliged to grant the adoptee a significant portion of his estate.[11] This reservation demonstrates that the adoptee is never quite on par with the oldest biological son. In the usual scheme of inheritance, the oldest biological son has the right to inherit the preferential share, a double share, while the younger sons receive a single share. According to this statute, the adoptee is to receive the same share as a younger son, with the proviso that the adoptee's share is not real estate.[12]

Other laws in the Laws of Hammurabi, LH 168–169, addressed the circumstances in which a son may be disinherited; if the son has committed grave offenses, and if an adoptee were fully on par with biological sons, similar stipulations would apply to the adoptee. However, LH 191 demonstrates that the adopter can cancel the adoption with appropriate compensation without the adoptee being charged with committing grave offenses. The implicit analogy between the statutes on this domain of adoption reflects scribal thinking, and it is the intellectual precursor of the explicit application of legal concepts. What applies to all members of one class, the young

[11] An adoptee whose adoption was cancelled retains the right to a share in his adopter's estate because it is to be assumed that the adoptee no longer has a share to his birth parent's estate due to his adoption into another family. Driver and Miles argued that it was his leaving his family that constitutes the break from inheritance (*The Babylonian Laws*, 1.387), but three pieces of evidence militate against this argument: (1) nowhere else is the leaving of a household the cause of disinheritance (one can think of other circumstances in which a person might abandon a family home without being adopted into another); (2) the adoptee does not necessarily inherit from the adopter with the same share as a natural-born son, so a right, perhaps limited, to the birth parent's estate might be warranted; (3) the adoption contracts demonstrate that an inheritance needs to be stipulated.

[12] Adoption contracts may provide that the adoptee enjoys the status of the oldest son. See Stone and Owen, *Adoption in Old Babylonian Nippur*, 35–36.

child not raised in adoption equal with the adopter's children (LH 190), is applied by the scribe to all the members of another class, the young child raised in adoption as equal with the would-be children (LH 191). The statutes are based on a common rationale by analogy: the adopter can cancel the adoption with appropriate compensation. The power and flexibility of the method of incremental variants allow the scribe to shape cases in adjoining statutes that show the significance of specific variables and how legal principles come into view.

In LH 191, the scribe has incorporated another method of composition, an explanation. The explanation is expressed in multiple parts. First, the scribe articulated the general remedy: "that child will not depart empty-handed." Then the scribe specified that the father who raised the adoptee will give him a one-third share of his property. Then the scribe added another clarification that while the adopter must give the adoptee a third of his estate, a sizable amount, he cannot give the adoptee any landed property from his estate. Presumably, that means that the adoptee receives chattels and silver so that he can (and most likely must) depart and need not be in proximity to the adopter who has disinherited him by reversing the adoption. This stipulation was most likely intended to prevent everyday friction between the adoptee whose adoption was reversed and the adopter who revoked the adoption.

But the question remains whether an adoptee can abrogate the relationship with the adopter.[13] The Laws of Hammurabi addresses only a limited subset of possibilities:

> LH 192
>
> If the child reared by a courtier or the child reared by a *sekretu* should say to the father who raised him or the mother who raised him, "You are not my father" or "You are not my mother," they shall cut out his tongue.
>
> LH 193
>
> If the child reared by a courtier or the child reared by a *sekretu* identifies with his father's house and repudiates the father who raised him or the mother who raised him and departs for his father's house, they shall pluck out his eye.

[13] Other types of misbehavior merit the disavowal of the adoption in the series *ana ittišu*. The series mentions the cancellation of an adoption and the concomitant disinheritance of the adoptee because he has misbehaved, run away, or hung out on the streets (Landsberger, *ana ittišu*, 47.3–48.16).

Why does a child adopted by people with specific status merit so severe a penalty if he tries to abrogate the adoption?[14] A comparison to SLEx 4′–6′ is instructive. It deals with a major principle of adoption law: whether the adopter or the adoptee may repudiate the relationship:

SLEx 4′
If (the adopted son) states to his father and mother, "You are not my father" or "You are not my mother," he shall forfeit house, field, orchard, slaves, and possessions, and they shall sell him (into slavery) for his full value.

SLEx 5′
(If) his (adoptive) father and mother state to him, "You are not our son," they shall forfeit . . . the estate.

SLEx 6′
If his (adoptive) father and mother state (to him), "You are not our son," they shall forfeit (the estate).[15]

The utterance by the adopter unilaterally of "You are not my child" did dissolve the bond and did nullify the adoption: adoption contracts were employed to prevent that from occurring by their penalty provisions.[16] The statutes in the Laws of Hammurabi address only the situation of a person adopted by those with specific status. What is omitted is the case of an adoptee repudiating an adopter in general.

[14] Driver and Miles argued that the purpose of the inclusion of adoption in the Laws of Hammurabi is to alter the nature of adoption because they think that the Laws of Hammurabi was legislation. Heretofore, Driver and Miles averred, adoption has been governed only by contract: a particular adoption was subject to the terms enumerated in the contract governing it. The stipulations of the Laws of Hammurabi, however, would apply generally to cases of adoption, and therefore adoption became a status: an adoptee had rights because of his status as an adoptee. But a specific contract could overrule those rights and modify the conditions of adoption. The question then is what was it that the Laws of Hammurabi is overturning? Driver and Miles argued that birth parents previously had the right to reclaim their child unless prevented so by the contract (*The Babylonian Laws*, 1.387). The Laws of Hammurabi prevented this if the adopter has brought up the child or if the child has been trained by an adopting craftsman or has been adopted by a palace official. However, it is not so clear that this is an innovation of the Laws of Hammurabi. It is clear from the statutes that the issue of reclaiming by the birth parents or the adoptee returning on his own to his birth parents mostly likely is the issue at hand since six out of nine statutes deal with this issue. It is possible to argue that the Laws of Hammurabi is innovating in quite the opposite way, by providing the circumstances in which an adoptee can return to the birth parents without the adopter's consent. Only if the child is adopted by a courtier or a *sekretu* is the adoption absolute.

[15] SLEx 5′ and 6′ appear to offer different formulations of the statement of repudiation.

[16] The usual penalty for the adopter is a huge fine, while the adoptee is threatened with being sold into slavery. A Middle Babylonian text provides for an unusually harsh penalty: the adoptee's head is to be smeared with hot asphalt and he is forced to pay a large penalty in silver (RBC 779 [= Amanda H. Podany, Gary M. Beckman, and Gudrun Colbow, "An Adoption and Inheritance Contract from the Reign of Iggid-Lim of Ḫana," *JCS* 43–45 (1991–1993), 39–51]).

This selectivity, focused on adopters of high status, shapes the punishment clause. In LH 192–193, the body part that performed the offensive action is removed.

> LH 192
>
> If the child reared by a courtier or the child reared by a *sekretu* should say to the father who raised him or the mother who raised him, "You are not my father" or "You are not my mother," they shall cut out his tongue.
>
> LH 193
>
> If the child reared by a courtier or the child reared by a *sekretu* identifies with his father's house and repudiates the father who raised him or the mother who raised him and departs for his father's house, they shall pluck out his eye.

LH 192 mandates the severing of the tongue of the adoptee who uttered a repudiation of his adopter, and LH 193 decrees the gouging of the eye of the adoptee who has searched for his (natural) father. Adoption contracts, by contrast, require the enslavement of the repudiating adoptee or the forfeiture of inheritance.[17] The statutes in the Laws of Hammurabi mandate poetic justice. With this, the scribe has systematized the statutes in two ways: he has employed a certain type of punishment across a number of statutes addressing a variety of cases, and he has ordained a single type of punishment in adjacent statutes, highlighting what the two statutes have in common: an adoptee who dares to repudiate an adopter of high status and therefore deserves mutilation, a type of punishment unique to the Laws of Hammurabi among the law collections. One further consideration: one might wonder what would happen to such an adoptee who dared to repudiate the adoption and was punished in such a manner. While it is arguable that the palace or temple would retain a mutilated person,[18] an adoptee of the status of courtier or *sekretu* who repudiated the adopter might well be sold into slavery or otherwise disposed of by an aggrieved adopter, akin to the usual punishment for an adoptee. But the emphasis of LH 192–193 is on repudiating the errant action of the adoptee. Therefore, the penalty of mutilation is highlighted, even if the adoptee would also have been sold into slavery.

[17] E.g., Stone and Owen, *Adoption in Old Babylonian Nippur*, 38–39.

[18] Driver and Miles based this argument on the biblical prohibition of a priest who is physically deformed (*The Babylonian Laws*, 1.404). See Lev 21:17–21.

The statutes on adoption in the Laws of Hammurabi exemplify the characteristic methods of composition employed by the scribe. Incremental variants are used to generate a series that presents a fuller picture of a focused section of a legal topic. The casuistic formulation of the statutes and the casuistic reasoning implied between statutes clarify the pertinent points and reveal the implicit conceptualization. They demonstrate the drafting scribe's flair for legal reasoning and decision-making on cases that were part of the repertoire of traditional cases rather than cases representative of reality. The scribe has also employed other methods of composition characteristic of other sets of statutes he composed: the incorporation of explanation and the application of specific types of punishment.

6

The Legal Authority of the Laws of Hammurabi

Much ink has been spilled over the legal authority of the Laws of Hammurabi. The discussion has focused on whether the Laws of Hammurabi was cited in legal records under the assumption that this would be evidence for its authority. As for the scope of its legal authority, scholars have debated a number of possibilities. Was the Laws of Hammurabi issued by Hammurabi as legislation amending existing law? If it was not legislation modifying law, did it originate in verdicts issued in specific disputes? And if so, did it incorporate Hammurabi's own judicial decisions or the verdicts of other judges in particular lawsuits? Alternatively, if the Laws of Hammurabi did not modify the law either as legislation or judicial decisions, is there evidence that the Laws of Hammurabi mirrors the law as it was practiced in Babylonia? But the crucial question is whether this approach accurately and effectively illuminates the nature of the legal authority of the Laws of Hammurabi.

6.1. The Laws of Hammurabi and Its Relationship to Law as Practiced

The Laws of Hammurabi does present itself as Hammurabi's judicial decisions (LH XLVII: 1–8), but finding legal records recounting those decisions has so far proved a failure. At most, there are legal records and royal correspondence that seem to reflect the same concerns as the Laws of Hammurabi, and we must consider whether this is evidence that the Laws of Hammurabi incorporated law as practiced, either as a legal ruling issued in a lawsuit, as legislation, or as existing law applied across many cases.[1]

[1] An Old Babylonian letter, A 3529, contains a reference to a stela on which the rules for wages were inscribed, but the sender of the letter is not accepting or rejecting the wage rules. Rather, the sender is instructing his representative to provide the workers with what they are demanding, then he will arrive and settle with them. See Roth, "The Law Collections of King Hammurabi," 22–23; Roth, *Law Collections*, 6.

The Laws of Hammurabi. Pamela Barmash, Oxford University Press (2020). © Oxford University Press.
DOI: 10.1093/oso/9780197525401.001.0001.

A legal record from the Ur III period recounts the case of a man who made accusations against his father and his brother, both temple officials with the title of ugula.[2] The accusation against his father was substantiated, but the death sentence decreed on the father was not carried out because the king issued a pardon. At a later date, the same man accused his brother, but this time the accusation was not substantiated. The accuser was sentenced to death.

(1 –9) Lugal-gizkim-zi, the son—and the eldest brother—of the ugula of the Inanna temple, brought suit under the jurisdiction of Amar-Suen. The suit was substantiated, and he (Amar-Suen) sentenced (the ugula) to death. The ugula of the Inanna temple fully satisfied him (Amar-Suen), and the king pardoned him. $Arad_2$-mu the sukkah-mah was the mashkim.

(10–25) A second time, he (Lugal-gizkim-zi) brought suit against the ugula of the Inanna temple: the charge of infringing a cultic taboo; the charge of diverting the sheep, butter, and flour for the royal offering; the charge of intercepting the butter for the regular offerings amounting to three silas per month, and the charge of diluting the butter of the regular offering. He (Lugal-gizkim-zi) initiated the proceedings against him (the ugula) before $Arad_2$-mu the sukkah-mah, Dada the ensi of Nippur, and Sag-nanna-zu. The suit was not substantiated, and he (Lugal-gizkim-zi) was sentenced to death.

(26–50) Furthermore, concerning the inheritance portion of Lugal-gizkim-zi, the ugula of the Inanna temple awarded to Lú-bal-sa_6-ga his son—the younger brother—the post of ugula of the Inanna temple, the residence and the associated paternal accoutrements including the royal and patrimonial possessions. Lú-bal-sa_6-ga, Sag-Enlil, Ur-Ababa swore by the king that they would not contest his (the ugula's) dividing (the estate) into thirds, the post of ugula of the Inanna temple, the residence and the associated paternal accoutrements, and patrimonial possessions. The case was concluded before Dada the ensi of Nippur. (Date and seals)[3]

[2] What is ironic is that the succession of one family to successive senior posts at the Inanna temple is employed by modern scholars as evidence of the power of a kin-based group. See William W. Hallo, "The House of Urmeme," *JNES* 31 (1972), 87–95; Roth, "A Reassessment of RA 71 (1977) 125ff," 9–14; Richard L. Zettler, "The Genealogy of the House of Ur-Me-me: a Second Look," *AfO* 31 (1984), 1–9. However, as can be seen in the machinations of the accuser, he did not display family solidarity: he accused both his father and brother of a capital offense.

[3] Jean-Marie Durand, "Une condamnation a mort a l'époque d'Ur III," *RA* 71 (1977), 125–127; Roth, "A Reassessment of RA 71 (1977) 125ff," 9–14.

The false accusation was deemed to merit the death of the accuser. This would appear to parallel two statutes in the Laws of Hammurabi, LH 1–2, where the false accuser is punished with the same penalty that the accused would have suffered:

> LH 1
> If a man accused another man, charging him with homicide (lit. laid upon him [the charge of] homicide), but then cannot bring proof against him, his accuser shall be killed.
>
> LH 2
> If a man accused another man of witchcraft but cannot bring proof, the one against whom witchcraft was charged will go down to the River and will dive in the water. If the River has overcome him, his accuser will carry away his estate. If the River has cleared that man and he has survived, the one who accused him of witchcraft shall be killed; the one who dove into the River will carry away the estate of his accuser.

The legal record and the statutes from the Laws of Hammurabi appear to be informed by the same principle: the false accuser is punished with the same penalty that the accused would have suffered. However, a number of caveats should be noted. This principle is nowhere stated as the reason for the penalty, either in the legal record or in LH 1–2. This may mean that another principle might inform the penalty, and we can only speculate what that might be: perhaps those who falsely accuse a family member are subject to the death penalty, or those who falsely accuse a temple official are subject to the death penalty, or the like. It must be noted that this case is from the Ur III period, not the Old Babylonian period, and the principle that the false accuser suffers the penalty the accused might have suffered is not found in the Laws of Ur-Namma, the only law collection extant from the Ur III period.[4]

The chronological gap is negligible in a recently published letter from Hammurabi that seems to echo the circumstances of a statute in the Laws of Hammurabi:

> The son of Ipqusha the goldsmith told me this: Last year, thieves broke through [the wall] of my house and took my property. Furthermore, they

[4] The Laws of Ur-Namma is preserved incompletely, so future discoveries might shed light on this issue.

have now again broken through [the wall] of my house but I was able to seize these thieves. That is what he told me. Now I have sent you this son of Ipqusha. Tie up the thieves whom he seized, place them under strong guard, and have them brought to me. Also, send me the witnesses of the son of Ipqusha.[5]

As was the king's prerogative, Hammurabi appeared to have wished to investigate this matter personally. The circumstances seem to echo LH 21, and the question is whether this statute derives from the sentence that the king may have issued at the conclusion of his investigation:

LH 21

If a man broke into a house, they shall kill him and hang him in front of that breach.

The letter suggests a connection because it mentions a theft made possible by a breach in the wall of a house. The hurdle is that we do not have evidence of the king's ruling. To make the case that statutes in the Laws of Hammurabi derive from Hammurabi's decisions requires much more specific evidence. A record stating that the remedy was hanging the thief in front of the breach would be decisive. But what we have, a letter that includes the circumstances but omits the penalty, is insufficient, especially when the penalty in the Laws of Hammurabi is so striking and singular. The circumstance of breaking through a wall by a thief may not be that unusual: the Covenant Code in the Bible mentions it as well (Exod 22:1–2).

Furthermore, the ruling in the Laws of Hammurabi is at odds with legal records.[6] In cases of theft from Hammurabi's reign, victimized homeowners sought the return of their lost property, either in kind or in reparations, but the Laws of Hammurabi envisions poetic justice in LH 21. The perpetrator is to be executed and put on display in front of the physical evidence of his crime, the breach at the house he broke into.

Another letter from Hammurabi contains a ruling, and here we inch tantalizingly closer to a relationship between a royal decision and a law collection. The question is whether this royal order was an application of a statute from the Laws of Hammurabi, or alternatively, whether the royal order in the

[5] AbB 13.12.

[6] Rivkah Harris, "The *nadītu* Laws of the Code of Hammurapi in Praxis," *Or* 30 (1961), 163–169.

letter may have been the individual case for which the statute was ostensibly generated as a general rule:[7]

> Speak to Lushtamar-Zamama and Bēlānum. Thus says Hammurabi. [In regard to] Sin-ana-Damrum-lippalis son of Maninum whom the enemy captured, give his merchant 10 shekels of silver from the temple of Sin and ransom him.[8]

The circumstances appear to echo a statute on redeeming captured soldiers:

> <u>LH 32</u>
> If either a soldier or a fisherman is taken captive while on a royal campaign and a merchant redeems him and helps him to return to his city, if there is sufficient means in his own estate for the redemption, he shall redeem himself; if there is not sufficient means in his estate to redeem him, he shall be redeemed by his city's temple; if there is not sufficient means in his city's temple, the palace shall redeem him, but his field, orchard, or house will not be given for his redemption.

According to the letter, the king had to issue special instructions for this man, presumably a soldier, to be ransomed. The statute, by contrast, presents a procedure to be followed in case a soldier is captured, with no need for the king to intervene and launch the process of redemption. It seems unlikely then that the action described in the letter is an application of the statute. Even more decisively, because the letter mentions only that the payment be issued from the temple and not a multistep process of checking whether the captured soldier's estate could provide the funds and then whether his city-temple could supply them, it is impossible to determine whether the statute was a general ruling occasioned as a result of the king's activities as reported in the letter. We could speculate that the statute records a regularization of the process of redemption for a captured soldier, but for proof, we would need more evidence of the intervening steps in the process.

[7] Bottéro, "The 'Code' of Hammurabi," 165; Charpin, *Writing, Law, and Kingship in Old Babylonian Mesopotamia*, 79–80.

[8] AbB IX, 32.

Another letter concerning a missing soldier has been adduced as evidence that the Laws of Hammurabi were applied.[9] It is known from two copies and may have been a school exercise:[10]

> Tell Sin-ay-abash: thus speaks Shamash-naṣir. May Shamash and Marduk give you life out of regard for me. Concerning the field of Sin-magir, the soldier: Sin-magir the soldier fled, and his field was given to Munawwirum. Today, his sons appeared, saying: We want to have possession of our father's field, and we will perform our father's *ilku*-service. The king said: Their field is returned to them, and they will have to perform their father *ilku*-service.

The question is whether this is an application of a statute in the Laws of Hammurabi. Charpin argued that this mirrors LH 28:

> LH 28
> If either a soldier or a fisherman has been taken captive while serving in a royal fortress and his son is able to perform his *ilku*-service, the field and the orchard shall be given to him, and he shall perform his father's *ilku*-service.

However, this letter is about a case where the soldier has fled, an issue addressed in different statutes:

> LH 30
> If either a soldier or a fisherman has abandoned his field, orchard, or house because of the *ilku*-service and has absented himself, and another person has taken possession of his field, orchard, or house and has performed the *ilku*-service for three years—if (the original possessor) then returns and claims his field, orchard, or house, it will not be given to him; the one who performed his *ilku*-service shall be the one to continue to perform the *ilku*-service.
>
> LH 31
> If he has absented himself only for one year and then he has returned, his field, orchard, and house shall be returned to him, and he himself shall perform the *ilku*-service.

[9] Charpin, *Writing, Law, and Kingship in Old Babylonian Mesopotamia*, 79.

[10] AbB XIV, 98. The second text was published by J. R. Kupper, "Lettres de Kiš," *RA* 53 (1959), 180. The second text has different personal names and only one son, so it may be that it is not a copy but an independent unrelated text.

While LH 28 provides for the son to take over the field, that remedy is to be applied when the father has been taken captive. LH 31 treats the case of a soldier who has fled and has not performed his *ilku*-service. It is not clear according to the Laws of Hammurabi that the heirs of a man who had a claim on crown lands could inherit if the man fled *ilku*-service voluntarily. The mismatch does not allow us to claim that the legal action recorded in the letter is an application of the statute in the Laws of Hammurabi.

Another intriguing reference to the Laws of Hammurabi being employed as legislation is found in AbB XIII, 13:10. Hammurabi instructs his official to adjudicate a case "according to the law (*dīnum*) that is currently applied in Emutbalum." However, this cannot be a reference to the Laws of Hammurabi for two reasons: (1) its statutes are called *dīnātum*, the plural form of the noun, and the reference cannot be to the Laws of Hammurabi as a unified composition (but could refer to an individual paragraph); and (2) the singular noun most likely refers to the current set of administrative rules that the king prescribed, not to a specific statute in the Laws of Hammurabi. In this case, a number of palace servants had deserted their posts, probably due to the disorder that ensued when Hammurabi conquered the city, and Hammurabi has ordered that they were to be dealt with in accordance with the rules and procedures that the king imposed on a newly acquired administrative unit.[11] Klaas Veenhof observed that this text serves as evidence that kings could impose laws, but this still does not clarify the link between the legal activities of the king and the Laws of Hammurabi itself.

The evidence from legal records and royal correspondence is insufficient to confirm that Hammurabi's judicial rulings or the rulings of judges were incorporated in the Laws of Hammurabi or that the Laws of Hammurabi was employed as legislation or reflected law as practiced in particular cases.[12] An alternative method of finding a link to the Laws of Hammurabi has been suggested by Dominique Charpin. He argued that the formulation of a legal decision in anonymous terms in royal correspondence, omitting the names of the parties in the dispute, is evidence that the statutes in the Laws of Hammurabi

[11] Veenhof, "The Relationship between Royal Decrees and 'Law Codes,'" 78.

[12] There is an important caveat to the omission of references to the Laws of Hammurabi in legal records. Driver and Miles noted that the parties to a contract did have the freedom to make the terms they wished in their contracts: no contract or report of a case would need to cite a section of the Laws of Hammurabi as its basis (*The Babylonian Laws*, 1.401). The consequence is that there would be no need to cite the Laws of Hammurabi in a contract because the terms of a contract were independent of the Laws of Hammurabi.

derive from royal rulings.[13] A letter records that Hammurabi's successor, Samsu-iluna, investigated two cases that affected *nadītu*-nuns, cloistered women dedicated to a god, and issued a decision regarding one case:

> They told me this, in addition: The judge Awil-Sin has a claim of money owed by Mar-Shamash, a man of Sippar. Because he did not repay (the claim), he seized Mar-Shamash and said, If you refuse to sell your goods to reimburse me and I receive nothing, I will seize the slave of your daughter, the *nadītu*-nun of Shamash, who lives in a cloister. That is what they told me.
>
> [Royal Decision] A *nadītu*-nun of Shamash whose father and brothers have provided the support for her to live and for whom they wrote a tablet and who lives in a cloister is not responsible for the debts or *ilku*-service of the house of her father and brothers. Her father and brothers shall perform their *ilku*-service. . . . Any creditor who seizes a *nadītu*-nun of Shamash for the debts or the *ilku*-service of the house of her father and brothers, that man is an enemy of Shamash.[14]

It is striking that the verdict is couched in language that does not name the parties involved. Does the generic language imply that this ruling is a ruling to be applied in general? It may be so: the linguistic form of the ruling is close to the linguistic form of the apodosis (penalty clause) of the statutes of the Laws of Hammurabi. However, the circumstances are not articulated in the conditional form characteristic of the statutes, which contain a protasis describing the factors of the situation. The ruling was a royal decision, but its relationship to the statutes in the Laws of Hammurabi is suggestive, not decisive. It was copied several times, and Charpin hypothesized that the verdict became a precedent, one that might have or should have been incorporated in a law collection. But since the Laws of Hammurabi were too recent, Charpin argued, Samsu-iluna never updated his father's law collection with cases his father never considered. His verdicts never appear in any law collection. The existence of this generic ruling is suggestive, but there is no

[13] Charpin, *Writing, Law, and Kingship in Old Babylonian Mesopotamia*, 73–74; Charpin, *Hammurabi of Babylon*, 155–157.

[14] C. Janssen, "Samsuiluna and the Hungry nadītums," *Northern Akkad Project Reports* 5 (1991), 3–40; Charpin, *Writing, Law, and Kingship in Old Babylonian Mesopotamia*, 73–74; S. Lafont, "Les actes législatifs des rois mésopotamiens," in *Auctoritates Xenia R. C. van Caenegem oblata: la formation du droit et ses auteurs* (Wetenschappelijk comite voor rechtsgeschiedenis koninklijke Academie voor wetensschappen; ed. Serge Dauchy, Jos Monballyu, and Alain Wijffels; Iuris scripta historica 13; Brussels: Peeters, 1997), 3–27; Roth, "The Law Collection of King Hammurabi," 23–28.

evidence for the circumstances under which a law collection may have been updated. This claim remains intriguing yet hypothetical.

Royal correspondence does not appear to shed light on whether rulings by a king in a specific dispute were generalized and incorporated into the Laws of Hammurabi. We do know that kings did issue *ṣimdât šarrim*, a royal decree that applied generally (in contrast to a ruling in a particular dispute), and we must investigate whether the genre of a royal decree has been incorporated in a law collection. The Laws of Hammurabi explicitly refers twice to *ṣimdât šarrim*, a royal decree, in LH 51 and U. Both paragraphs prescribe that a debtor has to repay in accordance with the decree issued by the king:

> LH 51
>
> If he does not have silver to repay, he shall give to the merchant, in accordance with the royal decree, <grain or> sesame according to their market value for the silver borrowed from the merchant and the interest on it.
>
> LH U
>
> If a man who has an interest-bearing loan does not have silver with which to repay, he (the merchant) shall take grain and silver in accordance with the royal decree and the interest on it at the royal decree and the interest on it at the annual rate of 60 silas per 1 kur (= 20 percent); if the merchant attempts to increase and collect the interest on the (silver) loan [up to the grain interest of 100 silas of grain] per kur (= 33 percent) [or in any other way beyond] 36 barleycorns [per shekel of silver (= 20 percent)], he shall forfeit whatever he had given.

Kraus suggested that the royal decree was incorporated in another statute in the Laws of Hammurabi:[15]

> LH T
>
> If a merchant gives grain or silver as a interest-bearing loan; he shall take 100 silas of grain per kur as interest (= 33 percent); if he gives silver as an interest-bearing loan, he shall take 36 barleycorns per shekel of silver as interest (= 20 percent).

[15] F. R. Kraus, "Akkadische Wörter und Ausdrücke XII, *ṣimdatum, ṣimdat šarrim*," *RA* 73 (1979), 62. See Veenhof, "The Relationship Between Royal Decrees and 'Law Codes,'" 75.

However, LH T deals with interest, and LH 51 and U deal with the right to repay in kind.[16] This right served as special protection for farmers since the price for crops was lowest at harvest time. It is possible that a royal decree contained multiple paragraphs, and only one dealt with the right to repay in kind. But why would a law collection need to refer to a royal decree? It already has the authority of the king. Perhaps the impetus to refer to a royal decree was to make reference to its content, not to infuse the statute with the authority that such a decree would manifest. It seems likely that the royal decree contained a table of conversions or list of equivalents.[17] Furthermore, if the evidence that LH 51 and U stemmed from a royal decree is that an explicit reference to a royal decree is made, that implies that the other statutes that do not mention a royal decree were not derived from one.

Possible evidence that a royal decree by Hammurabi was incorporated in the Laws of Hammurabi may be found in an isolated statute, LH 112, one that is not part of a set improvising on a typical case. This isolated statute echoes the reference in school texts to a royal decree, and this might indicate that Hammurabi issued a royal decree on this occurrence. A number of practice school texts dating from the time of Hammurabi's successors make reference to a royal decree dealing with consigned goods that were not delivered.[18] LH 112 addresses the case of goods given in consignment that were stolen by the person who was supposed to deliver them:

> LH 112
> If a man was engaged in a trading expedition and gave silver, gold, precious stones, or any other goods to another under consignment for transportation and that latter man did not deliver that which was consigned to him where it was to be consigned to but appropriated it, the owner of the consigned property shall charge and convict that man of whatever consignment he failed to deliver and that man shall give to the owner of the property 5 times the property that had been given to him.

It is striking that there is only a single statute on this topic. Does the fact that this is an isolate and not part of a set of statutes elaborated by means of

[16] LH Z refers to the exchange rate acceptable to merchants of products other than grain or silver.
[17] Veenhof, "The Relationship between Royal Decrees and 'Law Codes,'" 77.
[18] YOS 13:328, BM 78589, and YOS 13:436 are from the reign of Ammiditana. CBS 1153 dates from Ammi-ṣaduqa, and BM 97222A is damaged and does not have a date. See Veenhof, "The Relationship between Royal Decrees and 'Law Codes,'" 71.

incremental variants serve as evidence that it originated as (part of) a royal decree? The obstacle to advancing this argument is that the school texts deal specifically with nondelivery, while the paragraph in the Laws of Hammurabi addresses the case of the transporter appropriating the very goods he was to deliver.[19] The mismatch weakens the argument, yet the presence of an isolated statute is intriguing.

References to a royal decree in Old Babylonian texts after the promulgation of the Laws of Hammurabi have inspired the suggestion that a royal decree was issued by one of Hammurabi's successors in response to a ruling in the Laws of Hammurabi. This would indicate that the Laws of Hammurabi was put into practice, and a later ruler needed to modify it. LH 278 provides for a one-month guaranty if it should be discovered that a slave has epilepsy, and LH 279 stipulates that a seller must provide a warranty for any claims on the slave. LH 280–281 provide for slaves purchased abroad to be returned to their original owner.

<u>LH 278</u>
If a man bought a male or female slave and during his (first) month's service epilepsy has struck him, he may return him to his seller and the buyer shall take back the silver that he has paid.

<u>LH 279</u>
If a man bought a male or female slave and he or she is liable for a claim, the seller shall answer the claims.

<u>LH 280</u>
If a man has bought a man's male or female slave in a foreign country and then when he has returned to the (home) country, the owner of the male or female slave has recognized his male or female slave, if that male or female slave are natives of the (home) country, their release (from the buyer) shall then be granted without (any payment of) silver (and they shall return to their former owner).[20]

[19] Veenhof suggested that the statute in the Laws of Hammurabi might be an extension of the decree with the addition of the offense of appropriation, but if there were a decree, it is more likely the royal decree was issued by one of Hammurabi's successors using the formulation of LH 112 ("The Relationship between Royal Decrees and 'Law Codes,'" 72–73).

[20] The status of the slave after the release has been debated because the remedy has been erroneously understood as meaning "their release (from the buyer) shall then be granted without (any payment of) silver (and they shall go free)." Moses Schorr queried whether the slaves mentioned were runaway slaves or were stolen from their owner and sold abroad ("Die §§ 280–282 des Gesetzbuches Ḫammurabis," *Wiener Zeitschrift für die Kunde des Morganlandes* 22 [1908], 383–392). He assumed

LH 281

If (they are) natives of another country, the buyer shall declare before the god the silver that he has paid, and the owner of the male or female slave shall give to the merchant the silver that he has paid and shall redeem his male or female slave.

that LH 280 means that they were to be given their freedom and therefore they could not have been runaway slaves. They must have slaves stolen and brought abroad, so Schorr inquired why the buyer was to lose his money and why the native slave was to be manumitted while the foreign-born slave was to be restored to his owner. If this were the case, then LH 280 is inconsistent with LH 9–10, where the owner has the right of recovery of his property. Schorr suggested that underlying these statutes is a primitive Semitic law that if a native slave is sold abroad he goes free, reflected in the mishnaic law (Gittin 4:6) that rules that a Jewish slave sold to a non-Jew or outside the land of Israel is set free. Schorr argued that the ruling of LH 280, freeing a slave who has been forcibly returned to his home country, is in the public interest, but this raises the problem of why Schorr extrapolated from a law (in the Mishnah) about a slave deliberately sold abroad to a statute (in the Laws of Hammurabi) about a slave stolen and sold abroad (and/or a runaway). This also raises the questions of why the owner would bother to identify his slave, if he won't be able to take him or her back, and why the buyer would lose his money. Schorr suggested that the buyer acted in bad faith because he should have recognized that the slave was a native of his home country and could not have been abroad legally. However, such a law would have the consequence that a buyer would not buy slaves from his home country while abroad and bring them home if they have to be set free without compensation.

Koschaker argued that while a law forbidding the sale of native slaves abroad is the basis of LH 280, the correlation between LH 280–281 still begs the question of why the owner would lose his slave if his slave was stolen from him (or if his slave ran away) (*Rechtsvergleichende Studien zur gesetzgebung Hammurapis: Königs von Babylon*, 51–54). Koschaker argued that LH 280–281 is a mass of contradictions and therefore the lines that contain the distinction between native and foreign are a later interpolation.

Driver and Miles contended that LH 279–281 all deal with the warranty of title to a contract of sale of a slave: in LH 279, a third party makes a claim on a slave, and in LH 280–281, a buyer has bought slaves abroad and brought them to Babylonia (*The Babylonian Laws*, 1.478–482). The seller should be the one to answer the owner's claims, but he is abroad; the ordinary rule of the warranty by the seller cannot be enforced, and therefore the law has to find a remedy for the buyer who has to give up the slave to the owner. The law appears to compensate the loss to the buyer if there was not a reason for him to suspect that the title to the slave was dubious: if the slave was foreign, then there was no reason for the buyer to suspect that the seller did not have valid ownership of the slave. Driver and Miles admitted that Schorr's contention that it is forbidden to sell a slave abroad may be true, and it may be reflected in MAL C 3. The fact that the slave was native-born should have made the buyer suspicious as to how the slave reached the foreign land, and therefore he has no right to an indemnity. The difficulty remains as to why the buyer would buy a native-born slave and return him to Babylon. Furthermore, Driver and Miles questioned why the rule in LH 32 is not applied to the native-born slave but is applied to the foreign-born slave: If a merchant is repaid for redeeming a captured soldier, why should the buyer of a foreign slave but not a native slave be recompensed? They also posed the question of why the rule of LH 9—that the owner regains his property without payment—is not applied when the slave is foreign born. They suggested that the owner loses his right of recovery if a foreign slave reaches a foreign land beyond the jurisdiction of Babylonian courts, but they reject this reason as too modern.

However, the difficulty with LH 280 is cleared up once we realize that the remedy should be understood as "their release (from the buyer) shall then be granted without (any payment of) silver (and they shall return to their former owner)." The buyer of a native slave abroad does run the risk of the slave being identified by his owner, and the buyer would determine whether the risk is worth the price, since perhaps the risk is minimal and is only entailed if the owner comes across the slave. The consequence of this law is that if it were applied, a certain number of native slaves found abroad would be left in the foreign land, and the native owner would never have the opportunity to come across them and have them returned.

Many slave contracts from the Old Babylonian period stipulate three liabilities on the slave: "three days investigation (of the slave's legal status), one month epilepsy, and for claims on [the slave], he is responsible in accordance with the royal decree."[21] The last two stipulations mirror the statutes in the Laws of Hammurabi, but the first one about the warranty for the investigation of the slave's identity and status is not mentioned in the Laws of Hammurabi. Martin Stol argued that LH 280–281 are a concrete example of the investigation of a slave's identity and status and that the statutes mirror neatly the stipulations in the slave contracts.[22] However, since the contracts first appear about fifty years after Hammurabi, Stol hypothesized that a royal decree including all three stipulations was issued during the reign of a later king (perhaps Abiešuh). However, the term "investigation" (*teb'ītum*) is absent from LH 280–281, and the case of a slave purchased abroad as formulated in the Laws of Hammurabi hinges on whether the slave is a native or a foreigner. A buyer who purchases a foreign slave in (the buyer's) native country would assume that he would be less at risk for buying a slave owned by someone else and, therefore, deserves to be reimbursed. This distinction does not overlap with the investigation of the slave's identity as mentioned in Old Babylonian slave contracts, and the claim that a royal decree instituting three stipulations was issued in response to a provision in the Laws of Hammurabi does not hold.

Claus Veenhof took issue with Stol's argument and modified it. He argued that the proviso in contracts that a warranty is in accordance with a royal decree refers only to the final stipulation: the first two stipulations are independent nominal clauses, and the final one is a verbal phrase governed by the proviso.[23] The royal decree dealt only with claims by a third party on slaves. The royal decree, according to Veenhof, was not about slaves in particular but about claims of ownership on any goods purchased, and the evidence for this is that a warranty for claims according to the royal decree is specified in other sale contracts. However, why would a royal decree about warranty for claims in sales in general need to be made in reaction to a provision in the Laws of Hammurabi about native slaves purchased abroad? The Laws of Hammurabi addresses a narrow issue compared to the putative royal decree. Again the similarity is intriguing but not probative.

[21] M. Stol, *Epilepsy in Babylonia* (Cuneiform Monographs 2; Groningen: Styx, 1993), 133–135; Claus Wilcke, "Zu den spät-altbabylonischen Kaufverträgen aus Nord-Babylonien," *WO* 8 (1976), 258–262. See also Driver and Miles, *The Babylonian Laws*, 1.479–481.

[22] Stol, *Epilepsy in Babylonia*, 134–135.

[23] Veenhof, "The Relationship between Royal Decrees and 'Law Codes,'" 70–71.

However, we do have the texts of reform edicts from Hammurabi's successors, and as was discussed in chapter 2, the provisions in contracts to prevent a debt from being cancelled due to an edict is clear evidence that the edicts of equity were put into practice and enforced. By contrast, there are no clear-cut references in records of legal activities or in the edicts of equity that prove that the statutes in the law collections were enforced, with one exception. The edicts appear to void a statute of the Laws of Hammurabi. LH 117 prescribes that free people who are sold into debt-slavery were to be released after three years of service, while the Edict of Ammi-ṣaduqa 20 provides for their immediate release of debt-slaves if they are from particular towns. LH 118 and the Edict of Ammi-ṣaduqa 21 stipulate that a slave sold for debt-servitude does not go free.

LH 117
If an obligation was outstanding against a man (lit. a financial difficulty has seized a man) and he sold or gave into debt service his wife, his son or his daughter, they shall perform service in the house of their buyer or of the one who holds them in debt service for three years; their release shall be secured in the fourth year.

LH 118
If he gives a male or female slave into debt service, the merchant may extend the term (beyond the three years), he may sell him; there are no grounds for a claim.

Edict of Ammi-ṣaduqa 20
If an obligation results in foreclosure against a citizen of Numhia, Emutbalum, Idamaras, Uruk, Isin, Kisurra, or Malgium (so that) he (placed) his own person, his wife, his children in debt servitude or as a pledge, because the king has invoked equity (mīsharum) for the land, he is released; his freedom is in effect.

Edict of Ammi-ṣaduqa 21
If a house-born (female) or (male) slave of a citizen of Numhia, Emutbalum, Idamaras, Uruk, Isin, Kisurra, or Malgium . . . whose price . . . has been sold for silver or was given over for debt servitude or was made a pledge, his freedom shall not be effectuated.

The voiding of the automatic release provided for in the Laws of Hammurabi may be a sign that these two statutes in the Laws of Hammurabi were either put into practice or mirrored law as practiced. This proves only that the automatic release for the family members of a debtor was put into effect (as well as the right to sell a slave of a debtor), whether as a law of prior standing or due to Hammurabi's authority. This does not demonstrate that the statutes in the Laws of Hammurabi as a whole were considered authoritative.

Otherwise, the statutes in the Laws of Hammurabi share only a literary form—statutes in conditional sentences—with the edicts, not content. The literary form used in the statutes of the Laws of Hammurabi and other law collections derives from two sources, a general tendency to articulate law in casuistic form and the scholastic mindset and tradition of Mesopotamian scribal culture. These tendencies contributed to the development of a repertoire of typical cases through which a scribe demonstrated his flair by composing variants on these cases in statutes, whether through the technique of incremental variants, as in the Laws of Hammurabi, or the technique of maximal variants, as in the Laws of Eshnunna.[24] The Laws of Hammurabi became part of the scholastic legal tradition, a tradition that possessed a wealth of material. This tradition included compendia of legal terminology and contractual formulas, collections of model contracts and literary legal decisions, and student exercises.

One further matter must be noted. Public access to the Laws of Hammurabi was limited. While it was inscribed on a stela, a public monument, the Stela was placed in a temple, and even if the public had access to the temple, the number of passersby would be fewer than a stela set up in a thoroughfare or market. Furthermore, while scholars now argue that more people could read in Mesopotamia than was formerly conceded, literacy was still limited, and the Stela of the Laws of Hammurabi was inscribed in an archaic ductus, further limiting access.

Examining the evidence whether Hammurabi issued the law collection that bears his name as legislation modifying existing law or as

[24] The scholar who identified the technique employed in the Laws of Eshnunna, Barry Eichler, argued that the technique would appear to eliminate the possibility that the Laws of Eshnunna was the product of either legislation or exemplary legal decisions in actual court cases. The Laws of Eshnunna was part of the Mesopotamian scholastic tradition and, as Eichler argued, was designed for teaching legal thought and the understanding of the complexities of disputes. In other words, the choice of maximal variants was intentionally designed to inspire analysis of the gray areas, the variants that might be found in the real-life situations of actual disputes, rather than rote memorization of polar cases. It was a legal textbook, designed to inspire Socratic teaching. I agree with Eichler that the technique of maximal variants and polar cases is at work in the Laws of Eshnunna, but whether the technique of maximal variants would have been a more effective method of teaching legal thinking than incremental variants is debatable.

incorporating judicial decisions, whether his or a judge's, has yielded mesmerizing clues but no definitive evidence.[25] The Laws of Hammurabi does not seem to reflect the verdicts of the king or judges in particular lawsuits, nor does it appear to conclusively mirror the law as it was practiced in legal matters in Babylonia. This methodology also attempts to correlate the Laws of Hammurabi with specific lawsuits and legal acts mentioned in legal records and royal correspondence. It evaluates whether the references to royal decrees, whether issued by Hammurabi or his successors, have affected the statutes in the Laws of Hammurabi or were a reaction to them. The yield of the analysis is intriguing yet inconclusive. The question that must be examined is whether this approach accurately and effectively elucidates the nature of the legal authority of the Laws of Hammurabi. It assumes that citation or allusion is necessary to demonstrate its legal authority. I believe that a new tack is warranted, one that takes into account how law operated in antiquity.

6.2. Legal Precedent and the Nature of the Laws of Hammurabi

Mesopotamian scribes writing legal documents did not cite either law collections or previous legal cases.[26] The attempts by modern scholars to tie specific statutes in the Laws of Hammurabi to royal correspondence and decrees or legal records have not yielded probative evidence about the legal authority of the Laws of Hammurabi. Does this mean that the Laws of Hammurabi did not serve as law in any sense? The fact that the Laws of Hammurabi was not cited as precedent has been used as evidence that it did not serve as law, whether as legislation, a set of official verdicts, or a collection of standard law. But this is a misunderstanding of precedent and authority, and it is time to move beyond the limits of that discussion.

[25] The fact that the Laws of Hammurabi does not include every possibility should not be deemed evidence that it was not meant to be put into effect, nor does its prescription of remedy for offense mean that it was impractical (contra Yoffee, *Myths of the Archaic State*, 107). No collection of law can ever include every variable, every nuance, every possibility. Every collection of law can been seen as promoting a rosy vision of a time in which all perpetrators will be caught, all evidence of their crime will be unambiguous, and the punishment swift and certain. The Laws of Hammurabi is no different.

[26] Law that is inscribed in writing is no guarantee of fairness. See Rosalind Thomas, "Written in Stone? Liberty, Equality, Orality and the Codification of Law," in L. Foxhall and A. D. E. Lewis, *Greek Law in Its Political Setting: Justifications Not Justice* (Oxford: Clarendon Press, 1996), 9–31.

One determinative characteristic of a legal system, termed "the rule of law," is that it should be predictable and consistent.[27] The use of precedents, either as binding or persuasive, is one possible means of doing so but not the only one. It must be noted that oftentimes in appeals to precedents, references are made to specific precedents in order to argue that those precedents are *not* applicable and should *not* be applied and therefore the position argued does not conflict with previous cases.[28] In Mesopotamia, there was no concept of binding precedent in the form of previous cases or the authoritative text of a law collection. Past cases or legal texts are not cited as binding or persuasive. Seeking precedents as evidence for the legal authority of the Laws of Hammurabi is misplaced.[29] It is projecting contemporary assumptions about law into the past—assumptions that are faulty.

[27] Raymond Westbrook argued that Mesopotamian law was primitive in comparison to Greek law because a nonprimitive system exhibits rules that are reasonably predictable and their results mutually consistent ("The Early History of Law: A Theoretical Essay," in *Ex Oriente Lex: Near Eastern Influences on Ancient Greek and Roman Law* [ed. Deborah Lyons and Kurt Raaflaub; Baltimore: Johns Hopkins University Press, 2015], 228–229). Westbrook further contended that Mesopotamian law lacked three features that are necessary for nonprimitive law. Westbrook insisted that nonprimitive law possesses theoretical categories and definitions of abstract concepts. However, as we have seen, there is categorization and systematization in the Laws of Hammurabi. Furthermore, the Roman jurists were skeptical of abstract concepts, as we discussed in chapter 4.

Westbrook argued that the second characteristic of non-primitive law is making reference to an authoritative statute or precedent. As he states, "There was an orgy of citation" in Greek, Roman, and rabbinic legal texts. The question is whether the lack of references to the law collections in Mesopotamian legal records means that there was no legal precedent in Mesopotamian law. If the law collections reflected how skilled scribes demonstrated their legal flair, and if legal exercises reflected how students were taught legal terminology and institutions, that may mean that Mesopotamian law had a distinct notion of legal precedent different from that in Greek, Roman, and rabbinic legal texts. The argument that just because legal records did not record precedents does not mean that precedents were not articulated during legal proceedings: what was inscribed in writing was not a complete rendering of what happened during the resolution of a dispute. References could not have been required in written records. Furthermore, while Westbrook argued that citations are to be found in classical and rabbinic law, in order to prove his point he cited the Mishnah and a speech given in court by Demosthenes, neither of which is a legal record or document from a legal transaction (see Westbrook, "Cuneiform Law Codes and the Origins of Legislation," *RA* 79 [1989], 214).

Westbrook argued that the third characteristic of nonprimitive law is a lawyer, a professional expert in law. However, what does the absence of a term for a profession mean when there are references to individuals who served as professional judges and to scribes with expertise in law who acted in the capacity of lawyers? There are also a few references to a legal professional who could be hired to assist the plaintiff and win his case. See Mogens Trolle Larsen, *The Old Assyrian City-State and Its Colonies* (Mesopotamia 4; Copenhagen: Akademisk Forlag, 1976), 370; Klaas R. Veenhof, "Old Assyrian Law," in *A History of Ancient Near Eastern Law* (Handbook of Oriental Studies; ed. Raymond Westbrook; Leiden: Brill, 2003), 1.473.

[28] Even a quick search of the opinions of the Supreme Court of the United States shows that a large part of an opinion is devoted to analyzing prior verdicts and dismissing them as irrelevant to the particular case under review.

[29] Sophie Lafont argued that royal law was subsidiary to local standards and was invoked only when local law was inapplicable or challenged by one of the parties to a dispute. No wonder, then, that neither royal decrees nor law collections were cited in legal records ("Codification et subsidiarité dans le droit du proche orient ancien," in *La Codification des lois dans l'antiquité: actes du Colloque de Strasbourg, 27–29 Novembre 1997* [Travaux du Centre de Recherche sur le Proche-Orient et la Grèce

Furthermore, the use of precedents even in modern law is complex. First, a number of modern legal systems forbid the use of decisions in prior cases as a source of law.[30] Second, the rule of law may not mean that precedents must be followed, because that could easily lead to injustice: when a judge is forced to adjudicate according to fixed rules—such as mandatory sentencing, to offer a contemporary example—the rule of law may be weakened. When a judge is not permitted to take the social context or other factors of a case into consideration, legal institutions become less rational. When a judge is not authorized to decide which of the variables in a case are essential but is directed to elevate one variable above all others, injustice may result. Modern law values consistency, but slavish conformity can violate fairness.[31] A decision may appear to be predictable and consistent from one perspective but distorted and unjust from another.

Consistency means that like cases should be treated alike, and predictability allows people to adapt their behavior to follow the law and avoid disputes. However, determining which factors make one case like another and therefore determinative is far from obvious and straightforward. Allowing discretion to reach a verdict may have been perceived as more just.[32] Permitting law to be flexible and individualized may have been seen as more fair than forcing law to be inevitable, uniform, and efficient.[33] The particular circumstances of a dispute and its broader social context may shape a

Antiques; ed. Ed. Lévy; Paris: de Boccard, 2000]). However, there are references to royal edicts, and contractees could have always made their own agreements. Lafont contended that the appeal of the wronged man in the Laws of Hammurabi was an appeal to the king when local law did not provide justice ("Codification et subsidiarité dans le droit du proche orient ancien," 54).

[30] Those legal systems may have a law code as a source of law (the *Code civile* in France) or may designate only the decisions of particular courts as usable as precedent (the Federal Constitutional Court in Germany). See Adriaan Lanni, "Arguing from 'Precedent': Modern Perspectives on Athenian Practice," in *The Law and the Courts in Ancient Greece* (ed. Edward M. Harris and Lene Rubinstein; London: Duckworth, 2004), 168 n.2.

[31] Lanni, "Arguing from 'Precedent,'" 167.

[32] It is erroneous to think that the Mesopotamians deliberately weighed adjudicating by precedent and decided to go along without it. It is just that they did not adjudicate by citing precedent.

[33] In the records of legal speeches from Athens, orators did not make reference to statutes but appealed to what might be deemed extralegal considerations (Adriaan Lanni, "'Verdict Most Just': The Modes of Classical Athenian Justice," *Yale Journal of Law and the Humanities* 16 (2004), 278–280). Those extralegal arguments were considered critical to achieving justice. Athenian law prized flexibility in order to attain justice suited to the individual and the social context. Therefore, Athenian law focused on procedural law rather than on substantive law. The laws that survive do not define the offense in question or offer guidelines as to how the law should be interpreted but only name the legal procedures to be followed after the offense has allegedly been committed (Lanni, *Law and Justice in the Courts of Classical Athens* [New York: Cambridge University Press, 2008], 87). See also the discussion of the nature of Greek law in Lanni, *Law and Justice in the Courts of Classical Athens*, 4, 9–11.

decision. If the purpose of litigation and legal activity is a just resolution of a dispute, there may be tension between discretion and consistency, and discretion may count for more than the predictable application of generalized rules that may fit a particular situation poorly. There is no reason for law to be limited to the logical application of a discrete set of standardized rules. There is no need for the law of a particular culture to constitute a coherent and logical system: law may simply be eclectic, and individual cases may have merited such flexibility.

The interpretive flair that a scribe exhibited in composing statutes for a law collection such as the Laws of Hammurabi or for a legal exercise allowed the scribe to express what he conceived to be equitable and just.[34] Discretion in individual cases allowed Mesopotamian law flexibility. Legal systems in general face the tension between adherence to general rules and doing justice in specific cases.[35] Mesopotamian law did not articulate general rules, but scribes who wrote the law collections were educated in typical cases and legal terminology alongside other scribes who made a living writing legal documents. The scribes who wrote the law collections may have supported themselves by writing legal documents as well.[36] *The Laws of Hammurabi served as an articulation of what was just. While it did not serve as binding precedent or constitute a set of authoritative verdicts, it expressed what was legally appropriate and fair, and that served to educate scribes. This is so in two ways: composing law as improvisation on a repertoire of standard cases served to develop a sense of justice in the scribes who wrote the statutes and legal exercises, and studying and copying them instilled a sense of justice in the scribal students who read and copied them.*

This means of articulating justice sidesteps one problem of consistency in law that is a particular nettlesome issue in Mesopotamian culture: referring to previous decisions might be one way of achieving predictability, but to do so, one would need a means of accessing past decisions. It may seem problematic in a society of such limited literacy to require reference to past decisions in written documents, and searching through clay tablets presents physical and organizational challenges. The parties to a legal dispute may have had a general

[34] That individual scribes might have conflicting ideas about what is just and equitable is not an obstacle. There is no reason for a society to have a homogeneous systems of law controlling the behavior of all its inhabitants. See Laura Nader and H. F. Todd Jr., "Introduction," in *The Disputing Process* (ed. Laura Nader and H. F. Todd Jr.; New York: Columbia University Press, 1978), 33.

[35] Lanni, *Law and Justice in the Courts of Classical Athens*, 175.

[36] It must be noted that the Laws of Hammurabi is not fantasy purely detached from reality: it must have borne a resemblance to the law as it was actually practiced. Indeed, from where else would the drafters have shaped the particulars of a dispute and extrapolated from one case to another?

sense about what happened in past circumstances. And even if the parties to a legal dispute did have access to a repository, the records of past cases simply did not record sufficient information.[37] In the legal records from Mesopotamia, only one, the Nippur Murder Trial, has a discussion of the reasoning for the verdict, and this may be an outlier since it was transmitted as a model court case. The Laws of Hammurabi does have statutes in which an explanatory clause highlights the feature of a case that should prove decisive in the remedy. Scribal education and practice meant that scribes did have a general sense of what happened in the past, and the articulation of law by improvising on a repertoire of cases instilled thought-patterns of what constituted justice and fairness. While there is no evidence that there were repositories of past rulings that could be used as precedents, scribal students did copy law collections and model court cases and contracts and wrote legal exercises. This instilled a sense of justice in them, and the conflicting rulings they may have learned helped them to think through competing examples of what constitutes justice and to weigh the variables in a particular dispute.[38] It is no surprise, then, that many of the copies of law collections extant are student copies.

Even when scribes felt free to improvise, the distance between their rulings was relatively narrow. It is clear that Mesopotamian law collections exhibit shared norms. At the same time, the scribe of the Laws of Hammurabi veered away from the other law collections in the types of punishment prescribed. The scribe, for example, called for poetic justice far more frequently in the Laws of Hammurabi than in other law collections. The scribe deviated by stipulating mutilation and vicarious punishment for certain offenses, characteristic types of punishment in the Laws of Hammurabi. But otherwise the variation was no more than typical for the law collections. The relative consistency across the law collections meant that there was predictability. The deviation from the norm was not so wide. A scribe demonstrating his flair was demonstrating his grasp of fairness more than contradicting other scribes. By means of these methods of composing sets of statutes, Mesopotamian law manifested a tradition of reflective jurisprudence.

[37] See the observations about the lack of detailed records in ancient Athens in Lanni, *Law and Justice in the Courts of Classical Athens*, 125.

[38] By shifting away from the concept of a textual version of law employed as precedent, we gain a greater understanding of the context of law and how legal rulings were made. See Laura Cuthbertson, "Local Courts in Centralizing States: The Case of Ur III Mesopotamia," in *Social Theory in Archaeology and Ancient History: The Present and Future of Counternarratives* (ed. Geoff Emberling; New York: Cambridge University Press, 2016), 186–187.

7

The Afterlife of the Laws of Hammurabi

The Continuation of Scribal Improvisation outside Mesopotamia and the Creation of Commentaries in Mesopotamia

The Laws of Hammurabi is the culmination of one stream of tradition and a witness to the start of another. The tradition of a law collection associated with a royal patron appeared for the first time in the Laws of Ur-Namma, a law collection dating from about 2100 BCE. Scribes drafting a law collection would demonstrate their legal flair by composing statutes on a traditional repertoire of cases. They integrated the set of statutes into the textual structure of a royal inscription, and the composition as a whole was intended to demonstrate that the king has fulfilled his divine mandate to institute justice. The Laws of Hammurabi is the most developed of this stream of tradition in length and scope, and it is the apex of this Mesopotamian tradition. Strikingly, the tradition continued outside of Mesopotamia. In this chapter, we analyze how statutes were composed on a repertoire of traditional cases in the Hittite Empire and in ancient Israel, and we explore the possibility that this tradition spread to Greece and Rome. At the same time that the tradition of a law collection expanded outside of Mesopotamia, a new intellectual tradition arose in Mesopotamia: certain texts and their authors became esteemed and privileged in an unprecedented way. The Laws of Hammurabi was drawn into this new tradition. We investigate how Hammurabi was regarded and honored as a sage and how the Laws of Hammurabi became the subject of formal commentary.

7.1. The Continuation of Scribal Improvisation outside Mesopotamia

The tradition of Mesopotamian law collections linked to a royal patron started about 2100 BCE and continued to the time of Hammurabi. The royal

The Laws of Hammurabi. Pamela Barmash, Oxford University Press (2020). © Oxford University Press.
DOI: 10.1093/oso/9780197525401.001.0001.

scribes employed the textual structure of a royal inscription for the law collections, and they reshaped this textual structure by incorporating a set of statutes. They did so because in the Mesopotamian educational system, scribes learned textual structures for a number of genres, including royal inscriptions, and they also studied legal terminology, concepts, textual patterns, cases, and practices. Scribes knew this material thoroughly and used it to compose new works out of the words of earlier works. The practice of composing statutes on traditional cases was transmitted outside of Mesopotamia as part of a shared tradition.[1] Not surprisingly, scribes from other cultures reshaped the cases and textual structures as they saw fit, just like Mesopotamian scribes.

Let me illustrate this with the statutes on the case of the assault on a pregnant woman. This topic is found in two Mesopotamian law collections and in a school exercise text from Mesopotamia:

LL d
If [a . . .] strikes the daughter of a free man and causes her to lose her fetus, he shall weigh and deliver 30 shekels of silver.

LL e
If she dies, that male shall be killed.

LL f
If a . . . strikes the slave woman of a man and causes her to lose her fetus, he shall weigh and deliver 5 shekels of silver.

[1] My use of the term "shared tradition" is intentional. Raymond Westbrook developed the concept of a common legal tradition for ancient Near Eastern law, for which he received much criticism. Greatly problematic is his emphasis on the continuities far more than the culturally specific legal phenomena. His understanding the legal traditions of the ancient Near East as a common one—that is, a single legal system that can be reconstructed from any and all texts of a genre touching on law—is untenable; moreover, his use of the term "common"—a venerable term in legal history referring to "the common law," a legal system built up from judicial precedent and custom—is simply not accurate for the ancient Near East. He made a similar strong claim for Greek and Roman law. Westbrook qualified his claim in a posthumously published piece in which he argued that ideas travel lightly: cultural ideas are easily transmitted from one culture to another. See Westbrook, "The Nature and Origins of the Twelve Tables," *ZAR* 105 (1988), 74–121; "Cuneiform Law Codes and the Origins of Legislation," 201–222; "Drakon's Homicide Law" in *Symposium 2007: Vorträge zur griechischen und hellenistischen Rechtsgeschichte* (ed. E. Harris and G. Thür; Vienna: Österreichen Akademie der Wissenschaften, 2008), 3–16; "Barbarians at the Gates: Near Eastern Law in Ancient Greece," in *Ex Oriente Lex*, 59–69. The editors of (most of) his collected essays, which appear in *Law from the Tigris to the Tiber: The Writings of Raymond Westbrook* (ed. Bruce Wells and F. Rachel Magdalene; Winona Lake, Ind.: Eisenbrauns, 2009), introduce his oeuvre by modifying both his conceptualization and terminology to a shared tradition. See Martha T. Roth, "Errant Oxen, or the Goring Ox Redux," in *Literature as Politics, Politics as Literature: Essays on the Ancient Near East in Honor of Peter Machinist* (ed. David S. Vanderhooft and Abraham Winitzer; Winona Lake, Ind.; Eisenbrauns, 2013), 398 n.5.

SLEx 1′
If he jostles the daughter of a free man and causes her to miscarry her fetus, he shall weigh and deliver 10 shekels of silver.

SLEx 2′
If he strikes the daughter of a free man and causes her to miscarry her fetus, he shall weigh and deliver 20 shekels of silver.

LH 209
If a free man strikes a daughter of a free man and causes her to miscarry her fetus, he shall pay 10 shekels of silver for her fetus.

LH 210
If that woman dies, they shall kill his daughter.

LH 211
If he causes a daughter of a palace dependent / commoner to miscarry her fetus by the beating, he shall pay 5 shekels of silver.

LH 212
If that woman dies, he shall pay 30 shekels of silver.

LH 213
If he strikes a free man's slave woman and causes her to miscarry her fetus, he shall pay 2 shekels of silver.

LH 214
If that slave woman dies, he shall pay 20 shekels of silver.

All three texts share the typical case, but the scribes drafting each text had the freedom to go their own direction and to improvise on the case as they saw fit. The scribes of the Laws of Lipit-Ishtar and of the Laws of Hammurabi prescribed different punishments based on the consequence to the pregnant woman, whether she suffers miscarriage or death, as well as on her social status. They did not base punishment on the intention of the offending party. By contrast, in the Sumerian Laws Exercise Tablet, a distinction is drawn between involuntarily jostling a pregnant woman and assaulting her intentionally: the scribe drafting the school exercise takes into account a consideration that neither law collection mentions. Social class is taken into account in all three. The Laws of Hammurabi identifies three social categories; the Laws of Lipit-Ishtar recognizes only two; and while the Sumerian Laws Exercise Tablet mentions only the daughter of a free man, the specification implies other social categories. Other than social status, no other characteristics of the pregnant woman are taken into account. A woman may survive a miscarriage, while another woman may not because she possessed less robust health or has bad luck. The man who strikes her is responsible, even though his action may be only one factor leading to the woman's death. His action may not have determined the final outcome, but other factors are omitted. As the commonalities and differences demonstrate, all three texts improvise on the traditional case, but the scribes reshaped the case with modest variation.

The Middle Assyrian Laws follows in the same vein as the other law collections, but with more permutations:

> MAL A 21
> If a man strikes a daughter of the free class, causing her to abort her fetus, and they prove the charges against him and find him guilty, he shall pay 9,000 shekels of lead; they shall strike him 50 blows with rods; he shall perform the king's service for a month.

The scribe employed the traditional case, a miscarriage caused by an assault, but reimagined the remedy through the mode of multiple punishments characteristic of his law collection. Furthermore, the scribe did not place this statute in the context of other statutes dealing with miscarriage, as the other scribes did. Rather, he placed this statute in a set dealing with sexual crimes. Later in this tablet, the scribe presented in more detail a set of statutes dealing with miscarriage:

> MAL A 50
> [If a man] strikes [another man's wife and causes her to abort her fetus . . .] a man's wife [. . .] and they shall treat him as he treated her.[2] He shall make full payment of a life for her fetus. And if that woman dies, they shall kill that man; he shall make full payment of a life for her fetus. And if that woman's husband has no son, and his wife whom (the assailant) struck aborted her fetus, they shall kill that assailant for her fetus. If her fetus was a female, he shall make full payment of a life only.
>
> MAL A 51
> If a man strikes another man's wife who does not raise her child,[3] causing her to abort her fetus, it is a punishable offense; he shall give 7,200 shekels of lead.

2 Because the text is incomplete, it is not clear what the punishment is.

3 It is not clear what the specification "a wife who does not raise her child" means: Is she too ill to raise a child? Too neglectful? Does she have a wet nurse who would take care of her child? See G. R. Driver and John C. Miles, *The Assyrian Laws* (Oxford: Clarendon, 1935), 114–115.

MAL A 52

If a man strikes a prostitute causing her to abort her fetus, they shall assess him blow for blow; he shall make full payment for a life.

MAL A 53

If a woman aborts her fetus by her own action and then they prove the charges against her and find her guilty, they shall impale her. They shall not bury her. If she dies as a result of aborting her fetus, they shall impale her; they shall not bury her. If any person should hide that woman because she aborted her fetus . . .

In composing this set of statutes, the scribe has devised more variations than what is found in the earlier Mesopotamian law collections. A distinction is drawn based on social status, but the difference is based on marital and maternal status, not only between free and enslaved. The scribe varied the punishment on whether the fetus was male or female. The scribe improvised further by adding the case of the prostitute and the case of a woman who causes her own abortion.

Improvising on a typical case spread beyond the borders of Mesopotamia. A Hittite scribe composed statutes on the traditional case of an assault on a pregnant woman:

HL 17

If anyone causes a free woman to miscarry, [if] it is in her tenth month, he shall pay 10 shekels of silver; if it is her fifth month, he shall pay 5 shekels of silver. He shall look to his house for it.

Late version of 17

If anyone causes a free woman to miscarry, he shall pay 20 shekels of silver.

HL 18

If anyone causes a female slave to miscarry, if it is her tenth month, he shall pay 5 shekels of silver.

Late version of 18

If anyone causes a female slave to miscarry, he shall pay 10 shekels of silver.

Like the Mesopotamian scribes, the scribe of the Hittite Laws distinguished between social status, between free and slave. But he introduced a new consideration: how far along in the pregnancy the woman was before the miscarriage.[4] He did not address the death of the woman as a result of the miscarriage, nor did he consider the intention of the offending party, whether the woman had been jostled or assaulted. These factors are considered in the Mesopotamian law collections, but not in the Hittite Laws. The innovation of the Hittite scribe was to make a distinction based on how far along in the pregnancy the assault occurred. The Hittite scribe also articulated a distinction between earlier and later law, indicating that the scribe drafting the Hittite Laws was cognizant of a historical change in Hittite law. This awareness, almost unique among the law collections, serves as evidence that the Hittite Laws reflected law as it was applied.[5]

This traditional case, assault on a pregnant woman, is incorporated in the Covenant Code in the Hebrew Bible:

> Exodus 21:22–24
>
> If men brawl and knock against a pregnant woman so that a miscarriage results[6] but an *ason*[7] does not ensue, (the offender) shall surely be obliged according to whatever the husband may exact from him and pay according to the assessment.[8] But if an *ason* ensues, it shall be a life for a life. An eye for an eye, a tooth for a tooth, a hand for a hand, a leg for a leg, a burn for a burn, wound for a wound, bruise for a bruise.

[4] The duration of the pregnancy was counted in ten months of the calendar rather than in the nine-month length of gestation.

[5] One textually corrupt passage in the Laws of Ur-Namma, LU E3b, states that Ur-Namma modified the rule regarding the sale of slaves. This could also be an indication that the Laws of Ur-Namma contained law as practiced, but the problematic nature of the textual exemplar brackets such a conclusion. See Civil, "The Law Collection of Ur-Namma," 252.

[6] The Hebrew clause *ve-yetz'u yeladeiha* refers to a miscarriage. The possibility that it refers only to the early birth of a viable infant seems remote.

[7] The term אסון (*ason*) has been the subject of debate: Is the issue of an *ason* about the well-being of the pregnant woman or of her fetus? Among the more significant contributions to the discussion are Bernard S. Jackson, "The Problem of Exod. XXI 22–25 (*ius talionis*)," *VT* 23 (1973), 273–304; Moshe Weinfeld, "Hamatat ubar: emdatah shel masoret yisrael behashva'ah le-emdat ammim aḥerim," *Zion* 42 (1977): 129–142; Chaim Cohen, "The Ancient Critical Understanding of Exodus 21:22–25 and Its Implications for the Current Debate on Abortion," in *Mishneh Todah: Studies in Deuteronomy and Its Cultural Environment in Honor of Jeffrey H. Tigay* (ed. Nili Sacher Fox, David A. Glatt-Gilad, and Michael J. Williams; Winona Lake, Ind.; Eisenbrauns, 2009), 437–458; David Andrew Teeter, *Scribal Laws: Exegetical Variation in the Textual Transmission of Biblical Law in the Late Second Temple Period* (Forschungen zum Alten Testament 92; Tübingen: Mohr Siebeck, 2014), 141–155.

[8] The meaning of פללים (pelilim) as assessment was clarified by E. A. Speiser, "The Stem *PLL* in Hebrew," *Journal of Biblical Literature* 82 (1963), 301–306. For a number of recent studies, see Bernard S. Jackson, *Wisdom-Laws: A Study of the Mishpatim of Exodus 21:1–22:16* (Oxford: Oxford University Press, 2006), 209–227; William H. C. Propp, *Exodus 19–40* (Anchor Bible; New York: Doubleday, 2006), 223–225.

The biblical scribe addressed a somewhat different scenario from that in the Mesopotamian and Hittite law collections: a number of men are engaged in fisticuffs, and somehow a pregnant woman, who otherwise would be wise enough to remove herself from the scene of a brawl, is injured. Despite the difference, this case appears to be part of the scribal tradition represented in the cuneiform law collections. The variation is one of quantity, not magnitude. The case of the assault on a pregnant woman in the later cuneiform law collections (the Middle Assyrian Laws and the Hittite Laws) is more heterogeneous than in the earlier law collections, and this is so in the Covenant Code. Scribal tradition provides a repertoire of typical cases, and each law collection improvises on these types. The case of a miscarriage caused by a blow is a traditional legal case by which a scribe would show his legal flair, and later scribes seem willing to reshape it more.[9]

Another imprint of Mesopotamian law can solve an interpretive puzzle in this statute. What is the significance of the set of phrases at the conclusion of the statute: "a life for a life, an eye for an eye, a tooth for a tooth, a hand for a hand, a leg for a leg, a burn for a burn, wound for a wound, bruise for a bruise"? The inclusion of a list of very specific injuries echoes mesmerizingly the Mesopotamian and Hittite statutes on a similar set of specific injuries. A set of statutes in the Laws of Hammurabi addresses bodily injury:

LH 196
If a free man should blind the eye of a man of the free class, they shall blind his eye.

LH 197
If he should break the bone of a free man, they shall break his bone.

LH 198
If he should blind the eye of a palace dependent / commoner, he shall weigh and deliver 60 shekels of silver.

LH 199
If he should blind the eye of a free man's slave or break the bone of a free man's slave, he shall weigh and deliver one-half of (the slave's) value.

[9] The influence of this tradition appears to be limited to the Covenant Code. See Barmash, *Homicide in the Biblical World*, 140–147. This phenomenon is distinct from the independent invention of isolated statutes with identical content, such as LU 4 and Exod 21:4 or LE 53 and Exod 21:35.

LH 200

If a free man should knock out the tooth of another free man of his own rank, they shall knock out his own tooth.

LH 201

If he should knock out the tooth of a palace dependent / commoner, he shall weigh and deliver 20 shekels of silver.[10]

The case of physical assault with specific injuries is one more typical case on which a scribe would demonstrate his skill. The punishment of mutilation informed by poetic justice is characteristic of the Laws of Hammurabi in general. This type of punishment conflicts with other cases of nonfatal assault in other Mesopotamian law collections, where compensation is the mode of recompense (i.e., LE 44–46). In the Hebrew Bible, a formulary akin to the statutes on assault in the Laws of Hammurabi (but not based on them) has become a fixed set of phrases—"a life for a life, an eye for an eye, a tooth for a tooth, a hand for a hand, a leg for a leg, a burn for a burn, wound for a wound, bruise for a bruise"—and the scribe drafting the Covenant Code has applied it to a different case, the case of a pregnant woman assaulted in a brawl. The scribe did so, even though the penalty for assault in the Covenant Code follows a different principle, compensation for recuperation and healing (Exod 21:18–19). The formulary of "a life for a life, an eye for an eye, a tooth for a tooth, a hand for a hand, a leg for a leg, a burn for a burn, wound for a wound, bruise for a bruise" in the case of a pregnant woman assaulted expresses equivalence. The scribe of the Covenant Code did not refer to "a life for a life, an eye for an eye," etc., as a specific punishment, but he employed it to express equivalence as a principle of punishment.[11] He applied a formula based on cases of injury to body parts to the case of a pregnant woman assaulted.

Identifying the shared educational tradition solves the puzzle of the formulary of "a life for a life, an eye for an eye, a tooth for a tooth, a hand for a hand," and so on, in the Covenant Code. It also explains why the situation of a pregnant woman assaulted is one of the specific cases of assault treated in the Covenant Code.[12] Shared educational tradition also explains why many

[10] Many types of assault are omitted. While injuries to the eyes, teeth, and bones are included, no mention of injuries to the nose, ear, hand, or foot is made. No mention is made of an injury to the slave of the temple and the palace. No consideration is made of a case where the aggressor is a woman. Omissions as well are found in HL 7–16 and MAL A 7–8, A 9, A 21, A 50–52.

[11] See Barmash, *Homicide in the Biblical World*, 154–178.

[12] Another case in the Covenant Code originates in the shared tradition, the case of the goring ox. Cases involving oxen appear with frequency in Mesopotamian law collections and student

of the statutes in the Covenant Code are formulated in conditional sentences like the Mesopotamian law collections.[13] The royal inscription format,

exercises: oxen killed by lions, SLEx 9`, LOx 7–8, SLHF vi.16–22, 32–36, LH 244; lost oxen, LU C 3, 5, 6 (see Civil, "The Law Collection of Ur-Namma," 249–250), SLEx 10`, HL 66–67, 79, 71; rented oxen damaged, LL 34–37, LOx 1–5, *ana ittišu* IV.1–10, SLHF vi.11–15, LH 245–249, HL 78; damaged oxen, HL 74–76; drowned oxen, LOx 6, SLHF vi.23–31; stolen oxen, HL 70; dead oxen, HL 72; and a pregnant cow assaulted, HL 77a. This is not surprising for an agricultural society. However, the Covenant Code shares the specific case of an ox that gores other animals and human beings with the Laws of Hammurabi and the Laws of Eshnunna. For the classic scholarly exposition on the goring ox in Mesopotamian law, see J. J. Finkelstein, "The Goring Ox: Some Historical Perspectives on Deodands, Forfeitures, Wrongful Death and the Western Notion of Sovereignty." *Temple Law Quarterly* 46 (1973), 169–290, and *The Ox That Gored* (prepared by Maria deJ. Ellis; Publications of the American Philosophical Society; Philadelphia: American Philosophical Society, 1981).

Martha T. Roth argued that this case should be understood as a case of an errant ox, as another instance of cases involving oxen that are addressed in law collections and similar to those cases, not unusual or compellingly different ("Errant Oxen," 400). There is merit to her argument since a significant number of statutes in the law collections are devoted to oxen and in particular to errant oxen. The question that needs to be considered is whether the scribe conceived the statutes on the goring ox as part of a set of cases about oxen. This is indeed the case in the Laws of Hammurabi, where the statutes addressing the goring ox, LH 250–252, are part of a series starting in LH 241 on oxen. However, this is not the case in the Laws of Eshnunna, LE 53–55, where it is preceded by statutes on escaping slaves and is followed by statutes on vicious dogs and a tottering wall, more cases of death through negligence. In the Hebrew Bible, statutes on the goring ox (Exod 21:28–32) are preceded by laws on aggravated assault, but they serve as a pivot pointing to statutes on agricultural disputes. The statutes on an ox goring a person to death is followed by one on damage to oxen, which itself is followed by a statute on an ox gored by another ox; then the Covenant Code addresses agricultural cases. The scribe of the Laws of Eshnunna viewed the case on the goring ox as unlawful killing, while the scribe of the Covenant Code conceived them both as unlawful killing and as a subcategory of disputes over oxen.

The lines of evidence converge as proof that the Covenant Code is part of the shared educational tradition, even if some evidence is probative and other evidence is more suggestive. The literary form of the conditional sentence in the law collections and the frequent appearance of the statutes addressing the assault on a pregnant woman in the law collections are probative, while the case of the goring ox may be less compelling because (1) it is not as widespread as the case of assault on the pregnant woman and (2) it is a particular case about disputes about oxen. If only one of these pieces of evidence existed, the case for a shared tradition would be weak. Rather, we have a number of pieces of evidence of varying degrees of decisiveness whose cumulative effect and clustering in the Covenant Code strengthen the case for a shared tradition.

An ox goring in an agricultural-pastoralist society seems a likely eventuality: an ox is usually a docile animal, but considering the number of oxen in use, the case of an ox going berserk would occur from time to time. Not surprisingly then, the case of the goring ox is found in *The T'ang Code*, a Chinese law code, article 207, 2.193–195. But yet there is only one record of a case involving a goring ox in Mesopotamia, COS 3.121. However, arguing whether an occurrence is probable based on its presence in documents of actual cases is faulty, simply because so few legal documents, such as those extant from Mesopotamia, mention anything other than the sale of barley, slaves, donkeys, or orchards of date palms. This is not as odd as it seems. The vast bulk of legal documents in our contemporary society is also devoted to recording economic transactions, such as the sale of merchandise, automobiles, and homes. The nature of the differences between the biblical and cuneiform sources is already familiar to us from our analysis of the cuneiform law collections themselves.

[13] David P. Wright argued that the author of the Book of the Covenant derived its order and topics directly from the Laws of Hammurabi ("The Compositional Logic of the Goring Ox and Negligence Laws in the Covenant Collection (Ex 21:28–36)," ZAR 10 (2004), 93–142; *Inventing God's Law: How the Covenant Code of the Bible Used and Revised the Laws of Hammurabi* (New York: Oxford University Press, 2009). His arguments have met with much criticism. See Bruce Wells, "The Covenant Code and Near Eastern Legal Traditions: A Response to David P. Wright," *Maarav* 13

however, was not retained outside of Mesopotamia as the overarching textual structure, at least as far as the extant sources demonstrate.

7.2. Mesopotamian Scribal Learning outside of Mesopotamia

So far we have highlighted a specific traditional case that demonstrates that Mesopotamian legal learning spread outside of Mesopotamia. We must then ask, how did the scribes outside of Mesopotamia acquire knowledge of the case of a pregnant woman assaulted as well as other elements of Mesopotamian law? There is extensive evidence for a cuneiform educational system at the western periphery of the Near East for the mid- to late second millennium BCE, and less evidence for the first millennium BCE. Mesopotamian teachers trained local students in the curriculum of Mesopotamia because Akkadian became the lingua franca. It was used for diplomatic correspondence, even between two countries neither of whose language was Akkadian. The Hittite and Egyptian monarchies employed Akkadian as the language of communication. As much as Akkadian was a language attracting interest for practical reasons, it was also a language of prestige as the language of the superpower often dominant in the ancient Near East.[14]

(2006), 85–118; Wright, "The Laws of Hammurabi and the Covenant Code: A Response to Bruce Wells," *Maarav* 13 (2007), 211–260. See also Meir Malul's illuminating study of the comparative method, *The Comparative Method in Ancient Near Eastern and Biblical Legal Studies* (AOAT 227; Kevelaer and Neukirchener-Vluyn: Butzon & Bercker and Neukirchener Verlag, 1990).

[14] There was an analog to this development within Mesopotamia itself. The Sumerian language was considered prestigious, which may be why there was a (partial) translation of the Laws of Hammurabi into Sumerian. An Old Babylonian translation of the Laws of Hammurabi, probably from Sippar, contains the epilogue translated into Sumerian with Akkadian glosses (fragment w). See Åke Sjöberg, "Was There a Sumerian Version of the Laws of Hammurapi?" *Aula Orientalis* 9 (1991), 219–225. It is clear that it is a translation, not a Sumerian "original" text for the Laws of Hammurabi, because one of the two lines of the epilogue omitted and not translated into Sumerian is already damaged on the Stela excavated at Susa. This line must have been damaged in antiquity even before the Stela was carried off by the Elamites to Susa; otherwise the line would have been included in the Sumerian version. The second line was omitted because it would not make any sense without the first.

The Sumerian translation could either be a school text, as part of scribal training was in legal terminology, or yet another official document turned into Sumerian. In either case, the glosses were intended for clarification. If the first possibility were the case, then the tablet was a school text, and the bilingual text was meant to teach legal terminology, a strange goal considering that contracts and other legal documents were written in Akkadian. If the second, then the bilingual text reflects the continuing tradition of royal inscriptions in bilingual form. It may be speculated that since Sumerian was the language of prestige, the Akkadian glosses were for clarity since Sumerian was no longer spoken and had to be taught deliberately to students learning the scribal arts. See Sjöberg, "The Old Babylonian Eduba," 161–167.

The evidence offers snapshots into the instructional activities of Mesopotamian teachers. One foreign teacher residing in Emar offered instruction in cuneiform lexical lists, the primary stage of training in Sumerian and Akkadian.[15] He also wrote documents, such as a debt note (Emar 26). A Babylonian scribe active in Hattuša, the capital of the Hittite Empire, in the fifteenth century BCE founded a scribal family whose descendants were active in the scribal craft for at least two centuries.[16] Other Babylonian and Assyrian experts were present in Hattuša, whether as scribes, incantation priests, or physicians.[17] Mesopotamian teachers taught the cuneiform curriculum and practiced their craft.

The most extensive evidence for a cuneiform curriculum comes from Ugarit in the Late Bronze period. The material remains at Ugarit are replete with cuneiform lexical texts, precisely the texts used in the beginning stages of scribal education in Mesopotamia.[18] These texts run the progression from the simplest to the more difficult, most likely indicating that they were studied in an order meant to facilitate learning. Just as the evidence reveals education in Nippur in the Old Babylonian period, there are only student copies but no master text from which the students copied—evidence that the teacher knew the lexical series by heart and expected the students to memorize it as well. Among the lexical texts is the large series ḪAR-ra, whose first two tablets are of legal and administrative terminology.[19] One school archive collection omits most of this large series, except for the legal and administrative terminology, testifying to the importance of Mesopotamian law outside of Mesopotamia. There are ritual and literary texts extant, as well as one exercise tablet containing legal material that appears to be a contract. This tablet seems to be a school text because there is an alphabet at the end, perhaps appended when a less advanced student needed to practice (a scrap tablet?).

[15] There were other foreign scribes at Emar in this period, but they have left no trace of their involvement in the schooling of scribes. See Yoram Cohen, "Kidin-Gula—The Foreign Teacher at the Emar School," *RA* 98 (2004), 97–98.

[16] Gary M. Beckman, "Mesopotamians and Mesopotamian Learning at Ḫattuša," *JCS* 35 (1983), 104–108.

[17] It appears that there was a constant exchange of experts among Mesopotamia, Hatti, and Egypt during the Late Bronze Age (as well as a stream of diplomatic messengers). It may also be that the Egyptians learned their cuneiform from the Hittites. On Hittite scribal education and on the presence of foreign experts, see Gordin, *Hittite Scribal Circles*, 123–145 (esp. 138), 331.

[18] W. H. van Soldt, "Babylonian Lexical, Religious, and Literary Texts and Scribal Education at Ugarit and Its Implication for the Alphabetic Literary Texts," in *Ugarit: ein ostmediterraneas Kulturzentum im alten Orient: Ergebnisse und Perspektiven der Forschung* (ed. Manfried Dietrich and Oswald Loretz; Münster: Ugarit-Verlag, 1995), 172–212.

[19] Van Soldt, "Babylonian Lexical, Religious, and Literary Texts," 198.

However, there are traces of seals on the reverse, which would indicate that the tablet in question was an actual legal document.[20] The tablets containing literary and ritual texts in particular exhibit many mistakes, reflecting the low level of expertise the students had acquired. This raises the question of why students copied them, and the answer may be that these texts were part of the accepted curriculum for cuneiform, allowing the student to practice Sumerian and Akkadian, the foreign languages they were learning.

Scribes who were able to master the cuneiform curriculum would surely be able the master the far simpler alphabetic one of their native language, especially since the names of the scribes demonstrate that they were natives of Ugarit and so would have already spoken Ugaritic before being sent to school.[21] Scribal schools taught both the cuneiform and alphabetic curricula. Both linguistic worlds operated in tandem, with an alphabetic education existing alongside the complex cuneiform one. An alphabetic culture could have an extensive education system. At the same time, the prevalence of abecedaries suggests possibly a basic level of literacy, with upper-level literacy and reading limited to a minority.[22]

The use of clay tablets, a durable writing material, at Ugarit demonstrates that a culture could have an extensive Mesopotamian cuneiform educational system as well as a native educational network based on an alphabetic literature.[23] The nature of writing materials used in ancient Israel, such as leather and papyrus, meant that they disintegrated and have not left any physical remains for analysis. The evidence for cuneiform education in ancient Israel is more cursory than for Ugarit.

The evidence for schools in the geographic area of ancient Israel is found in the types of texts that have been discovered:

1. At Tel Megiddo, a fragment of the Epic of Gilgamesh has been excavated.[24]

[20] Van Soldt, "Babylonian Lexical, Religious, and Literary Texts," 176.

[21] Van Soldt, "Babylonian Lexical, Religious, and Literary Texts," 183–184.

[22] A different context of literacy may have existed in the Aegean. Erasures and other indications that what was written was only the initial transcription in Late Bronze in clay tablets from the eastern Mediterranean serves as evidence that scribes may have learned on the job. They possessed basic literacy and then trained onsite as scribes associated with a particular craft or even a workshop (Joanna S. Smith, "Writing Styles in Clay of the Eastern Mediterranean Late Bronze Age," in *Sea Routes: Interconnections in the Mediterranean 16th–6th c.* BC [Athens: University of Crete and the A. G. Leventis Foundation, 2003], 277–278, 281).

[23] Carr, *Writing on the Tablet of the Heart*, 52; William W. Hallo, "The Expansion of Cuneiform Literature," *Proceedings of the American Academy of Jewish Research* 46–47 (1980), 312.

[24] Wayne Horowitz and Takayoshi Oshima, *Cuneiform in Canaan: Cuneiform Sources from the Land of Israel in Ancient Times* (Jerusalem: Israel Exploration Society and the Hebrew University

2. A bilingual and perhaps a trilingual lexical text from Aphek has been found, as well as a bilingual one from Ashkelon.[25]
3. A school tablet with an excerpt from an identifiable lexical text HAR-RA = ḫubullu was discovered at Hazor.[26]

This evidence dates from the Late Bronze period, before the Israelites.[27] What evidence is there for the Israelites' learning Mesopotamian scribal practices? Of the ninety-four Akkadian texts excavated so far in Israel, eighteen texts have their provenance in Israelite sites dating from the First Temple period, four more texts might be from the First Temple period, and five from the Exilic and Second Temple periods.[28] The array of documentation attests to knowledge of Akkadian acquired either from a foreign scribe living in ancient Israel or by individual Israelites who studied in foreign lands. It is clear from the contents or clay of most of the texts that they were written in the land of Israel and were not imported.[29] It is, therefore, not necessary to assume that a text imprinted with Mesopotamian learning must have been composed while Israelites were living in Mesopotamia during the Babylonian Exile or later, although a Mesopotamian location might make the transmission of scribal learning more clear. And while a wide range of

of Jerusalem, 2006), has now been succeeded by Horowitz, Oshima, and Seth Sanders, *Cuneiform in Canaan: The Next Generation* (second edition; Winona Lake, Ind.; Eisenbrauns, 2018). The Gilgamesh text is found in Horowitz, Oshima, and Sanders, *Cuneiform in Canaan*, second edition, 105–108.

[25] Horowitz, Oshima, and Sanders, *Cuneiform in Canaan*, second edition, 27–30, 40–41.

[26] Horowitz, Oshima, and Sanders, *Cuneiform in Canaan*, second edition, 70–72.

[27] Inscribed liver models used for extispicy were discovered at Hazor, probably meant for the training of diviners. See Horowitz, Oshima, and Sanders, *Cuneiform in Canaan*, second edition, 64–66.

[28] Wayne Horowitz, Takayoshi Oshima, and Seth Sanders, "A Bibliographical List of Cuneiform Inscriptions from Canaan, Palestine/Philistia, and the Land of Israel," *JAOS* 122 (2012), 753–766; Horowitz and Oshima, *Cuneiform in Canaan*; Horowitz, Oshima, and Sanders, *Cuneiform in Canaan*. See also Karel van der Toorn, "Cuneiform Documents from Syria-Palestine: Texts, Scribes, and Schools," *Zeitschrift des deutschen Palästina-Vereins* 116 (2000), 98–113.

[29] William Morrow argued that scholars must clarify how Israelite scribes could have gained knowledge of Mesopotamian texts ("Cuneiform Literacy and Deuteronomic Composition," *Bibliotheca Orientalis* 62 (2005), 204–213). If a text like the Middle Assyrian Laws was unavailable to Israelite (and most Mesopotamian) scribes because it never entered the scribal curriculum of the Neo-Assyrian period, then it cannot have been a model for an Israelite text. This point is well taken, and I have offered the Middle Assyrian Laws as an example of how a repertoire of traditional cases were employed in Mesopotamian learning, not as a model followed by an Israelite scribe.

Morrow also made the important point that none of the texts from the Israelite period are school texts and suggested the possibility that Mesopotamian scribal learning passed through to the Israelites through Aramaean scribes in the ninth to eighth centuries ("Legal Interactions: The mišpāṭîm and the Laws of Hammurabi," *Biblitheca Orientalis* 70 [2013], 330–332). However, the evidence for Aramaean learning among the Israelites is also lacking.

dates have been offered for the Covenant Code,[30] access to Akkadian scribal learning was available to Israelite scribes over a long period of time.[31] Israelite scribes learning how to write Mesopotamian texts would acquire knowledge of narrative, hymns, and cultic, legal, and diplomatic literature, among other genres. They would then be able to adapt counterparts in their own language to the foreign textual tradition(s) they had learned. When they modified foreign traditions, they did so with the same freedom that Mesopotamian scribes had in the transformation from Sumerian to Akkadian.

While we do not have specific evidence of the study of the Laws of Hammurabi in the land of Israel during the First Temple period, the Exilic period, or the Second Temple period, fragments of a law collection in cuneiform expressed in conditional sentences have been found at Hazor and have been dated to the Middle Bronze Age.[32] The fragments are inscribed on local clay (so they are not imported texts) and appear to address a variety of bodily injuries.

The tradition of a repertoire of traditional cases continued in Mesopotamia itself. The Laws of Hammurabi continued to be copied in Mesopotamia well into the first millennium BCE.

This tradition is a special case of the stream of culture that diffused from Mesopotamia to the rest of the ancient Near East and the Mediterranean world. It is an analogous yet distinct phenomenon from the patterns of allusion, citation, and intertextuality manifested in biblical texts that echo, evoke, imitate, repeat, interpret, and replicate other texts.[33] The law collections do

[30] I have argued that the Covenant Code exhibits dates from the First Temple period based on linguistic evidence. See my discussion in "Determining the Date of Biblical Legal Texts," in *The Oxford Handbook of Biblical Law* (ed. Pamela Barmash; Oxford: Oxford University Press, 2019), 233–253.

[31] While it would seem easier for Israelites to have gained this knowledge in Mesopotamia, only scribes with Akkadian names are found among the extant documents, even the ones from Judahite exiles: this implies that Judahite exiles did not have their own scribes, unless they are using Akkadian names. See Laurie Pearce and Cornelia L. Wunsch, *Documents of Judean Exiles and West Semites in Babylonia in the Collection of David Sofer* (Cornell University Studies in Assyriology and Sumerology 28; Bethesda, Md.: CDL Press, 2014), 303–305.

[32] Wayne Horowitz, Takayoshi Oshima, and Filip Vukosavović, "Hazor 18: Fragments of a Cuneiform Law Collection from Hazor," *Israel Exploration Journal* 62 (2002), 158–176; Filip Vukosavović, "The Laws of Hazor and the ANE Parallels," *RA* 108 (2014), 41–44; Horowitz, Oshima, and Sanders, *Cuneiform in Canaan*, 86–88. For an understanding of how political circumstances provoked differing responses to education and cultural borrowing, see Sandra Jacobs, *The Body as Property: Physical Disfigurement in Biblical Law* (Library of Hebrew Bible / Old Testament Studies 582; London: Bloomsbury, 2014), 14–23; William S. Morrow, "Resistance and Hybridity in Late Bronze Age Canaan," *Revue Biblique* 101 (2008), 321–339.

[33] See the essays in Ziony Zevit, ed., *Subtle Citation, Allusion, and Translation in the Hebrew Bible* (Sheffield: Equinox, 2017); and Christopher B. Hays, "Echoes of the Ancient Near East?: Intertextuality and the Comparative Study of the Old Testament," in *The Word Leaps the Gap: Essays on Scripture and Theology in Honor of Richard B. Hays* (ed. J. Ross Wagner, C. Kavin Grieb, and Katherine A. Rowe; Grand Rapids, Mich.; Eerdmans, 2008), 20–43.

not intentionally echo one another but share a repertoire of traditional cases on which the scribe who composed statutes or the scribal student who wrote a student exercise articulated what is just and fair. The scribe or scribal student did not intentionally make an echo to an earlier text but reshaped, redrafted, and revised conventional cases. (Other scribes and scribal students did copy those exemplars as exactly as their skill allowed without improvisation and functioned more like copyists.)

At the same time that scribes were composing variants on a repertoire of cases, they were also basing the textual pattern of a law collection on more standardized textual patterns and even directly imitating earlier texts. The Laws of Hammurabi is likely based on other royal inscriptions of Hammurabi. The scribe composing the Laws of Hammurabi intended literary dependence, employing other royal inscriptions as a model. As we discussed in chapter 3, the scribe drew from these earlier texts of Hammurabi: we have identified a number of the textual patterns that served as models, and we are fortunate to have either the royal inscription on which the Laws of Hammurabi is based or on other royal inscriptions that share the textual model with the Laws of Hammurabi. By contrast, when composing statutes on a set of traditional cases, the scribe was more likely to have assimilated, and reflected on, a set of traditional legal problems rather than alluding to an earlier law collection. This mode of composition derives from the associations and mindset of the scribe rather than imitating and reshaping another text.

This twofold approach was only partially emulated in ancient Israel. The Israelite scribe who composed the Covenant Code followed the Mesopotamian tradition of reshaping traditional cases and did not imitate the model of royal inscriptions. While Mesopotamian legal culture did exert influence on other cultures, influence was far from a simplistic process.

One final consideration must be addressed: Why would an Israelite scribe adopt Mesopotamian scribal practices at all? Adopting and adapting Mesopotamian learning might have been seen as prestigious because of the political and cultural hegemony of Mesopotamia.[34] Mesopotamian learning provided a repertoire of usable cases and topics. It must be noted, however, that of the biblical legal corpora, only the Covenant Code manifests this mode of composition: reshaping a number of traditional cases and employing conditional sentences to formulate statutes.

[34] See the discussion of how prestige influences the composition of a text in Nathan Mastnjak, "Prestige, Authority, and Jeremiah's Bible," *Journal of Religion* 98 (2018), 542–558.

7.3. Did Mesopotamian Scribal Improvisation Spread to Greece and Rome?

The imprint of Mesopotamian scribal scholarship on the Hittite Laws and the Covenant Code is unmistakable. But we must ask whether the influence of Mesopotamian legal practices spread farther. In recent decades, scholars have shed light on the influence of the ancient Near East on ancient Greece and Rome, but Mesopotamian influence on Greek and Roman law has been more difficult to detect.[35]

The ancient Greeks themselves believed that their lawgivers had adopted their laws and reforms from foreign examples during their travels throughout the Mediterranean region. Solon was thought by Herodotus to have borrowed from Egyptian law:

> (Amasis) is the king who established the law requiring each Egyptian every year to declare how he made his living to the governor of his nome. If someone failed to do so, or if he revealed that his livelihood was not a just and honest one, his punishment was death. Solon the Athenian took this law and established it for the Athenians; it is an admirable law, and may it always be in force.[36]

Despite this claim, it is a legend inspired by Greek tropes of imagining their past.[37] The Greeks conceived that individual cultural elements were invented

[35] For analysis of the relationship between Mesopotamian culture and classical culture, see Stephanie Dalley and A. T. Reyes, "Mesopotamian Contact and Influence in the Greek World 1: To the Persian Conquest," in *The Legacy of Mesopotamia* (ed. Stephanie Dalley; Oxford: Oxford University Press, 1998), 85–106; Johannes Haubold, *Greece and Mesopotamia: Dialogues in Literature* (Cambridge: Cambridge University Press, 2013); Christopher Metcalf, *The Gods Rich in Praise* (Oxford: Oxford University Press, 2015). These authors build on the pioneering work of Walter Burkert, *The Orientalizing Revolution: Near Eastern Influence on Greek Culture in the Early Archaic Age* (Cambridge, Mass.: Harvard University Press, 1992); and Martin L. West, *The East Face of Helicon: West Asiatic Elements in Greek Poetry and Myth* (Oxford: Clarendon Press, 1997). Mary R. Bachvarova offers a new model of the transmission route in *From Hittite to Homer: The Anatolian Background of Ancient Greek Epic* (Cambridge: Cambridge University Press, 2016). For an analysis of the distinct political shape of Greece and Mesopotamia and some observations on their significance for law, see Kurt A. Raaflaub, "Do Ideas Travel Lightly? Early Greek Concepts of Justice in Their Mediterranean Context," in *Literature as Politics, Politics as Literature: Essays on the Ancient Near East in Honor of Peter Machinist* (ed. David S. Vanderhooft and Abraham Winitzer; Winona Lake, Ind.; Eisenbrauns, 2013), 355–379.

[36] *Histories* 2.177. Translation from *The Landmark Herodotus* (ed. Robert B. Strassler; trans. Andrea L. Purvis; New York: Anchor, 2007), 201.

[37] Kurt A. Raaflaub, "Early Greek Political Thought in Its Mediterranean Context," in *A Companion to Greek and Roman Political Thought* (ed. Ryan Balot; Malden, Mass.: Wiley-Blackwell, 2009), 37–56, 39–41; Raaflaub, "Do Ideas Travel Lightly?," 375.

only once, by a specific individual, and they held great admiration for ancient Egypt. Leaving aside the problem of the historicity of Solon's travels, Herodotus was associating two vastly different legal practices, which only superficially appear alike. An annual income declaration made sense in the Egyptian tax system. However, the annual census in Solon's time was about capability for military service, and although this was based on an individual's economic resources (and social class), the annual census was not linked to taxes until two centuries later. Greek historical imagination made a connection with an initiative of a pharaoh, but the two practices were independent inventions. We must seek a more exact echo.

A law collection was engraved on the wall of the agora in the Greek city of Gortyn about 450 BCE. The paragraphs are formulated in conditional sentences and are articulated casuistically:[38]

Law Code of Gortyn II:2–10

If a person rapes a free man or a free woman, he shall pay one hundred staters.

If on account of an apetairos, (he shall pay) ten (staters).

If a slave (rapes) a free man or a free woman, he shall pay double.

If a free man (rapes) a male serf or a female serf, (he shall pay) five drachmas.

If a male serf (rapes) a male serf or a female serf, (he shall pay) five staters.[39]

The statutes are formulated casuistically in a technique akin to the variants in Mesopotamian law collections. Does this literary formulation serve to demonstrate the influence of Mesopotamian law? We have observed that casuistic formulation may be prompted by factors other than a shared tradition. To prove Mesopotamian influence, we need more conclusive evidence. The decisive influence of Mesopotamian law upon biblical and Hittite law is unmistakable because of the common cases. But is that the case here? No, there is no evidence of common traditional cases. There is a literary likeness in the

[38] The use of conditional sentences is high in the Anglo-Saxon law codes, but it can only be speculated as to whether this is due to the psychological fit of the conditional form or the influence of biblical law. See Jürg R. Schwyter, "Syntax and Style in the Anglo-Saxon Law-Codes," in *Verschriftung und Verschriftlichung: Aspeckte des Medienwechsels in verschiedenen Kulturen und Epochen* (ed. Christine Ehler and Ursula Schaefer; Tübingen: Gunter Narr, 1998), 196–205.

[39] Ronald F. Willetts, *The Law Code of Gortyn* (Berlin: De Gruyter, 1967), 40.

use of casuistic statutes expressed in conditional form, but without shared cases, the evidence is not strong enough to prove dependence.

The use of conditional sentences in the formulation of statutes is found as well in the Roman XII Tables,[40] but again it is difficult to substantiate the imprint of Mesopotamian law without serious doubt.[41] If we investigate whether there are provisions in the XII Tables that seem to be an improvisation on a set of traditional cases like those in the Mesopotamian law collections, a number of statutes are worthy of consideration. The opening statutes of the Laws of Hammurabi deal with problems in legal procedure. The initial provisions in the XII Tables also deal with legal procedures.[42] Both the Laws of Hammurabi and the XII Tables employ the same pattern for organizing those statutes: they are arranged from the opening claim in litigation to posttrial issues.[43] This ordering seems logical and not necessarily dependent on a Mesopotamian tradition. Many copies of the Laws of Hammurabi were made during this time period, but there is no instance of another corpus of law from the ancient Near East or the Mediterranean basin in the thirteen-hundred-year gap between the Laws of Hammurabi and the XII Tables whose initial paragraphs address legal procedure. The parallel is intriguing but not probative.

The situation of a thief breaking in is a case found in the Mesopotamian law collections, the Covenant Code, and the XII Tables. In a number of statutes, a distinction is drawn between a theft occurring at night and one occurring in the daytime:

> LE 12
>
> A man who is caught in the field of a commoner / palace dependent among the sheaves at midday shall pay 10 shekels of silver. He who is caught at night among the sheaves shall die, he will not live.
>
> LE 13
>
> A man who is caught in the house of a commoner / palace dependent in the midst of the house at midday shall pay 10 shekels of silver. He who is caught at night in the midst of the house shall die, he will not live.

[40] David Daube observed that conditional sentences are exceedingly rare in Roman legislation (*Forms of Roman Legislation* [Oxford: Clarendon, 1956], 4–8).

[41] The Laws of Gortyn and the XII Tables also lack definitions and abstract categories, but given the reservations expressed by Roman jurists over definitions and abstract categories as discussed in chapter 4, their omission may not be that definitive.

[42] M. H. Crawford, ed., *Roman Statutes* (London: Institute of Classical Studies, University of London, 1996), 579.

[43] Westbrook, "Barbarians at the Gate," 67.

Exodus 22:1–2

If the thief is caught digging his way in and is struck and dies, there is no liability (for his death). If the sun has risen, there is liability (for his death). (The thief) shall definitely pay; if he cannot, he shall be sold for his theft.

XII Tables 8:12

If a thief commits a theft by night, if the owner kills the thief, the thief shall be killed lawfully.

XII Tables 8:13

By daylight . . . if the thief defends himself with a weapon . . . the owner shall shout.

All three make a distinction between theft at night and theft during the day. The Laws of Eshnunna makes a further distinction between the time of day and applies it to two situations: theft in a field and theft in a home. Exodus 22 does not address theft in a field but focuses on a thief tunneling into a home.[44] The leeway granted to repel the thief depends on the time of day. The XII Tables treats nighttime versus daytime theft, and it may be safe to presume that it addresses the actions of a homeowner despite the problematic text.

However, the situation of an intruding thief is addressed in the Laws of Hammurabi and the Hittite Laws without the issue of daytime versus nighttime:

LH 21

If a man breaks into a house, they shall kill him and hang him in front of that breach.

HL 93

If they seize a free man at the outset, before he enters the house, he shall pay 12 shekels of silver. If they seize a slave at the outset, before he enters the house, he shall pay 6 shekels of silver.

The question is whether the case of the intruding thief is distinctive enough to demonstrate that there was a tradition spreading beyond Mesopotamia into the Near East and Mediterranean region.[45] That is not so clear: the cases of the goring ox and the pregnant woman assaulted are so highly unusual

[44] See also Job 24:14–17 for an articulation of the fear aroused by offenses committed during the night.

[45] Greengus, *Laws in the Bible and in Early Rabbinic Collections*, 215–218.

that their appearance and their prevalence in cuneiform law collections and scribal exercises, at least for the pregnant woman assaulted, serve as decisive evidence for Mesopotamian influence. The case of an intruding thief, with and without the distinction of nighttime versus daytime incursion, appears too general and too commonplace.

Westbrook argued that the XII Tables contains another set of laws, on personal injury, that seems to mirror the Mesopotamian laws:

XII Tables 8:2
If anyone has broken another's limb, let there be retaliation in kind, unless he comes to an agreement on compensation.

XII Tables 8:3
. . . If a person has broken the hand of a freeman with hand or club, let him pay a penalty of 300 asses (a type of Roman coinage); or it of a slave, 150 asses.

XII Tables 8:4
If he commits *iniuria* to another, the penalty is (25 asses).

Westbrook observed that the statutes in the XII Tables seem to be akin to the statutes on personal injury and that a genetic relationship can been identified by the rule against *iniuria,* a minor physical assault that humiliates rather than causes physical pain.[46] The Laws of Hammurabi contain an extended series of statutes on such an assault, including a slap to the face, an injury that is intended to demean more than cause bodily injury (LH 202–205). Again, the parallel is indefinite because the Mesopotamian law names the offense as a slap on the face while the XII Tables refers to humiliation in general without articulating how it was accomplished.

Marc Van De Mieroop singled out another characteristic, the public promulgation of law, as evidence for the influence of Mesopotamian law on Greek law, but whether the public presentation of Greek law is based on Mesopotamian law is hard to say.[47] If there were more evidence of the public

[46] Westbrook, "The Nature and Origin of the Twelve Tables," in *Ex Oriente Lex*, 90–94. On the provisions about cheek slapping in Mesopotamian law, see Martha T. Roth, "Mesopotamian Legal Traditions and the Laws of Hammurabi," *Chicago-Kent Law Review* 71 (1995), 27–36.

[47] Van De Mieroop argued that the literary formulation and the public display are decisive proof of Mesopotamian influence (*Philosophy before the Greeks*, 206). Van De Mieroop also noted that it is not easy to read a public display of law, like that of the Laws of Gortyn, but it is the public display of law that reflects and influences a mindset (*Philosophy before the Greeks*, 177). There was a system of law in place in a society.

display of law in first millennium BCE Mesopotamia and especially in the Hittite Empire and Neo-Hittite states—cultures transmitting Mesopotamian culture westward—this claim would be on firmer ground.[48] We may also have doubts as to whether the placement of the Stela of the Laws of Hammurabi in a temple is public enough to warrant thinking of it as a public display. But without a tradition of public display of a law collection after the Laws of Hammurabi, it is difficult to claim that a public display of a law collection in Greece is necessarily dependent on Mesopotamian influence.

The tradition of improvisation on a repertoire of traditional cases persisted outside of Mesopotamia for a millennium and a half in texts from the Hittite Empire and ancient Israel. Whether this was true as well for ancient Greece and Rome is more difficult to discern. The evidence for a shared tradition is too equivocal and is not probative.

7.4. The Development of Commentaries in Mesopotamia

The Laws of Hammurabi is the culmination of one stream of tradition and a witness to the start of another. A new intellectual practice developed in Mesopotamia: specific texts and their authors became esteemed and

Michael Gagarin argued that Mesopotamian law did not influence Greek law because a higher percentage of the population in the Greek city-states could read and therefore the public display of the Laws of Gortyn was more accessible and had a greater impact on law as it occurred everyday because it could be consulted (*Writing Greek Law* [Cambridge: Cambridge University Press], 2008, 150–151). But if that is the case, Gagarin's argument is confronted by the same issue that was raised in regard to the Laws of Hammurabi: If written law were prescriptive, why was it not referred to in legal records? No citations are made to written law, for example, in speeches delivered in Athenian courts. Gagarin argued that the interest of the Laws of Gortyn reflected in the greater attention paid to legal procedure than in the Laws of Hammurabi demonstrates that the former was intended to have an influence on litigation (*Writing Greek Law*, 153–155). Gagarin contended as well that the reason there were no citations was to prevent law from degenerating into formalism and to allow greater flexibility in the interest of ensuring justice.

[48] Nonetheless, there is an importance to written law. First, the publication of law does have a decisive effect on law, as Euripides puts in the mouth of Theseus in the play *Suppliant Women*: "When the laws are written, the poor and the rich have equal rights." Second, written legal documents provide a measure of certainty for individual circumstances, while witnesses may lie or forget or not be available and those taking an oath before the gods be dishonest, an available written contract did not lie. For a Mesopotamian example, in a bitter letter-prayer, a creditor complained about trying to reclaim his loan to a repeat perjurer. When the loan was initially taken out, the creditor did not require a written document but was satisfied with an oath and symbolic gesture. He expressed his regret in the letter-prayer. See Benjamin A. Foster, *Before the Muses: An Anthology of Akkadian Literature* (third edition; Bethesda, Md.; CDL, 2005), 215–216. In general, sale documents and contracts were retained in order to serve as evidence if a dispute arose. Lastly, the publication of law in the name of the ruler gave the sense that there was a system of justice at work in a society, an expectation that contemporary people still hold (Van De Mieroop, *Philosophy before the Greeks*, 181).

privileged in an unprecedented way. Texts became the subject of formal commentaries, and those who were perceived to be their author were deemed prestigious. The Laws of Hammurabi was drawn into this new tradition. Hammurabi himself was regarded as a sage, and the Laws of Hammurabi was quoted in commentaries on other texts and was the subject of its own commentary.[49]

The tradition of composing law collections in Mesopotamia experienced a long hiatus after the Laws of Hammurabi. Many copies of the Laws of Hammurabi were inscribed, but no new law collection was written until the Neo-Babylonian Laws, of which we have only a single exemplar, poorly preserved, dating from about 700 BCE. It is damaged at the beginning and end, and only fifteen statutes dealing with free people are preserved. The linguistic form is different from the earlier law collections: relative clauses are employed in place of conditional formulation.[50] The Neo-Babylonian Laws also lacks the royal inscription superstructure common to the earlier tradition of law collections.[51] A modest revival of the tradition of law collections may have taken place in the Neo-Babylonian period and could have been the impetus for the Neo-Babylonian Laws. Another piece of evidence for this revival is found in a text that recounts the assiduousness of a Neo-Babylonian king, presumably Nebuchadnezzar II (r. 605–562 BCE), in composing a law collection in order to thwart injustice, but a law collection bearing his name is not extant.[52] This text makes allusions to

[49] Elnathan Weissert argued that a description of Sennacherib's chariot, *sāpinat raggam u ṣēnam*, "conqueror of the evil and wicked," may be an allusion to Hammurabi's description as *raggam u ṣēnam ana ḫulluqim*, "(Anum and Enlil . . . ordained Hammurabi . . .) to destroy evil and wickedness" in the prologue to the Laws of Hammurabi ("Creating a Political Climate: Literary Allusions to *Enūma Eliš* in Sennacherib's Account of the Battle of Haluel," in *Assyrien im Wandel der Zeiten: XXXIXe Rencontre Assyriologique Internationale, Heidelberg, 6.–10. Juli 1992* [Heidelberger Studien zum Alten Orient 6; Heidelberg: Heidelberger Orientverlag, 1997], 196 n.43). However, the verb employed in Sennacherib's text is not the one in the Laws of Hammurabi, and the syntax differs as well, making the allusion unlikely. Furthermore, this claim would be stronger if there were multiple allusions from the Laws of Hammurabi clustered in Sennacherib's text or if the phrase from the Laws of Hammurabi were alluded to repeatedly in Neo-Assyrian texts, showing that it had become a common phrase (Morrow, "Legal Interactions," 330 n.112).

[50] Roth, *Law Collections*, 143–144.

[51] Van De Mieroop, *Philosophy before the Greeks*, 149, 155. Van De Mieroop suggested that a change in royal ideology took place in Mesopotamian culture after the time of Hammurabi's reign: a public pronouncement in the form of a law collection that a king ensured justice was no longer necessary, perhaps because the ideals of law-giving changed. He speculated that since omens were called by the same term as legal verdicts (*purussû*), it may be that the gods instead of kings were seen as guaranteeing justice. See Francesca Rochberg, *The Heavenly Writing: Divination, Horoscopy, and Astronomy in Mesopotamia* (Cambridge: Cambridge University Press, 2004), 193–196.

[52] W. G. Lambert, "Nebuchadnezzar King of Justice," *Iraq* 27 (1965), 1–11. How the level of the Neo-Babylonian text is enhanced by the use of language borrowed from the Laws of Hammurabi

the Laws of Hammurabi to present the Neo-Babylonian king as a righteous and just ruler along the lines of Hammurabi. The name of Hammurabi is not mentioned in the extant text, but the use of allusions, if recognized by those listening to or reading the text, enhances the status of the Neo-Babylonian king.

While the writing of law collections went into a hiatus, the Laws of Hammurabi became a classic text. No other law collection was copied so often and for so long. It has been discovered in more than fifty copies, attesting to its central place in the scribal curriculum. This is in stark contrast to its predecessors, of which only a few copies remain. The prologue of the Stela was still being copied in the Persian period,[53] and the latest dated manuscript, containing LH 53–101, is from the fourth century BCE.[54] These late dates may mean that the Laws of Hammurabi circulated even later and farther afield. Stefan Maul speculated that knowledge of the Laws of Hammurabi may have extended into the Hellenistic period and that it is by no means improbable that it could have been discussed in the learned circles of Alexandria, but he noted that we lack any evidence for this.[55] Despite the long history of transmission of the Laws of Hammurabi, it was not employed as a legal precedent or as otherwise authoritative in legal actions, but it was used as a text in scribal education.

In its long history, the Laws of Hammurabi bears witness to another tradition, one in which it was esteemed and privileged. In the first millennium BCE, Hammurabi was envisioned as a sage. A late Babylonian list of literary

is explored by Hurowitz, "Hammurabi in the Mesopotamian Tradition," 507–512. It even borrows situations from the first five statutes of the Laws of Hammurabi, although it freely veers from the penalties prescribed in those statutes.

[53] A. Fadhil, "Der Prolog des Codex Hammurapi in einer abschrift aus Sippar," in *XXXIVeme Rencontre assyriologique internationale, Istanbul, 1987* (Ankara: Türk Trih Kurumu Basimevi, 1998), 726. The text states that the scribe saw the Stela at Susa and that the wording is according with the old Stela: while one can argue that this does not necessarily mean that the scribe copied the text off the Stela, the explicit reference means that at least there was an appearance of checking the text against the Stela. It is probable that few in the first millennium BCE could read the Stela, since even when it was inscribed in the second millennium, its archaic ductus served as a barrier to reading it.

[54] Stefan Maul, "Tontafelabschriften des 'Kodex Hammurapi' in altbabylonischer Monumentalschrift," *ZA* 102 (2012), 76–99; Van De Mieroop, *Philosophy before the Greeks*, 247 n.11; Joachim Oelsner, "Tontafeln aus drei Jahrtausenden—die Leipziger Sammlung von Keilschrifttexten," *ZAR* 18 (2012), 108 s.v. nB 8. There are a number of unpublished fragments from the Persian period, such as BM 54795, which is a copy of LH 53, written in the tenth year of the reign of the Achaemenid king Artaxerxes I (465–424 BCE). BM 59776, containing LH 275–277, is late first millennium BCE with its archaicizing script. See Gesche, *Schulunterricht in Babylonien: Im Ersten Jahrtausend v. Chr.*, 714.

[55] Maul, "Tontafelabschriften des 'Kodex Hammurapi' in altbabylonischer Monumentalschrift," 80.

texts calls the Laws of Hammurabi "A source book for learned scholars dealing with the more esoteric matters of Babylonian thought."[56]

That the Laws of Hammurabi enjoyed privileged status is reflected in that a commentary was written on it. A Late Babylonian fragment of the Laws of Hammurabi contains both semantic glosses of a simple kind as well as comments manifesting more intensive interpretational moves.[57] BM 59739, fragment v, lists a word from individual statutes and provides another word in explanation:

obv 2 ["He will subm]erge himself," $GIR_5.GIR_5$ means "to su[bmerge" . . .]
3 [The "divine River"] is Ea; the River god is a river [. . .]
4 ["If it (the river) overco]mes him," SAR means "to overcome" [. . .]
5 [. . .] "in a lawsuit": KU, read EŠ, means "in [. . .]
6 [. . .] "witness" [. . .]
rev 2 [. . .] "robber" (?) means "mur[derer . . .]
3 [. . .] "chief" means "mayor" [. . .]
4 [. . . KI] means "region," KI means "district" [. . .]
5 [. . .] "utensils" means "equipment" [. . .]
6 [Lemma]ta and oral explanations relating to "If [a man . . .]."
7 [Tablet] of Nabû-[. . .].[58]

This commentary text appears to be restricted to the statutes and did not extend to the prologue (and presumably the epilogue as well) because the incipit in the colophon reads "If [a man] . . . ," showing that the composition began with conditional sentences, that is, he literary form of the statutes. Obverse lines 3–4 refer to statute 2 of the Laws of Hammurabi; lines 5–6 refer to statute 3; reverse lines 2–4 refer to statute 23; and line 5 refers to statute 25. Although the text of the commentary is broken, it is likely that it treated the first twenty-five statutes. This text is too fragmentary to add to our understanding of these statutes in the Laws of Hammurabi, but it demonstrates

[56] W. G. Lambert, "The Laws of Hammurabi in the First Millennium," in *Reflets des deux fleuves, Volume de Mélanges offerts à André Finet* (Akkadica Supplementum 6; Leuven: Peeters, 1989), 97.

[57] Lambert, "The Laws of Hammurabi in the First Millennium," 96–97, with a new collation by Enrique Jiménez, "On the Commentary to the Code of Hammurapi and the Babylonian God of Ordeals," *NABU* 2014/84, and on the Yale Cuneiform Commentaries site <https://ccp.yale.edu/P461271>. See also Charpin, *Writing, Law, and Kingship in Old Babylonian Mesopotamia*, 81.

[58] Eckart Frahm, *Babylonian and Assyrian Text Commentaries: Origins of Interpretation* (Guides to the Mesopotamian Textual Record 5; Münster: Ugarit, 2011), 242.

that the Laws of Hammurabi was studied in the Late Babylonian period and that a commentary was produced.

The commentator provided a contemporary title for an Old Babylonian one: "chief" ([ra-b]a-an-nu) means "mayor" (^{lú}ḫa-za-nu). This is in line with the updating of the word "chief" ([ra-b]a-an-nu) with the contraction of -ia- and no mimation, as it would appear in Old Babylonian. In rev 3, "possessions," ([nu-ma]-tu), is given the gloss of "utensils" [u-na-a-tu], the common term in the first millennium BCE. These simple equivalents are accompanied by glosses of a more esoteric nature.[59] The commentator sought to offer an esoteric commentary in obv. 5: the preposition ina is glossed with a pseudo-Sumerian equivalent, KU^{eš}, apparently prompted by the lexical list Ea I: 180–181.[60] In obv. 2, GIR$_5$.GIR$_5$ is equated with *šalû*, attested in lexical texts, such as Diri II 44; thus GIR$_5$.GIR$_5$ means "to su[bmerge" . . .]. In obv. 4, sar is equated with kašādu; thus SAR means "to overcome" [. . .]. While no extant lexical list makes this equation, it is known from bilingual texts (CAD K 272a s.v. kašādu).

The commentator uses the same literary form for both types of glosses: the verb from the base text is cited and then equated with another work featuring that verb. But it may be observed that the esoteric glosses do not advance understanding of the text but rather make it more obscure. This commentary offers philological explanations serving to elucidate the text, but it is the only commentary on the Laws of Hammurabi that has been identified so far. Eckart Frahm made a striking observation: since the Laws of Hammurabi was so old and, therefore, most likely was difficult for the scholars of the first millennium to understand, it is astonishing that only one commentary on it has been identified.[61]

A number of texts appear to contain quotes from the Laws of Hammurabi. A commentary on a medical text incorporates a quotation from LH 117–118, but the exemplar is so broken that nothing further can be analyzed.[62] A commentary on a lexical text, Aa 16 commentary BM 41286, incorporates a brief quotation *a-na ni-pu-tú it-ta-pu*, "distrains an ox," from LH 241, *šum-ma a-wi-lum* GUD *a-na ni-pu-tim it-te-pí 1/3 ma-na* KÙ.BABBAR *i-ša-qal*, "If a

[59] Jiménez. "On the Commentary to the Code of Hammurapi and the Babylonian God of Ordeals."
[60] Civil, *Ea A = naqû, Aa A = naqû*, 186. See Lambert, "The Laws of Hammurabi in the First Millennium," 97.
[61] Frahm, *Babylonian and Assyrian Text Commentaries*, 242.
[62] R. Borger, "Die Weihe eines Enlil-Priester," *BiOr* 30 (1973), 175; Frahm, *Babylonian and Assyrian Text Commentaries*, 101; Lambert, "The Laws of Hammurabi in the First Millennium," 97 n.6.

man distrains an ox, he shall pay 1/3 maneh of silver."[63] Lambert argued that there is a quote from the opening line of the Laws of Hammurabi in an expository text BM 32574 *ina i-nu-um ᵈA-num ṣi-i-ru* "when august Anum."[64]

The rise of fixed texts and commentaries reflects a new attitude in which texts name themselves as interpretive and are formally dependent on another text. The Laws of Hammurabi was drawn into this new stream of tradition, the fixing of texts and the rise of formal commentary. Scribes and readers related to it as a fixed text in ways that were different from earlier attitudes. No longer was a law collection an improvisation frozen momentarily in written form. The Laws of Hammurabi became an object of study. Scribal students copied it out as exactly as they could, and if the text itself underwent any changes, it was either an inadvertent or one-time fix by a puzzled scribe. Eventually, it became the subject of formal commentaries, a radical change in orientation and attitude.

This radical change is reflected in a dramatic transformation in relating to texts that occurred during the Neo-Assyrian and Neo-Babylonian periods. In the Old Babylonian period, the knowledge that scribes possessed was oral, and the texts they wrote were aides de memoire. A large percentage of the texts they learned were in Sumerian, the language defining the educational attainment of scribes, even if they would rarely use it in what they wrote on a daily basis for their clients. They preserved a number of texts, especially lexical lists, faithfully, maintaining particularities and peculiarities. Alternatively, other texts were revamped, either to produce stable alternate versions or to be altered at will. They used the traditions of Sumerian literature to inspire them to create new compositions. Only rarely did the scribes demonstrate an antiquarian awareness in which they provided an Akkadian translation to a Sumerian text or glosses explaining unusual forms.

The written remains from the Old Babylonian period have been transmitted to us by serendipity: the houses in which they were discovered collapsed in a sudden disaster, preserving their contents, and a few of those houses were literally made of tablets as part of their building materials. A large part of the texts from the Old Babylonia period consist of the discarded exercises of students: schoolboys and a few schoolgirls. Those tablets were meant to be ephemeral. They were created as part of the process

[63] Frahm, *Babylonian and Assyrian Text Commentaries*, 101.
[64] Lambert, "The Laws of Hammurabi in the First Millennium," 97, but Frahm doubted it (*Babylonian and Assyrian Text Commentaries*, 101).

of memorization and by chance were preserved rather than recycled. We lack any evidence for the existence of libraries in this period—either private, temple, or royal libraries. In contrast, the first millennium BCE attests to the existence of libraries, private ones belonging to scribes, diviners, priests, and high government officials, and royal ones belonging to the king. The texts from the first millennium BCE were deliberately collected by certain scribes and kings in libraries. The overwhelming majority of texts they amassed were of omens and divination, and the copies themselves were checked to make sure that they were faithful copies of prior copies. Literary texts were marginal, and most of the texts were in Akkadian. The majority of Sumerian literature was lost.

When the Laws of Hammurabi became a fixed text, scribes perceived it through a new lens. Its words and sentences were seen as set, and the Laws of Hammurabi itself became an object of study, rather than the legal cases of the scribal repertoire whose circumstances could be altered as the scribe desired.

While understanding any text requires an implicit act of interpretation, the development of a fixed text and of interpretation that names itself as dependent on a fixed text is more than the rise of a new genre. It is a new attitude. This intellectual orientation makes a sharp disjunction between elevating one text above another and making them equal, between acknowledging the boundaries between texts and ignoring them, between assenting to the fixed existence of a text and its obscurities, on the one hand, and effacing the obscurities of a text by removing them, on the other hand. It is a radical change in intellectual life. The Laws of Hammurabi started as a royal inscription incorporating scribal improvisation on a repertoire of traditional cases and evolved into a fixed canonical text requiring formal interpretation.

Conclusion

I have in this volume approached the Laws of Hammurabi with the intent of providing a histoire totale of it, trying to comprehend the place of the Laws of Hammurabi in its own time and its legacy for later Mesopotamia and for cultures outside of Mesopotamia. The Laws of Hammurabi provides insight into human intellectual achievements and rationality in general and into the interplay between legal activity, jurisprudence, and political circumstances in Mesopotamia specifically.

The scribe who composed the Laws of Hammurabi probed toward legal principles and conceptualization in the statutes. Like earlier scribes, he improvised on a traditional repertoire of cases. Unlike earlier scribes, he advanced toward generalization and abstraction by employing innovative methods of composition. He created paradigmatic sets of statutes that illustrated legal principles by modifying variables, presenting a comprehensive treatment of a legal topic. He linked together cases in earlier law collections that were independent from one another in order to highlight conceptual links. He forged extensive clusters of statutes on broad legal topics, such as land tenure or family, and sets focused on specific types of disputes. The scribe sometimes even included explanations that clarified the basis for the prescribed punishment. He employed particular types of sanctions, especially mutilation on the privileged class and the punishment of an innocent person, as poetic justice integrating disparate offenses. By employing innovation and originality in methods of composition, the scribe advanced toward conceptualization and legal principles.

Although the scribe lived in a culture that did not have jurisprudential or philosophical writing about law, the statutes he composed manifest a significant instance of legal reasoning before the flowering of Roman law. The methods of composition he employed allow us to see early modes of legal thinking. Law as a theoretical problem was emerging in the Laws of Hammurabi.

The legal thinking of the scribe of the Laws of Hammurabi did not appear ex nihilo in Mesopotamian culture. Mesopotamian scribes had made nascent attempts at systematization through the creation of lexical lists, lists

The Laws of Hammurabi. Pamela Barmash, Oxford University Press (2020). © Oxford University Press.
DOI: 10.1093/oso/9780197525401.001.0001.

that brought together words that belonged together conceptually, whether trees or vocations. While the primary purpose of the lists was to teach the writing of cuneiform, the secondary effect and perhaps intended goal was to prompt reasoning about the commonalities or distinctions within a list. Mesopotamian scribes also formulated circumstances in casuistic description articulated in conditional sentences for scientific writing, such as in omen texts or medical texts. While this type of literary expression makes sense for law, its use in scholastic genres by Mesopotamian scribes most likely prompted its use in law collections. Casuistic formulation inspires casuistic reasoning, and the advances toward legal principles and conceptualization achieved by the scribe of the Laws of Hammurabi have deep roots in Mesopotamian scribal endeavors.

Equally enshrined in Mesopotamian scribal culture was the writing of royal inscriptions, and royal propaganda and legal reasoning are the two traditions melded in the Laws of Hammurabi. The two discursive modes are integrated in well-wrought craftsmanship. The scribe of the Laws of Hammurabi embedded the statutes in the overarching textual pattern of a royal inscription. He may have based this pattern on two royal inscriptions extant from the reign of Hammurabi or on a model that his composition and the royal inscriptions share. The scribe made significant changes in the general pattern of royal inscriptions. He incorporated two divine commissions of the king to highlight the king's purported activities in the legal realm in addition to the usual emphasis on a king's building activities and military successes. He presented the king's building activities as a timeless triumph using a verbose stream of participles and title rather than a narrative of accomplishments in chronological order. This enabled the scribe to make the king appear to have promulgated the laws immediately after he was bestowed with kingship. In so doing, the scribe highlighted the total and unalloyed fulfillment of the divine mandate of the king to fulfill justice. His adjustments to the textual pattern presents the king in everlasting and unassailable achievement, as a success in all undertakings, in unwavering piety, as an exemplar of royalty. Whether using a royal inscription pattern for a law collection was an innovation of the scribe of the Laws of Hammurabi or a prior tradition, the scribe intentionally employed and reshaped the royal inscription textual pattern with a set of statutes for the rhetorical purpose of demonstrating that the king fulfilled the divine mandate of ensuring justice.

The scribe employed the royal inscription pattern to glorify the king and manifest royal authority. The explicit audience of a royal inscription was the gods and successive kings, but the implicit audience was the king's subjects. His legitimacy was predicated on divine election and on his fulfillment of the duties of the royal office, and the Laws of Hammurabi placed special emphasis on his duty to maintain justice. The set of statutes is presented as his judicial decisions, implementing his mandate and affirming his right to serve as monarch.

The extant Stela on which the Laws of Hammurabi are incised amplified the goal of justifying Hammurabi's accession to the monarchy through the relief at its top. The image departed from more common images of presentation scenes before a deity by elevating Hammurabi as a near-equal to the god by removing routine elements from the scene and making his stance and clothing and adornment only slightly lesser than the god. The direct gaze between king and god symbolizes the eternality of their relationship, and the identification of the god as Shamash, the sun-god and the god of justice, accentuates Hammurabi's mandate to ensure justice that is the main point of the Stela. The text itself is inscribed in an eye-catching geometric pattern, and the imagery and design animate the text. Royal authority is manifested vividly.

The Laws of Hammurabi emanates from the political and social matrix of Old Babylonia. The Laws of Hammurabi is more than a tool of royal propaganda. While it was likely commissioned by the king himself, it was shaped through the expertise and aspirations of the scribal class in general and by the scribe composing it in particular. The sets of statutes incorporated in the Laws of Hammurabi emanate from the scribal realm despite their presentation as Hammurabi's judicial decisions. The scribe who composed the Laws of Hammurabi and the scribal group he belonged to held a social position dependent on their knowledge. As much as he glorified the king in his composition, he also glorified scribal expertise. By incorporating law so extensively, the scribe highlighted the role of those who enabled legal activities. The Laws of Hammurabi discloses and validates the scribal group in which its scribe resided and worked. It conveys how a scribe conceived of justice, which elements of a dispute he thought were decisive, and the types of punishment he believed an offense merited. Legal expertise was used by the scribal class to advance themselves, and it is hoped that future studies of Mesopotamian law will delve further in exploring this consideration.[1] To what extent did they use legal texts, whether law collections, contracts, and

[1] Niek Veldhuis identified a sea change in scribal practices during the Old Babylonian period that were prompted by the transformation in the social location of scribes from centralized positions in palaces and temples to scribes working as freelancers who may have had more humble origins and who rose to elite status (*History of the Cuneiform Lexical Tradition* [Guides to the Mesopotamian

so on to advance their interests? What more may we discern about their political, intellectual, or social agenda?

The inventiveness that the scribe displayed in composing the Laws of Hammurabi was not unique among scribes in the Old Babylonian period. They preserved knowledge from the previous millennium, and at the same time they interacted with that knowledge in a dynamic way. Besides law collections, they innovated with newly composed and expanded lists containing legal terminology and phrases.[2] To what extent was this effort paralleled or surpassed in other areas of scribal endeavor?

The Laws of Hammurabi was part of an elaborate and extensive project exalting the king, extending and cementing his authority. Hammurabi's dynasty started off as minor rulers who gradually expanded their dominion. Hammurabi extended the scope of the territory he ruled greatly. The year names of his reign mirror his progress: they exhibit how his aspirations changed from temple building to imperial and nationalistic aims. The composition of the law collection bearing his name was likely prompted by his ambitiousness, but we might well wonder to what extent this was the case for other rulers and their law collections. Perhaps the fragility of empire motivated the writing of a law collection. Hammurabi's territorial kingdom lasted only for the last twelve years of his reign and the first eight years of his successor Samsuiluna's, and it may be that a law collection was an attempt to surmount the stresses inherent in extending Hammurabi's dominion. The scribal tradition of law collections ceases after Hammurabi's reign, with a very modest revival in the first millennium BCE: Is the dearth of later law collections caused by chance, or does it reflect a change in royal and/or scribal traditions?

This study sheds light on other relationships besides literary dependence that texts can share. I argue that scribes outside of Mesopotamia adopted an educational tradition and reshaped it to fit their cultural circumstances. It was not a common legal system, but an educational system partially adopted outside of Mesopotamia. The selective representation of shared cases in the collections and their degree of overlap manifest scholarly study in the ancient Near East, not the general diffusion of legal tradition nor direct influence of one text on another.

Textual Record; Münster: Ugarit-Verlag, 2014], 225). To what extent was this manifested in their legal activities?

[2] Veldhuis, *History of the Cuneiform Lexical Tradition*, 188–194.

Knowledge of Mesopotamian educational tradition means that the scribe could either read Akkadian or had recourse to an intermediary tradition, such as an Aramaic translation. Since an Aramaic intermediary is only conjecture, the more likely scenario is one in which scribes acquired a basic proficiency in Akkadian and were exposed to the repertoire of traditional cases. The period in which Hittite scribes would have acquired this would be during the system of international relations in the Amarna Age in the mid-and late second millennium. For Israelite scribes, the period in which a number of northern and southern scribes were likely exposed to, and probably needed to learn, Akkadian was during the period of the Neo-Assyrian and Neo-Babylonian Empires. The Israelite states were at first satellite states and then later imperial provinces under the sphere of influence and domination of these great powers, and it stands to reason that Israelite scribes might want to leverage the prestige of the cultures of those empires, if not also present a critique. The adoption of another educational system provides a distinct model for the relationship between texts that transcends literary dependence or general cultural diffusion. It highlights an understanding of scribal education based on the evidence of student texts and on the continuities and discontinuities between texts from differing cultures. The processes of cultural interaction become more visible, and we gain a more nuanced perspective on the potentialities and dimensions of cultural influence.

This study poses a new viewpoint on tradition, which is often perceived as conservative and unchanging. What is striking is how inventive and original tradition could be. A. Leo Oppenheim highlighted how streams of tradition in Mesopotamian culture operated:

> When Assyriologists will be able to follow the fate of individual text groups through the history of their tradition, they will obtain insights into the working of this "stream" and, conceivably, light will be shed some day on the ideological and other preferences that neither the content or wording of these texts is likely to reflect directly.[3]

Oppenheim highlighted the aspects of preservation and transmission inherent in tradition, yet he noted that tradition is often reshaped. Oppenheim bestowed on later scholars with a strong caveat the task of illuminating the reshaping of tradition. The stream of tradition manifested in law collections

[3] Oppenheim, *Ancient Mesopotamia*, 16.

is both deeply faithful to transmitting that tradition's pattern yet at the same time responsive to political needs and local cultural patterns as well as the concerns of the individual scribe.[4]

This understanding of tradition highlights the nature of the authority of the Laws of Hammurabi. It did not have legal authority in the sense of a law code that was cited as authoritative law or that was used (without necessarily being cited) as authoritative law. It did possess authority in other modes. The Mesopotamian legal learning that it manifested was authoritative because that tradition of learning served to educate scribes. It developed a sense of justice in the scribes who wrote statutes and legal exercises, and studying and copying them instilled a sense of justice in the scribal students who read and copied them. This educational tradition eventually turned the Laws of Hammurabi into a classic, a prestigious text that was copied for over a millennium.

The afterlife of the Laws of Hammurabi in Mesopotamia serves as a witness to a new era of knowledge, one of interpretation of texts. The primary repository of knowledge was the tablet, and not surprisingly the Laws of Hammurabi became the subject of second-order reflections in the form of commentary and citation. In the first millennium, allusions and citations were made to the Laws of Hammurabi, even though otherwise it was not cited in legal texts. It gained authority as a literary classic, not as a legal authority whose rules served as mandates in resolving legal disputes. The concept of a legal text having authority through citation or reference did not yet exist.

While the Laws of Hammurabi has been known for more than a century, it has not been truly integrated in the study of legal history beyond a perfunctory mention here and there. Yet its study has much to contribute to the history of law. It attests to the richness and complexity of legal thinking before Roman law. The emerging legal mind of the Laws of Hammurabi manifests patterns of thinking that anticipate later developments in jurisprudence. It demonstrates the vitality of legal thinking, and its existence prompts a more complex story of legal development and imagination.

[4] See also Beate Pongratz-Leisten, "Tigridian Royal Representation, Text and Image Between Tradition and Innovation," 347–348; Eleanor Robson, "The Production and Dissemination of Scholarly Knowledge," in *The Oxford Handbook of Cuneiform Culture* (ed. Karen Radner and Eleanor Robson; Oxford: Oxford University Press, 2011), 557–560.

Bibliography

Abram, Mary. "A New Look at the Mesopotamian Rod and Ring: Emblems of Time and Eternity." *Studia Antiqua* 10 (2011): 15–36.

Abusch, I. Tzvi. "The Demonic Image of the Witch in Standard Babylonian Literature: The Reworking of Popular Conceptions by Learned Exorcists." In *Mesopotamian Witchcraft: Toward a History of Understanding of Babylonian Witchcraft Beliefs and Literature*, vol. 5. 1989. Ancient Magic and Divination, 27–58. Leiden: Brill, 2002.

Abusch, I. Tzvi. "'He Should Continue to Bear the Penalty of That Case': Some Observations on *Codex Ḫammurabi* 3–4 and 13." In *From Ancient Israel to Modern Judaism: Intellect in Quest of Understanding—Essays in Honor of Marvin Fox I.* Edited by Jacob Neusner, Ernest S. Frerichs, and Nahum M. Sarna. Brown Judaic Studies 159, 77–96. Atlanta: Scholars, 1989.

Abusch, I. Tzvi. "Witchcraft and the Anger of the Personal God." In *Mesopotamian Witchcraft: Textual, Historical, and Interpretative Perspectives.* Edited by I. Tzvi Abusch and Karel van der Toorn. Ancient Magic and Divination I, 51–57. Gröningen: Styx, 1999.

André-Salvini, Béatrice. *Le Code de Hammurabi.* Collection Solo. Paris: Réunion des Musées nationaux, 2003.

Aruz, Joan. "Seals of the Old Elamite Period." In *The Royal City of Susa: Ancient Near Eastern Treasures in the Louvre.* Edited by Prudence O. Harper, Joan Aruz, and Francoise Tallon, 117–118. New York: Metropolitan Museum of Art: Distributed by H. N. Abrams, 1992.

Ascalone, E., and L. Peyronel. "Two Weights from Temple N at Tel Mardikh-Ebla: A Link between Metrology and Cultic Activities in the Second Millennium BC?" *JCS* 53 (2001): 1–12.

Attenborough, F. L., ed. and trans. *The Laws of the Earliest English Kings.* Cambridge: Cambridge University Press, 1922.

Bachvarova, Mary R. *From Hittite to Homer: The Anatolian Background of Ancient Greek Epic.* Cambridge: Cambridge University Press, 2016.

Baker, Heather D. *The Prosopography of the Neo-Assyrian Empire* 2/I. Helsinki: Neo-Assyrian Text Corpus Project, 2000.

Barmash, Pamela. "Adoption." In OEBL, 1–9.

Barmash, Pamela. "Amnesty and Reform Decrees." In OEBL, 9–13.

Barmash, Pamela. "Determining the Date of Biblical Legal Texts," in *The Oxford Handbook of Biblical Law*, 233–253. Edited by Pamela Barmash; Oxford: Oxford University Press, 2019.

Barmash, Pamela. *Homicide in the Biblical World.* New York: Cambridge University Press, 2005.

Barmash, Pamela. "Scribal Initiative in the Clarification and Interpretation of Mesopotamian Law Collections." In *Birkat Shalom: Studies in the Bible, Ancient Near Eastern Literature, and Postbiblical Judaism Presented to Shalom M. Paul on the Occasion of His Seventieth Birthday.* Edited by Chaim Cohen, Victor Avigdor Hurowitz, Avi M. Hurvitz, Yochanan Muffs, Baruch J. Schwartz, and Jeffrey H. Tigay, 553–565. Winona Lake, Ind.: Eisenbrauns, 2008.

Bartor, Assnat. *Reading Law as Narrative: A Study in the Casuistic Laws of the Pentateuch*. Ancient Israel and Its Literature / Society of Biblical Literature. Atlanta: Society of Biblical Literature, 2010.

Beckman, Gary M. "Mesopotamians and Mesopotamian Learning at Ḫattuša." *JCS* 35 (1983): 97–114.

Bergmann, E. *Codex Hammurabi textus primigenius*. Rome: Pontificium Institutum Biblicum, 1953.

Biggs, Robert D. "Babylonian Prophecies, Astrology, and a New Source for 'Prophecy Text B.'" In *Language, Literature, and History: Philological and Historical Studies Presented to Erica Reiner*. Edited by Francesca Rochberg-Halton. AOS 67, 1–14. New Haven, Conn.: American Oriental Society, 1987.

Black, Jeremy. *The Literature of Ancient Sumer*. Oxford: Oxford University Press, 2004.

Blair, Ann. *The Theater of Nature*. Princeton, N.J.: Princeton University Press, 1997.

Blitz, Rudulph C., and Millard F. Long. "The Economics of Usury Regulation." *Journal of Political Economy* 73 (1965): 608–619.

Bodine, Walter R. *How Mesopotamian Scribes Learned to Write Legal Documents: A Study of the Sumerian Model Contracts in the Babylonian Collection at Yale University*. With a foreword by William W. Hallo. Lewiston, Maine: Edward Mellen, 2014.

Borger, Rykle. *Babylonisch-Assyrisch Lesestücke*. 2 volumes. 2d ed. Analecta Orientalia 54. Rome: Pontifical Biblical Institute, 1979.

Borger, Rykle. "Die Weihe Eines Enlil-Priesters." *Bibliotheca Orientalis* 30 (1973): 164–176.

Bottéro, Jean. "The 'Code' of Hammurabi." In *Mesopotamia: Writing, Reasoning, and the Gods*. Translated by Zainab Bahrani and Marc Van De Mieroop, 156–184. Chicago: University of Chicago Press, 1992.

Bottéro, Jean. "Désordre économique et annulation des dettes en Mèsopotamie à l'époque paléo-babylonienne." *JESHO* 4 (1961): 113–164.

Bottéro, Jean. "Le Noms de Marduk." In *Essays on the Ancient Near East in Memory of Jacob Joel Finkelstein*. Edited by Maria de Jong Ellis, 5–27. Memoirs of the Connecticut Academy of Arts and Sciences. Hamden, Conn.: Archon, 1977.

Bottéro, Jean. "L'Ordalie en la Mésopotamie Ancienne." *Annali Della Scuola Normale Superiore Di Pisa. Classe de Lettere e Filosofia* Serie III 9, no. 4 (1981): 1005–1067.

Burkert, Walter. *The Orientalizing Revolution: Near Eastern Influence on Greek Culture in the Early Archaic Age*. Cambridge, Mass.: Harvard University Press, 1992.

Canby, Jeanny Vorys. *The "Ur-Nammu" Stela*. University Museum Monographs 110. Philadelphia: University of Pennsylvania Museum of Archaeology and Anthropology, 2001.

Carr, David M. *Writing on the Tablet of the Heart: Origins of Scripture and Literature*. Oxford: Oxford University Press, 2005.

Carter, Elizabeth. "A History of Excavation at Susa: Personalities and Archaeological Methods." In *The Royal City of Susa: Ancient Near Eastern Treasures in the Louvre*. Edited by Prudence O. Harper, Joan Aruz, and Francoise Tallon, 20–24. New York: Metropolitan Museum of Art: Distributed by H. N. Abrams, 1992.

Charpin, Dominique. *Hammurabi of Babylon*. London: I. B. Tauris, 2012.

Charpin, Dominique. "'I Am the Sun of Babylon': Solar Aspects of Royal Power in Old Babylonian Mesopotamia." In *Experiencing Power, Generating Authority: Cosmos, Politics, and the Ideology of Kingship in Ancient Egypt and Mesopotamia*. Edited by Jane A. Hill, Philip Jones, and Antonio J. Morales, 65–96. Philadelphia: University of Pennsylvania Museum of Archaeology and Anthropology, 2013.

Charpin, Dominique. *Le clergé d'Ur au siècle d'Hammurabi*. Hautes études orientales 22. Geneva: Droz, 1986.

Charpin, Dominique. 'Le statut des "codes de lois" des souverains babyloniens." In *Le législateur et la loi dans l'Antiquité.Hommage à Françoise Ruzé. Actes du colloque de Caen, 15–17 mai 2003*. Edited by P. Sineux, 93–107. Caen: Presses Universitaires de Caen, 2005.

Charpin, Dominique. *Writing, Law, and Kingship in Old Babylonian Mesopotamia*. Translated by Jane Marie Todd. Chicago: University of Chicago Press, 2010.

Charpin, Dominique, Dietz Otto Edzard, and Marten Stol. *Mesopotamien: Die Altbabylonische Zeit*. Annäherungen. Fribourg: Academic Press; Göttingen: Vandenhoeck & Ruprecht, 2004.

Chevalier, Nicole. *Une Mission en Perse 1897–1912*. Paris: Réunion des Muesées Nationaux, 1997.

Chiera, Edward. *Legal and Administrative Documents from Nippur*. Publications from the Babylonian Section VIII. Philadelphia: University Museum, 1914.

Civil, Miguel. "Ancient Mesopotamian Lexicography." In *CANE*, 2305–2314.

Civil, Miguel. *Ea A = Naqû, Aa A = Naqû, with Their Forerunners and Related Texts*. Materials for the Sumerian Lexicon. Rome: Ponficium Institutum Biblicum, 1979.

Civil, Miguel. "The Law Collection of Ur-Namma." In *Cuneiform Royal Inscriptions and Related Texts in the Schøyen Collection*. Edited by A. R. George, with contributions by M. Civil et al. Cornell University Studies in Assyriology and Sumerology. Bethesda, Md.: CDL Press, 2011.

Civil, Miguel. "Lexicography." In *Sumerological Studies in Honor of Thorkild Jacobsen*. Edited by Åke Sjöberg. AS 20, 123–157. Chicago: University of Chicago Press, 1976.

Civil, Miguel. "On Some Texts Mentioning Ur-Namma." *Or* 54 (1985): 27–45.

Clayton, Jay, and Eric Rothstein. "Figures in the Corpus: Theories of Influence and Intertextuality." In *Influence and Intertextuality in Literary History*. Edited by Jay Clayton and Eric Rothstein, 3–36. Madison: University of Wisconsin Press, 1991.

Cohen, Boaz. *Jewish and Roman Law: A Comparative Study*. New York: Jewish Theological Seminary of America, 1966.

Cohen, Chaim. "The Ancient Critical Understanding of Exodus 21:22–25 and Its Implications for the Current Debate on Abortion." In *Mishneh Todah: Studies in Deuteronomy and Its Cultural Environment in Honor of Jeffrey H. Tigay*. Edited by Nili Sacher Fox, David A. Glatt-Gilad, and Michael J. Williams, 437–458. Winona Lake, Ind.; Eisenbrauns, 2009.

Cohen, Eran. "Functional Value of *Iprus* Forms in Old Babylonian *Šumma* Protases." In *Language and Nature: Papers Presented to John Huehnergard on the Occasion of His 60th Birthday*. Edited by Rachel Hasselbach and Naama Pat-El. Studies in Ancient Oriental Civilizations 67, 1–11. Chicago: Oriental Institute, 2012.

Cohen, Yoram. "Kidin-Gula—the Foreign Teacher at the Emar Scribal School." *RA* 98 (2004): 81–100.

Collon, Dominique. *First Impressions: Cylinder Seals in the Ancient Near East*. Chicago: University of Chicago Press; London: British Museum Publications, 1987.

Cooley, Jeffrey L. "An OB Prayer to the Gods of the Night." In *Reading Akkadian Prayers and Hymns: An Introduction*. Edited by Alan Lenzi. Society of Biblical Literature Ancient Near East Monographs 3, 71–83. Atlanta: Society of Biblical Literature, 2011.

Cooper, Jerrold. "Apodotic Death and the Historicity of 'Historical' Omens." In *Death in Mesopotamia: Papers Read at the XXVIe. Roncontre Assyriologique Internationale*. Edited by Bendt Alster, 99–105. Copenhagen: Akademisk Forlag, 1980.

Cooper, Jerrold S. "Medium and Message: Inscribed Clay Cones and Vessels from Presargonic Sumer." *RA* 79 (1985): 97–114.

Cooper, Jerrold S. "Paradigm and Propaganda: The Dynasty of Akkade in the 21st Century." In *Akkad: The First World Empire: Structure, Ideology, Traditions*. Edited by Mario Liverani. History of the Ancient Near East. Studies V. Padova: Sargon, 1993.

Cooper, Jerrold S. *Presargonic Inscriptions*. Sumerian and Akkadian Royal Inscriptions. New Haven, Conn.: American Oriental Society, 1986.

Cover, Robert. "Nomos and Narrative." In *Narrative, Violence, and the Law*. Edited by Martha Minow, Michael Ryan, and Austin Sarat. Law, Meaning, and Violence, 95–172. Ann Arbor: University of Michigan Press, 1993.

Crawford, M. H., ed. *Roman Statutes*. London: Institute of Classical Studies, University of London, 1996.

Curtis, John E., and William W. Hallo. "Money and Merchants in Ur III." *Hebrew Union College Annual* 30 (1959): 103–139.

Cuthbertson, Laura. "Local Courts in Centralizing States: The Case of Ur III Mesopotamia." In *Social Theory in Archaeology and Ancient History: The Present and Future of Counternarratives*, 185–202. Edited by Geoff Emberling. New York: Cambridge University Press, 2016.

Dalley, Stephanie, and A. T. Reyes. "Mesopotamian Contact and Influence in the Greek World: To the Persian Conquest." In *The Legacy of Mesopotamia*. Edited by Stephanie Dalley, with drawings by Stephanie Dalley and Marion Cox, Stephanie Dalley et al., 85–106. Oxford: Oxford University Press, 1998.

Daube, David. *Forms of Roman Legislation*. Oxford: Clarendon, 1956.

Daube, David. "Some Forms of the Old Testament Legislation." *Proceedings of the Oxford Society for Historical Theology* (1944–45): 36–46.

David, Martino. *Die Adoption im altbabylonischen Recht*. Leipzig: Weicher, 1927.

Delnero, Paul. "Variation in Sumerian Literary Compositions: A Case Study Based on the Decad." Ph.D. dissertation. University of Pennsylvania, 2006.

Dennis, Andrew, Peter Foote, and Richard Perkins, trans. *Laws of Early Iceland: Grágás, Volume 1*. University of Manitoba Icelandic Series III. Winnipeg: University of Manitoba Press, 1980.

Démare-Lafont, Sophie. "Women at Work in Mesopotamia: An Attempt at a Legal Perspective." In *The Role of Women in Work and Society in the Ancient Near East*. Edited by Brigitte Lion and Cécile Michel. Studies in Ancient Near Eastern Records. Boston: De Gruyter, 2–16.

Diakonoff, I. M. "On the Social Structure of Old Babylonian Society." In *Beiträge zur Sozialen Struktur des alten Vorderasien*. Edited by Horst Klengel. Schriften zur Geschichte und Kultur des Alten Orients, 26–31. Berlin: Akademie-Verl., 1971.

Diakonoff, I. M. "Socio-Economic Classes in Babylonia and the Babylonian Concept of Economic Stratification." In *Gesellschaftsklassen Im Alten Zweistromland und in Den Angrenzenden Gebieten; XVIII. Rencontre Assyriologique Internationale, München, 29. Juni Bis 3. Juli 1970*, 41–52. München: Verlag der Bayerischen Akademie der Wissenschaften; In Kommission bei Beck, 1972.

Diakonoff, I. M. "Some Remarks on the 'Reforms' of Urukagina." *RA* 52 (1958): 1–15.

Di Tullio, Daria. "Un articulo del codice di Lipit-Ištar." *NABU* 2004/43.

Donbaz, V., and H. Sauren. "NI 2553 + 2565: A Missing Link of the Hammurabi Law Code." *Or* 22 (1991): 5–28.

Dossin, G. "Prières Aux 'Dieux de la Nuit' (AO 6769)." *RA* 32 (1935): 179–187.

Driver, G. R., and John C. Miles. *The Assyrian Laws*. Ancient Codes and Laws of the Near East. Oxford: Clarendon, 1935.

Driver, G. R., and John C. Miles. *The Babylonian Laws I*. Volume 1: Legal Commentary. Oxford: Clarendon Press, 1952.

Driver, G. R., and John C. Miles. *The Babylonian Laws II*. Ancient Codes and Laws of the Near East. Oxford: Clarendon, 1955.

Durand, Jean-Marie. "Dagan et la fin du Mari." *NABU* 2004/51.

Durand, Jean-Marie. "Une condamnation a mort a l'époque d'Ur III." *RA* 71 (1977): 125–136.

Edzard, Dietz Otto. *Gudea and His Dynasty*. RIME 3/1. Toronto: University of Toronto Press, 1997.

Edzard, D. O. "'Soziale Reformen' imZweistromland bis ca. 1600 v. Chr.: Realität oder literarischer Topos." *Acta antiqua Scientiarum Hungaricae* 22 (1974): 145–156.

Eichler, Barry L. "Examples of Restatement in the Laws of Hammurabi." In *Mishneh Todah: Studies in Deuteronomy and Its Cultural Environment: In Honor of Jeffrey H. Tigay*. Edited by Nili Sacher Fox, David A. Glatt-Gilad, and Michael J. Williams, 365–400. Winona Lake, Ind.: Eisenbrauns, 2009.

Eichler, Barry L. "Exodus 21:22–25 Revisited: Methodological Consideration." In *Birkat Shalom: Studies in the Bible, Ancient Near Eastern Literature, and Postbiblical Judaism Presented to Shalom M. Paul on the Occasion of His Seventieth Birthday*. Edited by Chaim Cohen et al., 14–20. Winona Lake, Ind.: Eisenbrauns, 2008.

Eichler, Barry L. "Literary Structure in the Laws of Eshnunna." In *Language, Literature, and History: Philological and Historical Studies Presented to Erica Reiner*. Edited by Francesca Rochberg-Halton. American Oriental Society 67, 71–84. New Haven, Conn.: American Oriental Society, 1987.

Eidem, Jesper. *The Shemshara Archives 2: The Administrative Texts*. Historisk-Filosofiske Skrifter. Copenhagen: Kongelige Danske Videnskabernes Selskab, 1992.

Elsen-Novák, Gabriele, and Mirko Novák. "Der König der Gerechtigkeit.' Zur Ikonologie und Teleologie des '*Codex' Ḫammurapi*." *Baghdader Mitteilungen* 37 (2006): 131–155.

Eppihemer, Melissa. "Representing Ashur: The Old Assyrian Rulers' Seals and Their Ur III Prototype." *JNES* 72 (2013): 35–49.

Fadhil, A. "Der Prolog des Codex Hammurapi in einer abschrift aus Sippar." In *XXXIVeme Rencontre Assyriologique Internationale, Istanbul, 1987*, 717–729. Ankara: Türk Trih Kurumu Basimevi, 1998.

Falkenstein, Adam, and Wolfram von Soden. *Sumerische und Akkadische Hymnen und Gebete*. Die Bibliothek der Alten Welt. Zürich: Artemis-Verlag, 1953.

Feldman, Marian. "Object Agency? Spatial Perspective, Social Relations, and the Stele of Hammurabi." In *Agency and Identity in the Ancient Near East: New Paths Forward*. Edited by Sharon R Steadman and Jennifer C. Ross, 148–165. London: Equinox, 2010.

Fincke, J. C. "Omina, die göttlichen 'Gesetze' der Divination." *Jaarbericht Ex Oriente Lux* 40 (2006–2007): 131–147.

Finkel, Irving L. "On Late Babylonian Medical Training." In *Wisdom, Gods and Literature: Studies in Assyriology in Honor of W. G. Lambert*. Edited by A. R. George and I. L. Finkel, 137–223. Winona Lake, Ind.: Eisenbrauns, 2000.

Finkelstein, J. J. "Ammiṣaduqa's Edict and the Babylonian 'Law' Codes." *JCS* 15 (1961): 91–104.

Finkelstein, J. J. "The Genealogy of the Hammurapi Dynasty." *JCS* 20 (1966): 95–118.

Finkelstein, J. J. "The Goring Ox: Some Historical Perspectives on Deodands, Forfeitures, Wrongful Death, and the Western Notion of Sovereignty." *Temple Law Quarterly* 46 (1973): 169–290.

Finkelstein, J. J. "A Late Old Babylonian Copy of the Laws of Hammurapi." *JCS* 21 (1967): 39–48.

Finkelstein, J. J. "The Laws of Ur-Nammu." *JCS* 22 (1969): 66–82.

Finkelstein, J. J. "Mišpāṭ, hamishpat ba-mizrah ha-qadmon." In *Encyclopaedia Miqra'it*, 5.588–614. 9 volumes. Jerusalem: Mossad Bialik, 1968.

Finkelstein, J. J. "On Some Recent Studies in Cuneiform Law." *JAOS* 90 (1970): 131–143.

Finkelstein, J. J. *The Ox That Gored*. Prepared by Maria deJ. Ellis. Transactions of the American Philosophical Society 71/2. Philadelphia: American Philosophical Society, 1981.

Finkelstein, J. J. "Sex Offenses in Sumerian Law." *JAOS* 86 (1966): 355–372.

Finkelstein, J. J. "Some New Misharum Material and Its Implications." In *Studies in Honor of Benno Landsberger on His Seventy-Fifth Birthday*. Edited by Hans G. Güterbock and Thorkild Jacobsen, 233–246. AS 16. Chicago: University of Chicago Press, 1965.

Fischer, Claudia. "The Twilight of the Sun-God." *Iraq* 64 (2002): 125–134.

Flückiger-Hawker, Esther. *Urnamma of Ur in Sumerian Literary Tradition*. Orbis Biblicus et Orientalis. Göttingen: Vandenhoeck & Ruprecht, 1999.

Foster, Benjamin R. *Before the Muses: An Anthology of Akkadian Literature*. 3rd Edition. Bethesda, Md.: CDL Press, 2005.

Foster, Benjamin. "A New Look at the Sumerian Temple State." *JESHO* 24 (1981): 215–241.

Foster, Benjamin R. "Social Reform in Ancient Mesopotamia." In *Social Justice in the Ancient World*. Edited by K. D. Irani and Morris Silver, 165–177. Westport, Conn.: Greenwood Press, 1995.

Foxvog, Daniel A. "A New Legal Text Bearing on Uruinimgina's Reforms." *JCS* 46 (1994): 11–15.

Frahm, Eckart. *Babylonian and Assyrian Text Commentaries: Origins of Interpretation*. GMTR 5. Münster: Ugarit, 2011.

Frame, Grant, and A. R. George. "The Royal Libraries of Nineveh: New Evidence for King Ashurbanipal's Tablet Collecting." *Iraq* 67 (2005): 265–284.

Frankfort, Henri. *The Art and Architecture of the Ancient Orient*. 4th ed. Pelican History of Art. New Haven, Conn.: Yale University Press, 1970.

Frayne, Douglas. *Old Babylonian Period (2002–1595 B.C.)*. RIME 4. Toronto: University of Toronto Press, 1990.

Frayne, Douglas. *Presargonic Period (2700–2350 B.C.)*. RIME 1. Toronto: University of Toronto Press, 2008.

Frayne, Douglas. *Ur III (2112–2004 BC)*. RIME 3. Toronto: University of Toronto Press, 2008.

Gagarin, Michael. *Writing Greek Law*. Cambridge: Cambridge University Press, 2008.

Garner, Bryan A., editor in chief. *Black's Law Dictionary*. 9th edition. St. Paul, Minn.: West/Thomson Reuters, 2009.

Garroway, Kristine H. *Children in the Ancient Near Eastern Household*. Explorations in Ancient Near Eastern Civilizations. Winona Lake, Ind.: Eisenbrauns, 2014.

Gasche, H. *La Babylonia Au 17e Siecle Avant Notre Ere: Approche Archeologique, Problemes et Perspectives*. Ghent: University of Ghent, 1989.

Gasche, H., J. A. Armstrong, S. W. Cole, and W. G. Gurzadyan. *Dating the Fall of Babylon: A Reappraisal of Second-Millennium Chronology*. Mesopotamian History and

Environment 4. Ghent and Chicago: University of Ghent and the Oriental Institute of the University of Chicago, 1998.

George, A. R. *The Babylonian Gilgamesh Epic: Introduction, Critical Edition, and Cuneiform Texts*. Oxford: Oxford University Press, 2003.

George, A. R. "In Search of the é. d u b. b a. a: The Ancient Mesopotamian School in Literature and Reality." In *An Experienced Scribe Who Neglects Nothing: Ancient Near Eastern Studies in Honor of Jacob Klein*. Edited by Yitschak Sefati et al., 127–137. Bethesda, Md.: CDL Press, 2005.

George, A. R., and Gabriella Spada. *Old Babylonian Texts in the Schøyen Collection, Part Two: School Letters, Model Contracts, and Related Texts*. CUSAS: Cornell University Studies in Assyriology and Sumerology. University Park; Pennsylvania State University Press, 2019.

Gesche, Petra D. *Schulunterricht in Babylonien Im Ersten Jahrtausend v. Chr.* Alter Orient und Altes Testament, vol. 275. Münster: Ugarit-Verlag, 2000.

Ghirschman, Roman. "Suse Du Temps Des SUKKALMAH; Campagne de Fouilles 1963–1964." *Arts Asiatiques* 11, no. 2 (1965): 3–21.

Glassner, Jean-Jacques. "Pour un Lexique Des Termes et Figures Analogiques en Usage Dan la Divination Mésopotamienne." *RA* 77 (1983): 3–10.

Goetze, Albrecht. *The Laws of Eshnunna*. AASOR 31. New Haven, Conn.: American Schools of Oriental Research, 1956.

Gordin, Shai. *Hittite Scribal Circles: Scholarly Tradition and Writing Habits*. Studien zu den Bogazköy-Texten. Wiesbaden: Harrassowitz Verlag, 2015.

Graetz, Shirley. "To Whom Does a Wronged Man Turn for Help? The Agent in Old Babylonian Letters." Ph.D. dissertation, Ben-Gurion University of the Negev, 2012.

Greengus, Samuel. *Laws in the Bible and Early Rabbinic Collections: The Legal Legacy of the Ancient Near East*. Eugene, Ore.: Cascade, 2011.

Greengus, Samuel. "Redefining 'Inchoate Marriage' in Old Babylonian Contexts." In *Riches Hidden in Secret Places: Ancient Near Eastern Studies in Memory of Thorkild Jacobsen*. Edited by Tzvi Abusch, 123–139. Winona Lake, Ind.: Eisenbrauns, 2002.

Greengus, Samuel. "The Old Babylonian Marriage Contract." *JAOS* 89 (1969): 505–532.

Guinan, Ann K. "Laws and Omens: Obverse and Inverse." In *Divination in the Ancient Near East: A Workshop on Divination Conducted during the 54th Rencontre Assyriologique Internationale, Würzburg, 2008*. Edited by Jeanette C. Fincke and Jeanette C. Fincke, 105–121. Winona Lake, Ind.: Eisenbrauns, 2008.

Günbatti, Cahit. "The River Ordeal in Ancient Anatolia." In *Veenhof Anniversary Volume*, 151–160. Leiden: Nederlands Instituut voor het Nabije Oosten, 2001.

Hallo, William W. "The Expansion of Cuneiform Literature." *Proceedings of the American Academy for Jewish Research* 46 (1979–1980): 307–322.

Hallo, William W. "The House of Urmeme." *JNES* 31 (1972): 87–95.

Hallo, William W. "A Model Court Case Concerning Inheritance." In *Riches Hidden in Secret Places: Ancient Near Eastern Studies in Memory of Thorkild Jacobsen*. Edited by Tzvi Abusch, 141–154. Winona Lake, Ind.: Eisenbrauns, 2002.

Hallo, William W. "Notes from the Babylonian Collection II: Old Babylonian HAR-Ra." *JCS* 34 (1982): 81–93.

Hallo, William W. "Slave Release in the Biblical World in Light of a New Text." In *Solving Riddles and Untying Knots: Biblical, Epigraphic, and Semitic Studies in Honor of Jonas C. Greenfield*. Edited by Ziony Zevit, Seymour Gitin, and Michael Sokoloff, 79–93. Winona Lake, Ind.: Eisenbrauns, 1995.

Hallo, William W. "Toward a History of Sumerian Literature." In *Sumerological Studies in Honor of Thorkild Jacobsen*. Edited by Åke Sjöberg. AS 20, 181–203. Chicago: University of Chicago Press, 1976.

Harper, Prudence O. "Mesopotamian Monuments Found at Susa." In *The Royal City of Susa: Ancient Near Eastern Treasures in the Louvre*. Edited by Prudence O. Harper, Joan Aruz, and Françoise Tallon, 159–182. New York: Metropolitan Museum of Art, 1992.

Harris, Rivkah. "The *Nadītu* Laws of the Code of Hammurapi in Praxis." *Or* NS 30 (1961): 163–169.

Haubold, Johannes. *Greece and Mesopotamia: Dialogues in Literature*. New York: Cambridge University Press, 2013.

Hays, Christopher B. "Echoes of the Ancient Near East?: Intertextuality and the Comparative Study of the Old Testament." In *The Word Leaps the Gap: Essays on Scripture and Theology in Honor of Richard B. Hays*. Edited by J. Ross Wagner and C. Kavin Rowe & A. Katherine Grieb, 20–43. Grand Rapids, Mich.: William B. Eerdmans, 2008.

Heimpel, Wolfgang. "The River Ordeal in Hit." *RA* 90 (1996): 7–18.

Heinz, Marlies, and Marian H. Feldman, eds. *Representations of Political Power: Case Histories from Times of Change and Dissolving Order in the Ancient Near East*. Winona Lake, Ind.: Eisenbrauns, 2007.

Herman, Ellen. *Kinship by Design: A History of Adoption in the Modern United States*. Chicago: University of Chicago Press, 2008.

Holtz, Shalom E. "The Career of a Neo-Babylonian Court Scribe." *JCS* 60 (2008): 81–85.

Horowitz, Wayne. "Astral Tablets in the Hermitage, Saint Petersburg." *ZA* 90 (2000): 194–206.

Horowitz, Wayne, Takayoshi Oshima, and Seth Sanders. "A Bibliographical List of Cuneiform Inscriptions from Canaan, Palestine/Philistia, and the Land of Israel." *JAOS* 122 (2002): 753–766.

Horowitz, Wayne, and Takayoshi Oshima. *Cuneiform in Canaan: Cuneiform Sources from the Land of Israel in Ancient Times*. Jerusalem: Israel Exploration Society: Hebrew University of Jerusalem, 2006.

Horowitz, Wayne, Takayoshi Oshima, and Seth L. Sanders. *Cuneiform in Canaan: The Next Generation*. 2d ed. University Park, Penn.: Eisenbrauns, 2018.

Horowitz, Wayne, Takayoshi Oshima, and Filip Vukosavović. "Hazor 18: Fragments of a Cuneiform Law Collection from Hazor." *Israel Exploration Journal* 62 (2012): 158–176.

Horsnell, Malcolm J. A. *The Year-Names of the First Dynasty of Babylon*, Volume II: *The Year-Names Reconstructed and Critically Annotated in the Light of Their Exemplars*. Hamilton, Ontario: McMaster University Press, 1999.

Hruška, Blahoslav. "Die innere struktur de Reformtexte Urukaginas von Lagaš." *Archiv Orientalni* 41 (1973): 4–13, 104–132.

Hruška, Blahoslav. "Die reformtexte Urukaginas: der verspätete versuch einer konsolierung des stadtaates von Lagaš." In *Le palais et la royauté: XIXe recontre assyriologique internationale*. Edited by Paul Garelli, 151–161. Paris: Librairie orientaliste Paul Guethner, 1974.

Huehnergard, John. *A Grammar of Akkadian*. Harvard Semitic Studies. Winona Lake, Ind.: Eisenbrauns, 2000.

Hurowitz, Victor Avigdor. *Inu Anum Ṣirum: Literary Structures in the Non-Juridical Sections of Codex Hammurabi*. Occasional Publications of the Samuel Noah Kramer Fund. Philadelphia: University Museum, 1994.

Hurowitz, Victor Avigdor. "Spanning the Generations: Aspects of Written and Oral Transmission in the Bible and Mesopotamia." In *Freedom and Responsibility: Exploring the Challenges of Jewish Continuity*. Edited by Rela Mintz Geffen and Marcia Bryan Edelman, 11–30. Hoboken, N.J.: Ktav, 1998.

Jackson, Bernard S. "Historical Aspects of Legal Drafting in the Light of Modern Theories of Cognitive Development." *International Journal of Law and Psychiatry* 3 (1980): 349–369.

Jackson, Bernard S. *Law, Fact, and Narrative Coherence*. Legal Semiotics Monographs. Roby, Merseyside, U.K.: Deborah Charles Publications, 1988.

Jackson, Bernard S. "The Problem of Exod. XXI 22–25 (*ius talionis*)." *Vetus Testamentum* 23 (1973): 273–304.

Jackson, Bernard S. *Wisdom-Laws: A Study of the Mishpatim of Exodus 21:1–22:16*. Oxford: Oxford University Press, 2006.

Jacobs, Sandra. *The Body as Property: Physical Disfigurement in Biblical Law*. London: Bloomsbury, 2014.

Jacobsen, Thorkild. "Pictures and Pictorial Language (The Burney Relief)." In *Figurative Language in the Ancient Near East*. Edited by Murray Mindlin, Markham J. Geller, M. J. Geller, and John E. Wansbrough, 1–11. London: School of Oriental and African Studies, University of London, 1987.

Jacobsen, Thorkild. *The Harps That Once—Sumerian Poetry in Translation*. New Haven, Conn.: Yale University Press, 1987.

Jaffee, Martin S. *Torah in the Mouth: Writing and Oral Tradition in Palestinian Judaism, 200 BCE–400 CE*. New York: Oxford University Press, 2001.

Janssen, C. "Samsu-Iluma and the Hungry *Nadītums*." *Northern Akkad Project Reports* 5 (1991): 3–40.

Jean, Charles-F. *Lettres Diverses*. Archives Royales de Mari 2. Paris: Imprimerie nationale, 1950.

Jiménez, Enrique. *The Babylonian Disputation Poems: With Editions of the Series of the Poplar, Palm and Vine, the Series of the Spider, and the Story of the Poor, Forlorn Wren*. Culture and History of the Ancient Near East 87. Leiden: Brill, 2017.

Jiménez, Enrique. "On the Commentary to the Code of Hammurapi and the Babylonian God of Ordeals." *NABU* 2014/84.

Joosten, Jan. "Covenant." In *The Oxford Handbook of Biblical Law*, 7–18. Edited by Pamela Barmash. Oxford: Oxford University Press, 2019.

Jursa, Michael. "'Als könig Abi-Ešuh gerechte ordnung hergestellt hat' eine bemerkenswerte altbabylonisch Prozessurkunde." *RA* 91 (1997): 135–145.

Kanarek, Jane L. *Biblical Narrative and the Formation of Rabbinic Law*. New York: Cambridge University Press, 2014.

Klein, Jacob. *Three Šulgi Hymns: Sumerian Royal Hymns Glorifying King Šulgi of Ur*. Ramat-Gan: Bar-Ilan University Press, 1981.

Klein, Jacob, and Tonia M Sharlach. "A Collection of Model Court Cases from Old Babylonian Nippur (CBS 11324)." *ZA* 97 (2007): 1–25.

Kleinerman, Alexandra. *Education in Early 2nd Millennium BC Babylonia: The Sumerian Epistolary Miscellany*. Cuneiform Monographs 42. Leiden: Brill, 2011.

Koch, Ulla. *Mesopotamian Divination Texts: Conversing with the Gods, Sources from the First Millennium BCE*. GMTR 7. Münster: Ugarit Verlag, 2015.

Komoróczy, G. "Zur Frage des Periodizität der altbabylonischen *mīšarum-Erlässe*." In *Societies and Languages of the Ancient Near East: Studies in Honor of I. M. Diakonoff*.

Edited by M. A. Dandamayev, I. Gershevitch, H. Klengel, G. Komoróczy, M. T. Larsen, and J. N. Postgate, 196–205. Warminster, England: Aris & Phillips Ltd., 1982.

Koschaker, Paul. *Rechtsvergleichende Studien Zur Gesetzgebung Hammurapis: Königs von Babylon*. Leipzig: Veit & Comp., 1917.

Kramer, Samuel Noah. "BM 23631: Bread for Enlil, Sex for Inanna." *Or* 54 (1985): 117–132.

Kramer, Samuel Noah. "The Death of Ur-Nammu and His Descent to the Netherworld." *JCS* 21 (1967): 104–122.

Kramer, Samuel Noah. "Law and Justice: Gleanings from Sumerian Literature." In *Reflets des deux fleuves, Volume de Mélanges offerts à André Finet*. Edited by M. LeBeau and P. Talon. Akkadica Supplementum 6, 77–82. Leuven: Peeters, 1989.

Kramer, Samuel Noah. *The Sumerians: Their History, Culture, and Character*. Chicago: University of Chicago Press, 1963.

Kramer, Samuel Noah. "Sumerian Theology and Ethics." *Harvard Theological Review* 49 (1956): 45–62.

Kramer, Samuel Noah. "'Vox Populi' and the Sumerian Literary Documents." *RA* 58 (1964): 148–156.

Kraus, F. R. "Akkadische Wörter und Ausdrücke XII, *ṣimdatum, ṣimdat šarrim*." *RA* 73 (1979): 51–62.

Kraus, F. R. "Briefschreibübungen im altbabylonischen Schulunterricht." *Jaarbericht Ex Oriente Lux* 16 (1964): 16–39.

Kraus, F. R. "Codex Ḫammu-Rabi IV 32–44." *Wiener Zeitschrift für die Kunde des Morganlandes* 51 (1948): 173–177.

Kraus, F. R. *Ein Edikt de Konigs Ammi-Saduqa von Babylon*. Studia et Documenta Ad Iura Orientis Antiqui Pertinenta 5. Leiden: Brill, 1958.

Kraus, F. R. "Ein Sittenkanon in Omenform." *ZA* 43 (1938): 77–113.

Kraus, F. R. "Ein zentrales Problem des altmesopotamischen Rechtes: Was ist der Kodex Hammurabi?" *Genava* NS 8 (1960): 283–296.

Kraus, F. R. *Königliche Verfügungen in Altbabylonischer Zeit*. Studia et Documenta Ad Iura Orientis Antiqui Pertinentia, vol. 11. Leiden: E. J. Brill, 1984.

Kraus, F. R. *Vom mesopotamischen Menschen der altbabylonische Zeit und seiner Welt: Eine Reihe Vorlesungen*. Mededelingen der Koninklijke Nederlandse Akademie Van Wetenschapper 36/6. Amsterdam: North-Holland, 1973.

Kuhrt, Amelie. *The Ancient Near East*. Routledge History of the Ancient World. London: Routledge, 1995.

Kupper, J. R. "Lettres de Kiš (suite et fin)." *RA* 53 (1959): 177–182.

Laessøe, Jørgen. "On the Fragments of the Hammurabi Code." *JCS* 4 (1950): 173–187.

Lafont, Bertrand. "The Ordeal." In *Everyday Life in Ancient Mesopotamia*. Translated by Antonia Nevill, 199–210. Edinburgh: Edinburgh University Press, 2001.

Lafont, Sophie. "Les Actes Législatifs Des Rois Mésopotamiens." In *Auctoritates Xenia R. C. Van Caenegem Oblata: La Formation Du Droit et Ses Auteurs*, vol. Iuris scripta historica 13. Wetenschappelijk Comite Voor Rechtsgeschiedenis Koninklijke Academie Voor Wetensschappen, 3–27. Brussels: Peeters, 1997.

Lambert, M. "Les 'Reforms' Urukagina." *RA* 50 (1956): 169–184.

Lambert, W. G. *Babylonian Creation Myths*. Winona Lake, Ind.: Eisenbrauns, 2013.

Lambert, W. G. *Babylonian Wisdom Literature*. Winona Lake, Ind.,: Eisenbrauns, 1996.

Lambert, W. G. "The Laws of Hammurabi in the First Millenium." In *Reflets des deux fleuves, Volume de Mélanges offerts à André Finet*. Edited by M. LeBeau and P. Talon. Akkadica Supplementum 6, 95–98. Leuven: Peeters, 1989.

Lambert, W. G. "Nebuchadnezzar King of Justice." *Iraq* 27 (1965): 1–11.
Landsberger, Benno. "Babylonian Scribal Craft and Its Terminology." In *Proceedings of the Twenty-Third International Congress of Orientalists*. Edited by Denis Sinor, 123–127. London: Royal Asiatic Society, 1954.
Landsberger, Benno. "Die babylonischen Termini für Gesetz und Recht." In *Symbolae ad iura orientis antiqui pertinentes Paulo Koschker dedicatae*. Edited by J. Friedrich, J. G. Lautner, and J. Miles. SDIOAP, 219–234. Leiden: E. J. Brill, 1939.
Landsberger, Benno. "Jungfräulichkeit." In *Symbolae iuridicae et historicae Martino David dedicatae*, 41–105. Edited by J. A. Ankum et al. Leiden: Brill, 1968.
Landsberger, Benno. "Remarks on the Archive of the Soldier Ubarum." *JCS* 9 (1955): 121–131.
Landsberger, Benno. "Scribal Concepts of Education." In *City Invincible*. Edited by Carl Kraeling and Robert McC. Adams, 94–103. Chicago: Oriental Institute, 1967.
Landsberger, Benno. *Die serie* ana ittišu. Materials for the Sumerian Lexicon. Rome: Pontificii instituti biblici, 1937.
Langdon, S. *Sumerian and Semitic Religious and Historical Texts*. Oxford Editions of Cuneiform Inscriptions 1. London: Oxford University Press, 1923.
Lanni, Adriaan. "Arguing from 'Precedent': Modern Perspectives on Athenian Practice." In *The Law and the Courts in Ancient Greece*. Edited by Edward M. Harris and Lene Rubinstein, 159–171. London: Duckworth, 2004.
Lanni, Adriaan. *Law and Justice in the Courts of Classical Athens*. New York: Cambridge University Press, 2008.
Lanni, Adriaan. "'Verdict Most Just': The Modes of Classical Athenian Justice." *Yale Journal of Law and the Humanities* 16, no. 2 (2004): 277–321.
Larsen, Mogens Trolle. "The Babylonian Lukewarm Mind: Reflections on Science, Divination, and Literacy." In *Language, Literature, and History: Philological and Historical Studies Presented to Erica Reiner*. Edited by Francesca Rochberg-Halton. American Oriental Society 67, 203–225. New Haven, Conn.: American Oriental Society, 1987.
Larsen, Mogens Trolle. *The Old Assyrian City-State and Its Colonies*. Mesopotamia. Copenhagen: Akademisk Forlag, 1976.
Leemans, W. F. "King Hammurapi as Judge." In *Symbolae iuridicae et historicae Martino David dedicatae II*. Edited by J. A. Ankum, R. Feenstra, and W. F. Leemans, 105–128. Leiden: E. J. Brill, 1968.
Lemche, Niels Peter. "Andurārum and Mīsharum: Comments on the Problem of Social Ethics and Their Application in the Ancient Near East." *Journal of Near Eastern Studies* 38 (1979): 11–22.
Levi, Edward H. *An Introduction to Legal Reasoning*. Chicago: University of Chicago Press, 1949.
Lieberman, Stephen J. "Royal 'Reforms' of the Amurrite Dynasty." *Bibliotheca Orientalis* 46 (1989): 242–260.
Lindgren, James. "Measuring the Value of Slaves and Free Persons in Ancient Law." *Chicago-Kent Law Review* 71, no. 1 (1995): 149–217.
Lindsay, Hugh. *Adoption in the Roman World*. Cambridge: Cambridge University Press, 2009.
Liverani, Mario. "The Deeds of Ancient Mesopotamian Kings." In *CANE*, 2353–2366.
Liverani, Mario. "Review of H. Gasche et al, *Dating the Fall of Babylon*." *JNES* 64 (2003): 213–215.

Lyon, David Gordon. "When and Where Was the Code Hammurabi Promulgated?" *JAOS* 27 (1906): 123–134.

Malul, Meir. "Adoption of Foundlings in the Bible and Mesopotamia Documents: A Study of Some Legal Metaphors in Ezekiel 16:1–7." *Journal for the Study of the Old Testament* 46 (1990): 97–126.

Malul, Meir. *The Comparative Method in Ancient Near Eastern and Biblical Legal Studies*. Alter Orient und Altes Testament 227. Neukirchen-Vluyn: Neukirchener Verlag, 1990.

Martin, Malachi. *The Scribal Character of the Dead Sea Scrolls*. Bibliothèque Du Muséon, vol. 44–45. Louvain: Publications universitaires, 1958.

Mastnjak, Nathan. "Prestige, Authority, and Jeremiah's Bible." *Journal of Religion* 98 (2018): 542–558.

Matuszak, Jana. "'Und Du, Du Bist eine Frau?!'—Untersuchungen zu Sumerischen Literarischen Frauenstreitgesprächen Nebst einer Editio Princeps von Zwei Frauen B." Ph. D. dissertation, University of Tübingen, 2017.

Maul, Stefan M. "Tontafelabschriften Des 'Kodex Hammurapi' in Altbabylonischer Monumentalschrift." *ZA* 102 (2012): 76–99.

McCown, Donald E., and Richard C. Haines. *Nippur I: Temple of Enlil, Scribal Quarter, and Soundings*. Oriental Institute Publications 78. Chicago: University of Chicago Press, 1967.

Meissner, Bruno. "Altbabylonische Gesetze." *Beiträge zur Assyriologie* 3 (1898): 493–523.

Metcalf, Christopher. *The Gods Rich in Praise: Early Greek and Mesopotamian Religious Poetry*. Oxford Classical Monographs. Oxford: Oxford University Press, 2015.

Michalowski, Piotr. "Charisma and Control: On Continuity and Change in Early Mesopotamian Bureaucratic Systems." In *The Organization of Power: Aspects of Bureaucracy in the Ancient Near East*. Edited by McGuire Gibson and Robert D. Biggs. Studies in Ancient Oriental Civilization 46, 45–57. Chicago: Oriental Institute of the University of Chicago, 1991.

Michalowski, Piotr. "Sumerian Literature: An Overview." *CANE*, 2277–2289.

Michalowski, Piotr, and M. P. Streck. "Hammurapi," In RLA 15: 380–390.

Michalowski, Piotr, and C. B. F. Walker. "A New Sumerian 'Law Code.'" In *DUMU-E$_2$-DUB-BA-A: Studies in Honor of Aake Sjöberg*. Edited by Hermann Behrens, Darlene Loding, and Martha T. Roth. Occasional Publications of the Samuel Noah Kramer Fund 11, 383–396. Philadelphia: University Museum, 1989.

Mitchell, W. J. T. *Iconology: Image, Text, Ideology*. Chicago: University of Chicago Press, 1986.

Morrow, William S. "Cuneiform Literacy and Deuteronomic Composition." *Bibliotheca Orientalis* 62 (2005): 204–214.

Morrow, William S. "Legal Interactions: The Mišpāṭîm and the Laws of Hammurabi." *Bibliotheca Orientalis* 70 (2013): 310–332.

Morrow, William S. "Resistance and Hybridity in Late Bronze Age Canaan." *Revue biblique* 115, no. 3 (2008): 321–339.

Moscovitz, Leib. *Talmudic Reasoning: From Casuistics to Conceptualization*. Texte und Studien zum antiken Judentum. Tübingen: Mohr Siebeck, 2002.

Müller, D. H. *Die Gesetze Ḥammurabis und ihr Verhältnis zur mosaichen Gesetzebung sowie zu den XII Tafeln*. Wien: Alfred Hölder, 1903.

Nader, Laura, and Harry F. Todd, eds. *The Disputing Process: Law in Ten Societies*. New York: Columbia University Press, 1978.

Neusner, Jacob. *Judaism: The Evidence of the Mishnah*. Chicago: University of Chicago Press, 1981.

Nissen, Hans J. "The Education and Profession of the Scribe." In *Archaic Bookkeeping: Early Writing and Techniques of Economic Administration in the Ancient Near East*. Edited by Hans J. Nissen, Peter Damerow, and Robert K. Englund, translated by Paul Larsen, 105–115. Chicago: University of Chicago Press, 1993.

Obermark, Peter Raymond. "Adoption in the Old Babylonian Perod." Ph.D. dissertation, Hebrew Union College–Jewish Institute of Religion, Cincinnati, Ohio, 1992.

Oelsner, Joachim. "Tontafeln aus drei Jahrtausenden—die Leipziger Sammlung von Keilschrifttexten." *ZAR* 18 (2012): 79–126.

Oelsner, Joachim. "Zur Einteilung des Kodex Ḫammu-rāpi im Altertum." *ZAR* 18 (2012): 79–125.

Olivier, Hannes. "The Effectiveness of the Old Babylonian Mēšarum Decrees." *Journal of Northwest Semitic Language* 12 (1984): 107–113.

Oppenheim, A. Leo. *Ancient Mesopotamia*. Rev. ed. Completed by Erica Reiner. Chicago: University of Chicago Press, 1977.

Oppenheim, A. Leo. *Letters from Mesopotamia*. Chicago: University of Chicago Press, 1967.

Oppenheim, A. Leo. "A Note on the Scribes in Mesopotamia." In *Studies in Honor of Benno Landsberger*. Edited by Hans G. Güterbock and Thorkild Jacobsen. AS 16, 253–256. Chicago: University of Chicago Press, 1965.

Oppenheim, A. Leo. "The Position of the Intellectual in Mesopotamian Society." *Daedalus* 104 (1975): 37–46.

Ornan, Tallay. "Unfinished Business: The Relief on the Hammurabi Louvre Stele Revisited." *Journal of Cuneiform Studies* 71 (2019): 85–109.

Oshima, T. "The Babylonian God Marduk." In *The Babylonian World*. Edited by Gwendolyn Leick, 348–360. New York: Routledge, 2007.

Paul, Shalom M. *Studies in the Book of the Covenant in the Light of Cuneiform and Biblical Law*. Supplements to Vetus Testamentum 18. Leiden: E. J. Brill, 1970.

Pearce, Laurie E., and Cornelia Wunsch. *Documents of Judean Exiles and West Semites in Babylonia in the Collection of David Sofer*. Cornell University Studies in Assyriology and Sumerology (CUSAS). Bethesda, Md.: CDL Press, 2014.

Peiser, Otto. "Jurisprudentiae Babylonicae Quae Supersunt." Ph.D. dissertation. University of Berlin, 1890.

Petschow, Herbert. "Zur 'Systematik' in den Gesetzen von Eschnunna." In *Symbolae iuridicae et historicae Martino David dedicatae II*. Edited by J. A. Ankum, R. Feenstra, and W. F. Leemans, 129–143. Leiden: E. J. Brill, 1968.

Petschow, Herbert. "Zur Systematik und Gesetzestechnik im Codex Hammurabis." *ZA* 57 (1965): 146–172.

Podany, Amanda H., Gary M. Beckman, and Gudrun Colbow. "An Adoption and Inheritance Contract from the Reign of Iggid-Lim of Ḫana." *JCS* 43–45 (1991–93): 39–51.

Poebel, Arno. *Historical and Grammatical Texts*. University of Pennsylvania. The University Museum. Publications of the Babylonian Section., vol. V. Philadelphia: University Museum, 1914.

Pongratz-Leisten, Beate. "Tigridian Royal Representation: Text and Image between Tradition and Innovation." In *Text and Image Proceedings of the 61e Rencontre Assyriologique Internationale, Geneva and Bern, 22–26 June 2015*. Edited by P. Attinger et al. Orbis Biblicus et Orientalis 40, 347–354. Leuven: Peeters, 2018.

Postgate, J. N. *Early Mesopotamia: Society and Economy at the Dawn of History*. London: Routledge, 1992.

Postgate, J. N. "Royal Exercise of Justice under the Assyrian Empire." In *Le Palais et la Royauté, Archéologie et Civilisation: Compte Rendu*, Paul Garelli, 417–426. Paris: P. Geuthner, 1974.

Price, Ira M. "The Relation of Certain Gods to Equity and Justice in Early Babylonian." *JAOS* 52 (1932): 174–178.

Propp, William H. C. *Exodus 19–40*. Anchor Bible. New York: Doubleday, 2006.

Raaflaub, Kurt A. "Do Ideas Travel Lightly? Early Greek Concepts of Justice in Their Mediterranean Context." In *Literature as Politics, Politics as Literature: Essays on the Ancient Near East in Honor of Peter Machinist*. Edited by David S. Vanderhooft and Abraham Winitzer, 355–379. Winona Lake, Ind.; Eisenbrauns, 2013.

Raaflaub, Kurt A. "Early Greek Political Thought in Its Mediterranean Context." In *A Companion to Greek and Roman Political Thought*, 37–56. Edited by Ryan Balot. Malden, Mass.; Wiley-Blackwell, 2009.

Radner, Karen, and Eleanor Robson, eds. *The Oxford Handbook of Cuneiform Culture*. Oxford Handbooks. Oxford: Oxford University Press, 2011.

Reiner, Erica. *Astral Magic in Babylon*. Transactions of the American Philosophical Society. Philadelphia: American Philosophical Society, 1995.

Reiner, Erica. "Runaway—Seize Him." In *Assyria and Beyond: Studies Presented to Mogen Trolle Larsen*. Edited by J.G. Dercksen, 475–482. Leiden: Nederlands Instituut voor het nabije Oosten, 2004.

Reiner, Erica. *Your Thwarts in Pieces, Your Mooring Rope Cut: Poetry from Babylonia and Assyria*. Michigan Studies in the Humanities. Ann Arbor: Horace H. Rackham School of Graduate Studies at the University of Michigan, 1985.

Renger, Johannes. "Überlegungen zum akkadischen syllabar." *Zeitschrift für Assyriologie* 61 (1971): 23–43.

Richardson, M. E. J. *Hammurabi's Laws: Text, Translation and Glossary*. The Biblical Seminar 73. Semitic Texts and Studies 2. Sheffield: Sheffield Academic Press, 2000.

Ries, Gerhard von. *Prolog und Epilog in Gesetzen Des Altertums*. Münchener Beiträge zur Papyrusforschung und antiken Rechtsgeschichte. München: Beck, 1983.

Robson, Eleanor. "The Production and Dissemination of Scholarly Knowledge." In *The Oxford Handbook of Cuneiform Culture*. Edited by Karen Radner and Eleanor Robson, 557–576. Oxford: Oxford University Press, 2011.

Robson, Eleanor. "The Tablet House: A Scribal School in Old Babylonian Nippur." *RA* 95 (2001): 39–66.

Rochberg, Francesca. *The Heavenly Writing: Divination, Horoscopy, and Astronomy in Mesopotamian Culture*. Cambridge: Cambridge University Press, 2004.

Roth, Martha T. "The Because Clause: Punishment Rationalizations in Mesopotamian Laws." In *Veenhof Anniversary Volume*, 407–412. Leiden: Nederlands Instituut voor het Nabije Oosten, 2001.

Roth, Martha T., ed. *Law Collections from Mesopotamia and Asia Minor*. 2d ed. Contribution by Harry A. Hoffner, Jr. SBL Writings from the Ancient World Series. Atlanta: Scholars Press, 1997.

Roth, Martha T. "Errant Oxen or, The Goring Ox Redux." In *Literature as Politics, Politics as Literature: Essays on the Ancient Near East in Honor of Peter Machinist*. Edited by David S. Vanderhooft and Abraham Winitzer, 397–404. Wimona Lake, Ind.; Eisenbrauns, 2013.

Roth, Martha T. "Hammurabi's Wronged Man." *JAOS* 122 (2002): 38–45.

Roth, Martha T. "The Law Collection of King Hammurabi: Toward an Understanding of Codification and Text." In *La Codification des Lois dans l'Antiquité*. Edited by Ed. Lévy, 9–31. Paris: De Boccard, 2000.

Roth, Martha T. "Mesopotamian Legal Traditions and the Laws of Hammurabi." *Chicago-Kent Law Review* 71 (1995): 27–36.

Roth, Martha T. "On *Mār Awīlim* in the Old Babylonian Law Collections." *JNES* 72 (2013): 267–272.

Roth, Martha T. "On Persons in the Old Babylonian Law Collections: The Case of *Mār Awīlim* in Bodily Injury Provisions." In *Extraction & Control: Studies in Honor of Matthew W. Stolper*. Edited by Michael Kozuh, Wouter F. M. Henkelman, Charles E. Jones, and Christopher Woods. Studies in Ancient Oriental Civilization, 219–227. Chicago: Oriental Institute, 2014.

Roth, Martha T. "A Reassessment of RA 71 (1977) 125ff." *Archiv für Orientforschung* 31 (1984): 9–14.

Roth, Martha T. "Scholastic Tradition and Mesopotamian Law: A Study of FLP 1287, a Prism in the Collection of the Free Library of Philadelphia." Ph.D. dissertation, University of Pennsylvania, 1979.

Roth, Martha T. "'She Will Die by the Iron Dagger': Adultery and Neo-Babylonian Marriage." *JESHO* 31 (1988): 186–206.

Rutz, Matthew, and Piotr Michalowski. "The Flooding of Ešnunna, the Fall of Mari: Hammurabi's Deeds in Babylonian Literature and History." *JCS* 68 (2016): 15–43.

Sasson, Jack M. "King Hammurabi of Babylon." In *CANE*, 901–915.

Sassoon, John. *Ancient Laws and Modern Problems: The Balance between Justice and a Legal System*. Bristol, UK: Intellect Books, 2005.

Schauer, Frederick. "Giving Reasons." *Stanford Law Review* 47 (1994–1995): 633–659.

Scheil, V. *La Loi de Hammourabi Vers 200 Av. J.C.* Paris: Ernest Leroux, 1904.

Scheil, V. *Mélanges Épigraphiques*. Mémoires de la Délegation en Perse 28. Paris: Ernest Leroux, 1939.

Scheil, V. "Les Nourrices en Babylonie et le § 194 Du Code." *RA* 11 (1914): 175–182.

Scheil, V. *Textes Élamites-Sémitiques, Douxiéme Série*. Mémoires de la Délegation en Perse 4. Paris: Ernest Leroux, 1902.

Scheil, V. *Textes Élamites-Sémitiques, Quatrième Série*. Mémoires de la Délegation en Perse 10. Paris: Ernest Leroux, 1908.

Schmandt-Besserat, Denise. *When Writing Met Art: From Symbol to Story*. Austin: University of Texas Press, 2007.

Schorr, M. "Die §§ 280–282 Des Gesetzbuches Ḫammurabis." *Wiener Zeitschrift für die Kunde des Morganlandes* 22 (1908): 383–392.

Schorr, M. *Urkunden des altbabylonische Zivil- und Prozessrechts*. Leipzig: J. C. Hinrichs, 1913.

Schwartz, Hillel. *The Culture of the Copy: Striking Likenesses, Unreasonable Facsimiles*. New York: Zone Books, 1996.

Schwyter, Jürg R. "Syntax and Style in the Anglo-Saxon Law-Codes." In *Verschriftung und Verschriftlichung: Aspeckte Des Medienwechsels in Verschiedenen Kulturen und Epochen*. Edited by Christine Ehler and Ursula Schaefer, 189–230. Tübingen: Gunter Narr, 1998.

Seri, Andrea. *Local Power in Old Babylonian Mesopotamia*. Studies in Egyptology and the Ancient Near East. Sheffield: Equinox, 2006.

Shaffer, Aaron. "A New Look at Some Old Catalogues." In *Wisdom, Gods and Literature: Studies in Assyriology in Honor of W. G. Lambert*. Edited by A. R. George and I. L. Finkel, 429–436. Winona Lake, Ind.: Eisenbrauns, 2000.

Shepperson, Mary. "The Rays of Šamaš: Light in Mesopotamian Architecture and Legal Practice." *Iraq* 74 (2012): 51–64.

Sjöberg, Åke. "CBS 11319+. An Old Babylonian Schooltext from Nippur." *ZA* 83 (1993): 1–21.

Sjöberg, Åke. "Ein Selbstpreis des Königs Ḫammurabi von Babylon." *ZA* 54 (1961): 51–70.

Sjöberg, Åke. "The Old Babylonian Eduba." In *Sumerological Studies in Honor of Thorkild Jacobsen*. Edited by Åke Sjöberg. AS 20, 159–179. Chicago: University of Chicago Press, 1974.

Sjöberg, Åke. "Prayers for King Ḫammurabi of Babylon." In *Ex orbe religionum. Studia Geo Widengren, XXIV mense apr. MCMLXXII quo die lustra tredecim feliciter explevit oblata ab collegis, discipulis, amicis, collegae magistro amico congratulantibus*. Studies in the History of Religions, 58–71. Leiden: Brill, 1972.

Sjöberg, Åke. "Was There a Sumerian Version of the Laws of Hammurabi?" *Aula Orientalis* 9 (1991): 219–225.

Slanski, Kathryn E. "The Law of Hammurabi and Its Audience," *Yale Journal of Law and the Humanities* 24 (2012): 97–110.

Slanski, Kathryn E. "The Mesopotamian 'Rod and Ring': Icon of Righteous Kingship and Balance of Power Between Palace and Temple." In *Regime Change in the Ancient Near East and Egypt: From Sargon of Agade to Saddam Hussein*. Edited by Harriet Crawford, 37–59. Proceedings of the British Academy. Oxford: University Press, 2007.

Smith, Duane. "A Ritual and Incantation-Prayer against Ghost-Induced Illness." In *Reading Akkadian Prayers and Hymns: An Introduction*. Edited by Alan Lenzi. Society of Biblical Literature Ancient Near East Monographs 3, 197–215. Atlanta: Society of Biblical Literature, 2011.

Smith, Joanna S. "Writing Styles in Clay of the Eastern Mediterranean Late Bronze Age." In *Sea Routes: Interconnections in the Mediterranean 16th–6th c. BC*. Edited by Nicholas Chr. Stampolidis and Vassos Karageorghis, 277–289. Athens: University of Crete and the A. G. Leventis Foundation, 2003.

Smoak, Jeremy. "Describing Temple Space: The Ekron Dedication as Monumental Text." *JNES* 76 (2017): 319–336.

Soden, Wolfram von. *Assyrisches Handwörterbuch*. Wiesbaden: Otto Harrassowitz, 1959–1981.

Soden, Wolfram von. "Ein neues Bruchstück des assyrischen Kommentars zum Marduk-Ordal." *RA* 52 (1957): 224–234.

Soden, Wolfram von. "Schwer zugängliche russiche Veröffentlichungen altbabylonischer Texte—1. Ein Opfershaugebet bei Nacht." *ZA* 90 (2000): 305–308.

Soden, Wolfram von. "Der hymnisch-epische Dialekt des Akkadischen." *ZA* 40 (1931): 163–227.

Soden, Wolfram von. "Der hymnisch-epische Dialekt des Akkadischen II." *ZA* 41 (1933): 90–183.

Soldt, W. H. van. "Babylonian Lexical, Religious and Literary Texts and Scribal Education at Ugarit and Its Implication for the Alphabetic Literary Texts." In *Ugarit: Ein Ostmediterraneas Kulturzentum Im Alten Orient: Ergebnisse und Perspektiven der Forschung*. Edited by Manfried Dietrich and Oswald Loretz. Abhandlungen Zur Literatur Alt-Syrien-Palästinas, vol. 7, 171–212. Münster: Ugarit-Verlag, 1995.

Sollberger, Edmond. *Inscriptions Royales Sumériennes et Akkadiennes*. Littératures anciennes du Proche-Orient. Paris: Éditions du Cerf, 1971.

Sollberger, Edmond. "Two Old-Babylonian Royal Inscriptions." In *Essays on the Ancient Near East in Memory of Jacob Joel Finkelstein*. Edited by Maria de Jong Ellis. Memoirs of the Connecticut Academy of Arts and Sciences, 197–200. Hamden, Conn.: Archon, 1977.

Sollberger, Edmond, and Christopher Walker. "Hammu-rāpī à Mari et à Sippar." In *Miscellanea Babylonica: Mélanges Offerts à Maurice Birot*. Edited by J.-R. Kupper and J.-M. Durand, 257–264. Paris: Editions Recherche sur les civilisations, 1985.

Spada, Gabriella. "A Handbook from the Eduba'a: An Old Babylonian Collection of Model Contracts." *ZA* 101 (2011): 204–245.

Spada, Gabriella. *Sumerian Model Contracts from the Old Babylonian Period in the Hilprecht Collection Jena*. Texte und Materialien der Hilprecht Collection 11. Wiesbaden: Harrassowitz, 2018.

Spada, Gabriella. "Two Old Babylonian Model Contracts." *Cuneiform Digital Library Journal*, no. 2 (2014): 1–13.

Speiser, E. A. "The Stem *PLL* in Hebrew." *Journal of Biblical Literature* 82 (1963): 301–306.

Steele, Francis R. *The Code of Lipit-Ishtar*. Museum Monographs. Philadelphia: University Museum, 1949. Reprinted from *American Journal of Archaeology* 52 (1948).

Steele, Francis Rue. "An Additional Fragment of the Lipit-Ishtar Code Tablet from Nippur." *Archiv Orientalni* 18 (1950): 489–494.

Steible, Horst, and Hermann Behrens. *Die Altsumerischen Bau- und Weihinschriften*. Freiburger Altorientalische Studien, vol. 5. Wiesbaden: F. Steiner, 1982.

Steinkeller, Piotr. *History, Texts and Art in Early Babylonia*. Studies in Ancient Near Records. Berlin: De Gruyter, 2017.

Steinkeller, Piotr. "Labor in the Early States: An Early Mesopotamian Perspective." In *Labor in the Ancient World*. Edited by Piotr Steinkeller and Michael Hudson, 1–35. Dresden, ISLET, 2015.

Steinkeller, Piotr. "The Reform of UruKAgina and an Early Sumerian Term for 'Prison.'" *Aula Orientis* 9 (1991): 227–233.

Stephens, Ferris J. "Notes on Some Economic Texts of the Time of Urukagina." *RA* 49 (1955): 129–136.

Stol, Marten. *Epilepsy in Babylonia*. Cuneiform Monographs 2. Groningen: Styx, 1993.

Stol, Marten. "Muškēnu." In *Reallexikon der Assyriologie und Vorderasiatische Archäologie*. Volume 8, 492–493. Berlin: Walter de Gruyter, 1993–1997.

Stol, Marten. "Old Babylonian Ophthalmology." In *Reflets des deux fleuves, Volume de Mélanges offerts à André Finet*. Edited by M. LeBeau and P. Talon, 163–166. Leuven: Peeters, 1989.

Stol, Marten. *Studies in Old Babylonian History*. Uitgaven Van Het Nederlands Historisch-Archaeologisch Instituut Te Istanbul. Leiden: Nederlands Historisch-Archaeologisch Instituut te Istanbul, 1976.

Stol, Marten. *Women in the Ancient Near East*. Translated by Helen and Mervyn Richardson. Berlin: de Gruyter, 2016.

Stone, Elizabeth C., and David Owen. *Adoption in Old Babylonian Nippur and the Archive of Mannum-mešu-liṣṣur*. Mesopotamian Civilization 3. Winona Lake, Ind.; Eisenbrauns, 1991.

Strassler, Robert B., ed., and Andrea L. Purvis, trans. *The Landmark Herodotus*. New York: Anchor, 2007.

Streck, Michael P. "Hammurabi oder Hammurapi?" *Archiv Orientalni* 67 (1999): 665–669.

Sunstein, Cass R. *Legal Reasoning and Political Conflict*. New York: Oxford University Press, 1996.

Szlechter, Émile. "Des droits successoraux dérivés de l'adoption en droit babylonien." *RIDA* 14 (1967): 79–106.

Szlechter, Émile. "Le code de Lipit-Ištar (I)." *RA* 51 (1957): 57–82.

Szlechter, Émile. "Le code de Lipit-Ištar (II)." *RA* 51 (1957): 177–196.

Szlechter, Émile. "Le code de Lipit-Ištar (III)." *RA* 52 (1958): 74–90.

Tanret, Michel. *Per Aspera Ad Astra: L'Apprentissage Du Cunéiforme à Sippar-Amnanum Pendant la Période Paléobabylonienne Tardive*. Mesopotamian History and Environment. Gand: Université de Gand, 2002.

Tanret, Michel. "The Works and the Days: On Scribal Activity in Old Babylonian Sippar-Amnänum." *RA* 98 (2004): 33–62.

Teeter, David Andrew. *Scribal Laws: Exegetical Variation in the Textual Transmission of Biblical Law in the Late Second Temple Period*. Forschungen zum Alten Testament. Tübingen: Mohr Siebeck, 2014.

Thomas, Rosalind. "Written in Stone? Liberty, Equality, Orality and the Codification of Law." In *Greek Law in Its Political Setting: Justifications not Justice*. Edited by L. Foxhall and A. D. E. Lewis, 9–31. Oxford: Clarendon Press, 1996.

Thomsen, Marie-Louise. "Witchcraft and Magic in Ancient Mesopotamia." In *Witchcraft and Magic in Europe: Biblical and Pagan Societies*. Edited by Bengt Ankarloo and Stuary Clark, 1–91. Philadelphia: University of Pennsylvania, 2001.

Tigay, Jeffrey H. *The Evolution of the Gilgamesh Epic*. Philadelphia: University of Pennsylvania, 1982.

Tinney, Steve. "On the Curricular Setting of Sumerian Literature." *Iraq* 61 (1999): 159–172.

Tinney, Steve. "Texts, Tablets, and Teaching: Scribal Education in Nippur and Ur." *Expedition* 40, no. 2 (1998): 40–50.

Toorn, Karel van der. "Cuneiform Documents from Syria-Palestine Texts, Scribes, and Schools." *Zeitschrift des deutschen Palästina-Vereins* 116 (2000): 98–113.

Toorn, Karel van der. *Scribal Culture and the Making of the Hebrew Bible*. Cambridge, Mass.: Harvard University Press, 2007.

Ungnad, Arthur. *Babylonian Letters of the Hammurapi Period*. University of Pennsylvania. University Museum. Publications of the Babylonian Section 7. Philadelphia: University Museum, 1915.

Van De Mieroop, Marc. *Cuneiform Texts and the Writing of History*. Approaching the Ancient World. London: Routledge, 1999.

Van De Mieroop, Marc. "Hammurabi's Self-Presentation." *Orientalia* 80 (2011): 305–38.

Van De Mieroop, Marc. *King Hammurabi of Babylon: A Biography*. Blackwell Ancient Lives. Malden, Mass.: Blackwell, 2005.

Van De Mieroop, Marc. *Philosophy before the Greeks: The Pursuit of Truth in Ancient Babylonia*. Princeton, N.J.: Princeton University Press, 2016.

Vanstiphout, H. L. J. "The Importance of the Tale of the Fox." *Acta Sumerologica* 10 (1988): 191–227.

Vanstiphout, H. L. J. "How Did They Learn Sumerian?" *JCS* 31 (1979): 118–126.

Vanstiphout, H. L. J. "Lipit-Eštar's Praise in the Edubba." *JCS* 30 (1978): 33–61.

Vanstiphout, H. L. J. "Memory and Literacy in Ancient Western Asia." In *CANE*, 2181–2196.

Vanstiphout, H. L. J. "On the Old Babylonian Eduba Curriculum." In *Centres of Learning: Learning and Location in Pre-Modern Europe and the Near East*. Edited by Jan Willem Drijvers and Alasdair A. MacDonald. Brill's Studies in Intellectual History, vol. 61, 1–16. Leiden: E. J. Brill, 1995.

Veenhof, Klaas. "Old Assyrian Law." In *A History of Ancient Near Eastern Law*. Edited by Raymond Westbrook. Handbook of Oriental Studies. Leiden: Brill, 2003.

Veenhof, Klaas. "The Relation between Royal Decree and 'Law Codes' of the Old Babylonian Period." *Jaarbericht Ex Oriente Lux* 35/36 (1997): 49–83.

Veldhuis, Niek. *History of the Cuneiform Lexical Tradition*. Guides to the Mesopotamian Textual Record. Münster: Ugarit-Verlag, 2014.

Veldhuis, Niek. "On the Curriculum of the Neo-Babylonian School." *JAOS* 123 (2003): 627–633.

Veldhuis, Niek. "TIN TIR = Babylon, the Question of Canonization and the Production of Meaning." *JCS* 50 (1998): 77–85.

Vukosavović, Filip. "The Laws of Hazor and the ANE Parallels." *RA* 108 (2014): 41–44.

Waetzoldt, Hartmut. "Die Entwicklung der Naturwissenschaften und des Naturwissenschaftlichen Unterrichts in Mesopotamien." In *Naturwissenschaftlicher Unterricht und Wissenskumulation: geschichtliche Entwicklung und gesellschaftliche Auswirkungen*. Edited by Johann Georg Prinz von Hohenzollern and Max Liedtke. Schriftenreihe Zum Bayerischen Schulmuseum Ichenhausen, Zweigmuseum Des Bayerischen Nationalmuseums, vol. 7, 31–49. Bad Heilbrunn/Obb.: J. Klinkhardt, 1988.

Walters, Stanley D. "The Sorceress and Her Apprentice: A Case Study of an Accusation." *JCS* 23 (1970): 27–38.

Wasserman, Nathan. "CT 21, 40–42': A Bilingual Report of an Oracle with a Royal Hymn of Hammurabi." *RA* 86 (1992): 1–18.

Watson, Alan. *The Spirit of Roman Law*. Athens: University of Georgia Press, 1995.

Weinfeld, Moshe. "Hamatat ubar: emdatah shel masoret yisrael behashva'ah le- emdat ammim aḥerim." *Zion* 42 (1977): 129–142.

Weissert, Elnathan. "Creating a Political Climate: Literary Allusions to *Enūma Eliš* in Sennacherib's Account of the Battle of Haluel." In *Assyrien im Wandel der Zeiten: XXXIXe Rencontre Assyriologique Internationale, Heidelberg, 6.–10. Juli 1992*. Heidelberger Studien Zum Alten Orient, vol. 6, 191–202. Heidelberg: Heidelberger Orientverlag, 1997.

Wells, Bruce. "The Covenant Code and Near Eastern Legal Traditions: A Response to David P. Wright." *Maarav* 13 (2006): 85–118.

Wells, Bruce. "The Cultic versus the Forensic: Biblical and Mesopotamian Judicial Procedures in the First Millennium BCE." *JAOS* 128 (2008): 205–232.

West, Martin L. *The East Face of Helicon: West Asiatic Elements in Greek Poetry and Myth*. Oxford: Clarendon Press, 1997.

Westbrook, Raymond. "The Adoption Laws of Codex Hammurabi." In *Kinnattutu ša darâti: Raphael Kutscher Memorial Volume*, 195–204. Tel Aviv: Institute of Archaeology, 1997.

Westbrook, Raymond. "Barbarians at the Gates: Near Eastern Law in Ancient Greece." In *Ex Oriente Lex*. Edited by Kurt Raaflaub and Deborah Lyon, 59–69. Baltimore, Md.; Johns Hopkins University Press, 2015.

Westbrook, Raymond. "Codex Hammurabi and the Ends of the Earth." In *Law from the Tigris to the Tiber: The Writings of Raymond Westbrook*. Edited by Bruce Wells and Rachel Magdalene, 133–139. Winona Lake, Ind.: Eisenbrauns, 2009.

Westbrook, Raymond. "Codification and Canonization." In *La Codification des Lois dans l'Antiquité*. Edited by Ed. Lévy, 33–47. Paris: De Boccard, 2000.

Westbrook, Raymond. "Cuneiform Law Codes and the Origins of Legislation." *ZA* 79 (1989): 201–222.

Westbrook, Raymond. "Drakon's Homicide Law." In *Symposium 2007: Vorträge zur griechischen und hellenistischen Rechtsgeschichte*, Edited by E. Harris and G. Thür, 3–16. Vienna: Österreichen Akademie der Wissenschaften, 2008.

Westbrook, Raymond. "The Early History of Law: A Theoretical Essay." In *Ex Oriente Lex: Near Eastern Influences on Ancient Greek and Roman Law*. Edited by Kurt Raaflaub and Deborah Lyon, 220–233. Baltimore: Johns Hopkins University Press, 2015.

Westbrook, Raymond. *Ex Oriente Lex: Near Eastern Influences on Ancient Greek and Roman Law*. Edited by Kurt Raaflaub and Deborah Lyon. Baltimore: Johns Hopkins University Press, 2015.

Westbrook, Raymond. "Hard Times: *CT* 45 37." In *Veenhof Anniversary Volume*, 547–551. Leiden: Nederlands Instituut voor het Nabije Oosten, 2001.

Westbrook, Raymond. "LH §§ 7 and 123—A Contradiction?" *NABU* 2007/27.

Westbrook, Raymond. "The Nature and Origins of the Twelve Tables." *ZAR* 105 (1988): 74–121.

Westbrook, Raymond. *Old Babylonian Marriage Law*. Archiv für Orientforschung. Horn, Austria: Berger & Söhne, 1988.

Westbrook, Raymond. "The Old Babylonian Term 'Napṭarum.'" *JCS* 46 (1994): 41–46.

Westbrook, Raymond. "Social Justice in Ancient Near East." In *Social Justice in the Ancient World*. Edited by K. D. Irani and Morris Silver, 149–163. Westport, Conn.: Greenwood Press, 1995.

Westbrook, Raymond. *Studies in Biblical and Cuneiform Law*. Cahiers de la Revue Biblique. Paris: J. Gabalda, 1988.

Westbrook, Raymond, and Claus Wilcke. "The Liability of an Innocent Purchaser of Stolen Goods in Early Mesopotamian Law." *Archiv für Orientforschung* 25 (1974): 111–121.

Whybray, R. N. *The Making of the Pentateuch: A Methodological Survey*. Journal for the Study of the Old Testament Supplement Series. Sheffield: JSOT Press, 1987.

Wiggerman, F. A. M. "Ring und Stab." In RLA 11: 414–421.

Wilcke, Claus. "Der Kodex Ur-Namma (CU): Versuch einer Rekonstruktion." In *Riches Hidden in Secret Places: Ancient Near Eastern Studies in Memory of Thorkild Jacobsen*. Edited by I. Tzvi Abusch, 291–332. Winona Lake, Ind.; Eisenbrauns, 2002.

Wilcke, Claus. *Early Ancient Near Eastern Law: A History of Its Beginnings—the Early Dynastic and Sargonic Periods*. Winona Lake, Ind.; Eisenbrauns, 2007.

Wilcke, Claus. "Genealogical and Geographic Thought in the Sumerian King List." In DUMU-E$_2$-DUB-BA-A: *Studies in Honor of Åke W. Sjöberg*, 557–569. Edited by Hermann Behrens, Darlene Loding, and Martha T. Roth. Philadelphia: University Museum, 1989.

Wilcke, Claus. "Politik im Spiegel der Literatur, Literatur als Mittel der Politik im älteren Babylonien." In *Anfänge politischen Denkens in der Antike, die nahölichen Kulturen und die Griechen*. Schriften des Historisches Kolleg, Kolloquien 24. Edited by K. Raaflaub, 29–75.. Munich: R. Oldenbourg, 1993.

Wilcke, Claus. "Die Sumerische Königsliste und erzählte Vergangenheit." In *Vergangenheit in Mündlicher Überlieferung*. Edited by Jürgen von Ungern-Sternberg und Hansjörg Reinau. Colloquium Rauricum 1, 113–140. Stuttgart: B. G. Teubner, 1988.

Wilcke, Claus. *Wer las und schrieb in Babylonien und Assyrien: Überlegungen zur Literalität im Alten Zweistromland*. Munich: C. H. Beck, 2000.

Wilcke, Claus. "Zu den spät-altbabylonischen Kaufverträgen aus Nord-Babylonien." *Welt des Orients* 8 (1976): 254–285.

Willetts, Ronald F. *The Law Code of Gortyn*. Berlin: De Gruyter, 1967.

Winckler, H. "Einige neuveröffentliche texte Hammurabis, Nabopolassars und Nebukadnezars." *ZA* 2 (1887): 122–123.

Winitzer, Abraham. *Early Mesopotamian Divination Literature: Its Organizational Framework and Generative and Paradigmatic Characteristics*. Ancient Magic and Divination 12. Leiden: Brill, 2017.

Winitzer, Abraham. "The Generative Principle in Old Babylonian Divination." Ph.D. dissertation, Harvard University, 2006.

Winter, I.J. "Touched by the Gods: Visual Evidence for the Divine Status of Rulers in the Ancient Near East." In *Religion and Power: Divine Kingship in the Ancient World and Beyond*. Edited by N. Brisch, 75–101. Chicago: Oriental Institute, 2008.

Wiseman, D. J. "The Laws of Hammurabi Again." *Journal of Semitic Studies* 7 (1962): 161–172.

Wolff, Hans Julius. *Roman Law, an Historical Introduction*. Norman: University of Oklahoma, 1951.

Worthington, Martin. *Principles of Akkadian Textual Criticism*. Studies in Ancient Near Eastern Records, vol. 1. Berlin: De Gruyter, 2012.

Wright, David P. "The Compositional Logic of the Goring Ox and Negligence Laws in the Covenant Collection (Ex 21:28–36)." *ZAR* 10 (2004): 93–142.

Wright, David P. *Inventing God's Law: How the Covenant Code of the Bible Used and Revised the Laws of Hammurabi*. New York: Oxford University Press, 2009.

Wright, David P. "The Laws of Hammurabi and the Covenant Code: A Response to Bruce Wells." *Maarav* 13 (2007): 211–260.

Yaron, Reuven. *The Laws of Eshnunna*. 2d ed. Jerusalem: Magnes Press, 1988.

Yaron, Reuven. "The Nature of the Early Mesopotamian Collections of Laws: Another Approach." In *La Codification Des Lois dans l'Antiquité: Actes Du Colloque de Strasbourg, 27–29 Novembre 1997*. Edited by Ed. Lévy, 65–76. Travaux du Centre de Recherche sur le Proche-Orient et la Grèce Antiques. Paris: De Boccard, 2000.

Yoffee, Norman. "Context and Authority in Early Mesopotamian Law." In *State Formation and Political Legitimacy*. Edited by Ronald Cohen and Judith D. Toland. Political Anthropology VI, 95–113. New Brunswick, N.J.: Transaction Books, 1988.

Yoffee, Norman. "The Decline and Rise of Mesopotamian Civilization: An Ethnoarchaeological Perspective on the Evolution of Social Complexity." *American Antiquity* 44 (1979): 5–35.

Yoffee, Norman. *The Economic Role of the Crown in the Old Babylonian Period*. Malibu, Calif.: Undena Publications, 1977.

Yoffee, Norman. *Myths of the Archaic State: Evolution of the Earliest Cities, States and Civilizations*. Cambridge: Cambridge University Press, 2004.

Zettler, Richard L, with an appendix by Martha T. Roth. "The Genealogy of the House of Ur-Me-Me: A Second Look." *Archiv für Orientforschung* 31 (1984): 1–9.

Zevit, Ziony, ed. *Subtle Citation, Allusion, and Translation in the Hebrew Bible*. Sheffield: Equinox, 2017.

Index of Subjects and Authors

Abram, Mary, 22, 285
absent husband, 152–154
Abusch, I. Tzvi, 166, 169–170, 183, 285
abuse by officials, 51, 55–59
Adab, 110, 111
Adad, 110, 111, 115, 126, 128
adoption, 123, 196, 219–229
adultery, 151–152, 171, 174–176, 187, 190
Akkad, 39, 40, 41, 47, 65, 72, 80, 82, 83, 90, 91, 92, 112, 113–114, 115, 133, 134
ama.r-gi$_4$ (term and concept of debt release), 52, 54–55, 60, 62, 66–67, 79, 80
Ammi-ṣaduqa, 41, 68–70, 80–82
Andre-Salvini, Béatrice, 47, 285
Anum, 40, 43, 65, 84, 89, 90, 91, 92, 96, 101, 102, 103, 104, 106, 117, 125, 126, 127, 129, 131, 276
Anunnaki, 30, 129
Armstrong, J. A., 17, 291
Artaxerxes I, 273
Aruz, Joan, 20, 285
Ascalone, E., 22, 285
Assur, 71, 113
Assurbanipal, 218
Athenian law, 248–250
Attenborough, F. L., 167, 285
Ayya, 94, 95, 97, 98, 104, 106

Babylon, 30–31, 45, 71, 75, 94, 96, 100, 101, 102, 104, 105, 106, 112, 115, 119, 131
Bachvarova, Mary R., 266, 285
bailment, 173
Baker, Heather D., 17, 285
Barmash, Pamela, 4, 51, 121, 167, 169, 171, 181, 186, 208, 219, 257, 258, 264, 285
Bartor, Assnat, 157, 286
Beckman, Gary M., 227, 261, 286, 287
Bergmann, E., 198, 286
Bible, relationship to Mesopotamian legal tradition, 56, 256–265, 283
Biggs, Robert D., 169, 286
Black, Jeremy, 205, 286
Black's Law Dictionary, 15–16
Blair, Ann, 3, 286
Blitz, Randolph C., 69, 286
Bodine, Walter, 207, 286
Borger, Rykle, 9, 102, 110, 112, 181, 275, 286
Borsippa, 107, 108
Bottéro, Jean, 6, 8, 15, 20, 42, 67, 106, 113–114, 170, 191, 235, 286
Britain, laws of the early kings, 167
builder of faulty construction, 192
Burkert, Walter, 266, 286

Canby, Jeanny Vorys, 23, 286
Carr, David M., 203, 204, 211, 262, 286
Carter, Elizabeth, 47, 286
casuistics, 70, 71, 137, 156–164, 199, 200, 245, 267, 280
Charpin, Dominique, 34, 40, 50, 76, 215, 216, 217, 220, 235, 236, 237, 238, 274, 286–287
Chevalier, Nicole, 31, 287
Chiera, Edward, 66, 287
Civil, Miguel, 72, 73, 206–207, 208, 210, 256, 259, 275, 287
Clayton, Jay, 142, 287
Code civile (France), 248
Cohen, Boaz, 157, 287
Cohen, Chaim, 256, 287
Cohen, Eran, 71–72, 287
Cohen, Yoram, 261, 287
Colbow, Gudron, 227, 297
Cole, S. W., 17, 291
Collon, Dominique, 20, 22, 287
commentaries, 4, 14, 15, 251, 271–277, 284
Cooley, Jeffrey L., 118, 287

Cooper, Jerrold, 8, 56, 72, 287–288
Cover, Robert, 132, 288
Crawford, M. H., 268, 288
Curtis, John E., 207, 288
Cuthbertson, Laura, 250, 288

Dagan, 111, 114
Dalley, Stephanie, 266, 288
Damkina, 110
Darius, 218
Daube, David, 184, 268, 288
David, Martino, 219, 288
death of a spouse, case of, 148–150, 184–185
death penalty, 152, 179, 188–194, 196
debt, 52, 54–59, 67–70, 79–82, 85, 244. *See under* distraint
Delnero, Paul, 208, 288
Démare-Lafont, Sophie (Lafont, Sophie), 187, 288
Dennis, Andrew, 15, 288
Diakonoff, I. M., 58, 65, 288
Dilbat, 108
distraint, 85, 154–155, 188–189, 190, 193
Di Tullio, Daria, 143, 288
Donbaz, V., 198, 288
Dossin, G., 118, 288
Driver, G. R., 6–7, 73, 100, 133, 142, 170, 175, 178, 180, 183, 185, 186, 194, 195, 198, 220, 224, 225, 227, 228, 237, 242, 243, 254, 289
Durand, J.-M., 111, 232, 289

Ea, 93, 96, 97, 103, 105, 110, 117, 126, 127, 134
Eabzu, temple, 104, 106
Eanna, temple, 104, 106
Ebarbar temple, 30, 37, 76, 104, 106, 129
Edzard, Dietz Otto, 38, 40, 57, 58, 59, 289
Egalmah temple, 107
Egishnugal temple, 104, 106
Eichler, Barry L., 147, 152, 245, 289
Eidem, J., 218, 289
Ekur temple, 31, 65, 91, 103, 104, 106, 127, 128, 129
Elamites, 20, 26, 31, 33, 47
Elsen-Novák, Gabriele, 22, 289
Emah temple, 110, 111
Emeslam temple, 110, 111
Emeshmesh temple, 113
English Draft Criminal Code, 15
Eninnu temple, 59, 61, 109
Enlil, 31, 37, 90, 91, 96, 101, 102, 103, 105, 106, 117, 126, 127, 129
Enlil-bani, 65–66, 78
Emeslam temple, 108, 110
Enki, *see under* Ea
Enmetana temple, 54–55, 59, 62, 78, 79, 80
Eppihemer, Melissa, 27, 289
equity
  act of, 12, 51–66, 76–78
  edicts of, 9, 51–52, 66, 68, 70, 77–78
  relationship with law collections, 76–86
Eridu, 104, 105, 106
Erra, 108, 111
Esagila temple, 30–31, 75, 98, 104, 106, 117, 119, 120, 122
Eshnunna, 71, 76
Eudgalgal temple, 110
Eulmash temple, 112
excavation of Stela, 2, 19–20, 31, 89
explanation, statutes with, 183–188, 279
Ezida temple, 43, 108

Fadhil, A., 273, 289
Falkenstein, Adam, 59, 289
false accusation, 165–172, 175, 176
Federal Constitutional Court (Germany), 248
Feldman, Marian, 22, 44, 289
Fincke, J. C., 199, 289
Finkel, Irving L., 217, 289
Finkelstein, J. J., 9–10, 15, 49, 57, 67, 71, 76–78, 99, 115, 144, 145, 146, 147, 166, 181, 198, 259, 289–290
Fischer, Claudia, 34, 290
Fluckiger-Hawker, Esther, 72, 73, 290
Foote, Peter, 15, 288
Foster, Benjamin R., 51, 52, 54, 58, 271, 290
Foxvog, Daniel, 57, 290
Frahm, Eckart, 274, 275, 276, 290
Frame, Grant, 205, 216, 290
Frankfort, Henri, 20, 25, 290
Frayne, Douglas, 25, 33, 54, 55, 56, 65, 68, 290

Gagarin, Michael, 271, 290
Garroway, Kristine H., 219, 221, 222, 290
Gasche, H., 17, 210, 290–291
George, A. R., 121, 205, 207, 209, 210, 216, 290, 291
Gesche, Petra D., 207, 291
Ghirshman, Roman, 210, 291
Girsu, 109, 111
Glassner, Jean-Jacques, 146, 291
gods, role of in justice, 34–41
Goetze, Albrecht, 74, 144, 291
Gordin, Shai, 216, 261, 291
goring ox, 258–259
Graetz, Shirley, 121, 291
Grágás (medieval Icelandic laws), 15
Greek law, 266–268, 270–271. *See under* Athenian law; Laws of Gortyn
Greengus, Samuel, 142, 151, 170, 180, 269, 291
Gudea, 40, 59, 62, 63, 78
Guinan, A., 199, 291
Gunbatti, Cahit, 170, 291
Gurzadyan, V.G., 17, 291

Haines, Richard C., 209, 296
Hallo, William W., 81, 206, 207, 211, 232, 262, 288, 291
Hammurabi
  date, 17
  date of promulgation of Laws of Hammurabi, 75–76
  extent of empire, 44–46
  latest dated manuscript of the Laws of Hammurabi, 273
  name, 17
Harper, Prudence O., 19, 20, 27, 33, 292
Harris, Rivkah, 234, 292
Hattusha, 71
Haubold, Johannes, 266, 292
Hays, Christopher B., 264, 292
Heimpel, Wolfgang, 170, 292
Heinz, Marlies, 44, 292
Herman, Ellen, 219, 292
Hittites, 45, 261, 283
Hoffner, Harry A., Jr., 198, 298
Holtz, Shalom E., 214, 292
homicide, 165–172
Horowitz, Wayne, 118, 262, 263, 264, 292
Horsnell, J. A., 76, 292
Hruška, Blahoslav, 22, 57, 58
Huehnergard, John, 30, 292
humanitarianism, 222
Hurowitz, Victor Avigdor, 31, 89, 90, 91, 98, 99, 102, 103, 105, 109, 111, 113, 116, 118, 122, 133, 273, 293
Hursagkalamma temple, 107

Iddin-Dagan, 40
inchoate marriage, 142–146, 150, 177
incremental variants, 13, 146–156, 160, 161, 164, 172, 180, 181–183, 245, 279
innkeeper, 81, 171, 186–187, 188, 190, 191
Irra-Imite, 66
Ishme-Dagan, 40
Ishtar, 93, 97, 103, 104, 106, 107, 110, 111, 112, 113, 117, 126, 128, 131, 134
Isin, 66, 71, 107

Jackson, Bernard R., 158, 184, 256, 293
Jacobs, Sandra, 264, 293
Jacobsen, Thorkild, 20–22, 59, 293
Jaffee, Martin, 214, 293
Janssen, C., 238, 293
Jean, Charles-F., 120, 293
jilted bridegroom, 142–146
Jimenez, Enrique, 168, 274, 275, 293
Joosten, Jan, 56, 293
Julian, 158
Jursa, Michael, 68, 69, 293

Kanarek, Jane, 132, 293
Karkara, 110
Kassite dynasty, 45
Kesh, 108
Kish, 107
kittum, 52–54, 118, 124, 130
Klein, Jacob, 63, 207, 293
Kleinerman, Alexandra, 208, 212, 293
Koch, Ulla, 160, 199, 294
Komoróczy, G., 67, 294
Koschaker, Paul, 75, 151, 174, 178, 185, 224, 242, 294
Kramer, Samuel Noah, 34, 37, 52, 59, 62, 72, 206, 294
Kraus, F. R., 6, 8, 10, 15, 58, 65–66, 67, 68, 76, 81, 113, 147, 159, 171, 239, 294

Kuhrt, Amelie, 73, 168, 170, 294
Kupper, Jean-Robert, 25, 236, 294
Kutha, 108

Laessøe, Jørgen, 32, 294
Lafont, Bertrand, 170, 294
Lafont, Sophie (Démare-Lafont, Sophie), 187, 238, 247–248, 294
Lagash, 54, 55, 59, 109, 111
Lambert, M., 58, 294
Lambert, W. G., 42, 54, 127, 168, 272, 274, 275, 276, 294–295
Landsberger, Benno, 159, 168, 171, 189, 212, 213, 218, 221, 224, 226, 295
Langdon, Stephen, 26, 295
Lanni, Adriaan, 248, 249, 250, 295
Larsa, 55, 104, 106, 111, 114
Larsen, Mogens Trolle, 159, 216–218, 247, 295
"law code" versus "law collection," 15
Leemans, W. F., 49, 295
legal precedent, 246–250
Lemche, Niels Peter, 54
Levi, Edward H., 160, 162, 295
Lieberman, Stephen J., 68, 71, 81, 207, 295
Lindgren, James, 15, 295
Lindsay, Hugh, 219, 295
Lipit-Istar, 65, 73
literacy, 29, 116–117, 120–121, 214–218, 245, 262
Liverani, Mario, 17, 87, 88, 295
Long, Millard F., 69, 286
Louvre, 2, 19, 47
Lucius Javolenus Priscus, 158
Lyon, David Gordon, 30, 296

Malgium, 110
Malul, Meir, 221, 260, 296
Mama, 108
Manishtusha, 47
Marduk, 30, 31, 42, 52, 53, 84, 90, 91, 92, 93, 94, 96, 97, 98, 101, 102, 103, 104, 105, 106, 116, 117, 119, 120, 121, 122, 126, 127, 130, 134, 236
Mari, 111
Martin, Malachi, 204, 296
Mashkan-shapir, 110
Mastnjak, Nathan, 265, 296
Matuszak, Jana, 172, 296
Maul, Stefan, 273–274, 296
McCown, Donald E., 209, 210, 296
Meek, T. J., 116, 120
Meissner, Bruno, 2, 296
Meslamtea, 135
Metcalf, Christopher, 266, 296
Michalowski, Piotr, 72, 73, 75, 76, 111, 132, 212, 213, 215, 296, 299
Miles, John C., 6–7, 73, 100, 133, 142, 170, 175, 178, 180, 183, 185, 186, 194, 195, 198, 220, 224, 225, 227, 228, 237, 243, 254, 289
mīsharum, 9, 52–54, 118, 124, 130
Mitchell, W. J. T., 20, 296
model contracts, 207–208
Morgan, Jacques de, 2
Morrow, William, 263, 264, 272, 296
Moscovitz, Leib, 157–158, 160, 161, 163, 296
Müller, D. H., 89, 296
Mursilis I, 45
muškēnum (commoner/palace dependent), meaning of term, 65–66, 154, 155, 156, 194–195
mutilation as punishment, 186, 194–196

Nader, Laura, 249, 296
Nanna, 39
Nanshe, 38
Nergal, 126, 129
Neusner, Jacob J., 147, 296
Ninazu, 112
Ningirsu, 38, 56, 58, 59–61, 111
Ninkarrak, 126, 128
Ninlil, 37, 91, 126, 127
Ninmah, 111
Nin-sumun, 41
Nintu, 108, 126, 129
Nippur, 31, 102, 103, 104, 106, 113
Nisaba, 38, 39, 208
Nissen, Hans J., 216, 297
Novák, Mirko, 22, 289
number of scribes involved in writing the Laws of Hammurabi, 176

Obermark, Peter Raymond, 220, 297
Oelsner, Joachim, 17, 199, 273, 297

Olivier, Hannes, 27, 67, 68, 70, 297
omens, 8, 16, 77, 159–160, 199
Oppenheim, A. Leo, 8, 38, 46, 213, 215, 283, 297
organization of laws in clusters, 176–183, 279
Ornan, Tallay, 20, 22, 25, 26, 297
Oshima, T., 127, 262, 263, 264, 292, 297
Owen, David, 219, 220, 225, 228, 301

Pa-tibira, 55
Paul, Shalom M., 20, 297
Pearce, Laurie, 264, 297
Peiser, Otto, 1, 297
Perkins, Richard, 15, 288
Petschow, Herbert, 149, 297
Peyronel, L., 22, 285
physician at fault, 194–196
Podany, Amanda H., 227, 297
Poebel, Arno, 186, 297
poetic justice, 183–195, 228, 233–234, 258
pointillism, 146. *See under* polar variants
polar variants, 147–156, 160, 172, 245
Pomponius, 158
Pongratz-Leisten, Beate, 29, 284, 297
Postgate, J. N., 54, 66, 215, 297–298
pregnant woman, assault on, 252–258, 259, 260
Price, Ira M., 38, 298
Propp, William H. C., 256, 298
punishment as means of systematization, 188–196, 279
Purvis, Angela, 266, 301

Raaflaub, Kurt A., 266, 298
Radner, Karen, 4, 298
Reiner, Erica, 35, 155, 170, 298
Renger, Johannes, 216–217, 298
Reyes, A. T., 266, 288
Ries, Gerhard, 88, 90, 102, 298
Rim-Sin, 26, 100
river ordeal, 170–171, 186, 233
Robson, Eleanor, 4, 207, 284, 298
Rochberg, Francesca, 272, 298
Roman law, 4–5, 158, 167, 247, 266–271
Roth, Martha T., 16, 17, 41, 47, 64, 73, 74, 84, 116, 120, 121, 122, 123, 140, 144, 146, 148, 165, 179, 181, 183, 185, 187, 207, 231, 232, 238, 252, 259, 270, 272, 298–299
Rothstein, Eric, 142
royal emblems of authority, 20, 22, 41
royal inscription pattern, 11, 78, 87–132, 280–281
royal legislation, 6–7, 231–246
royal propaganda, 9–10, 101–132, 280–281
Rutz, Matthew, 76, 111, 132, 299

Samsu-iluna, 238, 282
Sanders, Seth L., 263, 264, 292
Sargon I, 113
Ṣarpanitum, 98, 120
Sasson, Jack M., 17, 299
Sassoon, John, 195, 299
Sauren, H., 198, 288
Schauer, Frederick, 187, 299
Scheil, Victor, 2, 31, 32, 89, 186, 299
Schmandt-Besserat, Denise, 20, 22, 23, 24, 27, 29, 42, 299
Schorr, M., 70, 241–242, 299
Schwartz, Hillel, 214, 299
Schwyter, Jürg R., 267, 299
scribal education, 11, 137, 141–142, 159–160, 203–218, 250, 260–265, 279–280
scribes as legal experts, 203–204, 212–214, 249–250, 281–282
Seri, Andrea, 51, 299
Shaffer, Aaron, 160, 300
Shamash, 11, 20, 22, 23, 24, 25, 26, 27, 30, 34–41, 42, 53, 76, 88, 94, 95, 96, 97, 98, 101, 102, 103, 104, 105, 106, 115, 118, 119, 124, 125, 126, 128, 168, 169, 236, 238
Shamshi-Adad, 27
Sharlach, Tonia, 207, 293
Shepperson, Mary, 37, 38, 300
Shulgi, 41, 62–64, 72, 78, 209, 218
Shutruk-Nahhunte I, 47
Sin, 103, 104, 105, 106, 115, 126, 128, 131, 235
Sin-Kashid, 66–67
Sin-muballit, 91, 93, 115
Sippar, 30–31, 45, 47, 71, 94, 95, 96, 104, 105, 106, 216

Sjöberg, Å. W., 132, 134, 207, 209, 210, 211, 213, 260, 300
Slanski, Katherine P., 22, 300
slavery, 155–156, 177, 179, 241–245, 253, 255
Smith, Duane, 118, 300
Smith, Joanna, 262, 300
Smoak, Jeremy, 43, 300
social concord, 60–61, 63, 79
social reform, 51–76. *See under* equity: acts of *and under* equity: decrees of
Soden, Wolfram von, 59, 100, 118, 170, 289, 300
Soldt, W. H. van, 261–262, 300
Sollberger, Edmond, 25, 41, 133, 301
Spada, Gabrielle, 207, 291, 301
Speiser, E. A., 256, 301
Steele, Francis R., 2, 73, 301
Steible, Horst, 54, 301
Steinkeller, Piotr, 40, 55, 59, 62, 65, 160, 301
Stela of the Vultures, 27
Stephens, Ferris J., 57, 301
Stol, Marten, 65, 133, 187, 197, 243, 287, 301
Stone, Elizabeth C., 219, 220, 225, 228, 301
Strassler, Robert B., 266, 301
Streck, M. P., 17, 75, 296, 302
Suma-la-el, 45, 115
Sunstein, Cass R., 158, 160, 302
Supreme Court of the United States of America, 247
Susa, 2, 30, 31, 32, 47
Szlechter, Émile, 73, 219, 302

Tablet of Destinies, 42, 121
talion. *See under* poetic justice
Tanret, Michel, 213, 216, 302
Teeter, David Andrew, 256, 302
Teletum see Ishtar, 110
theft, 178–183, 192, 269
thematic linking of cases, 165–176
Thomas, Rosalind, 246, 302
Thomsen, Marie-Louise, 171, 302
Tigay, Jeffery H., 211, 302
Tinney, Steven, 206, 208, 302
Tishpak, 111
Todd, H. F., Jr., 249, 296
Toorn, Karel van der, 206, 263, 302
Tuttul, 111
Tutu, 108

Ungnad, Arthur, 25, 302
Uniform Commercial Code, 15
Ur, 39, 66, 71, 104, 106, 216, 217
Urash, 108
Uruinimgina, 55–59, 62, 78, 79, 82, 85
Ur-Namma, 25, 62, 72–73
Uruk, 55, 104, 106
Utu. *See under* Shamash

Van De Mieroop, Marc, 22, 45, 65, 116, 160, 177, 198, 213, 215, 270, 271, 272, 273, 302
Vanstiphout, H. L. J., 168, 206, 207, 208, 213, 215, 302–303
Veenhof, Klaus, 67, 76, 78, 237, 239, 240, 241, 243, 247, 303
Veldhuis, Niek, 206, 207, 211, 281–282, 303
Victory Stela of Naram-Sin, 27, 28, 40, 47
Vukosavović, Filip, 264, 292, 303

Waetzoldt, Hartmut, 210, 303
Walker, C. B. F., 72, 73, 132, 296, 300
Walters, Stanley D., 168, 303
Warad-Sin, 100
Wasserman, Natan, 31, 32, 115, 303
Watson, Alan, 158, 303
Weinfeld, Moshe, 256, 303
Weissert, Elnatan, 272, 303
Wells, Bruce, 170, 259–260, 303
West, Martin L., 266, 303
Westbrook, Raymond, 10, 54, 70, 146–147, 149, 151, 167, 179, 182, 187, 192, 219, 220, 247, 252, 268, 270, 303–304
wet-nurse, 185–186
Whybray, R. N., 100, 304
widows and orphans, motif of, 38, 62–63, 84–85, 94
Wiggerman, F. A. M., 22, 304
Wilcke, Claus, 34, 56, 57, 72, 73, 182, 215, 217, 243, 304–305
Willetts, Ronald F., 267, 305

Winckler, H., 25, 305
Winitzer, Abraham, 8, 146, 199, 305
Winter, Irene, 22, 305
Wiseman, D. J., 67, 305
witchcraft, 166, 169–173
Wolff, Hans Julius, 4–5, 305
Worthington, Martin, 110, 112, 305
Wright, David P., 259–260, 305
wronged man, 120–123, 134
Wunsch, Cornelia L., 264, 297

Yaron, Reuven, 66, 74, 144, 148, 153, 185, 192, 305
Yoffee, Norman, 43, 45, 49, 50, 51, 214, 246, 305

Zababa, 93, 97, 107, 117, 126, 128, 134
Zabala, 110
Zettler, Richard L., 232, 305
Zevit, Ziony, 264, 305
Zimri-Lim of Mari, 217

Index of Texts

XII Tables, 268
8:2, 270
8:3, 270
8:4, 270
8:12, 269
8:13, 269

A 3529, 231
Aa 16 Commentary BM 41286, 275–276
AbB XIII, 10, 237
AbB XIII, 12, 234
AbB XIV, 98, 236
AbB IX, 32, 235
Advice to a Prince, 54
ana ittišu, 206, 221, 224, 226, 259
ARM 2.132, 120
ARM 24.249, 170

BIN 2 75, 220
BM 32574, 276
BM 54795, 273
BM 59739, 274–275
BM 59776, 273
BM 78589, 240
BWL 119, 172

COS 3.121, 259
CT 21, 40–42, 32, 115
CT 45, 18, 174
Curse of Akkad, The, 40

Digest of Justinian, 158

Edict of Ammi-ditana, 68
Edict of Ammi-ṣaduqa
4, 68
6, 70
7, 69
8, 68
9, 69
16–17, 81
18, 81
20, 80–81, 82, 244
21, 82, 244–245
Edict of Samsu-iluna, 68, 70
Enlil in the Ekur 37
Enuma elish, 116
Euripides, Suppliant Women 271
Exodus
21:4, 257
21:18–19, 258
21:22–24, 256
21:28–32, 259
21:35, 257
22:1–2, 234, 269
Epic of Gilgamesh, 121, 211, 262

Fable of the Fox, 168–169

Gaius, Institutes, 158
Gudea Cylinder A, 38
Gudea Cylinder B, 40, 84, 85
Gudea Statue B, 84, 85

Herodotus 2.177, 266
Hittite Laws, 71, 73, 74
1, 165
7–16, 258
17, 255
18, 255
57, 197
58, 197
59, 198
66, 259
67, 259
70, 259
71, 259
72, 259
74–76, 259
77a, 259
78, 259
79, 259

93, 139, 269
197, 176
198, 150, 176
Hymn to Nanshe, 39
Hymn to Ningirsu, 59–60, 61
Hymn to Shamash, 35–37

Iddin-Dagan B, 40
Ishme-Dagan A+V, 40, 64

Job 24:14–17, 269

Law Code of Gortyn 268
II. 2–10, 267
Laws of Eshnunna, 39, 71, 74, 103, 137, 188
1-4, 10
12, 139, 188, 189, 268
13, 139, 188, 189, 268
15, 192
17, 148, 149
18, 148, 149
22, 154
23, 154
24, 154, 188, 189
25, 143, 144, 145, 152
26–28, 175
26, 152, 188, 189
27, 150, 151, 152, 172
28, 150, 151, 152, 172, 188, 189
29, 149, 152, 153
30, 149, 152, 153
36–37, 175
40, 181
41, 187
42–47A, 195
44–46, 258
50, 149
53–55, 139, 259
53, 139, 257
58, 188, 189, 192
59, 149
60, 188, 189
Laws of Hammurabi
I:1-49, 95, 96, 99, 100, 101
I:14–26, 131
I:27-49, 84, 131
I:32-44, 40
I:50-62, 103–104
I:63–II:1, 104
II:2–12, 104
II:13–21, 104
II:22–31, 104
II:32-36, 104
II:37-47, 104
II:48–54, 107
II:55–67, 107
II:68–III:6, 108
III:7–16, 108, 131
III:17–23, 108
III:24–35, 108
III:36–46, 109
III:47–54, 110
III:55–64, 110
III:65–69, 110
III:70–IV:6, 110
IV:7–22, 110
IV:23–31, 111
IV:32–44, 111–112, 131
IV:45-52, 112
IV:53–58, 112–113
IV:59–63, 113
IV:60–66, 131
IV:64–66, 113
IV:64–V:5, 133
IV:67–V:13, 115
V:3–12, 133
V:14–19, 92, 99
V:14–25, 53, 84, 116, 130, 131
V:20–24, 92
V:25, 92, 96, 97
1–5, 172, 176, 178
1, 165, 166, 168, 176, 188, 189, 233
2, 166, 168, 188, 189, 233
3, 166, 171, 188, 189
4, 166, 171
5, 166, 167, 168
6–13, 178, 179, 180
6–25, 177
6, 178, 179, 180, 188, 190, 191
7, 178, 179, 180, 184, 188, 190, 191
8, 179, 180, 188, 190, 191, 197
9–12, 181
9–13, 178, 183

9, 180, 181, 182, 184, 188, 190, 192, 242
10, 181, 182, 184, 188, 190, 242
11, 181, 182, 184, 190
12, 182, 184
13, 182
14, 178, 188, 190
15, 155, 188, 190
16, 155, 188, 190
17, 155
18, 155, 171
19, 156, 188, 190
20, 156
21, 139, 188, 190, 234, 269
22, 188, 190
25, 188, 190, 192
26–65, 177
26, 188, 190, 198
28, 236–237
30, 236
31, 236–237, 242
33, 82, 188, 190
34, 82, 85, 188, 190
35, 198
36, 198
51, 187, 239–240
53, 273
57, 146
58, 147
59, 138
60–62, 31
G, 85
H, 198
L–CC, 100–126, 176, 177
M, 188, 189
N, 188, 189
U, 187, 239–240
T, 239–240
X, 85
Z, 85, 187, 240
BB, 188, 189
108, 81, 186, 188, 190, 191
109, 81, 171, 188, 190
110, 188, 190
111, 187
112, 240, 241
113, 198
115, 155
116, 85, 155, 188, 189, 190, 192
117–119, 198
117–118, 275
117, 80, 81, 244
118, 82, 244
119, 85
120–121, 198
120, 198
122–132, 172, 175, 176
122, 173, 178
123, 172, 173, 178
124, 172, 173
125, 173, 179
126, 152, 173, 174
127–194, 176, 177
127, 151, 152, 172, 174, 176, 196
128, 151, 152, 172
129, 150, 151, 152, 172, 174, 186, 188, 190
130, 152, 172, 174, 188, 190
131, 152, 172, 175
132, 152, 175, 176
133a, 153, 187
133b, 153, 186, 187, 188, 10
134, 149, 153
135, 153
136, 153, 185
143, 186, 187, 188, 190
148, 138
153, 188, 189
155, 186, 187, 188, 190
157, 188, 190
159, 145
160, 145
161, 144, 145
162, 149
163, 149, 184, 185
164, 150, 184, 185
165, 140, 224
166, 140
167, 138, 140
168–169, 225
170, 139, 224
171, 139, 149, 224
172, 149, 179
177, 85
185, 222, 223

186, 222, 223
187, 222, 223
188, 222, 223
189, 222, 223
190, 222, 223, 224, 226
191, 223, 224, 225, 226
192, 223, 226, 228
193, 223, 226, 228
192–194, 196
194, 185
195, 196
196, 195, 257
197, 195–196, 257
198, 257
199, 257
200, 196, 258
201, 258
202, 196, 270
203, 178
205, 178, 196
208, 178
209, 138
210, 138, 188, 189, 190, 192, 253
213, 138, 253
215–277, 177
215, 194
216, 194
217, 155, 194
218, 194, 195
219, 194
223, 155
226, 194
229, 188, 189, 192
230, 188, 189, 190, 192
232, 179, 192
235, 179
241–243, 10
241, 259, 275
244, 259
245–249, 259
247, 141
248, 141
250–252, 139, 249
250, 139
251, 139
252, 129
253, 192, 196
256, 192, 196
259–260, 191
275–277, 273
278–282, 177
278, 241
279, 241, 242
280, 241, 242
281, 242
282, 196
XLVII:1, 158
XLVII:1–8, 97, 116, 130, 231
XLVII:9–10, 93, 97
XLVII:9–21, 117
XLVII:11–77, 93–94
XLVII:15–21, 41, 134
XLVII:22–29, 93, 97
XLVII:22–39, 117, 134
XLVII:32–39, 131
XLVII:40–45, 131
XLVII:40–58, 117
XLVII:59–61, 85
XLVII:59–78, 30, 117, 131
XLVII:74–78, 32
XLVII:79–83, 114, 117, 119
XLVII:84–XLVIII:2, 119, 131
XLVIII:3–19, 119
XLVIII:3–58, 98
XLVIII:6–7, 31
XLVIII:20–38, 120, 131, 134
XLVIII:39–58, 120
XLVIII:59–74, 123
XLVIII:75–85, 123
XLVIII:86–94, 124, 131
XLVIII:95–XLIX:1, 53, 124
XLIX:1–17, 125
XLIX:2–52, 42–43
XLIX:18–52, 125, 131
XLIX: 45–52, 127
XLIX:53–80, 127
XLIX:81–97, 127
XLIX:98–L:13, 127
L:14–40, 128
L:41–63, 128, 131
L:64–80, 128
l:81–91, 128
L:92–LI:23, 128–129
LI:70–83, 30

manuscript S, 186, 198
manuscript r, 166, 181, 198
manuscript t, 198. *See under* BM 59739 (a commentary on LH)
Laws of Lipit-Ishtar, 39, 71, 73, 74, 79, 80, 132, 165, 181, 208
A iii 9–23, 80
d, 138, 252–254
e, 138, 252–254
f, 138, 252–254
9, 139
10, 138
17, 168
24, 138
25, 139
28, 138
29, 143, 145
31, 139–140
32, 139–140
34–37, 259
35, 140
36, 140
37, 140
Laws about Rented Oxen
1–5, 259
1, 140
2, 140
3, 141
4, 141
6, 259
Laws of Ur-Namma 71, 72–73, 74, 79, 80, 132, 181, 233
A i 31–42, 84
A ii 87–92, 82
A ii 114–124, 82
A iii 104-113, 38, 84
A iii 125–134 (= C i 1–10), 79, 80
A IV 162–168 (= C ii 30–39), 62, 85
C ii 43–51, 84
C 3, 259
C 5, 259
C 6, 259
E3b, 73, 256
1, 165
4, 257
6, 176
14, 176
15, 142
16–22, 195
28, 168
29, 168
LIH 95, 90–94, 134. *See* RIME 4, E4.3.6.7
Lipit-Ishtar Hymn 208–209

Middle Assyrian Laws, 71, 75, 165
A 3–6, 181
A 7–8, 258
A 9, 258
A 15, 150
A 21, 254, 258
A 40, 171
A 47, 170, 171
A 50, 254, 258
A 51, 254, 258
A 52, 255, 258
A 53, 255
C 3, 242
Mishnah Gittin 4:6, 242

Neo-Babylonian Laws 71, 75, 188, 272
Nippur Murder Trial 171

RA 71 (1997) 125ff, 64, 232
RIME 4, E4.2.13.20-29, 100
RIME 4, E4.2.14.20, 100
RIME 4, E4.3.6.2, 94–100, 134
RIME 4, E4.3.6.7, 90–94, 98–100, 134

Shir-Namshub Hymn to Shamash 50-56, 37
Shulgi Hymn B, 63
Shulgi Hymn F, 62
Shulgi Hymn P, 41
Shulgi Hymn X, 63
Sumerian Laws Exercise Tablet 208
1`-2`, 138, 253
4`, 227
5`, 227
6`, 227
9`, 259
10`, 259
Sumerian Laws Handbook of Forms, 181, 259, 259, 259

T'ang Code, 259
TCL XVII 76, 67
TJA 28, 220

UET 5 260, 221
Ur-Namma Hymn
A, 83
C, 56, 80, 83
F, 83

YOS 8 120, 220
YOS 13:328, 240
YOS 13:436, 240